TCCB

The Test and County Cricket Board Collection

GREAT
TESTS
RECALLED

Original reports of the memorable matches

TCCB

The Test and County Cricket Board Collection

GREAT TESTS

RECALLED

Original reports of the memorable matches

WRITERS INCLUDE
NEVILLE CARDUS, JOHN ARLOTT,
R. C. ROBERTSON-GLASGOW,
E. W. SWANTON AND
MATTHEW ENGEL

Edited by Peter Hayter

BLOOMSBURY

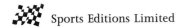 Sports Editions Limited

Managing Director	Richard Dewing
Art Director	Mary Hamlyn
Senior Designer	Rob Kelland
Designer	Sandra Cowell
Design Assistant	Lyndon Brooks
Editor	Leslie Smillie
Editorial Assistant	Joanna Mawson
Picture Research	Rob Kelland
	Abigail Sims

First published in 1990 by
Bloomsbury Publishing Limited
2 Soho Square
London
W1V 5DE

ISBN 0-7475-0723-6

Produced, edited and designed by
Sports Editions Limited
3 Greenlea Park, Prince George's Road
London, SW19 2JD

Typeset in Joanna and 20th Century by Sports Editions Limited

Origination, printing and binding by Butler and Tanner, Frome

· CONTENTS ·

· P R E F A C E ·

A bowler runs up to bowl, a batsman prepares and fieldsmen wait. The possibilities are endless. That is the essence of cricket and it is constant from the beaches of Barbados to the lush lawn of Lord's — as it has been in all kinds of places since the start of play some three centuries ago.

Recording what happens next has the effect of making the event real and permanent, not only for the participants but also for those not present, even for those unborn. If, on occasions, the word becomes as much, if not more than the deed, writers should be forgiven. Cricket is nothing if it fails to fire the imagination.

Here the task of an editor has been to select pieces which do justice to the moment, the cricket and the writers. The hardest part, as is the case for all selectors, has been deciding what to leave out. Where possible, the reports appear exactly as they did when first published. Minor corrections have been made.

My thanks go to all the writers and the players; to the Test and County Cricket Board; to Mary Hamlyn and her team of designers; to Rob Kelland for his outstanding efforts, including tireless picture research; to Sandra Cowell; to Leslie Smillie, Joanna Mawson and Matthew Hamlyn for being a second, third and fourth pair of eyes; and to Reg Hayter's Sports Agency for invaluable research.

PETER HAYTER · OLD TRAFFORD · AUGUST 1990

THIS WAS THE TEST that brought the Ashes, right, into being. In a low scoring match which lasted just two days England were asked to score a mere 85 in their second innings to win and, with a batting order which featured Yorkshire's George Ulyett, Richard Barlow from Lancashire and the great Dr W. G. Grace, doing so should not have taxed them unduly. The Australians, however, were in no mood to surrender, and were further inspired when Grace ran out Jones for six while he was prodding the pitch. When England, having cruised to 51 for two lost Grace

for 32, suddenly Frederick Spofforth, the 'demon' of the Australian attack who had rattled through England's batsmen in the first innings, taking seven for 46, found another gear. As England's batting fell into panic, Spofforth sent the wickets tumbling to repeat his first day feat and finished with seven for 44. His match analysis was 14 for 90; England's last five wickets had fallen for seven runs. The following day *The Sporting Times* carried a mock obituary notice stating that the body of English cricket would be cremated and the Ashes taken back to Australia.

An original engraving of the Test match at the Oval between England and Australia in 1882 which brought The Ashes into being. Inset: the advertisement in the personal columns of 'The Times' newspaper which started the legend of The Ashes.

CRICKET.
THE AUSTRALIANS v. ENGLAND

Rarely, if ever, has there been so large an attendance on an English cricket-ground to witness a match as that which assembled yesterday on Kennington Oval, and the contest was quite worthy of the distinction it received. The third team of Australians have illustrated in a most marked manner their skill at the "noble game", and whether winning (which has usually been the case) or losing they have shown that thoroughness which gives to most pastimes their greatest charm. A team representing the combined talent of England, both amateur and professional, had been selected to play against them, and the encounter has been looked forward to with warm interest. Many of the general public even who do not as a rule take much interest in cricket have concerned themselves about this match. Up to the present time the Australians have played 29 games; 18 of these have been placed to their credit, three they have lost, and eight have been left in an unfinished state. On a wicket which did not play so true as one could have wished the Australians went in first, but the superb fielding of England (especially that of Dr. Grace at point) and the destructive bowling of Barlow and Peate prevented them making much headway. The attacks of the Lancastrian were particularly effective, and his analysis is worthy of especial note, as he captured half the wickets at the cost of a little less than four runs apiece. The fact of an "England" team proving itself competent to dispose of the Australians for the meagre total of 63 was received with considerable gratification by the sightseers, who, by the way, were by no means grudging of their cheers at any noteworthy piece of play on the part of the Australians. Far better things were expected of the English in batting than they accomplished. The early collapse of Dr. W. G. Grace was the cause of much chagrin. Barlow played with his wonted care for some time. Ulyett, although he batted at the outset with a great amount of uncertainty, improved towards the close of what proved to be the highest innings of the day's play. Read's

exploit in the late contest between the Players and the Australians has caused him to be quite a favourite, and yesterday he justified his confidence, as he carried his bat for the second best score of the day. Mr. Steel also hit with judgment. Although the Australians were deprived of the services of Mr. Palmer, their renowned player Mr. Spofforth bowled in a style which showed that he has lost none of his

Dr. W. G. Grace's early collapse: "was the cause of much chagrin."

skill. The English had by far the worst light, which towards evening was at times very deceptive. At the close of the first day the game may be considered to be left in a fairly even state. Altogether there were over 20,000 spectators present.

At a quarter to 12 the bell rang to clear the ground, which was promptly done, and it soon became known that the Australians, having won the toss, had, as a matter of course, elected to go in. Ten minutes after noon the English team entered the field, and were soon afterwards followed by Messrs. Bannerman and Massie. Peate led off from the gasometer wicket, the field to his bowling being distributed as follows:— Hon. A. Lyttelton, wicket keeper; Dr. W. G. Grace, point; Mr. Lucas, deep cover point, Mr. Steel slip; Mr.

C. T. Studd, extra mid-off; Ulyett, cover-point; Barlow, long-slip; Barnes, mid-off; Read, long-off; and Mr. Hornby, mid-on short. Ulyett was the other bowler, and to his attacks the Hon. A. Lyttelton kept wicket, Dr. Grace was at point, Mr. Studd cover-point, Mr. Steel slip, Peate cover-slip, Barnes third man, Barlow mid-off, Mr. Hornby mid-on, Mr. Lucas short leg, and Read long leg. The last ball of the opening over Mr. Bannerman drove well to the off for three. Ulyett started with a maiden. A single from each batsmen and a bye were scored off the next six balls, after which Mr. Massie was bowled by Ulyett, the ball striking his leg-stump. The loss of so valuable a batsman was certainly a most disastrous commencement. Mr. Murdoch came in. His first hit was a very clean cut to the boundary off Ulyett. Ten runs were the result of nine overs. Soon after this Mr. Murdoch made six by two square-leg hits and an on-drive, all from Ulyett. This bowler then gave way to Barlow, but runs still came. Fourteen maidens were now sent down in succession, and a single to Mr. Murdoch was the sole result of 17 overs and then the Australian captain had the misfortune to play the ball on to hs wicket. Two for 21. Mr. Bonnor was well cheered on joining Mr. Bannerman. The usual widening of the field was made to suit his hard hitting. This precaution however, did not prove necessary, as in the third over after his arrival a very fast ball of Barlow's hit his middle and off stumps. Three for 22. Mr. Horan came next on the list, and Mr. Bannerman relieved the tardy run-getting by a late cut for three from Barlow. This proved his last score, as in the subsequent over a remarkably fine catch low down at point got rid of him. Four for 26 was not at all hopeful for the Australians. Mr. Giffen made his appearance, but both he and Mr. Horan were by no means at home with the bowling. Only four runs were added, and then both of them were dismissed. Mr. Horan had his leg-stump taken by Barlow, and Mr. Giffen was clean bowled by Peate. Six for 30. Messrs. Blackham and Garrett became partners. Soon afterwards the bowling showed that a run had been obtained in ten overs for two wickets. Mr.

Garrett made four by an on-drive at each end. Forty runs were the outcome of 1 hour and 40 minute's play. Soon after a twofold change was tried, Mr. Steel going on at the gasometer wicket, and Ulyett resuming at the Pavilion. A single only was secured in four overs, and then luncheon was announced.

The usual interval of three-quarters of an hour having elapsed the game was continued. Peate and Barlow were once more intrusted with the attack. The last ball of the Yorkshireman's first over Mr. Garrett lifted to deep long-off, where it was well judged and held by Read. Seven for 45. Mr. Boyle's stay was brief, as after a couple of singles he retired clean bowled. Eight down. Messrs. Blackham and Jones kept together for a few overs. The former cut a ball of Peate's for four, and drove one of Barlow's straight with a like result. This freedom soon received a check, for at 59 Mr. Blackham skied a ball which point stepped back and easily secured. Nine for 59. Mr. Spofforth made one solitary hit, an on-drive for four, but then lost the company of Mr. Jones, who was easily caught by third man. Total, 63. Duration of the innings, two hours and a quarter.

The England batting was opened by Barlow and Dr. Grace a few minutes before half-past 3. Mr. Spofforth (gasometer wicket) bowled the first over. His field was disposed as follows:— Mr. Blackham, wicket-keeper; Mr. Murdoch, point; Mr. Bannerman, forward-point; Mr. Garrett, cover-point; Mr. Bonner, slip; Mr. Jones, cover-slip; Mr. Massie, mid-off; Mr. Boyle short mid-on; Mr. Giffen, long-on; and Mr. Horam, short-leg. From the pavilion wicket the attack was opened by Mr. Garrett who was supported by his field as follows:— Mr. Blackham, wicket keeper; Mr. Murdoch, point; Mr. Bannerman forward point; Mr. Giffen, cover point; Mr. Bonner, slip; Mr. Horan, third man; Mr. Spofforth, mid-off; Mr. Massie, extra mid-off; Mr. Jones, deep behind bowler; and Mr. Boyle, short mid-on. Four runs were made in as many overs. Eight (including a square-leg hit for a couple and an on drive for three by Barlow) were then scored. This promising state of affairs did not last long, as at 13 Dr. Grace was bowled, leg

stump. One down. Ulyett gave a chance of being stumped before he had scored. The misfortune of losing the Gloucestershire captain was quickly followed by another, as Barlow was taken splendidly at forward point. Two for 18. Mr. Lucas aided Ulyett, who drove a ball of Mr. Garrett's for four. The score was then augmented by four byes. A square-leg hit for four by Mr. Lucas was the most important item until 40 was reached, this number having taken 60 minutes to obtain. A single later Mr. Spofforth crossed over, and Mr. Boyle superseded Mr. Garrett. At half-past 4 the 50 was completed. Speedily afterwards the English team suffered a serious loss, as Ulyett, who had been getting a little too venturesome, got out of his ground and paid the penalty. With only two singles added in eight overs Mr. Lucas was caught at wicket. Mr. Studd's stay was very brief; he was dismissed by a bailer without having scored. Half the wickets for 60 runs. The vacancy was filled by Read. When the total of the Australians had been reached Mr. Lyttelton had the misfortune to be caught at wicket off his hand. Barnes then joined Read, and it was hoped that this pair would repeat the success they achieved in the recent Players' match. But these hopes were soon dispelled as after making a deep square-leg for four and a single, the Notts batsman was bowled by Mr. Boyle. Seven for 70. This state of affairs was changed for a short while by Read and Mr. Steel. Five overs produced three singles, when the Surrey representative made a very clean cut through the slips for three. This he quickly supplemented by an on-drive for four. Mr. Steel having made six by two leg-hits, Mr. Boyle, at 88, handed the ball over to Mr. Garrett. In his first over Mr. Steel cut him to the boundary and Read obtained four from Mr. Spofforth by an on drive. Before anything further could be done Mr. Steel played on. Eight for 96. Read cut a ball of Mr. Spofforth's for three, and a single by the new arrival, Mr. Hornby, caused the "100" to be registered. A single only was obtained, and then the innings quickly terminated. Mr. Hornby was bowled, leg stump, and Peate well caught at mid-off. Play now ceased for the day.

ENGLAND V. AUSTRALIA.

Day Two

The Daily Telegraph 30/8/82

The match at Kennington Oval yesterday ended, not only in a surprise, but also in a scene of excitement scarcely, if ever, equalled on any cricket ground. Notwithstanding the threatening appearance with which the morning opened, such was the public interest awakened by the first day's play that by ten o'clock some thousands of persons were gathered at the enclosure, and as the day wore on the crowd increased until there were, it is believed, at the close of the match, not far from twenty-five thousand spectators; and asssuredly it may be said that all the elements were present to sustain the interest in the play from the beginning to the end. We ventured yesterday to say that the Colonials had played an exceedingly uphill game with such spirit as to give fine proof of their quality, and that although the English team had 38 runs in hand on the first innings the issue was still an open one. How well the Australians deserved this praise was shown when they went in for their second innings. The wicket was even more decidedly against the batsman and in favour of the bowler than on the previous day. Nevertheless, our visitors nearly doubled their score, making 122 as against 63. There was, perhaps, some slight falling off in the English bowling. Barlow—who bowled almost the whole of the preceding afternoon with remarkable steadiness and success, taking five wickets for only 19 runs—was less effective, and even Peate did not succeed as he had in the first innings in the long succession of maiden overs which made his analysis so striking. Still, on the whole, the bowling was remarkably good, especially in the latter part of the Australian innings. It will be seen by the score that only three of the Colonials reached double figures, including Massie's fine achievement of 55, the highest individual total of the match. Two noteworthy incidents marked the Australian innings. The first of these showed the strictness with which the game was played. Murdoch and Jones were together when the captain made a hit to short leg. Mr. Lyttelton, the wicket keeper,

F. R. Spofforth, Australia's first demon bowler. Many have noted a resemblance to a later practitioner of the noble arts of fast bowling, D. K. Lillee.

Lyttelton, and so very smartly closed the Australian captain's innings for an admirably played 29. A neater or more expeditious piece of fielding has rarely been seen.

In the end the whole Australian team was disposed of for 122 runs, thus leaving the home side 85 to win. This for one of the most perfect batting elevens the country could select seemed no great feat, and the odds were supposed to be largely in their favour. Dr. W. G. Grace and Mr. Hornby opened the innings, their appearance at the wickets being the signal for hearty cheering. Both played with considerable animation, but when the score had reached 15 the Lancashire captain was bowled by Spofforth for 9. Barlow, one of the steadiest batsmen in England, followed, but was immediately bowled also by "the demon", as he is called, for 0. Ulyett followed, and for a while the spell of the Colonial bowling seemed to have been broken. Runs came with fair rapidity; 20, 30, 40, 50 were successively exhibited on the board, and the hopes of an English triumph rose high. At length Ulyett gave a chance to Blackham, who never misses one, and Mr. A. P. Lucas took his place. There were thus three wickets down and 34 runs were required. But the overthrow of Ulyett was a great encouragement to the Australians, and when very soon afterwards Dr. Grace was caught by Bannerman at mid off—having made 32 out of a total of 53—their elation naturally knew no bounds. The Hon. A. Lytteleton now joined Mr. Lucas. It would be hard to name two more accomplished batsmen, but they found it hard to play Spofforth and Boyle. Both were bowling in their best style, Spofforth especially seemed to be irresistible. It was no small feat that two gentlemen guarded their wickets against twelve splendid maiden overs in succession, and shortly after five o'clock it was known that they had raised the score by the most careful play to 65.

This was the crisis of the game. Twenty runs were wanted, and to get them there were Lucas and Lyttelton still in; Read, Steel, Studd, Barnes, and Peate to follow. At 66 Mr. Lyttelton was bowled by

fielded, and threw in the ball, which was recieved by another member of the team and dropped at the wicket. The ball however, was not "dead"—the wicket keeper having for the moment only acted as fielder, and Jones, forgetting this important fact, left his ground, and Mr. Grace, observing the movement, instantly picked up the ball and removed the bails. There was some momentary complaining on the part of the sympathisers with the

Colonists, but no kind of protest was made, or was, indeed, possible. The second incident followed shortly afterwards when Murdoch, having made a fine drive to the off, was attempting a second run—on the strength of the fact that Mr. Hornby, who was fielding, would be unable to throw in on account of an injury to his arm. This calculation proved unsound. Mr. Hornby passed the ball to Mr. C. T. Studd, who threw it to Mr.

The Australians of 1882: Standing (left to right): S. P. Jones, A. C. Bannerman, G. J. Bonner, F. R. Spofforth, J. McC. Blackham, G. Eugene Palmer, G. Giffen, T. W. Garrett, H. H. Massie, Percy S. McDonnell. Seated (left to right): W. L. Murdoch, H. F. Boyle and T. Horam.

Spofforth—19 runs wanted and five wickets to fall. The excitement now grew apace. It was visible everywhere—in the pavilion, on the stands, throughout the dense ring of spectators, and in the field itself. The Australians were congratulating each other openly—meeting in groups whenever a wicket fell, and displaying an eagerness and elation seldom seen in a cricket-field. On the other side every ball was watched and every single run cheered as though it had been a phenomenon. Mr. Lucas had just played a 4 through the slips, greatly to the delight of the on-lookers, when Mr. Steel was caught and bowled by Spofforth. Another accession of anxiety— fifteen runs wanted, four wickets to fall. Maurice Read, the hope of Surrey, succeeded. Great was the enthusiasm with which he was greeted. In previous matches with the Colonials he had greatly distinguished himself. He was bowled by Spofforth's second ball. Fifteen runs still wanted, and three wickets to fall. Barnes followed, and presently drove the fast

bowler for 2; then 3 were run for a bye; and then came another disaster. Lucas played on — and 10 runs were yet needed, and there were now only two wickets to fall. The excitement reached a pitch which mere words can hardly convey, and it was not lessened when Barnes sent a catch to Murdoch, and left Mr. C. T. Studd and Peate, the last men, in face of the Australian bowlers, with still 10 runs to win. Peate scooped the first ball to leg for 2, but this was the end. The last ball of the over—Mr. Studd never having had a single ball—disarranged the professional's wicket, and the English team were beaten by 7 runs. The Australians were warmly cheered by the crowd who were generous enough to admit that our visitors had fairly won, and by means of splendid cricket. And so ended the most important of the contests between English cricketers and the Australians; a contest fought out with indomitable pluck by the winners, and which will long be remembered by those who had the good fortune to witness it.

FINAL · SCORES

AUSTRALIA — First Innings

A. C. Bannerman, c Grace, b Peate	9
H. H. Massie, b Ulyett	1
W. L. Murdoch, b Peate	13
G. J. Bonner, b Barlow	1
T. Horan, b Barlow	3
G. Giffen, b Peate	2
J. McC. Blackham, c Grace, b Barlow	17
T. W. Garrett, c Read, b Peate	10
H. F. Boyle, b Barlow	2
S. P. Jones, c Barnes, b Barlow	0
F. R. Spofforth, not out	4
Extras (b 1)	1
Total	**63**

Fall of wickets: 1-6, 2-21, 3-22, 4-26, 5-30, 6-30, 7-48, 8-53, 9-59, 10-63

Bowling: Peate 38-24-31-4, Ulyett 9-5-11-1, Barlow 31-22-19-5, Steel 2-1-1-0

ENGLAND — First Innings

Barlow, c Bannerman, b Spofforth	11
Dr. W. G. Grace, b Spofforth	4
Ulyett, st Blackham, b Spofforth	26
A. P. Lucas, c Blackham, b Boyle	9
Hon. A. Lyttleton, c Blackham, b Spofforth	2
C. T. Studd, b Spofforth	0
Read, not out	19
Barnes, b Boyle	5
A. G. Steel, b Garrett	14
A. N. Hornby, b Spofforth	2
Peate, c Boyle, b Spofforth	0
Extras (b 6, lb 2, nb 1)	9
Total	**101**

Fall of Wickets: 1-13, 2-18, 3-57, 4-59, 5-60, 6-63, 7-70, 8-96, 9-101, 10-101

Bowling: Spofforth 36.3-18-46-7, Garrett 16-7-22-1, Boyle 19-7-24-2

AUSTRALIA — Second Innings

A. C. Bannerman, c Studd, b Barnes	13
H. H. Massie, b Steel	55
W. L. Murdoch, run out	29
G. J. Bonner, b Ulyett	2
T. Horan, c Grace, b Peate	2
G. Giffen, c Grace, b Peate	0
J. McC. Blackham, c Lyttleton, b Peate	7
T. W. Garrett, not out	2
H. F. Boyle, b Steel	0
S. P. Jones, run out	6
F. R. Spofforth, b Peate	0
Extras (b 6)	6
Total	**122**

Fall of wickets: 1-66, 2-70, 3-70, 4-79, 5-79, 6-99, 7-114, 8-117, 9-122, 10-122

Bowling: Barlow 13-5-27-0, Ulyett 6-2-10-1, Peate 21-9-40-4, Studd 4-1-9-0, Barnes 11-5-15-1, Steel 7-0-15-2

ENGLAND — Second Innings

Barlow, b Spofforth	0
Dr. W. G. Grace, c Bannerman, b Boyle	32
Ulyett, c Blackham, b Spofforth	11
A. P. Lucas, b Spofforth	5
Hon. A. Lyttleton, b Spofforth	12
C. T. Studd, not out	0
Read, b Spofforth	0
Barnes, c Murdoch, b Boyle	2
A. G. Steel, c & b Spofforth	0
A. N. Hornby, b Spofforth	9
Peate, b Boyle	2
Extras (b 3, nb 1)	4
Total	**77**

Fall of wickets: 1-15, 2-15, 3-51, 4-53, 5-66, 6-70, 7-70, 8-75, 9-75, 10-77

Bowling: Spofforth 28-15-44-7, Garrett 7-2-10-0, Boyle 20-11-19-3

·1908·

ENGLAND WON BY ONE wicket courtesy of a 39-run last wicket stand between Sidney Barnes and Arthur Fielder, right, although as the winning run was being scampered, cover point Gerry Hazlitt narrowly missed with a shy at the stumps. Montague Noble, a quite exemplary Australian cricketer and captain, led his side with 61 and 64 in either innings, and Warwick Armstrong added a punchy 77 as Australia set England 282 to win. England's heroes of the first innings, Jack Hobbs and Kenneth Hutchings, both missed

Barnes & Fielder

out. Hobbs had marked his England debut with 83 while Hutchings cracked 126. The second innings relied on modest contributions from all the top and middle order, Essex's Freddie Fane the only man to go past 50, and Australia appeared to have the match won when no. 11 Fielder joined Barnes at the wicket. Barnes, who came out of the minor counties with Staffordshire to tour Australia, farmed as much of the strike as possible and went on to hit 38 not out as England achieved a remarkable win.

Montague Noble:
*"A quite exemplary
Australian cricketer."*

Mr. M. A. Noble

SECOND TEST MATCH.

ALL DAY AT THE WICKETS

By MAJOR PHILIP TREVOR.

MELBOURNE, Wednesday.

Having won the toss and thus secured the great advantage of batting first on a perfect wicket, the Australian batsmen wisely decided to run no risks.

The huge crowd present appeared rather disappointed with the defensive nature of the batting, but undoubtedly the Colonials played the right game.

At the drawing of stumps the Australians had scored 255 for seven wickets.

For the most part the batting was sternly defensive in character, Cotter alone playing an enterprising game.

The English bowling was good, especially that of Fielder and Crawford.

Macartney and Trumper, who was unusually cautious, played sound, steady cricket, and their example was followed by Armstrong and Noble.

Armstrong showed no inclination to hit, and was playing extremely well when he was finally caught by Hutchings at second slip.

Undoubtedly the cause of the slow scoring was the excellence of the English bowling.

Crawford has not bowled so well for weeks. Fielder also did good work, while Barnes, Braund, and Rhodes kept an accurate length.

The Englishmen have no reason to be dissatisfied with the result of the day's play.

The English bowling was good, especially that of Fielder and Crawford. Early in the day the fielding lacked cleanness, but it improved as time went on.

Trumper, after a bright start, soon became slow for him; but he played an attractive innings, his defences being watchful and his hitting all-round very clean. He was batting for eighty-three minutes, his figures including five 4's.

After luncheon Hill joined Macartney, the attendance having by this time increased to 20,000. Crawford and Fielder shared the bowling.

With 9 runs added Macartney was bowled. He had played excellent cricket for over an hour and a half, his footwork being good and his cutting very neat.

Noble was next in, and the 100 went up when the innings had lasted a trifle more than an hour and three-quarters.

Runs came slowly till at 111 Hill was bowled. He took thirty-seven minutes to score his 16.

On joining Noble, Armstrong was warmly cheered.

Fielder and Crawford bowled admirably, making the ball turn, and being very accurate in length. However, no wicket fell, so at 140 Fielder gave way to Barnes.

At 145 the umpires examined the ball, and ordered a new one.

The game had been in progress about two hours and fifty minutes when the score reached 150.

The batting remained careful to a degree, and at the tea interval the total was 160 for three wickets.

Eight runs were put on, and then a brilliant catch in the slips, with the right hand, got rid of Armstrong. Four wickets for 168.

Armstrong played a very quiet, defensive innings. He hit three 4's and was batting for sixty-four minutes.

At 185 Barnes displaced Fielder. Noble completed his 50 in an hour and fifty-three minutes, but when he had made two more runs he was missed being stumped off Barnes.

With the score 197 McAlister was foolishly run out. Hobbs returned the ball smartly from deep third man, and Humphries put the wicket down in brilliant style.

Ransford came in, and 200 went up as the result of three hours and three-quarters' cricket and at 214 Noble was caught at slip off Rhodes. Patience was the chief feature of Noble's innings. He played well, and hit five 4's, but in scoring his 61 he was at the wickets for over two hours and a half.

MELBOURNE, Thursday

The Englishmen did great things in the Test match here today, finishing off the Australian innings for an addition of 11 runs and then scoring 246 for three

Kenneth Hutchings

wickets. As the result of their fine play they left off in a very good position, being only 20 runs behind with seven wickets in hand. Interest in the match was well sustained, the crowd numbering 18,000 before the end of the afternoon. Lord Northcote, Governor-General of the Commonwealth, was present. During the greater part of the day the cricket was even quieter in character than on Wednesday, the batting being very orthodox and unenterprising. Hutchings, however, brought about a complete change, hitting in the last hour with the utmost brilliance and rousing the spectators to enthusiasm. The Australian bowling was accurate, but on the fast, true-playing wicket it had little or no sting. As regards the fielding, a fairly good standard was maintained. Warm, pleasant weather prevailed all day.

With seven wickets down for 255, the Australians went on batting Ransford, not out 22, and Carter, not out 10, facing the bowling of Fielder and Crawford. Both batsmen began cautiously, but at 261 Ransford was unluckily run out, slipping down in trying to regain his crease. Hazlitt failed, Crawford bowling him for a single. Nine wickets for 265. Saunders was bowled without scoring, the innings, which lasted five hours and six minutes, ending for 266.

It was agreed by every one that in getting Australia out for such a modest total the Englishmen had accomplished a fine performance. They were warmly cheered as they walked back to the pavilion. Crawford's bowling was exceptionally good.

Fane and Hobbs opened the English innings to the bowling of Cotter and Saunders. Runs came steadily, and when the score had reached 27 Noble went on for Saunders and Armstrong for Cotter. The second of these changes proved successful, Armstrong's third ball bowling Fane off his pads. At this point luncheon was taken.

When the game was continued, Gunn joined Hobbs. Saunders shared the bowling with Armstrong. Play went on in a very quiet way, only 20 runs being added in half an hour. Noble fielded at short mid-on to Armstrong and Trumper at "silly point" to Saunders. As no wicket fell, a double change was tried at 49, Hazlitt and Cotter going on. Armstrong had bowled nine overs, three maidens for eight runs and a wicket. When 50 went up the innings had been in progress 69 minutes.

The total having been increased to 61, Gunn was out leg-before-wicket. He was greatly dissatisfied with the decision. Hutchings joined Hobbs, and the game proceeded just as uneventfully as before.

Hobbs completed his 50 after batting for just upon an hour and three-quarters. At 82 Saunders displaced Hazlitt, and Armstrong bowled again for Cotter. It was very hard to get runs from Armstrong, his pitch being so accurate. Macartney relieved Saunders at 93. The 10o went up as the result of two hours and five minutes' batting. Cotter bowled once more for Armstrong at 105, but without

Jack Hobbs. The master.

effect. At the tea interval the total was 113 for two wickets, Hobbs having made 59 and Hutchings 25.

When the game was resumed, Macartney and Armstrong were the bowlers. Nothing of any consequence happened till Hobbs, with his score at 69 gave a chance off Armstrong to Macartney at square leg. Noble went on at 129, Macartney giving way to him. Hobbs was

now batting with more freedom, but Hutchings continued to play a much slower game than usual. At 150 Cotter was tried again in place of Armstrong, and with ten runs added he bowled Hobbs. Three wickets for 160. Hobbs scored his 83 in about three hours and ten minutes, showing great patience and very strong defence. His innings, which included eight fours, was thought worthy of Hayward. So far, Hutchings had made 47.

Braund came in, and Hutchings reached his 50 after batting for an hour and 25 minutes. Macartney bowled for Noble at 194, and, as it happened, this change was followed by an astonishing change in the character of the cricket. From the first ball bowled by Macartney, Hutchings made a magnificent hit for six, and the next ball he drove for four. When 200 went up, the innings had lasted exactly 200 minutes. Hutchings was loudly cheered when he passed Hobb's score. He was now playing in great form, and changes of bowling were powerless to check his hitting.

Hazlitt and Armstrong were tried in turn, but to no purpose. Hutchings reached his hundred in two hours and eight minutes, having doubled his score in less than three-quarters of an hour. In the hope of getting a wicket before the drawing of stumps, Cotter was put on once more in place of Hazlitt, but nothing happened. At the closed, the total was 246 for three, Hutchings not out 117. Braund, playing a strictly defensive game, made 15 runs while Hutchings was getting 70.

Trott commenting on the game, said that the Englishmen played better cricket than in the last Test match. He was greatly impressed by the slashing play of Hutchings. Trumble considered that Hutchings's hitting of the fast bowling all over the field was the feature of the play, and added that he could not remember seeing fast bowling hit so hard.

Horan said, "The Englishmen were more confident to-day. It was delightful to watch Hutchings." Laver and other well-known cricketers, while praising Hutchings's fine display, were of the opinion that Hobbs's sound and stubborn game helped to kill the bowling.

SPORTING INTELLIGENCE.

CRICKET.
M.C.C. v. AUSTRALIA.
THE SECOND TEST MATCH.

MELBOURNE, Friday.

In the Test match here to-day the Australians played up in great style and recovered nearly all their lost ground. At the drawing of stumps they were only 20 runs behind, with all ten wickets to fall in their second innings. In doing so well they were indebted first to the excellent bowling of Cotter and Saunders, and at the end of the afternoon to some brilliant hitting by Noble and Trumper.

Bright weather again favoured the game, and the interest of the public was well sustained, the crowd numbering 10,000. So far, the feature of the match has been Hutchings's innings. It is the general opinion that nothing finer has been done by a batsman from England since Ranjitsinhji was here ten years ago. His power of wrist and forearm is considered marvellous, and the way in which he flicked the ball away on the leg side filled old Test match players with amazement.

The Englishmen went on with their innings, having, in face of a total of 266, scored 246 for three wickets, and Hutchings, not out 117, and Braund, not out 15, were opposed by Cotter and Armstrong. At the start runs came quickly and the Australian score was soon passed, the innings having then been in progress just upon four hours and 25 minutes. However, at 268 Hutchings was bowled by a "yorker" from Cotter. His magnificent innings of 126, which lasted nearly two hours and three-quarters, included a six and 21 fours. He had an enthusiastic reception as he walked back to the pavilion. Up to this point Braund had made 28. Hardstaff came in and the game proceeded quietly. At 281 Saunders displaced Cotter and Noble took the ball from Armstrong. In three-quarters of an hour only four runs had been scored from Armstrong and 30 from Cotter, but the latter had taken Hutchings's wicket. The batting was very cautious, and the total had only been increased to 287 when

Hardstaff was bowled. He hit two fours, but in getting his 12 runs he was at the wickets 34 minutes.

An hour's cricket had only produced 41 runs. Rhodes joined Braund, and the play remained painfully slow. At 290 Macartney relieved Noble, and other changes soon followed, Cotter at 294 displacing Saunders, who crossed over to Macartney's end. At lunch time, however,

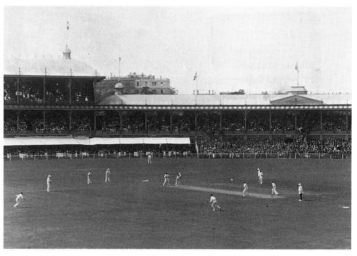

the two batsmen were still together. The total was 299 for five wickets, Braund having made 39 and Rhodes seven.

When the game was continued Saunders and Cotter shared the bowling as before. Three hundred went up as the result of just under five hours and 20 minutes' batting. Runs came steadily, and at 320 Saunders, from whom by this time 70 had been scored, gave way to Hazlitt. Then, at 325, Braund was bowled by Cotter. His innings was marked by extreme caution and strong defence. Running no risks, he was batting for two hours and 24 minutes. Still, he made some good hits, including five fours.

Crawford was next in, and at 336 Saunders bowled again in place of Cotter. Slow cricket followed till, at 353, Crawford, in hitting out at Saunders, was brilliantly caught at long-off. Barnes joined Rhodes, and Armstrong at once resumed bowling at Hazlitt's end. Rhodes had been playing with great restraint for over an hour and a half, but at last he lost his self-control, and, hitting wildly at a

ball from Saunders, was clean bowled. His innings included four fours. Eight wickets were now down for 360. Humphries did not stay long, Cotter going on at 369 and at once bowling him. Barnes and Fielder were together at the tea interval, the total being 381 for nine wickets. With one run added after resuming, Barnes, from a half hit, was caught at mid-on, the innings thus ending for 382.

Test cricket played against the background of Victorian grandeur at the Melbourne cricket ground.

The Australians, in starting their second innings, had a balance of 116 runs against them. Changing the previous order of batting, Noble went in himself with Trumper, and the experiment proved brilliantly successful. In recognition of his fine work in the first innings, Fane let Crawford begin the bowling with Fielder. It was soon evident that both batsmen were in form. Noble made nine runs in Fielder's first over, and the score rose rapidly. At 37 the first change was tried, Barnes displacing Crawford. At the end of half an hour's play the total was 45. Then, at 47, Fielder, from whom only 13 runs had been hit, gave way to Braund. Fifty went up in 40 minutes, the game being now quieter in character. Rhodes went on in place of Barnes at 76, but without effect. Continuing to play bright, attractive cricket the batsmen were indifferent to changes of bowling. At 86 Crawford resumed for Braund, and with ten runs added stumps were drawn. Noble and Trumper were warmly cheered for their splendid play.

Day Four

The Age
6/1/08

A FLUCTUATING GAME
AT AN EVEN STAGE.

AUSTRALIA'S SECOND INNINGS.

SEVEN WICKETS FOR 360 RUNS.

BY MID-ON

The intense public interest felt in the test matches of this season between the M.C.C. English Eleven and Australia was further demonstrated on Saturday by the assembling of 20,073 spectators at the Melbourne Cricket ground to witness the fourth day's play in the second match. The gate receipts for the day amounted to £854 13s 9d, making an aggregate of £3574 5s, and a total attendance of 75,297 spectators for the four days. The gate record for a test match is £4004, and it is probable that if the weather be again fine today that amount will be exceeded and a world's record established for Melbourne—it is at present held by Sydney. Fortunately for both the players and spectators on Saturday the intense heat was in a measure relieved by a light southerly breeze, but for which it would have been one of the most trying days of the season. Amongst the visitors to the pavilion were Archbishop Clarke, the State Premier, and the Lord Mayor of Melbourne. Cricketers were also pleased to see the English captain, Mr A. O. Jones, present, and looking much better than could have been expected after his recent severe attack of pneumonia. Mr. Jones had come on from Bowenfella, in the Blue Mountains, and has recovered 11 lbs. of the 2 st. which he lost in weight during his illness. He will proceed with the team to Adelaide, where the third test match commences next Friday, but will not be able to take part in the game.

The present match, which has already covered four days, has provided quite an unusual number of varied situations, first one side and then the other holding distinct advantage on figures. When the Englishmen in their first innings got within 20 runs of the Australian's first total and

had still seven wickets to fall they appeared to have victory well within their grasp. Even after those remaining seven wickets had failed to add more than 136 runs, England was still in a winning position with a lead of 116 runs, but when on Friday evening Noble and Trumper had, without being separated, wiped 96 runs off Australia's deficit, the chances of success were as even as at the start. On Saturday, however, a series of disasters overtook the Australians, and at one stage the prospect was even more in favor of England than it had been when the play ceased on the second day. Trumper, who had made 63, was out l.b.w.; Noble, having scored 64, was bowled by a full pitch to leg, which cannoned from his arm on to the wicket; Hill—the most consistent of Australian batsmen in test matches—had his wicket "skittled" after making 3, and when McAlister was run out for 15, Australia, with four of the best batsmen in the team disposed of, were only 46 runs ahead of England's first innings score. The situation was, however, if not saved, amazingly improved by a splendid stand made by Armstrong and Macartney—the Goliath and David of the team—who while together put on 105 runs for the fifth wicket, leaving the Australians 182 runs ahead, and with half their wickets—in number if not in value—still to fall. Althought the third hundred was reached before another wicket fell, the lead had only been increased to 187 when Macartney was disposed of, and at the fall of the seventh wicket (Ransford's) the Australians were still 195 to the good. As in the first match at Sydney, however, Carter and Cotter, though played respectively solely for wicketkeeping and bowling, came to the rescue of their side with the bat, and, putting on 48 runs, these two played out time, and left the game at the drawing of the stumps once again as even as at the start, Australia being 264 runs ahead, with three wickets to fall.

Much, of course, will depend upon the performance of Australia's "tail" to-day, but while on figures the chances appear to be almost as even as possible, the situation is perhaps slightly in favor of Australia. Assuming that no change in weather takes

place before the resumption of play to-day, it is hardly to be expected that the wickets will remain as good as it has been to the finish, and therefore if the Englishmen have to make about 300, which seems probable, the runs will "take some getting". Cricket is, however, not a game at which prophecy can be indulged in with any degree of certainty. The one fact at present beyond question is that on the termination of Australia's second innings England's representatives will be called upon to "set the teeth and stretch the nostril wide, and show us here the mettle of their pasture." The team contains a large proportion of young players, who are on their trial as representatives of their country, and if they succeed in pulling this match off, all England will be aglow with enthusiastic appreciation of their prowess when the cabled news of their success reaches the old country. They certainly have a nerve testing task on hand, and if they accomplish it successfully they may depend on the spectators bestowing applause on them ungrudgingly. The experience of this match as far as it has gone indeed must have satisfied the "new chums" in the English team that much they have heard about the Australian "barracker" is imaginary and unjust. He will be heard if he desires to express admiration or disapproval, as the case may be, but in bare justice it may be unreservedly asserted that he has nothing to learn in the matter of fairness from his prototype at Lord's or the Oval, at Bramall-lane or Old Trafford. Be the performer a Trumper, a Noble or a Hutchings or a Hobbs, he is, while at the wickets, to the Australian barracker merely a player whom he has paid his shilling to see, and, provided he gets his "bob's worth", the last consideration of the barracker is as to which side he represents. Let Cotter hit a sixer, the barracker will chance splitting his throat in yelling his approval, but should Cotter half an hour afterwards misfield a ball that same barracker will stentoriously recommend him to "get a bag." He is certainly no respecter of persons, but he is just as certainly, according to his lights, as fair in his criticism as he is noisy.

Noble (50) and Trumper (46) resumed Australia's second innings with no wickets down for 96 to the bowling of Fielder and Crawford. Fielder's first over was a maiden to Noble, and after Trumper had made a single off Crawford, noble hit him to the on for 3 and brought up 100, made in 86 minutes. Trumper, cutting Crawford for 2 and 1, reached 30, made in an hour and a half, and with the total at 106 each

The great Victor Trumper.

batsman had made 53. Although the wicket was playing as well as ever, it was politic of the Australians to subject it to prolonged wear and tear. England having to play the fourth innings on it, and the batting was therefore less forcible than on the previous evening. Noble scoring a single, equalled his fist innings score of 61 and wiped off Australia's deficiency of 116. Trumper drove Fielder and hit him cleverly to leg for 4 each in one over, but

in Crawford's next over he was out l.b.w. 1-63-126. Noble had then also made 63. Trumper was at the wickets an hour and 52 minutes, and hit seven 4's. Hill followed, and after scoring 2, cocked Crawford up to the on weakly, but not within dangerous distance of any fieldsman. Hill was not at his best when playing his first over from Fielder, and quickly lost Noble, who in trying to hook a full pitch from Crawford, missed and was bowled, the ball cannoning off his elbow on to the wicket 2-64-131. Noble had been batting 2 hours and 2 minutes and hit six 4's. McAlister joined Hill and started by hitting Crawford to square leg for 3, but Hill, who had shaped streakily for him, was clean bowled by Fielder, and with 2-3-135 up, the outlook for Australia had within the last few minutes changed materially for the worse. Armstrong joined McAlister, and it was felt that much depended on the partnership of the two Victorians. It opened uneventfully, and at the end of an hour's play 50 runs had been added to the overnight total. Then Armstrong, by a powerful off drive, sent Fielder to the grandstand rails and the score had then reached 152. Barnes deposed Fielder, who had taken one wicket for 20 runs. McAlister neatly took out Barnes for 2, and at 156 Rhodes replaced Crawford, whose two wickets had cost 61 runs. The partnership came to an unfortunate termination, Armstrong played Rhodes to cover point and ran. McAlister, after calling "No," started to save his partner's wicket and was run out. Fielder returned the ball wide, but Humphries took it expertly and turned it on to the wicket 4-15-162. The players then adjourned for lunch, Armstrong having made 14.

After the interval Macartney joined Armstrong and Fielder and Crawford bowled. Macartney received a hard blow in the ribs from Fielder, the ball bouncing to square leg for a bye. Hardstaff retired from the field, his place being taken by Young and Armstrong, who had reached 20, cut a no-ball from Fielder for 4, and drove Crawford to the boundary. Macartney, who had started carefully, glanced Fielder beautifully for 4, and

reached double figures by playing the same bowler to the on for 3. Hardstaff returned to the field just in time to see Armstrong drive Crawford splendidly for 4, and snick 2 in the same over. At 195 Braund replaced Fielder, who had taken one wicket for 57, and Armstrong having cut him for 3, a single to Macartney brought up 200, made in 3 hours and a quarter. In Crawford's next over a fast one went to the boundary for 4 byes, and at 204 Barnes replaced Braund, off whom 26 runs had been hit. Armstrong got into the forties by driving Barnes for 3, and Macartney pulled Crawford twice consecutively for 4, the first 4 being run out. Armstrong drove Barnes for 3, Hobbs smartly saving the 4 on the rails, and at 233 Rhodes again relieved Crawford, whose two wickets had cost 34 runs. Macartney hooked Barnes high to the on, but out of Gunn's reach, and Armstrong reached 32 by again driving Barnes for 3. He had then been at the wickets 98 minutes. At 239 Barnes again gave place to Braund, and Armstrong, after hitting Rhodes for 2, got him past fine slip to the rails. Macartney twice hit Braund to square leg for 2, Hutchings fielding both balls splendidly, and Armstrong, by a fine square cut for 4 off Rhodes, reached 66, and became top scorer for the innings. At 258 Fielder went on again instead of Braund, and bowled a maiden to Armstrong. Rhodes retired in favor of Crawford, and Armstrong reached 70 by cutting him for 3. The Victorian champion evoked loud applause by hitting Fielder straight for 4, the eminently useful partnership having then added 102 runs to the score. A single to Armstrong brought the total to 266, tying Australia's first innings total. At the 4 o'clock adjournment four wickets were down for 267, Armstrong 76, Macartney 36.

Only a single had been added by Armstrong after the interval when Barnes bowled him 5-77-268. Armstrong had been at the wickets 2 hours and a quarter, and hit seven 4's. The partnership had put on 105 runs for the fifth wicket at a critical juncture, and neither had given a chance though Macartney had nothing to spare when he survived an appeal by Barnes for l.b.w. Ransford followed, and

Macartney reached 40, hitting Crawford to the square leg boundary. Ransford had made a couple when he glanced Barnes nicely for 4, and Macartney cleverly hooked a fast rising one from Crawford for 3. At 259 Braund replaced Crawford, and Macartney, playing him to leg for a single, reached 50, made in 2 hours and 22 minutes. Macartney hit Braund to square leg, and Crawford slipping, the ball reached the boundary. The third hundred appeared after 5 hours and 10 minutes' play, and immediately afterwards Macartney cocked Barnes up and was easily caught by the wicketkeeper 6-54-303. Macartney, without giving a chance, had been at the wickets 2 hours and a half, and hit five 4's. Carter followed, and swept Braund round to leg for 2, but soon lost Ransford, who was caught in the slips by Hutchings, off Barnes 7-18-312. Cotter joined Carter, and after 3 byes were run, Cotter drove Braund for 4. In Braund's following over, Cotter hit the first and second balls to square leg for 2 and 4 respectively, and the sixth similarly for 2, but the 4 was the only clean hard hit of the three. Carter, emulating his partner, hit Barnes to leg for 4, and Cotter again skied Braund to square leg for 2, dangerously, but out of reach. Again lifting Braund, Cotter, who had made 30, was badly missed at mid-on by by Fielder, and at 345 Rhodes replaced Barnes. Carter cut Rhodes for 1 and Cotter, who narrowly escaped being run out, repeated the stroke. Crawford went on again in place of Braund, and Carter hit Rhodes to to square leg for 4. When the stumps were drawn, seven wickets were down for 360. Cotter 27, Carter 22. The unfinished partnership had added 48 runs to the score. The Englishmen generally fielded well, particularly good work being done by Hutchings and Hardstaff in the country and by Barnes at point, while Humphries further demonstrated that he is a veritable champion behind the wickets, worthy of being placed in the highest class amongst wicketkeepers—the class which has included such a trio of stars as Blackham, Pilling and Lilley.

The match will be resumed at noon today.

THE TEST MATCH.

A GREAT STRUGGLE.

ENGLAND'S HARD TASK.

AUSTRALIA - 1st Inns., 266 ; 2nd, 397.
Noble, 61.   Armstrong, 77
ENGLAND - 1st Inns., 382; 2nd, 159 (4 wkts.).
Hutchings, 126.   Fane, 50.

By MAJOR PHILIP TREVOR.

MELBOURNE, Monday.
After another day of stern cricket here in the Test match, the issue remains as open as ever, the Englishmen having 6 wickets to fall and wanting 123 runs to win. It cannot be denied that, keen as it was, the play often became wearisome.

When England went in with 282 to get, the batsmen played an entirely defensive game, running no risks.

Noble managed the Australian bowling with great skill. He and Macartney bowled splendidly, and Armstrong, with his good head work and extreme accuracy of length, was always able to keep down the runs.

The fielding was smart, Ransford, in particular, saving many runs by his brilliancy in the outfield.

Play went on under trying conditions, the temperature being 90.5 in the shade and 140.5 in the sun. Public interest was fully sustained, 9,000 people being present before the end of the afternoon.

So far, the aggregate attendance numbers 64,386, the takings amounting to £3,950. This sum is only £50 below record.

A hot wind was blowing when Carter, not out 22, and Cotter, not out 27, continued Australia's second innings, the total standing at 360 for 7 wickets. Crawford and Fielder started the bowling.

Before he had added a run to his score, Carter was missed in the slips by Hutchings off Fielder. Then, at 361, Cotter was out leg before wicket.

Hazlitt came in, and Carter scored freely, his cutting being very clean.

The English total was passed when the innings had extended over six hours and a quarter.

At 391 Barnes relieved Fielder, and with his third ball he bowled Hazlitt. Nine wickets for 392. Saunders joined Carter, who made 5 more runs before being caught at mid-on, the innings ending for 397.

In making this score the Australians were batting for six hours and thirty-five minutes. Carter played excellent cricket for nearly an hour and twenty-five minutes, his hits including seven 4's. The fielding in the closing part of the innings was not by any means first-rate.

Considering the score, Barnes's figures were extraordinarily good.

England's task of getting 282 runs to win was begun by Hobbs and Fane, Cotter and Saunders sharing the bowling. Both batsmen started cautiously, and the cricket all round was keen to a degree.

When the score had slowly reached 20 Saunders, from whom 9 runs had been hit, gave way to Armstrong.

At lunch time the total was 26 for no wicket the batsmen having made 10 each.

Upon resuming, Saunders bowled with Cotter. Runs came steadily, 50 going up when the innings had been in progress fifty-four minutes. Armstrong and Noble then took up the bowling.

The second of these changes soon met with success, Hobbs being bowled by Noble at 54. Hobbs had played a patient, watchful game for an hour and six minutes. Among his hits were two 4's.

Gunn failed, being out leg before wicket with the score still at 54. At this point Noble had taken two wickets for 1 run.

Hutchings was warmly cheered on joining Fane. For some time after this the cricket was very dull, the batsmen risking nothing and trying to wear the bowling down by sheer defence.

In the course of half an hour Fane scored 1 run and Hutchings 13. Meanwhile Saunders at 62 displaced Armstrong, who had bowled six overs, two maidens, for nine runs.

At 69 another change was tried, Hazlitt relieving Noble. So far, Noble's figures were 6-2-5-2.

As no wicket fell, Cotter and Noble bowled again at 83. At the tea interval the total was 93, Fane having made 34 and Hutchings 24.

On starting afresh Cotter and Noble still bowled. The 100 went up as the result of just under two hours and twenty minutes' cricket. Then at 114 Cotter, from whom 47 runs had been scored, made way for Armstrong.

Fane completed his 50 in two hours and thirty-four minutes, but without getting another run he played a ball gently on to his wicket. He hit two 4's in his very patient innings, and gave no chance. Three wickets for 121.

Braund came in, and Macartney at once bowled in place of Noble, whose analysis now showed two wickets for 18 runs.

The change proved effective, as with 10 runs added Hutchings was caught at mid-off. He had batted with great self restraint for nearly an hour and a half. Among his hits were three 4's. Four wickets for 131.

Hardstaff joined Braund and caring little for runs, both batsmen set themselves to play out time.

Anxious to get another wicket, Noble bowled again in place of Armstrong at 144, and put on Saunders for Macartney.

Play was naturally very slow, and Braund had been batting for fifty minutes when his score reached 10.

At 155 Cotter was tried again for Noble, and off his bowling, Braund, who had made 16, was missed by the wicket keeper standing back.

Just before the drawing of stumps Noble went on once more, but nothing happened, the total at the close being 159.

MELBOURNE, Monday.

The newspapers generally agree that the match is one of the most remarkable ever played, and this opinion is shared by the mass of the public. Some of the old players think the English batting was over-cautious, but others are of the opinion that it was the correct game to play in the circumstances. Horan believes that Hutchings was compelled to go slow owing to the state of both game and pitch.

SECOND TEST MATCH.

A SENSATIONAL FINISH.

VICTORY FOR ENGLAND.

BY ONE WICKET AND 1 RUN.

BY MID-ON

The sixth and last day's play on Tuesday attracted 7002 spectators, and as the receipts amounted to £119 4s 3d, the aggregates for the match were:- Spectators 89,385, gate receipts £4070 8s 3d. It was incorrectly announced that the previous record was £4004, for the match between Australia and Stoddart's team, at Melbourne, in 1895. As a matter of fact Sydney still has the gate record, the receipts from the famous match played between Warner's team and Australia in the season 1903-4, amounting to £4274. The finish of the match was in every way worth of its interesting character throughout. When Braund (39), Hardstaff (19), Rhodes (15), and Crawford (10) had been dismissed, and with 8 wickets down, England still wanted 73 to win, it looked any odds on Australia. Then, however, it was that the unexpected (which is the charm of cricket) happened. Barnes and Humphries took the total to 263 for the ninth wicket, and with England's chance appearing to be still utterly forlorn, the last man, Fielder, joined Barnes. How these two successfully defied the various changes which Noble made in his bowling will always be remembered when the great matches of the world are fought o'er again. The opportunity of a lifetime had come to Barnes, and in truth he turned it to good account. Playing all the bowling with consumate ease and perfect confidence he amassed a not out score of 38 runs, and eventually made the winning hit. Fielder's contribution being 19 not out. England wanted 39 runs to win when Fielder joined Barnes, and although odds of 10 to 1 and more were laid on Australia, the Englishmen won a victory which for its sensational character has seldom been equalled and never excelled. In vain did

Noble ring the changes to his bowling. Runs came steadily, and when eventually Barnes made the winning hit, it was generally admitted that a more exciting match had never been witnessed. England won by one wicket and one run, nine being out for 282. Barnes (36) and Fielder (18) carrying out their bats. Barnes was at the wickets an hour and a half, and put up a good performance which satisfied all good judges of the game that he must be reckoned with as a batsman—especially at a tight pinch.

Braund (17) and Hardstaff (17) resumed England's second innings to the bowling of Noble and Cotter, four wickets being down for 159. The former's first over produced three angles, but Hardstaff, hooking Cotter's first ball high and deep to leg was caught near the boundary by Ransford and with 5-19-182 up Rhodes joined Braund. Rhodes had only made 2 when McAlister missed him in the slips off Cotter—a sharp chance—and in the same over Cotter appealed unsuccessfully against Braund for lbw. The batsmen were playing under the weight of a keen sense of responsibility in a serious position, and the Australians were strenghtened by the material improvement in their chance of success which had been brought about by the dismissal of Hardstaff. With 170 up and 112 runs still required to win, the Englishmen had still a big task on hand, and runs came slowly and in singles. Braund got Noble through the slips for 3, and four leg byes were scored in the same over. Braund cutting Cotter for 2, the Englishmen got into their last hundred, 99 being wanted to win. At 184 Saunders replaced Noble, who had taken two wickets for 31 runs, and Braund hit him splendidly to leg for 4. Rhodes drove Cotter for 3, and at 196 Cotter, who had taken one wicket for 67, retired in favour of Armstrong. The latter fairly beat and bowled Braund, who had reached 30 in 1 hour 43 minutes, and the record was 6-30-196. Crawford joined Rhodes, with 86 still wanted, and a cessation of play took place while refreshments were brought out for the fieldsmen. Armstrong, as usual, was sticking up the batsman, who were playing under painfully apparent restraint,

Day Six

The Age 8/1/08

every run being cautiously felt for. Rhodes cut Saunders to third man, and foolishly started for a most risky run, which Crawford wisely declined, and, Armstrong returning to Carter, Rhodes was run out, 7-15-198. Barnes, who followed, got Saunders's next ball past third man for 2, and 200 appeared, made in 4 hours and 41 minutes. Crawford livened the game by hitting Armstrong clean out of the playing ground for 6, but off the next ball he was missed by Saunders at mid-on. In the latter's next over, however, Crawford mis-hit, and was caught at third man by Armstrong, 8-10-308. Humphries, who followed, scored 2 to leg off Saunders, and in the latter's next over drove him brilliantly for 4. At 216 Cotter replaced Armstrong, and bowled a maiden to Humphries. Noble relieved Saunders, and at the adjournment for lunch eight wickets were down for 221, each batsman having made 7, and 61 runs still required to win.

On resuming, Saunders and Cotter bowled, and runs came in singles, the batsmen, for two "tail enders", showing remarkable cleverness and judgment in the running between wickets. At 231 Armstrong replaced Cotter, and Barnes played him to the on for 2. The two batsmen were showing very distinctly by their confident play how badly judged was the policy which had enduced their predecessors to be over-awed by the serious aspect of the game, when it was much less so than at this later stage. The silence of the spectators was significant of their pent up interest, not a sound being heard as ball after ball was played. An occasional burst of applause relieved the stillness, especially when Barnes played Saunders to leg for 3, and Humphries hit Armstrong to leg for 4. The partnership was, however, at length dissolved by Humphries, who had made 16, being given out lbw to Armstrong, and with 9-16-243 up the last man, Fielder, joined Barnes. The latter played each bowler with deliberate judgment, and amidst intense excitement the score was gradually raised to 261, leaving 21 to get to win, when refreshments were again brought out, and a temporary cessation of play in consequence followed. Each stroke was

watched amidst breathless excitement as the score rose steadily. Noble changed his bowling, going on himself at 254 in place of Saunders, and putting Cotter on for Armstrong at 261. Barnes, however, continued to play a dogged game, smothering the good ones, and scoring at every available opportunity. He succeeded in obtaining most of the bowling, and eventually made the winning hit, England

Arthur Fielder's last wicket stand with Sidney Barnes secured England's sensational win.

winning by one wicket and 1 run, nine wickets being down for 282—Barnes 36, and Fielder, 18, being not out. Although the English innings totalled only 282 for nine wickets, it had occupied 6 hours and 3 minutes.

FINAL · SCORES

AUSTRALIA — First Innings

V. Trumper, c Humphries, b Crawford	49
T. Macartney, b Crawford	37
C. Hill, b Fielder	16
M. A. Noble, c Braund, b Rhodes	61
W. W. Armstrong, c Hutchings, b Crawford	31
P. McAlister, run out	10
V. Ransford, run out	27
A. Cotter, b Crawford	17
E. H. Carter, not out	15
G. Hazlitt, b Crawford	1
J. Saunders, b Fielder	0
Extras (lb 1, w 1)	2
Total	**266**

Fall of wickets: 1-84, 2-97, 3-111, 4-168, 5-197, 6-214, 7-240, 8-261, 9-265, 10-266
Bowling: Fielder 27.5-4-77-2, Crawford 29-1-79-5, Barnes 17-4-30-0, Braund 16-5-41-0, Rhodes 11-0-37-1

ENGLAND — First Innings

F. L. Fane, b Armstrong	13
Hobbs, b Cotter	83
Gunn, lbw, b Cotter	15
K. L. Hutchings, b Cotter	126
Braund, b Cotter	49
Hardstaff, b Saunders	12
Rhodes, b Saunders	32
Crawford, c Ransford, b Saunders	16
Barnes, c Hill, b Armstrong	14
Humphries, b Cotter	6
Fielder, not out	6
Extras (b 3, lb 3, w 1, nb 3)	10
Total	**382**

Fall of wickets: 1-27, 2-61, 3-160, 4-268, 5-287, 6-325, 7-353, 8-360, 9-367, 10-382
Bowling: Cotter 38-4-142-5, Saunders 34-7-100-3, Armstrong 34.2-15-36-2, Noble 9-3-26-0, Hazlitt 13-1-34-0, Macartney 12-2-34-0

AUSTRALIA — Second Innings

V. Trumper, lbw, b Crawford	63
M. A. Noble, b Crawford	64
C. Hill, b Fielder	3
P. McAlister, run out	15
W. W. Armstrong, b Barnes	77
T. Macartney, c Humphries, b Barnes	54
V. Ransford, c Hutchings, b Barnes	18
E. H. Carter, c Fane, b Barnes	53
A. Cotter, lbw, b Crawford	27
G. Hazlitt, b Barnes	3
J. Saunders, not out	0
Extras (b 12, lb 8)	20
Total	**397**

Fall of wickets: 1-126, 2-131, 3-135, 4-162, 5-263, 6-303, 7-312, 8-361, 9-392, 10-397
Bowling: Fielder 27-6-74-1, Crawford 38-6-125-3, Barnes 27.4-4-72-5, Braund 18-2-68-0, Rhodes 16-6-38-0

ENGLAND — Second Innings

F. L. Fane, b Armstrong	50
Hobbs, b Noble	28
Gunn, lbw, b Noble	0
K. L. Hutchings, c Cotter, b Macartney	39
Braund, b Armstrong	30
Hardstaff, c Ransford, b Cotter	19
Rhodes, run out	15
Crawford, c Armstrong, b Saunders	10
Humphries, lbw, b Armstrong	16
Barnes, not out	38
Fielder, not out	18
Extras (b 9, lb 7, w 1, nb 2)	19
Total (9 wkts)	**282**

Fall of wickets: 1-54, 2-54, 3-121, 4-131, 5-162, 6-196, 7-198, 8-209, 9-243
Bowling: Cotter 21-8-82-1, Armstrong 23-10-58-3, Noble 16.4-7-41-2, Hazlitt 2-1-8-0, Macartney 9-3-21-1, Saunders 30-9-58-1

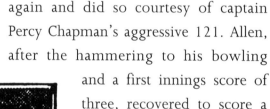

·1930·

LORD'S
SECOND TEST

KUMAR DULEEPSINHJI, right, in his first Test, hit 173 as England batted first, making what seemed an impressive 425. Then Bill Woodfull (155), Bill Ponsford (81), Alan Kippax (83) and Don Bradman (254) helped Australia easily overhaul England's efforts. They piled up a first innings score of 729 for 6 declared. Bradman batted for 339 minutes and found the boundary 25 times, in what was then the highest Test score in England. G. O. 'Gubby' Allen, on his debut, suffered figures of none for 115. England needed 305 to make the tourists bat

K. S. DULEEPSINHJI

again and did so courtesy of captain Percy Chapman's aggressive 121. Allen, after the hammering to his bowling and a first innings score of three, recovered to score a dogged 57. Leg-spinner Clarrie Grimmett bowled 53 overs and was rewarded with figures of six for 167. Australia needed only 72 to win but were given a nervy start at 22 for three with Bradman back in the pavilion, caught brilliantly by Chapman for only a single. Woodfull and Stan McCabe then steadied the ship with a 50 partnership and led Australia to a seven wicket win.

Spectators wait
patiently for entry
to Lord's. Some had
queued all night.

Day One

The Daily Telegraph 28/6/30

ENGLAND'S FINE START IN SECOND "TEST"

RECOVERY AFTER A POOR OPENING

MAGNIFICENT PERFORMANCE BY DULEEPSINHJI

ANOTHER ALL-NIGHT QUEUE AT LORD'S FOR TO-DAY'S PLAY

ENGLAND : 405 for 9

There was another all-night queue at Lord's last night, the first arrival—a man—taking up his place at 5.45 last evening—before play had finished in the first day of the Test match. By midnight there were about three hundred outside the ground and these were continuously increased during the early hours.

After a disappointing opening—Hobbs was out for one at 13, and six wickets had fallen for 239—England recovered brilliantly yesterday.

Duleepsinhji, playing in his first Test match against Australia, was the hero of the day.

In a sound innings, marked by some dazzling cuts, he made with Tate a fine seventh-wicket stand of 98 and then, by setting up a total of 173, passed his uncle Ranjitsinhji's famous 154 not out in his first Test match, and secured the highest score ever made against Australia at Lord's.

Woolley fully justified the faith of the selection committee in including him in the side, and his innings of 41 produced some of the most graceful and powerful strokes of the day.

Before the game began both teams were presented to the Duke of York, who remained until the luncheon interval. The Prime Minister, Miss Ishbel MacDonald and the Maharaja of Nawanagar (Ranjitsinhji) were among the crowd of 25,000 spectators.

Play will be resumed this morning at eleven o'clock. The weather forecast predicts bright periods with local showers and a lower temperature.

WOOLLEY JUSTIFIES SELECTION

By M. D. LYON

LORD'S, Friday

There is something about the atmosphere of a Test Match against Australia at Lord's that places it above the other games, although Manchester and Leeds usually provide the vital matches so far as the actual result of the rubber is concerned.

In the end the three wise men did not chip Woolley, for which I was grateful, for his innings this morning was a gem. He was caught, alas! after an all-too-brief forty-five minutes, in the course of which he played at least half a dozen strokes that for grace and power far outshone any made to-day or in the match at Nottingham. He is still the incomparable left-hand batsman of the world.

Hobbs, for once, made a poor shot at a good-length ball from Fairfax that pitched a little outside the off stump and ran away an inch or two. He was well caught by Oldfield, rather low down. Indeed, Oldfield kept so well that up to the luncheon interval he took every ball, whether from bowler or fieldsman, absolutely clean.

WALL'S BRILLIANT CATCH

Woolley was beaten by two balls from Grimmett, and he was nearly bowled by one from Fairfax that just cleared the top of his off stump. Finally, however, he was out, in a sense most unluckily. For he cut a shortish ball from Fairfax right off the face of the bat just behind point. Wall's catch was brilliant. He took the ball with both hands three or four inches from the ground, just in front of his feet.

Woodfull made a bad mistake in not having Wall on for Duleepsinhji when the latter first came in. It is only when he is starting that "Duleep" plays fast bowling with a certain lack of confidence.

Richardson missed Hammond in the slips off Wall. I say "missed" but hardly anyone else could have got to the catch at all.

Grimmett once again defeated Hammond in the flight, the ball drifted in a little in the air, touched Hammond's pad—he would have been l.b.w.—then hit his wicket. Hammond only really timed one ball, a perfect off drive past extra cover resulting. His form this year is sufficient condemnation of the Australian method of playing with no time-limit, for it is clear that the many long innings he played over there, when the clock did not exist so far as Tests were concerned, have left him without that joyousness at the wicket that characterised his batting two or three years ago.

A FINE PARTNERSHIP

The most valuable partnership between "Duleep" and Hendren, lasted until half-past three. Hendren, who was out most unluckily, caught at deep long leg by

Kumar Duleepsinhji pulls Grimmett to the boundary during his record-breaking debut innings for England. "The crowd cheered him for quite two minutes as he passed three figures." Bert Oldfield is the wicket-keeper.

McCabe, batted, I thought better than anyone. Never at any time did he look like getting out.

After lunch Hornibrook bowled accurately for a long spell from the nursery end, keeping both batsmen very quiet.

Everyone, I am sure, felt genuinely sorry for Woodfull when he dropped Duleepsinhji at square leg off McCabe. It was by no means a difficult chance in this class of cricket, although the ball travelled fairly fast, reaching Woodfull knee-high on his right side, but straight enough to enable him to use two hands, he is usually such a safe catch.

Bradman did not always pick up the ball cleanly, but he ran like a stag in the country, and his throwing was a delight to the eye.

Chapman played a Chapman innings. The taking of the new ball made a great difference to the state of the game, although Fairfax and Wall made it lift occasionally. Maybe the ball was particularly hard—they do vary a little.

Duleepsinhji played a sterling innings, sound rather than brilliant, but as he came in when two wickets had fallen cheaply he played the right game for his side. Subdued as he was, he made some dazzling cuts.

His great popularity was clearly shown when the crowd cheered him for quite two minutes as he passed three figures. Wall dropped him when 98—a sharp chance in the gully, but by no means such a difficult catch as that by which Wall dismissed Woolley.

It seems a pity that Grimmett should have to field at cover. He is no longer in his 'teens, and the running and sidestepping and picking up he has to do in that position must tend to tire him.

STEADY BOWLING

Duleepsinhji and Tate went along merrily after tea, the latter punching the ball heartily when not being hit on the fingers or being beaten by Grimmett's spinners. "Duleep" never drove the ball in front of the wicket until the last quarter of an hour. He has developed rather into a back player, facing the bowler too much, so that he cannot change his position soon enough to bring his left shoulder over the ball to make a full-blooded drive. He played Grimmett very well.

The Australian bowling was steady rather than dangerous, Fairfax probably bowling best.

On the whole it was a pro forma day's cricket, distinguished from the ordinary only by a few shots from Woolley, Duleepsinhji's batting, and Oldfield's superb wicket-keeping.

Day Two

The Daily
Telegraph
30/6/30

BRILLIANT STAND BY OPENING BATSMEN·

ENGLAND BOWLERS DEFIED

BRADMAN'S GENIUS

By COLONEL PHILIP TREVOR

ENGLAND .. .. .. 1st inns., 425
AUSTRALIA .. 1st inns., 404 (2 wkts).

After a day of brilliant batting at Lord's on Saturday, Australia scored 404 runs for the loss of two wickets. They are thus only 21 runs behind England with eight wickets in hand. The King was present during the afternoon, and the game was stopped while the players were presented to him.

All the strength of the England attack, changed often and cunningly, failed to shake the determination of Ponsford and Woodfull in their opening stand, or to check the exuberance of Bradman, who, coming in after Ponsford had left, hit out from the start and scored twice as fast as his captain.

Although England were not at full bowling strength, and the pitch played well all day, the greatest credit is due to the Australians for their skill and judgement.

With one exception—that which cost Ponsford his wicket—no chance was given to the field; the bowlers, indeed, although generally keeping a good length, never looked like taking a wicket.

Bradman's innings of 155 not out was masterly to a degree. Driven occasionally to defence by Tate, beaten once or twice by Robins, he nevertheless played with complete confidence. His placing was delightful; it outwitted the field time and again.

ENGLAND'S LAST WICKET

When the day's play began at eleven the last England wicket had still to fall. There was a little more hitting before Duckworth was caught by the wicket-keeper, Oldfield, standing back. The partnership between Duckworth and White produced 38 runs.

At five and twenty minutes to twelve began England's long day in the field. Australia's opening batsmen were restrained. Ponsford being cautious and Woodfull super-cautious. Still, neither made the semblance of a bad stroke, and neither, indeed, even looked as if he could get out. Tate, G. O. Allen, J. C. White, and R. W. V. Robins failed in turn to make the slightest impression on either of them on that excellent wicket. Struck twice on the leg, high up, by fast balls bowled by Allen, Ponsford remained imperturbable.

Neither he nor Woodfull is a stylist, yet neither was guilty of the slightest sin of omission. It took Woodfull an hour and a half to get twenty runs. Ponsford then scoring twice as fast as his partner. However, in the half hour before luncheon both men added runs more quickly. The score at the interval was 96—Woodfull 35, Ponsford 59.

When the game was resumed Woodfull began to catch Ponsford up, and he had all but done so when the game was momentarily suspended by the arrival of the King. In the first over bowled afterwards Ponsford was caught in the slips; for just over three hours the pair had successfully defied the England bowlers.

BRADMAN'S FINE STYLE

Don Bradman immediately raised the whole tone of the performance. Looking just as safe as Woodfull or Ponsford, he brought into play all of his many scoring strokes. The straight ball which was even slightly under-pitched he forced easily to the square-leg boundary. The slightly under-pitched one on the off-side he cut square to the off boundary. As he also jumped out to drive, he scored very fast.

Bradman has the knack of doing his clever wristwork at the very last moment, and he can use his feet as quickly as he uses his wrists. It took him only forty-five minutes to get his 50, and he got his 100 (out of 152 made while he was at the wicket) after batting just over a hundred minutes. He was at his very best from the first ball bowled him. His daring delighted the real cricketer without ever making him anxious. His was a great—a superb display.

At twenty minutes to six, with the total 325, Woolley was given a trial with the ball. By that time the crowd had begun to laugh as well as cheer. Probably not one of them had ever seen the England bowling so powerless in a Test match played in this country against Australia. I myself, at least, have never seen anything like it.

Yet in the circumstances I am not inclined to anathematise any of the Englishmen who bowled. The batting was just far too good for the bowling—and that is the long and short of it.

BOWLERS CRITICISED

The Australians had to face a total of 425. They proceeded to get more than 400 of these runs by batting that was always correct and subsequently brilliant. It was only natural that the English bowlers should have been severely criticised.

But the bowling was not definitely bad. Tate and White at any rate each kept their length, and Robins bowled fewer loose balls than he did in the first Test match. Allen, it is true, did not succeed in conveying the idea that the Australians did not like fast bowling, while Hammond just kept up an end unobtrusively.

Members of the M.C.C. asked one another if what they saw was really the best bowling which the country could produce.

There was nothing at all the matter with the England ground-fielding. It was all very good, and Chapman, wherever he stationed himself, was superb.

A little before close of play Woodfull was stumped. The Australians have still a long way to go, but they have already done what is practically unique, and an actual win for them is well within the bounds of probability.

No one in this country has yet seen a side open a Test match, get more than 400 runs, and at the end of the second day's play have to ask themselves if they are going to be beaten.

AUSTRALIANS MAKE CRICKET HISTORY.

Day Three

The Daily Mail

1/7/30

Cricket history was made at Lord's yesterday in the second Test match of this year's series.

The Australian batsmen—young Don Bradman in particular—shattered Test cricket records which had stood for many years.

Bradman's innings of 254 is:

The highest score in this country; and

The highest score by an Australian.

The Australian total, 729 for 6 wickets, is a record, the previous highest being England's 636 at Sydney.

The previous highest individual innings in this country and the highest Australian was W. L. Murdoch's 211 in 1884.

Bradman, when the English captain put an end to his innings, was only 33 runs short of R. E. Foster's absolute record for Test matches—287 at Sydney in 1904.

At the end of yesterday's play England, faced with the task of making 304 to avoid an innings defeat, had lost two wickets for 98.

There was an amusing problem at the score board on the popular side yesterday when Australia's total reached 702. The figures could not be turned into position—such figures had never been used—and in the end a diminutive 7 had to be hung in the vacant place. The scene when Bradman reached 200, too, was amazing. He was cheered again and again, and an Australian spectator who seized the ball on the boundary kissed it before throwing it back.

AUSTRALIA.

FIRST INNINGS.

W. M. WOODFULL, st Duckworth, b Robins	155
W. H. PONSFORD, c Hammond, b White	81
D. G. BRADMAN, c Chapman, b White	254
A. F. KIPPAX, b White	83
S. McCABE, c Woolley, b Hammond	44
V. Y. RICHARDSON, c Hobbs, b Tate	30
W. A. OLDFIELD, not out	43
A. FAIRFAX, not out	20
Extras (b. 6, l.b. 8, n.b. 5)	19
Total (6 wkts., dec.)	**729**

CHAPMAN'S GREAT LEAP.

By H. J. HENLEY.

The second Test match continued its dramatic course at Lord's yesterday—and it would be foolish to predict the result of a game that has already upset so many things that were regarded as probabilities.

When Australia declared their innings closed they had batted 10 hours and 10 minutes. In the meantime records and bowlers' hearts had been broken and much harsh criticism had been hurled at these bowlers—and at the English Selection Committee.

The Australian total was 729 with only six men out. Had the match been one of the play-to-a-finish variety the team might have gone on to score a thousand.

Few people who follow cricket ever dreamed that they would live to see a score of over 700 made against England at Lord's; but none begrudged the Australians their success. They had begun their innings against a score so large that it would have overawed most teams—and the innings of Bradman was such that those who saw the first part of it will tell the tale to their grandchildren in the years to come.

SLOW PROGRESS

Although Australia, with two wickets down, were only 21 runs short of England's total when the game was resumed, the batsmen did not attempt to force the pace; in the two hours before lunch the total was increased by no more than a hundred.

Even D. G. Bradman toned down his game and those who had not seen him bat before must have thought that the descriptions of his play on Saturday, so full of superlatives, were wildly exaggerated.

But it must be taken into account that when he went in on Saturday the English bowling had already grown tired. Yesterday he met it at its freshest, and, after all with two days remaining in which to give his team a chance to win, there was no reason why he should take big risks.

Yet the change in his methods was remarkable. He actually allowed maiden overs to be bowled to him—something undreamed of on Saturday. Then he had taken only an hour and 14 minutes to score his first hundred. Yesterday he took three hours to gather his last 99. A. F. Kippax scored at about the same pace, and the slow rate of progress of the two batsmen, with their side already safe from defeat, suggested that the English bowling was not so awful as some people had believed.

CHAPMAN WAS THERE!

Bradman found no difficulty in beating the previous biggest score in this country. But when he had made 254 he lifted the ball for the first time in an innings that had lasted five and a half hours—and this slight indiscretion cost him his wicket.

It was not a bad stroke, for the ball was hit hard and clean from the full centre of the bat blade; but Chapman happened to be in the vicinity of the stroke, which travelled in the direction of extra cover. England's captain made a leap sideways, threw out his long right arm, and held a catch that in its splendour provided a worthy end to a splendid innings. Bradman hit 25 fours.

J. C. White, who was the bowler, recaptured yesterday the mastery of length which had eluded him on Saturday. In the same over he bowled Kippax, who tried to cut a ball off his middle stump. Kippax had taken three hours to score 83—a sound, solid, solemn innings, without trimmings. V. Y. Richardson played the hit-or-miss kind of innings that the position of his side invited and banged up 30 in 25 minutes; S. McCabe also went for the bowling to the extent of 44. The rest of the innings was something of an anti-climax, with runs coming slowly against beaten bowlers and weary fieldsmen.

When the innings was declared closed at the tea interval England needed 304 to save an innings defeat—surely a unique position in a Test match for a team which had opened with a total of 425.

When England began their second innings an hour and 40 minutes remained for play—a very dangerous period at the end of the day, of course, for a team that had every reason to feel tired and dispirited. Especially was it a very uncomfortable position for such a pair of veterans as Hobbs and Woolley, whose united ages amount to 90.

They began confidently, but Woolley gave a "just-possible" chance to the wicket-keeper when he had made 5, and a little later Hobbs played inside and outside and all round a ball which bowled him.

Most English people were prepared for the worst then, and, to worsen matters still further, Woolley, who had settled down, trod on his wicket in the course of a stroke that hit the ball to the boundary!

But Hammond and K. S. Duleepsinhji showed that there was still some fight left in the side.

A CRICKET ROBOT.

By G. A. FAULKNER,
the former South African all-rounder.

It is England's turn now to be up against it—and it is very doubtful indeed whether she will extricate herself from her extremely uncomfortable position. The odds are very much against her, for the wicket, though not actually bad, is slightly worn in places, and it seems to be C. V. Grimmett's turn to win the game for Australia.

The Australians' innings left one gasping. Record after record was smashed while Don Bradman and Kippax remained together.

The pace they set was tedious, but they were obviously following out a well-conceived plan; the result proved them right.

Bradman never looked like getting out. In the whole of his long innings I can hardly remember a ball going off his bat in any direction but one he chose. His tenacity of purpose was remarkable; the placing of his shots certain and convincing; and his confidence in himself unshakable. I have always wondered how the England bowlers were ever able to get him out on good wickets—and I am wondering now as much as ever. He is a cricket robot.

A GORGEOUS SMITE

Richardson and McCabe livened the proceedings up for us. Richardson was always out for runs, and he lifted the ball once right into the stands next to the screens at the Nursery end—a gorgeous

Don Bradman's 254 was the highest score in England and the highest score by an Australian. According to G. A. Faulkner: "Bradman never looked like getting out."

smite. McCabe looked as good as ever. I liked the crispness of his batting, and it will surprise me if a century does not come his way before very long.

Of the England bowlers Tate commanded the most respect—though his analysis might not lead one to suppose so.

The Australians simply laid themselves out to wear him down. Although J. C. White claimed three wickets he hardly worried the batsmen, and G. O. Allen did not by any means come up to expectations. R. W. Robins only appeared dangerous occasionally.

GRIMMETT'S MENACE.

By G. C. DIXON,
who has an intimate knowledge of
Australian cricket.

Only rain can save England to-day. Even if the wicket remained perfect it would be a great performance to save an innings defeat.

As for batting long enough to save the match—well, frankly, I think that is out of the question.

The wicket is still quite good—but it is not as good as it was. At each end it is worn just enough to enable the slow bowlers to turn the ball a little, and on this sort of wicket Grimmett is the best bowler in the world.

He showed his quality early by breaking through Hobbs's defence—the master had one of the worst Tests in his great career.

Later he beat Woolley, Hammond, and Duleepsinhji with cleverly disguised spin and variations of flight.

England's batsmen will need to be super-batsmen to save the game against him to-day.

FIRST RATE

Australia's batting was again first-rate, though not quite as amazing as on Saturday.

Bradman was not nearly so dashing and electrical, but it was pleasing to see that always the side's interests came first. Knowing how ambitious he is, I haven't the slightest doubt that he was terribly keen to beat the 287 of R. E. Foster. But, far from playing safe when the record was within his grasp, he repeatedly ran five or six yards down the pitch to White, and, in the end, jumping out to one that he could not quite get on top of, he threw his wicket away.

SUPERB

England's fielding was again superb. And if ever a man deserved a statue it is lion-hearted Maurice Tate. In the course of the innings he bowled 400 balls, and you could count the bad ones on the fingers of one hand.

TEST MATCH

FOR

AUSTRALIA.

Day of Many Thrills.

CHAPMAN.

121 Runs and a Brilliant Catch.

By Cricketer.

LORD'S, Tuesday

There is a passage in "Tom Jones," greatest of English novels, where Henry Fielding, having got his plot terribly complicated, calls on all the high Muses, in person and severally, for aid, because, as he tells us, without their guidance "I do not know how I am going to bring my story to a successful conclusion." As I write these lines, after a day of wonderful cricket, I feel also the need of inspired and kindly forces. The day's play, in the old term, simply beggars description. England lost the match at noon, nearly won it again at the last hour, and lowered the flag only when forced down by sheer odds.

When twelve o'clock struck in the clock covered with ivy near the nursery, England were 147 for five, with Hobbs, Woolley, Hammond, Duleepsinhji, and Hendren all gone and 157 still needed to save themselves from defeat by an innings. Grimmett was master. Against his spin Hammond, Duleepsinhji, and Hendren had been batsmen sorely troubled and helpless. Now Chapman came in, and before making a run he mis-hit Grimmett's spin and sent the easiest of catches conceivable in a Test match. Victor Richardson seemed to lose sight of the ball, which fell

to the grass. Chapman's lucky star has never shone with to-day's brightness; he lived to play one of the most astonishing innings I have ever seen. Allen helped him in a stand which, coming as it did after the impotence of Hammond and Hendren, was incredibly secure once Chapman had found that he could kick Grimmett's breakaway with legs and pads which were quite indecently unconcerned with any academic relationship between a batsman's footwork and his bat. Chapman and Allen were undefeated at lunch, by which time they had taken England's score from 147 for 5 to 262 for 5. After the interval Grimmett's straight ball baffled Allen at 272. The sixth English wicket scored 125 in 95 minutes.

Allen's courage and his trustfulness in the forward stroke, defensively and offensively, put rather to shame the aimlessness and shiftlessness which we had witnessed (very painfully) when some of his superiors in technique were at the wicket. The day indeed was a triumph for courage and optimism—and an exposure of that professionalism which is too often content to work according to its own routined machinery and has too little use for the influences of imagination. Chapman's innings was no doubt technically very bad at parts, but probably the hardened county expert was inclined to look indulgently upon Chapman's many and fortunate mis-hits. But if Chapman's innings could not be called batmanship in the strict technical sense, it was something better than that in the eyes of Providence—it was an act of faith and cheerfulness. Before Chapman arrived at the wicket technique (of a sort) had proved useless for England in a dark hour—useless because it was technique and nothing else, lacking as it did the beard of men determined not to look at difficulties save to see them as hills that could be scaled granted the effort and the risk.

While Hammond and Hendren tried to tackle Grimmett, you would have sworn the wicket was sticky; each batsman thrust out a bat protectively and groped for the ball. Hendren, true, hit a beautiful four through the covers and a desperate on-drive against the spin, but the stroke which got him caught at "silly" mid-off was a purely speculative stab in the dark. Hendren's innings was distressingly touched with mortality and not worthy of a Test match player.

CHAPMAN AND GRIMMETT

After Allen's wicket fell, Chapman's innings went gloriously insane, yet retained some method in its madness. No cricketer, no matter how blessed by the gods, can hope to hit Grimmett simply by flinging his bat at the air. As a fact, Chapman by a curious compound of push work with his pads and a delayed forward stroke, quite upset Grimmett's tactics at the beginning of his innings, even while England's position was at its worst. Grimmett packed the off-side field to Chapman, and pitched his leg break wide of the off stump. As soon as Chapman had got sight of the ball, he pulled Grimmett round to the on, often in the grand manner, and sometimes sending the ball to fine leg with a very likeable lack of intent. Three times he achieved colossal on-drives from Grimmett for six. When his score was in the nineties and everybody on the ground save Chapman in a state of proud and affectionate anxiety, Chapman gorgeously mis-hit a ball over the slips for four, and he seemed to enjoy the escapade even more than he enjoyed those of his hits which observed the unities.

In an hour after lunch Chapman plundered 69 runs from the Australian attack, and his most remunerative, if not his most violent strokes were square-leg hits from Grimmett, a straight drive from Grimmett, a clout into the people on the mound stand from Grimmett, a hit to long leg from Grimmett, a pull toward leg from Hornibrook, another clout into the mound stand, a drive to long-on from Hornibrook, a thoroughly characteristic snick from Hornibrook, and then another six, all the more delightful because four of the runs were given away for nothing by overthrows which sent the crowd into fits of laughter and applause. Seldom can an innings in a Test match have caused more jubilation and hubbub amongst a crowd. Probably we should have to go as far back as Jessop's great routing of the Australians

in 1902 to find an equal to this innings by Chapman—that is, an equal as far as animal spirits are concerned, for of course Jessop's greatest innings was not only energy, strong and fearless, but energy concentrated and made whole by a masterful range of strokes all over the field. Nearly all of Chapman's major strokes to-day were drives theoretically or in practice. He came to the wicket when most of us were looking up trains for home. By the time he had been batting two hours we were as busy ringing up our hotels asking for a room for one night longer. Chapman fell to a clever catch by Oldfield at 354. In two hours and a half he made 121 out of a total of 207 scored while he was at the wicket.

THE MYSTERIOUS SPOT

The less said of the remainder of the English innings the better. There was a spot on the pitch at the pavilion end, I am told on excellent authority that it was there all Monday. The English bowlers were very remiss not finding it out with Grimmett's alacrity. It must be recorded as a curiosity that when Chapman batted the imp of evil in the turf seemed temporarily to become exorcised, or, if it remained there at all, had no intent more malicious than to provide that impetus which always makes a snick behind the stumps a certain four. Grimmett apart, none of the Australian bowlers were troublesome. Chapman played himself in to the fast bowling of Wall. Fairfax was for a while curiously neglected.

The day so far had been hectic enough, and thousands of throats must have hurt from the shouts that had punctuated every hit by Chapman. But sensation had not finished with us yet. She had yet another shriek to set our hearts beating. At ten minutes to four Woodfull and Ponsford walked confidently into the sunshine to score the mere 72 needed for an Australian victory. Against Hammond and Tate Ponsford batted as though eager to hit off the score himself, and two fours from Tate set his innings into excellent motion. Woodfull when one only hit a ball hard to Duleepsinhji at mid-on. To Chapman the chance would have been easy, but

Duleepsinhji could not hold the catch. Scarcely had the crowd subsided from this alarum than Ponsford was bowled by Robins. The first Australian wicket—it was not to be the last—fell in Robin's first over; indeed Ponsford was out the very next ball. Robins found the spot at the pavilion end, and his spin was excellent and, for a while, his length of the sort that keeps the batsman tortuously in two minds.

A WONDERFUL CATCH

It was not good bowling but marvellous fielding that captured the second Australian wicket at 17. Bradman cut Tate magnificently; it was one of the best strokes of the match. The ball flashed hard toward the ground quicker than sight could follow. The crack of the bat was triumphant. Chapman took the ball at his feet with both hands and threw it in the air almost before we knew what had happened. I have never seen a finer catch or a more beautiful one for that matter, and I have never seen a finer or more beautiful fieldsman than Chapman. Bradman could scarcely believe his eyes, and he walked slowly back to the pavilion. The ovation to Chapman was probably heard a mile away.

Then came another of those dramatic silences which fall on a cricket field after a moment of tumult. Robins bowled Kippax, the ball spun, and Kippax tried a cut. Duckworth's clamant crow split the skies, and another roar from the crowd went up as the finger of the umpire was seen pointing on high. The appeal of Duckworth was worthy of the word great; the occasion demanded it. His catch was a masterpiece of clean alacrity. And now Australia were 22 for 3 and the whole of Lord's was a bedlam, the heat of the afternoon was as though thrown out from action. Voices everywhere were asking could England, after all, win? Was it possible? "You never know," said a man in white spats non-committally. And he added, as though discovering an entirely new and original thought, "It's a funny game is cricket." When McCabe came in Woodfull went towards him to meet him. Words were spoken. The scene and the

The R101 passes over Lord's.

FINAL · SCORES

ENGLAND — First Innings

Hobbs, c Oldfield, b Fairfax	1
Woolley, c Wall, b Fairfax	41
Hammond, b Grimmett	38
K. S. Duleepsinhji, c Bradman, b Grimmett	173
Hendren, c McCabe, b Fairfax	48
A. P. F. Chapman, c Oldfield, b Wall	11
G. O. Allen, b Fairfax	3
Tate, c McCabe, b Wall	54
R. W. V. Robins, c Oldfield, b Hornibrook	5
J. C. White, not out	23
Duckworth, c Oldfield, b Wall	18
Extras (b 2, lb 7, nb 1)	10
Total	425

Fall of wickets: 1-13, 2-53, 3-105, 4-209, 5-236, 6-239, 7-337, 8-383, 9-387, 10-425

Bowling: Wall 29.4-2-118-3, Grimmett 33-4-105-2, Fairfax 31-6-101-4, Hornibrook 26-6-62-1, McCabe 9-1-29-0

AUSTRALIA — First Innings

Woodfull, st Duckworth, b Robins	155
Ponsford, c Hammond, b White	81
Bradman, c Chapman, b White	254
Kippax, b White	83
McCabe, c Woolley, b Hammond	44
Richardson, c Hobbs, b Tate	30
Oldfield, not out	43
Fairfax, not out	20
Extras (b 6, lb 8, w 5)	19
Total (6 wkts dec.)	729

Fall of wickets: 1-162, 2-393, 3-585, 4-588, 5-643, 6-672

Bowling: Allen 34-7-115-0, Tate 64-18-148-1, White 51-7-158-3, Robins 42-1-172-1, Hammond 35-8-82-1, Woolley 6-0-35-0

ENGLAND — Second Innings

Hobbs, b Grimmett	19
Woolley, hit wkt, b Grimmett	28
Hammond, c Fairfax, b Grimmett	32
Duleepsinhji, c Oldfield, b Hornibrook	48
Hendren, c Richardson, b Grimmett	9
Chapman, c Oldfield, b Fairfax	121
Allen, lbw, b Grimmett	57
Tate, c Ponsford, b Grimmett	10
Robins, not out	11
White, run out	10
Duckworth, lbw, b Fairfax	0
Extras (b 16, lb 13, w 1)	30
Total	375

Fall of wickets: 1-45, 2-58, 3-129, 4-141, 5-147, 6-272, 7-329, 8-354, 9-372, 10-375

Bowling: Wall 25-2-80-0, Fairfax 12.4-2-37-2, Grimmett 58-13-167-6, Hornibrook 22-6-49-1, Bradman 1-0-1-0, McCabe 3-1-11-0

AUSTRALIA — Second Innings

Woodfull, not out	26
Ponsford, b Robins	14
Bradman, c Chapman, b Tate	1
Kippax, c Duckworth, b Robins	3
McCabe, not out	25
Extras (b 1, lb 2)	3
Total (3 wkts)	72

Fall of wickets: 1-16, 2-17, 3-22

Bowling: Tate 13-6-21-1, Hammond 4.2-1-6-0, Robins 9-1-34-2, White 2-0-8-0

occasion were obviously trying to Woodfull himself let alone to a young cricketer with his spurs still to win. Woodfull again was Australia's good anchor. He watched Robins's spin to his bat, yet had one or two narrow escapes from edged strokes through the slips. McCabe, reliant as Woodfull, playing finely, meeting the ball cleanly and confidently. Here is another great batsman in the making.

Sad to say the end was anticlimax. Robins raised our hopes by a spell of bowling clever and as waspish of spin as anything achieved in the match by Grimmett. Then, with a quite sickening suddenness, his length went to pieces. Thirteen were hit from one over—and once again the Australians' crown on the stand lifted up heart and voice. The winning hit was made at five o'clock, and a memorable day was at an end.

CHAPMAN'S MATCH

As the cricketers came from the field sunshine fell on them, touching them with a lovely light. It might well have been a light cast by immortality, for this match will certainly never be forgotten. Australia won against a first innings score of 425; England, though compelled to bat needing 304 to avoid defeat in an innings, made 375 on the fourth day of a match played at Lord's in dry weather—a gallant performance. Victors and vanquished emerge from the game the better and the more historical for it. The finish when Australia were sweating by the brow to score 72 for victory was ironical. Only the day before they had waxed fat to the strength of 729 for six. The game of cricket played by men of true sport is incomparable.

Perhaps in years to come this match will be known as Chapman's match. Though for the first time he is a defeated English captain, his renown has been increased thereby, and not only because of a lion-hearted century. The match's greatest cricket was Chapman's fielding; it was fielding unparalleled. The catch that dismissed Bradman was a good crown for work which, by its swiftness, its accuracy, and for its beauty, will assuredly go down for good and all in the most precious annals of the game.

·1933·

THE THIRD TEST MATCH of the 1932/33 tour, in which England were victorious by no fewer than 338 runs, will go down in history as probably the most unpleasant ever played. So hostile was the feeling of the Australian public against England's captain Jardine, *right*, that on the days before the game started people were excluded from the ground when the Englishmen were practising. When Australia went in to bat and Woodfull was hit over the heart again, while Oldfield had to retire owing to a blow he received on the head, the majority of the spectators completely lost all hold of their feelings. Insulting remarks were hurled at Jardine, and when

Larwood started to bowl he came in for his share of the storm of abuse. Altogether the whole atmosphere was a disgrace to cricket. Jardine did not shrink from his line of action and showed great pluck in often fielding near to the boundary where he became an easy target for offensive remarks. Much as they disliked his methods, all the leading Australian critics were unanimous in their praise of his skill as a leader. (From *Wisden*, 1933.)

Harold Larwood, the centre of controversy during a Test match described in 'Wisden' as: "probably the most unpleasant ever played." Larwood was the chief protagonist of leg-theory or "bodyline" bowling designed to counter the brilliance of Don Bradman.

Day
One

The Times
14/1/33

ENGLAND'S POOR START

FINE STAND BY WYATT AND LEYLAND

FROM OUR SPECIAL CORRESPONDENT
ADELAIDE, SOUTH AUSTRALIA,

After a gallant fight England regained much of the ground they had lost early in the innings in the third Test Match, which was begun at the Adelaide Oval to-day in perfect weather. Jardine succeeded in winning the toss this time, but England had lost four leading batsmen at luncheon-time for 37. Then a magnificent partnership between Leyland and R. E. S. Wyatt stemmed the tide and when stumps were pulled up England had scored 236 for the loss of seven wickets, a good score in the circumstances, but hardly good enough for the first innings of a Test Match on a wicket which, if not perfect, was by no means bad. The Australians, therefore, are temporarily in the ascendant.

Jardine, having performed a captain's duty for the first time in this series, decided to take first innings. The problem of finding a partner for Sutcliffe to open the innings has been troubling the selectors and, despite his recent failures, Jardine stepped into the breach. The teams were not announced until the last minute, when some surprise was caused by the omission of the Nawab of Pataudi. Bowes also was out of the team and Verity and Paynter were included, with Brown as twelfth man. Ponsford replaced O'Brien, who was twelfth man for Australia.

EARLY DISASTER

Within the first hour England suffered the worst reverse she has experienced since the Sydney Test Match in 1925. Wall opened the bowling with O'Reilly and Jardine was always uncomfortable when facing the former, who has probably never bowled so fast in his career. Jardine showed a tendency to leave the leg stump unguarded and Wall knocked it back in the fourth over, when Jardine had made only three. Hammond was inclined to

flick at rising balls from Wall and after scoring two was out to a fine catch by Oldfield. Wall had taken two for ten runs in six overs, including two maidens. Jardine again altered the batting order and sent in Ames in next. Ames began on the defensive. In playing O'Reilly Sutcliffe hit the ball towards mid-on and Wall flung himself at full length on the ground, holding the ball a few inches from it.

Three wickets thus had fallen for 16 when Leyland came in. He immediately began to go for the bowling, doubtless mindful of the axiom that attack is the best defence. However, after an hour's play only 23 runs were on the board. Three runs later Wall was relieved by Ironmonger, who bowled Ames middle stump in his fourth over with a fast spinner. Ames made three in 39 minutes.

Leyland and Wyatt then began their invaluable, dogged partnership. They batted aggressively and enterprisingly and scored 156 runs before they were separated. Wyatt and Leyland, in fact, saved a complete disaster and eventually mastered the bowling, scoring easily off every bowler. It was evident that the wicket had lost its earlier pace and the Australian bowlers, particularly Grimmett, came in for much punishment. Wyatt lifted Grimmett into the stand twice within a few minutes and, later, he hit a short ball from Wall out of the ground. They put on 156 in 145 minutes.

THE STAND BROKEN

Leyland was the first to go. After an appeal for lbw had not been sustained O'Reilly bowled him. He had made 83 in three hours, hitting 13 4's in a fearless innings. The fifth wicket stand of 156 runs was 36 runs short of the English record. Paynter then joined Wyatt, who was soon caught by Richardson off Grimmett. Wyatt batted for 164 minutes, and hit three 6's and three 4's. It was a magnificently confident innings. Then after many l.b.w. appeals by all the bowlers Allen had to go when he got in front of a ball from Grimmett. He had made 15. Playing in his first test match Paynter batted well and, with Verity, played out time.

Day
Two

The Times
16/1/33

ENGLAND'S GRAND RECOVERY

CHEAP AUSTRALIAN WICKETS

FROM OUR SPECIAL CORRESPONDENT
ADELAIDE, SOUTH AUSTRALIA,

At the close of play in the third Test Match here to-day England, having effected a remarkable recovery, had the game in their favour. Paynter and Verity followed the excellent example set them on the first day by R. E. S. Wyatt and Leyland, putting on 94 runs for the eighth wicket, and England's score had been increased from 236 for seven to 341 before the last wicket fell. Australia started dismally against the bowling of Larwood and G. O. Allen and had four wickets down for 51. Then, however, Ponsford and Richardson stayed together till stumps were pulled up with the score 109 for four wickets. It is generally held that Australia need a lead of at least 100 on the first innings if they are to hold a chance of winning, and if the present partnership between Richardson and Ponsford fails they are not likely to obtain it, as there are no other notable batsmen to follow them even though some runs may be expected from the Australian "tail." The wicket so far is wearing wonderfully well but Australia have to take the fourth innings on it when there must be some signs of wear. Hitherto, however, it has been described as aa batsman's paradise. The outlook for Australia, still 232 behind with four of their best batsmen out, cannot be said to be a bright one.

In spite of frequent bowling changes Paynter and Verity continued their dogged stand uperturbed. Paynter was very impressive in his first Test Match innings. He used his feet well against Grimmett's slow bowling, hitting him freely past cover-point, and Verity at times played like an opening batsman. After luncheon Grimmett was unable to turn the ball, but Wall's increasing pace enabled him to finish with the good analysis of five for 72, a great performance for a fast bowler on the Adelaide wicket.

Within an hour of the beginning of their innings Australia were in a desperate position, having lost three leading batsmen, Fingleton, Bradman, and McCabe, for a total of 34. These valuable wickets were lost by weak strokes, and with the exception of Woodfull, who was hit in the chest by a ball from Larwood which obviously hurt him, and was unlucky into the bargain, all the batsmen gave chances, and did not show their best form.

EARLY SUCCESSES

Larwood began by bumping the ball disconcertingly, and after Fingleton had been dismissed by Allen he switched over to leg theory. At one time he had only two men on the off side. He was successful in trapping McCabe and Bradman, who fell surprisingly easy victims. This did not meet with the approval of the crowd, who made hostile demonstrations when the batsmen ducked. Vehement protests followed when Woodfull was hit over the heart and had to leave the ground in order to receive massage. As in the case of England the fifth-wicket partnership stemmed the tide of disaster, though both batsmen played shakily throughout.

Australia's desperate situation is causing much comment and despondency, and Australia's comparative failure on a perfect wicket is keenly discussed. M. A. Noble urges the batsmen to "dig themselves in" and so tire the bowling. Praise is due to the resourceful captaincy of both Jardine and Woodfull, particularly in their bowling tactics, which kept the batsmen playing all the time and never gave them a chance to settle down. A feature of the match has been the large number of appeals which were disallowed. So far only one batsman has been out lbw. Numerous appeals were made during the partnership of Ponsford and Richardson, which has already had three of four escapes. Voce had to leave the field after bowling five overs owing to an ankle injury and it is probable that Voce will not be able to go on again in the match.

Jardine's Fiery Quartette.

The three M.C.C. fast bowlers and Voce, who is as near fast as doesn't matter.

Above and below: how the 'Illustrated Sporting and Dramatic News' presented "Jardine's Fiery Quartette" prior to England's departure for the most controversial series in Test cricket history.

THE BID TO PIERCE AUSTRALIAN DEFENCES: ENGLAND'S FOUR PACE BOWLERS

There will be protests at including Voce among the fast bowlers at D. R. Jardine's disposal. Cricketers who play him from the pavilion are unanimously of the opinion that he is not above medium pace. Cricketers who bat against him regularly in the middle are not so sure. Anyhow, England has great hopes that Voce will succeed where F. R. Foster succeeded. Of the three orthodox fast bowlers, Larwood still appears to be supreme, but Bowes the most promising. Allen, at his best, can possibly leave both of them for sheer pace. But he is selected as an all-rounder. He is the only man in English cricket who may open for England both batting and bowling in a Test match.

ENGLAND'S LEAD

FINE INNINGS BY PONSFORD

FROM OUR OWN CORRESPONDENT

ADELAIDE, SOUTH AUSTRALIA,

England, as a result of the third day's play in the Test Match here, are in a winning position. They are now 204 runs ahead with nine wickets to fall, and as Australia will have to bat last victory seems assured for England. Although Sutcliffe is out, a big score is probable for England, and the Australians will have to face a substantial deficit. The wicket is wearing well, and the Australian spin bowlers are unlikely to receive any assistance from it. It is evident that Larwood is at present master of the situation, and Allen has proved himself to be a formidable second string. There had been mild demonstrations early to-day when Ponsford was hit on the body, but when Oldfield was struck on the head by a ball from Larwood the crowd of over 35,000 gave vent to their feelings. Larwood was then bowling to an orthodox off field, and Oldfield swung at a rising ball which seemed to fly off the edge of the bat on to

Oldfield's temple. Oldfield staggered away and collapsed, and after receiving treatment had to retire. The indignant crowd abused Larwood and Jardine, and continued their wild shouting when England opened their innings. Oldfield is suffering from concussion and shock, but is expected to play to-morrow.

Everything to-day depended upon the partnership between Ponsford and Richardson, and it was serious for Australia when it was broken. Richardson, after having played a dogged innings, dragged a ball on the off-side on to his wicket. This was the end of the last dependable pair, and Australia were in a serious position. Larwood was quickly changing his method of attack from leg to off theory, and the batsmen were frequently hit. Ponsford, however, batted with great confidence and skill, and Oldfield, in a great fighting innings, showed that Australia's tail did not begin with the fall of the fifth wicket. Ponsford was magnificent, for he held the innings together when the batting threatened to collapse entirely.

When England began their second innings Jardine again partnered Sutcliffe, who again failed, being out to a wonderful catch on the boundary by O'Brien, fielding as a substitute. After giving several chances Jardine and Wyatt played out time in a period of dull and lifeless cricket.

The moments that shaped history. Australia's Bert Oldfield is hit on the head by a ball from Larwood, above, and is forced to retire. Examination revealed a linear fracture of the skull. The irony is that the incident arose not from a ball delivered to a leg theory, but orthodox off side field.

*"Smith's Weekly"
was in no doubt.
The tactics of
England's captain
Douglas Jardine and
the bowling of
Larwood had
brought "sudden
death to the
traditions of the
game."*

"It's Not Cricket"—But Woodfull Always Plays the Game

BOARD OF CONTROL SHOULD STATE ITS VIEWS TO THE M.C.C. IN ENGLAND

Jardine Is Answerable For Larwood's Bowling Tactics

MAURICE TATE AN ONLOOKER IN TESTS

TO-DAY the man who "plays cricket," in a fine sportsmanlike way that nobody in the world can excel, is W. M. WOODFULL, captain of the Australian Eleven.

He took his knock over the heart from savage bowling. He played his innings, and he scored runs. Then he told Manager "Plum" Warner, plainly and simply, what he thought of the —

"Plum" Warner

SUDDEN DEATH TO TRADITIONS OF GAME

— bowling tactics of the English Eleven.

He made no complaint to anybody else; neither to the newspapers, nor to the big public who listened to him on the broadcast.

That's a man, if you like. All the honors are with him, and none are with Warner or Jardine.

On the Monday of the Test, the same bowler stunned Oldfield, in the middle of a match-saving score. "IT'S NOT CRICKET."

W. M. WOODFULL, Australian Captain.

D. R. JARDINE, English Captain.

ENGLAND WINNING

STEADY PROGRESS AT ADELAIDE

FROM OUR OWN CORRESPONDENT
ADELAIDE, SOUTH AUSTRALIA.

England, taking their time on a wicket which appears to be wearing well, established a big lead to-day and at the close of play had increased their advantage to 415 with four wickets still to fall. Their position would have been even more satisfactory had not Hammond thrown his wicket away to the last ball of the day, a bad one from Bradman, when he had made 85 by excellent cricket. It is probable that Paynter will be able to bat to-morrow. England's batting throughout the day was steady and patient, only 211 runs being scored in the day, but these tactics were sound, for the more wear they have out of the wicket the worse will be Australia's chance in the fourth innings.

There was a small attendance of spectators, indicating a waning interest in a game which Australia are not now likely to win. The play was certainly dull, but there was no reason why the Englishmen should hit out. The wicket was easy and gave the bowlers little help. D. R. Jardine justified himself as an opening batsman, after his recent failures, and although he was painfully slow his innings was of immense value to his side. Grimmett and O'Reilly by their excellent length kept the batsmen quiet. It has been the hottest day during the Test Match, and this affected the fielding, although Wall's two catches were magnificent. The fielding of the Australians naturally was weakened through the absence of Oldfield, who was unable to play on account of his injury. Richardson kept wicket well, but he was missed in the field. Ironmonger's slowness also was a handicap.

SLOW BATTING

Jardine and Wyatt started with great caution and only 45 runs were put on before luncheon. Jardine got himself well set and averaged only 12 runs an hour for four and a half hours. Wyatt was more enterprising and showed an inclination to hit hard, but the good-length bowlers kept his score down. Allen was sent in at the fall of the second wicket. He began briskly enough, but soon slowed up his rate of scoring, and after he had made 15 he reached forward in order to smother Grimmett's breaks and, after succeeding four times, missed the ball and once again was out leg-before-wicket for the same score and to the same bowler as in the first innings. Grimmett, although he was keeping a good length, presented no great difficulty and seems to be losing a great deal of his terrors.

In the absence of Paynter, who wrenched his ankle badly yesterday, Hammond followed Allen. He, too, was enterprising at first, but later became much more subdued. Leyland's innings was the brightest of the day and he quickly reached double figures, hitting hard. Woodfull put Bradman on to bowl in the last over of the day, and the first ball, a full-pitch outside the leg stump, Hammond tried to hit too hard and only turned it on to his stumps. Hammond's innings consolidated England's position and his partnership with Leyland may prove to have won the match. Hammond made many powerful shots to the off and he used his feet well against Grimmett. He seemed well set and immovable and must be deemed unlucky to have lost his wicket in such a way.

To-day was comparatively quiet after yesterday's excitements.

One English newspaper's answer to leg theory.

A sequence of photographs, right to left, showing Harold Larwood's perfect bowling action. With his pace and

Day Five

The Times
19/1/33

ENGLAND'S WINNING POSITION

AUSTRALIA PROTEST AT LEG-THEORY

FROM OUR OWN CORRESPONDENT
ADELAIDE, SOUTH AUSTRALIA,

England seem almost certain to beat Australia in the Third Test Match for, after scoring 412 in their second innings and leaving the Australians 532 to make in order to win, they succeeded in dismissing four of their best batsmen in the second innings for 120 before stumps were pulled up to-day. At the close of play Ponsford, Fingleton, McCabe, and Bradman were all out, and Woodfull and Richardson may be regarded as Australia's last hope, though Oldfield, if he is able to go in, which seems unlikely, is capable of a good performance. The wicket was still in excellent order when Australia went in a second time. On the form of this match the English team have proved themselves superior all round.

This morning Woodfull varied his tactics almost desperately in order to dismiss the remaining English batsmen. These however, seemed quite capable of dealing with the situation. The Australian bowlers may have got little help from the wicket, but it is significant that, later on, Larwood, Verity, and Allen soon accounted for four of the best of Australian batsmen. The English team gave a great exhibition of consistent batting. Larwood refrained from leg-theory bowling against Fingleton and Ponsford, but even while not employing this form of attack, about which there has been such a pother, had little difficulty in dismissing them. He is definitely a great bowler and the master of the Australian batting.

The only bright feature of the match from the Australian point of view was Bradman's bright innings to-day. In a little over an hour he showed his best form. He hit the the bowling hard at a critical period, and he made it look playable, which other Australians have hitherto failed to do. The crowd applauded heartily while Jardine kept his bowlers to the off theory, but when he reverted to leg theory against Bradman, who seemed to be getting the better of the bowling, they howled and hooted loudly. Except for Bradman, who practically threw his wicket away through over-eagerness, no Australian played the bowling with any confidence, although Woodfull was steady.

ENGLAND MAKE SURE

There was rain last night, but the showers had the effect of binding the wicket and it is still good for many hundreds more. It was evident at the start of play that Jardine wanted every possible run in order to make victory certain. Even when England had set Australia an almost impossible task he sent in Paynter, who was still suffering badly from a sprained ankle. Leyland ran for Paynter, who was seriously handicapped in his footwork and clearly in pain. England were distinctly lucky before luncheon when the Australian fielding was poor and chances were missed, particularly behind the wicket. Richardson, however, did well in Odfield's presence behind the wicket and the consequent presence of Richardson in the field might have served substantially to reduce England's score.

Ames batted well after a lean period in Test matches, but he gave two chances. Verity played a dogged innings and confirmed himself as a good batsman. He showed a nice variety variety of strokes. O'Reilly varied his pace and flighted the ball well towards the end of the innings and finished with the best figures for Australia.

When Australia went in Larwood began bowling to an off-field. His first few opening overs were very fast and he completely beat Fingleton with his pace. Ponsford went in at the fall of the first wicket. He began well, but was out to a good stroke. Larwood had, so far, taken two for one run. Larwood continued bowling to an orthodox field for a few overs, but, after Bradman had begun to score freely off him, he reverted to the leg theory. Woodfull and Bradman continued to make runs off Larwood and Bradman hit eight 4's and a 6 before he was caught and bowled by Verity.

The Australian Board of Control have cabled a protest against "body-line bowling" to the M. C. C. (See panel opposite).

accuracy, he was the perfect weapon in Jardine's leg theory armoury.

Day Six

The Times
20/1/33

"A MENACE TO THE GAME"

ADELAIDE, Wednesday.

The Australian Cricket Board of Control have sent this cable to the M.C.C. on the subject of the leg-theory controversy:

"Body-line bowling has assumed such proportions as to menace the best interests of the game, making protection of the body by the batsmen the main consideration.

" This is causing intensely bitter feeling between the players as well as injury. In our opinion it is unsportsmanlike.

" Unless stopped at once, it is likely to upset the friendly relations existing between Australia and England.
(Signed) Board of Control."

'Asked if he would make any comment on the leg-theory controversy, Mr. Warner, joint manager of the English team, said he would not make any statement to-day.

"Like Bismarck," he added, "I can be silent in seven languages!"—Reuter.

ENGLAND'S SUCCESS

A CONSISTENT PERFORMANCE

FROM OUR CRICKET CORRESPONDENT

The news yesterday morning that the Test Match at Adelaide had come to an end, quite apart from a natural satisfaction that England had been victorious, was received in this country with that feeling of relief which comes to a man when a turbulent tooth ceases to ache. It was indeed a sorry business, and so long as the technical and ethical points arising from the so-called "body-line bowling" are sub judice it would be improper here to discuss a matter which in due course the M.C.C. will no doubt settle satisfactorily.

But as we have hitherto heard only the Australian point of view, it is permissible to suggest that there has been a form of interference quite as serious as the alleged unfairness of the "leg-theory" bowling. Larwood has had to bowl under the disability that if a batsman as a result of his own negligence were hit the blame would be assumed by the mass of spectators to lie with the bowler. The knowledge of this, had it weighed with Larwood, could only tend to limit the value of a fast bowler, and it is to the credit of Larwood and his captain that they stuck imperturbably to their work in distressing circumstances.

CONSOLING FEATURES

If for a moment we can penetrate the fog of nonsense which has enveloped this match we can find a wealth of splendid cricket to console us. Regarded dispassionately it was, in fact, in many ways an excellent game, and granted that Australia had the worst of the luck in that they lost both the toss and their wicket-keeper, nothing can depreciate the merit of England's complete success. England after a disastrous start in their first innings, when they lost four of their best batsmen with only 30 runs on the board, fought back magnificently, thanks to the resolution of Leyland, R. E. S. Wyatt, Paynter, and Verity. During that time, and again in England's second innings when a winning advantage was being rubbed in, the bowling of O'Reilly, Ironmonger, and Wall, wisely and courageously directed by Woodfull, and supported by unflagging work in the field, must have been magnificent.

The bowling of the Australians in these three Test matches, even if Grimmett is no longer the terror he was, has been one of the finest features of the play, and has received scant recognition. When it came to be Australia's turn to bat there was again a grand exhibition of the fighting spirit, and it is doubtful whether a better innings has been seen during this unhappy tour than Ponsford's 85. England's bowling, however, was too good for most of the Australian batsmen, and when Jardine serenely and sedately consolidated an already big lead in the second innings it was obvious that not even the genius of Bradman could save his side from defeat. It was left to Woodfull, by a display of valour and steadfastness typical of the man, to finish the match on a high note, and it is earnestly to be hoped that the suggestion that this great cricketer will take no further part in these present Test matches is without foundation.

A TEAM IN BEING

It is good to feel that in achieving this success every member of the English side played his part—dare one say except Sutcliffe, who for once in a lifetime was not in the picture? The team as a whole showed a combined strength which has been lacking in recent years, with a welcome volume of all-round players to stiffen the middle and tail end of the side. Allen has been a great success, proving himself in every respect worthy of the high opinion in which he was held by the Selectors. He is one of those "busy" cricketers whom a captain loves to have on his side. Verity, whose bowling was more valuable than his analysis suggests, has been known in Yorkshire to be a batsman of high possibilities, and his form in this game recalls one's mind to the example of

Rhodes. It is early days yet to suggest that Verity may in time go in first for England, but it is not beyond the bounds of likelihood.

Whether Ames had made runs in the second innings or not his wicket-keeping alone seems now to have earned him his place in the English team, which but for a little discomfort in finding a suitable order of batting has now taken something like a definite and pleasant shape. For the Australians in their attempt to find a worthy team it is not easy to speak so cheerfully. They have four or five good batsmen, and three bowlers who have done all that could be asked of them, but there is a lack of that solidity which is usually the hall-mark of an Australian team.

THIRD TEST MATCH WON

AUSTRALIAN CHANGES PROBABLE

FROM OUR OWN CORRESPONDENT

ADELAIDE, JAN. 19

England won the third Test Match to-day by 338 runs. To-day's play was uninteresting, but served further to prove the mastery of the English attack and weakness of the Australian tail-end batsmen, who again failed.

It seems certain that big changes will be made in the next Australian Eleven after this sensational match. It is possible that Grimmett and Fingleton will be dropped and an attempt made to strengthen the bowling and batting by the inclusion of Oxenham or Nagel and O'Brien. Oxenhaim would be a suitable choice for Brisbane, where his home is, and O'Brien could open the innings with Woodfull, making two defensive batsmen to start with. Ironmonger should be retained on account of the possibility of rain in Queensland. Nagel, who was omitted after one trial in the first Test Match, has a good chance, and left-handers in Darling and Nitschke may also be included. The absence of a good all-round player is being regretted, as McCabe has so far been a

disappointment. After Richardson was out to-day the rest of the side were dismissed for a few runs and, by allowing Woodfull to make singles, the bowlers were able to get at the tail-enders, who made a poor showing. The wicket again was perfect and Larwood and Allen were in fine form, with Verity very dangerous as a relief bowler. They were all wonderfully accurate and the fast bowlers showed great speed. Richardson was unlucky, as he played the only stroke possible to a ball which got up high and, touching it with his hand, gave an easy catch. He has been a consistent scorer, but has not been able to make a big score so far.

Woodfull carried his bat through the innings for the second time in the Test matches. He was always confident and showed that he still has great batting qualities. The strength of the bowling can be gauged by the fact that Richardson was unable to increase his score of 15 for 20 minutes. Allen beat Richardson several times by pace alone, and although the wicket was not helping him, Larwood ocasionally made the ball get up hastily, the batsmen being forced to duck quickly. After a few overs the leg-theory was employed. Larwood developed a tremendous pace again.

Oldfield was unable to bat. A medical examination has revealed a linear fracture of the frontal bone of his forehead and he was not well to-day. There is a possibility that he may not play in any further Test matches this season. A complete rest is needed and an X-ray will be taken before the Brisbane Test Match. The match has revealed the excellent quality of the Adelaide wicket, on which more than 1,100 runs were scored.

The aggregate attendance for the match was 173,300.

THE LEG-THEORY

AUSTRALIAN COMMENT

FROM OUR OWN CORRESPONDENT

SYDNEY, JAN. 19

The *Sydney Sun*, in a leading article on the subject of the Australian Cricket Board of Control's protest, says:—

"The Board of Control seems to have become somewhat confused between the verbs to cable and to burble. M.C.C. might be forgiven, after reading the appalling suggestions of Imperial disruption, if it replied to the board that it pack its several heads in ice. However, it is obvious that the cricket authorities in England are going to receive the representations in a friendly, inquiring spirit despite the board's weakness in diplomacy."

The *Daily Telegraph* says:— "The relations between Australia and England have survived much greater shocks, but the Board of Control is hardly noted for its sense of proportion. Why not talk the matter over before pushing ahead with an ultimatum? It is certain that all feeling against the practice is not on the Australian side."

FROM OUR OWN CORRESPONDENT

MELBOURNE, JAN. 19

Mr. Kent Hughes, Minister of Sustenance in this State's Ministry and a former Olympic athlete, who knew Mr. D. R. Jardine at Oxford, has telegraphed to Mr. Jardine: "Mailey's suggested conferences are one matter, but the accusation of unsportsmanlike play is very different. As an ex-international, I strongly object to the boorish, bitter, insulting wording of the Control Board's protest. The English attitude in 1921 was very different."

Mr. Hughes, when interviewed, recalled Gregory's tactics in England. He said: "If a conference is held, Australia must attend as fellow-sinners. The position of the fieldsmen is immaterial. It is the fast bumping ball about which the question of danger has arisen."

The *Melbourne Herald* editorial states: "While the Board's cable to Marylebone is justified by the disclosure of bitter feelings among the players and spectators, the reference to upsetting friendly relations between England and Australia is an hysterical exaggeration."

It recommends a conference between P. F. Warner, D. R. Jardine, J. B. Hobbs, W. M. Woodfull, M. A. Noble, and the Control Board to consider the question of fast body-line bowling with a packed leg field, which is different to fast bowling wiht an orthodox field.

SOUTH AFRICAN OPINION

CAPETOWN, Jan. 19.

South African cricketers regard Australia's leg-theory protests as absurd. H. W. Taylor says there is no danger if the batsmen play forward. The trouble with the Australians is, he says, that the leading batsmen, especially Ponsford, Bradman, and Kippax, are prone to play back against the fast bowling. Taylor described the Australian Board of Control's cable as "futile." He said that McCabe was a good forward player, who was successful against the M.C.C. Taylor concluded by saying that he considered that the Australians were not entitled to "squeal."

A. D. Nourse said that the Australian objections were unreasonable. He recalled that in 1921 Gregory had bumped the ball round the batsmen's heads and said that in Durban that bowler knocked his own cap spinning from his head.

H. B. Cameron, who captained the South African team in Australia last season, recalled the match at Lord's when he was knocked out by Larwood. He said that it was a pure accident, and at that time Larwood was not bowling leg-theory. Undoubtedly Oldfield's injury was a similar accident.—*Reuter*

M.C.C. TEAM'S STATEMENT

ADELAIDE, JAN. 19

After a meeting of the M.C.C. touring team to-day the following statement was issued:—

Members of the M.C.C. and the English team do not desire to enter into public controversy, for they deplore the introduction of any personal feeling into the records of a great game.

In view, however, of statements which have been given space in some sections of the Press to the effect that there has been dissension and disloyalty in their team, they desire to deny this definitely and absolutely, while assuring the public of England and Australia that they are, and always have been, utterly loyal to their captain, under whose leadership they hope to achieve an honourable victory.

FINAL · SCORES

ENGLAND — First Innings

Sutcliffe, c Wall, b O'Reilly	9
D. R. Jardine, b Wall	3
Hammond, c Oldfield, b Wall	2
Ames, b Ironmonger	3
Leyland, b O'Reilly	83
R. E. S. Wyatt, c Richardson, b Grimmett	78
Paynter, c Fingleton, b Wall	77
G. O. Allen, lbw, b Grimmett	15
Verity, c Richardson, b Wall	45
Voce, b Wall	8
Larwood, not out	3
Extras (b 1, lb 7, nb 7)	15
Total	341

Fall of wickets: 1-4, 2-16, 3-16, 4-30, 5-186, 6-196, 7-228, 8-324, 9-336, 10-341

Bowling: Wall 34.1-10-72-5, O'Reilly 50-19-82-2, Ironmonger 20-6-50-1, Grimmett 28-6-94-2, McCabe 14-3-28-0

AUSTRALIA — First Innings

W. M. Woodfull, b Allen	22
J. Fingleton, c Ames, b Allen	0
D. G. Bradman, c Allen, b Larwood	8
S. McCabe, c Jardine, b Larwood	8
W. H. Ponsford, b Voce	85
V. Y. Richardson, b Allen	28
W. A. Oldfield, retired hurt	41
C. V. Grimmett, c Voce, b Allen	10
T. W. Wall, b Hammond	6
W. J. O'Reilly, b Larwood	0
H. Ironmonger, not out	0
Extras (b 2, lb 11, nb 1)	14
Total	222

Fall of wickets: 1-1, 2-18, 3-34, 4-51, 5-131, 6-194, 7-212, 8-222, 9-222

Bowling: Larwood 25-6-55-3, Allen 23-4-71-4, Hammond 17.4-4-30-1, Voce 14-5-21-1, Verity 16-7-31-0

ENGLAND — Second Innings

Sutcliffe, c sub (O'Brien), b Wall	7
D. R. Jardine, lbw, b Ironmonger	56
Hammond, b Bradman	85
Ames, b O'Reilly	69
Leyland, c Wall, b Ironmonger	42
R. E. S. Wyatt, c Wall, b O'Reilly	49
Paynter, not out	1
G. O. Allen, lbw, b Grimmett	15
Verity, lbw, b O'Reilly	40
Voce, b O'Reilly	8
Larwood, c Bradman, b Ironmonger	8
Extras (b 17, lb 11, nb 4)	32
Total	412

Fall of wickets: 1-7, 2-91, 3-123, 4-154, 5-245, 6-296, 7-394, 8-395, 9-400, 10-412

Bowling: Wall 29-6-75-1, O'Reilly 50.3-21-79-4, Ironmonger 57-21-87-3, Grimmett 35-9-74-1, McCabe 16-0-42-0, Bradman 4-0-23-1

AUSTRALIA — Second Innings

W. M. Woodfull, not out	73
J. Fingleton, b Larwood	0
D. G. Bradman, c & b Verity	66
S. McCabe, c Leyland, b Allen	7
W. H. Ponsford, c Jardine, b Larwood	3
V. Y. Richardson, c Allen, b Larwood	21
W. A Oldfield, absent hurt	—
C. V. Grimmett, b Allen	6
T. W. Wall, b Allen	0
W. J. O'Reilly, b Larwood	5
H. Ironmonger, b Allen	0
Extras (b 4, lb 2, nb 5, w 1)	12
Total	193

Fall of wickets: 1-3, 2-12, 3-100, 4-116, 5-171, 6-183, 7-183, 8-192, 9-193, 10-193

Bowling: Larwood 19-3-71-4, Allen 17.2-5-50-4, Voce 4-1-7-0, Hammond 9-3-27-0, Verity 20-12-26-1

·1938·

IT HAD BEEN EIGHT YEARS since Don Bradman had become the first man to score a triple hundred in a Test match between England and Australia. In 1934 Bradman repeated the feat, scoring 304, also at Leeds. Now it was the turn of Yorkshire and England opener Len Hutton, *right*. Hutton lost partner Bill Edrich early but established a second wicket stand of 382 with Maurice Leyland (187). Hutton went on to score 364 in 13 hours 17 minutes, a world record, while Leslie Fleetwood-Smith took one for 298 in 87 overs. Hutton's demise did not

signal the end of the torture for Australia. Joe Hardstaff carried on where Hutton left off, scoring 169 not out. With Yorkshire wicket-keeper Arthur Wood (53), 106 runs were added for the seventh wicket. England declared at 903 for seven, once captain Walter Hammond realised that Bradman and Jack Fingleton would not be able to bat because of injuries picked up in the field. Bradman hurt himself after bowling just 14 balls. Without them, Australia collapsed to 201 and 123 for defeat by an innings and 579 runs.

Len Hutton receives the congratulations of Don Bradman, whose world record score he has just beaten at the age of 22, and team-mate Joe Hardstaff.

Day One

The Manchester Guardian 22/8/38

ENGLAND AND THE OVAL ON TOP

Poverty of Australia's Attack Exposed by Yorkshire

HUTTON'S SHARE IN BIG PARTNERSHIP

By Neville Cardus (Cricketer)

THE OVAL, Saturday.

A week or two ago I suggested in these columns that for the Oval Test match the Yorkshire team should be chosen to represent England. People laughed at the idea and said it was one of my little jokes. But I was serious; I would not dream of

Don Bradman (left) and Walter Hammond (right) toss up. Looking on is the legendary groundsman "Bosser Martin".

making little jokes about a Test match. To-day England have scored 347 runs and only one batsman, a Middlesex man, has got out. Two Yorkshiremen have taken the total from 29 for one wicket to its present altitude. If Sutcliffe had been playing instead of Edrich the chances are that England would not be less comfortably placed than they are as it is. I do not remember a single instance of a plain, unmistakable failure in Test cricket by a chosen Yorkshireman.

Bradman was terribly unlucky to lose the toss again on the easiest wicket conceivable, easier even than Nottingham's. In the absence of McCormick, said to be suffering from neuritis, the Australian attack was the weakest ever seen in representative cricket. O'Reilly laboured alone on the lifeless hearthrug. Fleetwood-Smith turned one or two balls, and off one of them Hutton gave an easy chance of stumping when he was not more than forty. Waite and McCabe, as opening bowlers in a Test match, whetted the appetites of all batsmen present. Bradman was compelled to ask Sidney Barnes to bowl, much to the curiosity of the authentic Sydney Barnes, who looked on and probably wondered what it was all about. Edrich faltered woefully at twenty

minutes past twelve; after that, for five hours, Hutton and Leyland played exactly as they wished to play. There was hardly ever a hint of the fall of a wicket. During one period which came under my observation not a ball beat the bat in an hour. Leeds was revenged—by two Yorkshiremen who took no part in the recent atrocities there. They will begin again on Monday. If the wicket holds good an England score of 600 at least should be attained comfortably. And on a wicket of the same docility there is every reason to suppose that Bradman will, in one of his two innings, stay in until the beginning of the match is lost in the mists of antiquity.

The English batting was watched by an astonishingly small crowd. Less than 13,000 paid at the gates, and on the whole it was an apathetic crowd. A voice said, "They're not trying"—meaning the Australians—"they know they've got the Ashes." The statement was as untrue as it was hoarse; O'Reilly bowled his hardest, so did his colleagues. They were beaten by Yorkshiremen and by a ridiculous wicket, of which we have not yet heard the last.

A SOLEMN OCCASION

Edrich and Hutton began quietly, and the crowd also was quiet; it was almost a congregation. For half an hour Waite and McCabe bowled with the new ball, both of them amiable as two Cheeryble brothers. McCabe beat Edrich and appealed for leg before wicket, but Walden, with presence of mind, said, or indicated, not out. Edrich seemed unhappy and far away from Lord's. At twelve o'clock England were twenty for none. Then O'Reilly came on with Fleetwood-Smith. The stage was ready; the scene-shifters had got the setting in order. Hutton played confidently and forward to O'Reilly. Edrich played back and interrogatively. He missed a quicker one, and Chester's finger went up terribly when the ball struck the pads. This was O'Reilly's hundredth wicket in nineteen Test matches. Poor Edrich departed in silence: he has eaten of the bitter bread of irony this season. On this occasion he suffered seventy-five minutes with the rest of us, for twelve penitential runs.

Leyland came in, thick in the arms and broad in the pads. I expected cheerfulness at once, but the cold weather was not encouraging. Shortly before Edrich got out Hutton committed a swift late cut off McCabe; he then pulled himself together. And even Leyland put levity momentarily aside. Thus in an atmosphere of gathering depression England contrived to score 89 for one wicket in two hours. Lunch mercifully intervened. I could not endure this kind of play so I took a walk and met J. N. Crawford and Braund, who recalled an occasion at Melbourne when K. L. Hutchings scored 128 against Australia and hit a six and twenty-five fours. It is often more thrilling to talk to an old cricketer than to watch a contemporary one. Towards ten minutes past one Leyland atavistically drove two brilliant fours in front of the wicket off Fleetwood-Smith.

No other incident ruffled the face of the day until after lunch Hutton was given his second innings by Barnett, who missed a most luscious chance of stumping off a ball from Fleetwood-Smith which spun a foot and Hutton was a long way out of his ground ploughing the off side. Hutton's score was now 40 and England's 91 for one. He then drove O'Reilly through the covers for four, with his body falling beautifully forward; it was a stroke of thanks-giving. Leyland watched it with admiration, and obviously it reminded him of a cricket-match, for he struck Fleetwood-Smith promptly for a four to the off, a real drive which went racing along the earth with the illusion of increasing velocity every yard. Next he was bowled by a no-ball from O'Reilly, much to his amusement. The match began to wake up and stretch itself. McCabe bowled from the Vauxhall or Houses of Parliament end while O'Reilly changed over; Leyland drove McCabe straight and powerfully, and, of course, no fieldsman protected the boundary behind the bowler. Then Leyland reached 50 in a hundred minutes, and a moment or two later Hutton also reached 50—in the more seemly time of two and a quarter hours. The sun came out, as though to see what all the sudden noise was about, and witnessed another boundary, a perfect

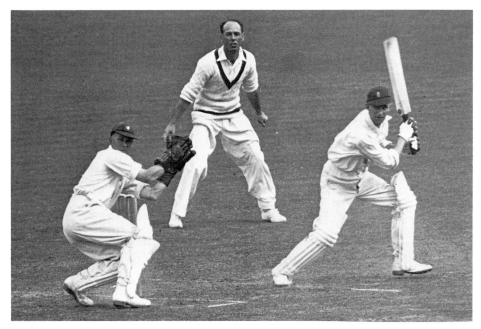

Hutton hits on the off-side early in his historic innings.

forcing hit to the on by Hutton off O'Reilly. Hutton was a model No. 1 batsman, sound yet watchful for the really loose ball, and always a Yorkshireman.

LEYLAND GREETS WAITE

Bradman persistently changed the bowling, probably for want of something better to do, and as soon as he asked Waite to try off-breaks Leyland smote a four to the off, and after doing so stood still as a post and watched the ball's progress towards Westminster. Both batsmen appeared as comfortable now as old inhabitants in their favourite club chairs. O'Reilly made his windmill movements to the wicket, head down, arms wheeling about him, but the drowsy turf changed his arts into merely hopeful industry. He mopped his brow at an over's end and, I thought, took refuge in muttered words. At three o'clock England was 147 for one; the fall of another wicket seemed dependent on some act of absent-mindedness on the part of Hutton and Leyland. Seldom did a ball elude the bat; sixty runs were scored in fifty minutes after lunch, as safely and as inevitably as any shelling of peas. Never a ball rose abruptly, seldom a ball spun. Bradman

and his men waited for something to turn up, and once, at the end of an over, O'Reilly threw the ball to the other bowler and seized his cap from the umpire with no attempt to disguise his disgusted helplessness. He could make no more impression on Leyland than an argumentative voice on a deaf man; Leyland played him with a rich, comic, wooden sort of assurance, as though saying all the times, "Hey, Bill, tha'rt a good un, but Ah know all about thi." So Fleetwood-Smith came to O'Reilly's assistance, and Leyland hit his first ball for four, as though continuing his discourse, "And tha'rt not what Ah'd call surprising either."

Still, Fleetwood-Smith found the edge of Leyland's bat, and Leyland at 68 was glad to snick an isolated spinning-away ball for two—which was the first ghost of a chance the Australian attack had seen since the failure of Edrich nearly two hours ago. Waite's hypothetical off-spinners, from round the wicket, recalled the age of innocence; McCormick's pace was badly missed. But Leyland, at 70, gave another diverting trace of fallibility by prodding a ball from Waite between his back foot and the leg stump, as though saying now, "Go on, lads, get me out—it can be done; Ah'm pla-ayin' for mi place in t' team, remember." Another exquisite late cut by Hutton, off Waite this time, told us that England v. Australia is one thing and Lancashire v. Yorkshire another. At 175 for one wicket Bradman resorted to Barnes, who experimented with three or four practice balls to McCabe, or

"Bosser" Martin makes sure his groundstaff put their backs into the job of rolling the wicket.

somebody, before launching upon his first over. Probably he wished to make sure which really was his bowling arm, right or left. I myself am not sure yet.

Hutton when he was 86 was nearly caught at first slip off a full-toss from Fleetwood-Smith; I mention this fact as an indication of how unlikely it seemed hereabouts that a wicket would fall in a way relating effect to cause. Two gorgeous fours in an over by Fleetwood-Smith, one to Leyland and one to Hutton, relegated the doldrums of the morning to a primal and empirical past; the English innings came out of the vapours and dispersed them. The Australian attack apparently entered bankruptcy; Barnes as a bowler meant that the brokers were in. At ten minutes to four Hutton achieved another century; he had exhibited a finely organised craftsmanship for more than

four hours, and now and again he modulated into aesthetic; his forward strokes were elegant and effortless and occasionally fruitful in the eyes of the scorers.

CERTAINTY BORNE OUT

Just before tea Leyland came to his destined century after some three and a quarter hours of ripeness; it was as certain as harvest-time that he would score plenteously against this Australian bowling; I have never doubted it. Leyland is always an England batsman; for the purposes of Test matches he should be regarded as in form whenever he is not suffering from a broken leg or a splintered finger. He began soberly to-day while he investigated the attack; "Let's be careful for a bit" he seemed to say. "There's no hurry; we can play this match till Christmas. We'll begin when we're ready." From O'Reilly's first ball after tea Leyland allowed himself to be bowled—by a no-ball; this was the second time he had allowed O'Reilly to bowl him with a no-ball. He is a man of humour. "Live and let live; give him a bit of encouragement—it costs nowt."

A slight shower fell before tea, not of much consequence but scarcely a promise

of fine weather over the week-end. At half-past four the game went forward, with great white clouds in a sky of blue, clouds with castles on the edges of cliffs, clouds like islands in a sea. The gasholder, now painted a severe grey, became transcendental in the soft evening light.

Hutton kept pace with Leyland; he forced Fleetwood-Smith twice in an over with his wrists to the on; he played back strongly and with poise. His footwork was quick and clean; seldom, if ever, did he lose balance or employ the wrong stroke. Even allowing for the poor attack, Hutton's cricket was a guarantee of many long scores for England for days to come, here and in Australia. Leyland, less studious than Hutton, attended to the humanities; his drives were related to the man himself. Sometimes he bent down and enjoyed a late cut, a humorous dab at the ball, a chuckle which contrasted with the broader laughs of his drives.

On and on the Australian bowlers toiled up while the score mounted up and up—29 for one, 50 for one, 100 for one, 150 for one, 200 for one, 250 for one, 300 for one, and so on until the day's end. Think of the suspense suffered in the countless homes of Australia, where whole families were gathered round the radio, listening to a ball-by-ball narrative, while outside the winter winds blew—and there are indeed wintry winds in Melbourne and Goulburn. Can a more searching trial to the spirit be imagined than that of a patriotic Australian, as he sits looking into a box, while hour after hour his beloved O'Reilly toils in vain, over after over until midnight comes and the fire dies down and the beer and whisky run out? At half-past five, English time, the score became 300 for one, and the crowd let out a roar so loud and abrupt that I thought the gasholder (or O'Reilly) had gone off.

In the last hour the scoring slackened to fifty or fewer; the batsmen rubbed home their lesson. Leyland put his bat to the dog-tired bowling, and it said, as broad and plain as Ilkley Moor, "So if tha wants Test matches played to a finish, well, here's the way to get off the mark before the Leagues and Littlewood's begin, properly like."

Day Two

The Daily Mail

23/8/38

HUTTON 300, AND STILL UNSATISFIED

Biggest Ever Score for England

By RONALD T. SYMOND

Final Test (Second Day).—At the Oval: England have scored 634 for 5 wickets against Australia.

Hungry Hutton has not yet finished his enormous meal of runs. The lad has been eating steadily for well over 11 hours, but shows no sign of repletion.

So far he has hit 27 fours, and gobbled up the record for the best score ever by an England batsman against Australia.

This morning he intends to attack Don Bradman's historic 334, the best score ever in these Tests.

The style and execution of Hutton's batting, equally with his monumental patience, have been worthy of a record which will probably live long in cricket history. Steadfast and conscientiously disciplined in superlative degree, his great innings has not lacked the graces of delightful stroke play.

Apart from the insatiable—not to say gl(h)uttonous—Yorkshireman, our batsmen did not shine with great brilliance yesterday. Australia's well-maintained attack was never properly mastered and thrashed, nor was the keen field ever worried into raggedness.

THAT WICKET

However, we have a pretty useful-looking total, and may safely regard our team as being on the high road to victory. Iniquitously perfect as the wicket has been, it cannot continue indefinitely to support such mammoth scoring. A shower of rain delayed the start until 11.55, when Leyland and Hutton resumed for a further 75 minutes their record partnership, which surpassed England's previous best by 59 runs.

Fleetwood-Smith began with a couple of loose overs, but afterwards bowled extremely well, while O'Reilly gave less trouble than usual.

So comfortable were the batsmen that there was only one way to take a wicket, particularly as the only risk they ran was that of stealing runs. Perhaps with a view to trapping the batsmen into indiscretions, some of the Australian misfielding looked suspiciously non-accidental.

Be this as it may, Leyland was at last run out in attempting a rash second run. Hassett threw in smartly from deep mid-off to the bowler's end, where Don Bradman was waiting to perform the bail-removing operation.

SOLID VIRTUE

Good batmaster Maurice Leyland hit 17 fours in his display of solid virtue, and was deservedly given a tumultuous ovation by the well-pleased multitude.

Walter Hammond used the big stick at once, caning Fleetwood-Smith for 12 in an over, but Hutton, who scored only 31 runs all morning, elected grimly to continue the wearing process without haste and without mercy.

After lunch the scoring proceeded slowly for an hour, and meantime Fingleton left the field owing to a pulled muscle in the left calf.

Hutton now began to score faster than Hammond, who spent 80 minutes gathering 21.

At 4.5 with the scoreboard reading 534 for two, Fleetwood-Smith bowled a maiden to Hammond. Never have I seen the Australian bowl so well with such meagre reward. Rarely have I seen a great batsman carry reasonable care to such absurd excess.

Fifteen minutes later Fleetwood-Smith won the success he had so richly deserved for his great-hearted persistence in the face of discouragement. Hammond was out, and Paynter followed him with small delay.

At tea-time Hutton, having batted faultlessly for nearly ten hours, was just 24 runs short of R. E. Foster's long-standing record for the highest individual score for England v. Australia (287 at Sydney, 1903-4).

Another shower delayed play until 5 o'clock, and in the second over Compton played over a ball from Waite. The time was now 5.5, and the score-board showed 555 for 5. Three wickets had fallen for 9 runs!

Hardstaff began quietly, but was very soon hitting the ball crisply. He despatched Fleetwood-Smith to the square leg boundary with stunning force, and off-drove the same bowler for the handsomest boundary of the day.

NOT SUICIDE, BUT—

Meanwhile the remorseless Hutton slowly but surely pushed R. E. Foster off his pedestal—a feat which the knowledgeable crowd hailed with terrific applause at 5.40.

Standing in O'Reilly's suicide squad at silly mid-on, McCabe demonstrated that

THE MARATHON
By TOM WEBSTER

the dangers of this position are not imaginary. A violent drive by Hardstaff caught him on the thigh, and set him limping painfully for several minutes.

At 6.17 a furore of cheering, lasting a full minute, greeted Hutton's treble century, and directly afterwards the players left in the field in a poor light with gentle rain falling.

The attendance was approximately 31,500 of whom 24,691 paid for admission at the turnstiles.

THE SCORES

ENGLAND.—First Innings

HUTTON, not out	300
EDRICH, lbw, b O'Reilly	12
LEYLAND, run out	187
W. R. HAMMOND, lbw, b Fleet-wood-Smith	59
PAYNTER, lbw, b O'Reilly	0
COMPTON, b Waite	1
HARDSTAFF, not out	40
Extras (b 10, lb 18, w 1, nb 6)	35
Total (5 wkts.)	634

BOWLING TO DATE

	O.	M.	R.	W.
Waite	61	13	121	1
McCabe	29	8	59	0
O'Reilly	66.2	19	144	2
F.-Smith	70	8	235	1
Barnes	17	2	40	0

FALL OF WICKETS

1	2	3	4	5
29	411	546	547	555

(Daily Mail Copyright.

Day
Three

Daily
Telegraph
& Morning
Post

24/8/38

HUTTON SMASHES ALL RECORDS

ENGLAND CERTAIN TO WIN FARCICAL TEST

Bradman Fractures Shin Bone While Bowling : Three Australians Out

By HOWARD MARSHALL

Hutton making his record score of 364 in the final Test match at Oval, Bradman being carried off the field with a fractured shin bone, England declaring at the phenomenal total of 903 for seven wickets—these were the outstanding events in one of the most remarkable day's cricket ever played.

That Australia lost three wickets for 117 after tea seemed entirely unimportant. The match is over, to all intents and purposes, and all that remains is to add up the records. As you will see in the accompanying panel (see over), eight new records have been set up in this fantastic affair.

Records do not make cricket, however, and we can only hope that these fresh ones will prove to be eight stout nails in the coffin of timeless Tests, played on wickets which turn a great game into a farce.

First of all, though, let us praise Hutton for his tremendous exhibition of concentration, endurance and skill. He gave point and purpose to the early hours, for the excitement was intense as he slowly and surely approached Bradman's record of 334, the previous highest individual score in test matches between England and Australia.

We could almost feel the huge crowd willing Hutton to succeed, and when, with a beautiful square-cut, he hit the decisive four off Fleetwood-Smith, a roar went up which must have shaken the Houses of Parliament across the river.

Bradman raced up to shake his hand, and while drinks came out and all the

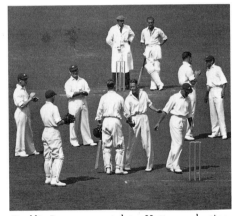

Freddie Brown congratulates Hutton on beating Bradman's world record.

Australians toasted him in the middle of the pitch the crowd cheered, and sang "For he's a jolly good fellow," and cheered and cheered again.

An astonishing scene, and Hutton richly deserved this wonderful ovation. When at last his concentration wavered and he was caught at cover by Hassett off O'Reilly, he had batted for 13 hours and 20 minutes, and hit 35 fours, 15 threes, 18 twos and 143 singles.

A prodigious effort, and if Hutton's innings was immensely prolonged, it was also logically and strictly in accordance with the conditions imposed by such a wicket and such a match.

That Bradman should have slipped and fractured his shin-bone while bowling was an ironical commentary on the state of affairs. This was a tragic misfortune for Australia, who have also lost Fingleton

with a strained muscle, and it is doubtful if he will be able to bat.

As it happens, even Bradman could not have hoped to stave off defeat, and while we may reasonably be pleased at England's mastery, I cannot believe that any true lover of cricket will be easy in his mind about the conditions in which it was achieved.

The wicket, so prepared that the bowlers were helpless, has completely destroyed the balance of the game. A groundsman perhaps, might conceive it his duty to prepare such a wicket, and regarded the result as a triumph, but it is surely high time the authorities stepped in and made an end of such harmful nonsense.

Half-an-hour of the Leeds Test was worth a whole day of the Oval travesty. At Leeds there was life in the wicket and the balance was held even between batsman and bowler. At the Oval, on turf completely dead, the only weapons left to the bowler were flight and accuracy, and the dice were so loaded in favour of the batsmen that winning the toss meant winning the match unless rain interfered.

IF THEY HAD WON THE TOSS

It is absurd that the spin of the coin should be given such entirely disproportionate importance. It is absurd that batsmanship should be reduced to a dead level of competence. And, by the same token, it is monstrous that the lovely arts of bowling should thus arbitrarily nullified.

If the boot had been on the other leg, and Australia won the toss, we should have thought it a serious matter indeed. It remains a serious matter with England in the winning position, serious for cricket as a whole.

It was pathetic to see a fine player like Hardstaff pottering about in the afternoon with 800 runs on the board playing half-volleys back to weary and indifferent bowlers, but he also was a victim of circumstances.

Time did not matter, runs were still important, so why should he take risks against a perfectly-set defensive field? That, I imagine, is how he viewed the situation, and how a match played in such conditions reacts upon a batsman.

I hope profoundly, at any rate, that we shall never again see such a total on the score-board in England, and that if we are

The Oval scoreboard shows that Hutton has just passed Bradman's world record Test score of 334.

to have these matches played to a finish, it shall never be upon wickets which make such absurdities possible.

At least we must pay tribute to the remarkable Australian fielding, which did not flag throughout 15 and a quarter hours. Bradman set his team a great example, and it was most unfortunate that

RECORD-SMASHING TEST

Hutton established a world's "endurance" record for the longest individual innings—13 hours and 20 minutes.

His 364 beat Bradman's 334 at Leeds in 1930, the previous highest in an England-Australia Test; passed Hammond's 336 not out against New Zealand at Auckland in 1933 (formerly the biggest innings in any Test), and made a record for the Oval, exceeding Bobby Abel's 357 for Surrey v. Somerset in 1899.

Hutton and Leyland, by putting on 382, set up a record for the second England wicket in a Test against Australia. They beat the 188 by Sutcliffe and Hammond at Sydney in 1932.

Hardstaff, who scored his first Test century against Australia, and Hutton, in adding 215, created a new record for the sixth England wicket, beating the 186 by Hammond and Ames at Lord's this season.

England's total of 903 for seven (declared), exceeding their 658 for eight (declared) at Nottingham in June, was not only their highest against Australia, but the biggest in any Test. Australia's highest is 729 for six (declared) at Lord's in 1930.

The England total is also the biggest made in a first-class match in this country, beating Yorkshire's 887 v. Warwickshire at Edgbaston in 1896.

Three Yorkshiremen (Hutton, 364; Leyland, 187, and Wood, 53) obtained 604 of the score in an innings lasting 15 hours and a quarter—the longest in Test history.

his final reward should be a fractured shin-bone.

SUN BLAZED DOWN

The weather changed completely overnight, and the sun blazed down when England continued their innings. All our interest was centred in Hutton's attempt to beat Bradman's record, and he and Hardstaff proceeded quietly against the bowling of O'Reilly and Fleetwood-Smith.

Hutton looked as fresh as a daisy, and

extremely certain and confident, but the Australians attacked him with the utmost hostility. The runs came slowly, and when Hutton was 315 O'Reilly made him edge the leg-break, and threw back his head in despair as the ball fell safely to ground.

At 670, Bradman took the new ball, and Waite and McCabe used it accurately, but Hutton forged steadily on, and at 688 the climax came when O'Reilly returned to the attack. A single to Hutton, a beautiful square-cut off Fleetwood-Smith, two more singles, and the record was within Hutton's grasp.

WOOD ATTACKS BOWLING

Suddenly O'Reilly bowled, Hutton flailed mightily and missed, as if concentration had deserted him, but it was a no-ball, and four runs were all he needed. Another pause, an irrepressible murmur of excitement from the crowd, a leg-break from Fleetwood-Smith, which Hutton cut gloriously to the boundary, and a storm of score-cards fluttered in the air as the crowd roared its satisfaction at Hutton's splendid triumph.

After that tremendous moment the tension relaxed. Hutton, still calm and judiciously masterful, did not alter his method, and Hardstaff stayed with him until the luncheon interval. Soon afterwards, Hutton was out and Wood came in to attack the bowling.

BRADMAN'S OVER

At 798 Bradman himself took the ball and sent down a maiden over, but by that time all reality had left the game. The total was 876 before Wood, much to his annoyance, was caught and bowled by Barnes, and Verity kept Hardstaff company until Hammond mercifully declared.

Australia, footsore and weary, began disastrously. Badcock was caught off Bowes by Hardstaff at short-leg in the second over of the innings. McCabe went with only 19 runs on the board, and it was left to Hassett to show us the true beauty of attacking batsmanship. Hassett played splendidly, and made his 42 out of 51 runs scored while he was at the wicket, and when he left Barnes and Brown quietly played out time.

Day
Four

The Times
25/8/38

THE FINAL TEST MATCH

ENGLAND WIN EASILY

AUSTRALIA'S BIG HANDICAP

FROM OUR CRICKET CORRESPONDENT

England beat Australia in the last Test Match of the present series at the Oval yesterday by an innings and 579 runs, the end coming at 20 minutes to 4 on the fourth day. That the game came to so abrupt a conclusion after elaborate arrangements had been made for its continuance, irrespective of time, was largely due to the fact that Australia when their turn came to bat were without D. Bradman.

This implies no lack of appreciation of the share which Hutton and others had played in building up England's enormous total of 903; nor does it overlook the splendid bowling of Bowes and of K. Farnes, but it is a plain statement of fact that this Australian team bereft of Bradman is a very ordinary batting side, bearing but a feeble resemblance to recent Australian team which contained such players as W. M. Woodfull and W. H. Ponsford.

Had Bradman and Fingleton been able to bat there is no knowing how many runs Australia would have made, or how long the game would have lasted, although it was generally admitted that England, having won the toss and having made full use of a perfect wicket, had already won the match.

No praise could be too high for the manner in which W. J. O'Reilly, who confirmed his claim to be regarded as the best bowler in the world, and L. O. B. Fleetwood-Smith, had toiled away while England's score grew and grew, and it is certain that none of the Australian teams of the past could have fielded with greater enthusiasm and accuracy.

England, for their part, took the heaven-sent chance they were offered, and if they were able to do no more than draw the rubber they supported the contention that this season they have been able to field a team capable of better things than the record of the Leeds match had suggested. Regarded from a more general point of view, it was almost universally agreed that the play in the early stages of this match, when the quality of the cricket was subordinated to the quantity of runs scored, was a severe condemnation of that spurious form of the game known as a time-limitless Test Match.

There was a feeling of unreality when play was begun in the morning, akin to a performance of Hamlet without the Prince. Had Bradman been there Australia would still have been struggling against the inevitable, but at least their death agony would have been relieved by a gay and gallant challenge to fate. During that long, and sometimes wearisome, period when England were amassing a score which might have run into four figures but for the merciful decision of their captain to declare the innings closed. Bradman's fielding and his continual liveliness of spirit were a reminder that even a time-limitless Test Match can provide its measure of enjoyment. His unhappy injury not only denuded the game of all meaning that it had ever possessed, but it robbed us of an opportunity of admiring the greatest of living batsmen in conditions in which he assuredly would have given of his best and most brilliant.

The absence of Fingleton rubbed in the hopeless handicap under which Australia were labouring, for he could have been relied upon to give some stability to a side which was beginning to bear the appearance of a clock when a small boy has begun to pull its inside to pieces.

YORKSHIRE'S MATCH

The score in the morning stood at 117 for three wickets with Brown and Barnes facing Farnes and Bowes, and it was not long before Barnes was surprised by the pace of a ball from Farnes which flew off his bat only just short of second slip's feet. Brown batted in the manner expected of an Australian, apparently unconcerned by the horror of the situation, taking his runs easily and placidly whenever the occasion came his way to put the ball away on the leg side. Barnes, too, forced the ball here and there with an ease which showed that at least there was nothing to fear in the state of the pitch.

The score had been taken to 145 before Barnes chopped a ball from Bowes on to

Bradman is helped from the field after fracturing a shin bone while bowling.

---

his wicket, and in the same over, with only two runs added, Barnett was out to a good catch by Wood, who kept wicket as well for England as he habitually does for Yorkshire—and there could be no higher praise. Waite, as soon as he had arrived, hit one of Bowes's slower balls straight for 4, and he banged another of more normal pace away to the square-leg boundary.

That was the limit of his contribution, for in trying to force a ball of good length away to leg he was bowled.

When O'Reilly was caught at the wicket, waving his bat for no particular purpose, seven wickets were down for 160 runs. With Fleetwood-Smith staying in long enough Brown, the excellence of whose batting seemed wasted in so drab a setting, found time to drive Edrich away to long on and to cut a no-ball to the boundary past deep third man.

SOUND JUDGMENT

There was an unusual occurrence when Hutton, with the intention perhaps that Fleetwood-Smith should receive the first ball of the next over, helped a stroke by Brown on to the boundary with his foot. The umpire, however, acting according to the instructions issued by the M.C.C. which say that "the runs which have been arranged for a boundary hit are to be added to the runs already made should a fieldsman wilfully cause the ball to reach the boundary," signalled five runs, and Brown gained the bowling. Fleetwood-Smith in the meantime had driven a ball over the bowler's head with a gloriously cross bat, and he had hooked another away to deep square-leg, an affair so serious that Leyland was put on to bowl.

Hammond, too, came on to be hit to leg by Fleetwood-Smith, who was playing one of the longest and most prolific innings of his career. The eighth, and last, wicket fell when Hammond, fielding at leg slip, held a catch at the second attempt from a sweep to leg by Brown.

Australia accordingly went in again soon after 1 o'clock 702 runs behind. This time the runs came fairly freely from the first few overs, Badcock once making a beautiful off-drive off Bowes before his leg stump was sent hurtling out of the ground. In the very next over McCabe, flourishing his bat in a manner significant of what the batsman thought of the state of affairs, was caught at the wicket, and at the luncheon interval, with a score at 31 for two wickets, it was no more than a question of time before the game was over.

The spectators had no sooner swallowed their sandwiches and regained their seats before Hassett was leg-before wicket to Bowes, and a few minutes afterwards Brown was caught at short leg. Barnett, declining to surrender his wicket before he had gained some reward for putting on his pads, hit two balls insuccession from Farnes with a glorious thump to the square-leg boundary. With Verity on at one end Hammond bethought himself of trying Leyland as a left-handed bowler of a different variety at the other, Barnes at once driving him past cover-point for 4. When Farnes came on again Barnes cut him square to the boundary, and Barnett with a true left-hander's off-drive and a deflection to leg showed that even if Australia were to be beaten there would at least be one stand made against England's bowlers.

THE END

Verity continued bowling at one end, which accordingly remained, if not closed, at least ajar, in so far as scoring was concerned, and he took the next wicket when Barnes, attempting a little too much in trying to hit the ball among the trams, was leg-before-wicket. Waite was out first ball, caught at silly point, and two runs later Barnett had one of his stumps uprooted by Farnes. O'Reilly treated himself to two full blows off Verity into the deep field, from the second of which he should have been caught.

It was the custom when the last man was in and a catch was offered in the deep to Denton, to remove the bails without watching the ball fall to rest in his certain hands. Wood, considering that Hardstaff was equally reliable, pulled up the stumps to keep as a souvenir of a pleasant engagement at the Oval, but Hardstaff dropped the catch, and Chester had to replace the stumps.

Not for long, however, as Fleetwood-Smith gave a catch to mid-on which was held, and the crowd were free to pour across the ground to pay the conventional compliments to Englishmen and Australians alike.

It was certainly a decisive victory, which would have have been all the more satisfactory had the score card not borne those unkind words "absent hurt."

FINAL · SCORES

ENGLAND — First Innings

Hutton, c Hassett, b O'Reilly	364
Edrich, lbw, b O'Reilly	12
Leyland, run out	187
W. R. Hammond, lbw, b Fleetwood-Smith	59
Paynter, lbw, b O'Reilly	0
Compton, b Waite	1
Hardstaff, not out	169
Wood, c & b Barnes	53
Verity, not out	8
Extras (b 22, lb 19, w 1, nb 8)	50
Total (7 wkts dec.)	**903**

Fall of wickets: 1-29, 2-411, 3-546, 4-547, 5-555, 6-770, 7-876

Bowling: Waite 72-16-150-1, McCabe 38-8-85-0, O'Reilly 85-26-178-3, Fleetwood-Smith 87-11-298-1, Barnes 38-3-84-1, Hassett 13-2-52-0, Bradman 3-2-6-0

AUSTRALIA — First Innings

C. L. Badcock, c Hardstaff, b Bowes	0
W. A. Brown, c Hammond, b Leyland	69
S. J. McCabe, c Edrich, b Farnes	14
A. L. Hassett, c Compton, b Edrich	42
S. Barnes, b Bowes	41
B. A. Barnett, c Wood, b Bowes	2
M. G. Waite, b, Bowes	8
W. J. O'Reilly, c Wood, b Bowes	0
L. O'B. Fleetwood-Smith, not out	16
D. G. Bradman, absent hurt	0
J. H. Fingleton, absent hurt	0
Extras (b 4, lb 2, nb 3)	9
Total	**201**

Fall of wickets: 1-0, 2-19, 3-70, 4-145, 5-147, 6-160, 7-160, 8-201

Bowling: Farnes 13-2-54-1, Bowes 19-3-49-5, Edrich 10-2-55-1, Verity 5-1-15-0, Leyland 3.1-0-11-1, Hammond 2-0-8-0

AUSTRALIA — Second Innings

C. L. Badcock, b Bowes	9
W. A. Brown, c Edrich, b Farnes	15
S. J. McCabe, c Wood, b Farnes	2
A. L. Hassett, lbw, b Bowes	10
S. Barnes, lbw, b Verity	33
B. A. Barnett, b Farnes	46
M. G. Waite, c Edrich, b Verity	0
W. J. O'Reilly, not out	7
L. O'B. Fleetwood-Smith, c Leyland, b Farnes	0
D. G. Bradman, absent hurt	0
J. H. Fingleton, absent hurt	0
Extras (b 1)	1
Total	**123**

Fall of wickets: 1-15, 2-18, 3-35, 4-41, 5-115, 6-115, 7-117, 8-123

Bowling: Farnes 12.1-1-63-4, Bowes 10-3-25-2, Leyland 5-0-19-0, Verity 7-3-15-2

Hutton returns to the pavilion having scored a world record 364 to secure his place in history.

·1939·

THE MOST FAMOUS TIMELESS Test produced 1,981 runs and only ended after 10 days, with England 42 runs short of victory, because they had to catch their ship home. South Africa batted first and with van der Bijl and Nourse making centuries reached 530. In reply, Les Ames top scored with 84 and Lancastrian Eddie Paynter made 62 as England reached 316. South Africa kept up the pressure in their second innings, hitting 401 with Melville this time going into three figures. England needed 696 to win and began well with Yorkshire's Paul Gibb making 120, his highest

score in Test cricket, while fellow Yorkshireman and opener Len Hutton made 55. Following Hutton's dismissal, Walter Hammond amassed a delightful 140 before Bill Edrich, *left*, with his highest Test score of 219, gave England a tremendous chance of victory. Paynter followed his first innings half century with 75 before falling to Gordon, who conceded 174 runs. With a two-day train journey required to reach their boat in Cape Town, the match ended prematurely, England having made the highest final innings score in Test history, 654 for five.

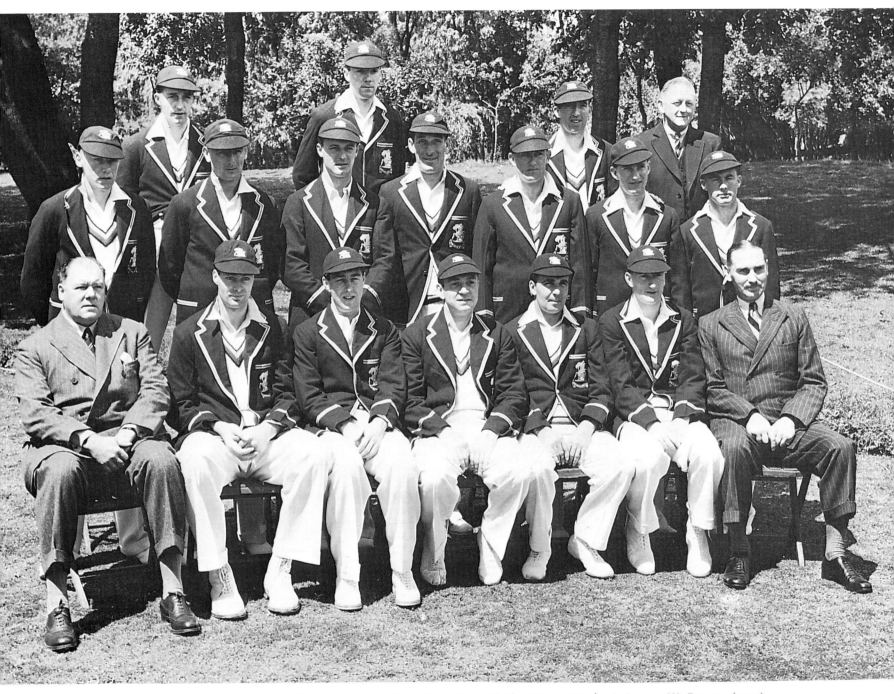

M.C.C.'s party to tour South Africa, 1938-9. Back row (left to right) : *W. J. Edrich, D. V. P. Wright, E. Paynter, W. Ferguson (scorer).*
Middle row (left to right): *L. L. Wilkinson, H. Verity, H. T. Bartlett, T. W. Goddard, R. T. D. Perks, L. Hutton, P. A. Gibb.*
Front Row (left to right) : *C. R. Ridgeway (S.African manager), K. Farnes, N. W. D. Yardley, W. R. Hammond (capt.), L. E. G. Ames,*
B. H. Valentine, Flt. Lieut. A. J. Holmes (Manager).

Day
One

Daily
Express
4/3/39

Van der Byl takes all day for 105

SOUTH AFRICANS CREEP ON

No need to hurry

Fifth Test.—At Durban. South Africa have scored 229 for two wickets in their first innings.

By WILLIAM POLLOCK,

Daily Express Cricket Reporter, who is the only staff reporter of a British national newspaper with the M.C.C. team.

DURBAN, Friday.

South Africa, winning the toss at last, have made a slow but sure start in the last and timeless Test.

Peter Van der Byl, who got "blues" for cricket and boxing at Oxford, stayed in all day battling gallantly while time marched slowly on.

The day ended with South Africa sitting well, if not exactly pretty.

When Melville produced a "tickey" (South African for threepenny-bit), Hammond was so surprised at not seeing the usual half a crown that he called "tails" when he should have called "heads". For the first time in nine, Hammond was wrong.

Perks and Farnes made five appeals in the first half-hour, four of them for lbw.

Van der Byl bent so cautiously that his body was almost at right angles to the bat. He took forty-five minutes before he made his first run.

When the first lot of drinks were brought out after an hour's cricket, South Africa's total was 26.

Wright, Verity and Hammond had turns of bowling. The fielders crept in closer and closer, and the scoreboard crept, too. Real timeless Test cricket. Batsmen were taking not the slightest risk. They were quite content with ones and twos from time to time.

SLOW MOTION

The bowlers concentrated on length.

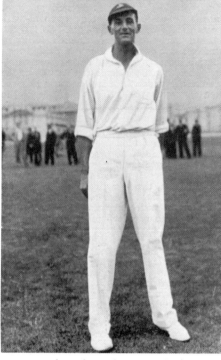

Peter Van der Byl scored 105 on the first day of the fifth and "timeless" Test.

Even Wright bowled to a close-set field with Edrich, Hutton and Paynter dotted a few yards from Van der Byl's strokeless bat.

There was 105 minutes of it, then lunch and only 49 runs on the slow-motion scoreboard.

A ball from Perks, quite inappropriately, hit Van der Byl on the funny-bone, causing him to holler.

Then a remarkable thing happened. Melville hit a boundary. It was the first 4 of the match. It occurred half an hour after lunch, off a no-ball by Perks.

This achievement was the start of brighter things. Van der Byl actually struck a ball from Wright for 3, and Melville showed such an inclination to see if Verity could be hit that Hammond took all the slips away.

After batting 152 minutes, Melville got 50. Van der Byl was not then half-way to 50. Mostly, he just stopped the ball with his bat so dead that it had hardly strength to trickle as far as the close-set fielders.

Paynter once had a real chance to run out Melville, but threw badly from cover.

Next thing we knew was Van der Byl straight-driving Verity for his first boundary. He had then been in more than three hours.

The partnership had an unlucky end at 131. Melville hit a leg-ball from Wright to the boundary and knocked his wicket down at the same time. Apart from its slowness, it was a fine innings, helping to lay the foundation of who knows what.

BIG HITTING

Having lost Melville, Van der Byl suddenly proceeded to act most queerly. He became such a hitter that he took 22 in one over off Wright.

This thoroughly woke up the crowd, who shouted for Wright to be kept on, but Hammond refused to oblige. And so to tea, with South Africa 162 for one.

When Van der Byl, then 70, hit a full toss from Wright straight back, the bowler let the ball through his hands.

Wright, like Verity, had no slips. Once Van der Byl, swinging at a leg-ball from him, hit it for 6 to the roof of the stand.

This Van der Byl is an extraordinary mixture. For long periods he plays gentle pat-ball, then suddenly lets fly and crashes the ball into wide, open spaces with the power of a giant.

He had battled 287 minutes when, at long last, his century went up from a stroke within a yard of being a catch at square leg.

For purposes of timeless Test cricket, it was a valuable innings, but, except during two or three patches, when he seemed to think he had earned a little fun, it was burdensome.

Van der Byl was hit about the body so often by Farnes and Perks that he must have been black and blue by the time he put away his bat for the day. Rowan helped him to add 88 for the second wicket. It did not matter how long it took runs to come so long as they did come.

Day
Two

Daily
Express

6/3/39

England should aim at 1,000

*From WILLIAM POLLOCK
Daily Express Cricket Reporter,
who is the only staff reporter of a
British national newspaper with
the M.C.C.*

DURBAN, Sunday

The South Africans have got this timeless Test all wrong. Evidently they think that the big idea is to stay in a long as you can and score as slowly as you like.

They have not thought enough about it. The thing is to get as many runs as possible, preferably a soon as possible. Runs count, not how long the team batted.

Peter Van der Byl stayed in more than seven hours. His scoring rate was about seventeen runs an hour. He went out nearly knocked out.

He was hit so often by Farnes that the crowd at one time shouted to Hammond: "Take that bowler off!" But mainly it was all the batsman's own fault. He takes guard on the leg stump and as the ball comes up moves across to the off stump, leaving bowlers no stumps in view.

POTTERING

Nourse, one of the best stroke players the South Africans have, has been pottering and poking about for more than four hours for 77. South Africa should have comfortably scored, say, 600 in the two days' batting.

Walter Hammond.

So far Verity has bowled forty-three eight-ball overs and had only 67 runs scored off him in about twelve hours.

You would have thought by the way the South Africans batted that Verity was using his hands to make mesmeric passes at them.

There is only one thing to do now: when South Africa are out, probably some time tomorrow, England must go in and make sufficient runs to win by an innings.

There is no reason why England should not make 1,000 runs. Hutton once made 364 himself. This time he had better go in and make 365. It is a handier number. Anyhow, the boat still sails on March 17.

Day
Three

Daily
Telegraph
& Morning
Post

7/3/39

ENGLAND'S TASK IN TIMELESS TEST

SOUTH AFRICA'S RECORD SCORE

P. A. GIBB OUT FOR 4— RAIN STOPS PLAY

DURBAN, Monday.

South Africa made a record score against England here to-day. Their 530 beat their previous best of 513 for 8 wickets at Cape Town during the 1930-31 tour, and as they captured the wicket of P. A. Gibb before rain prevented any further cricket—at 4.46—they appear to have secured a firm grip on this play-to-a-finish Test.

As the weather experts forecast more rain the England batsmen may face a stern task in their effort to catch up. In view of the uncertain weather the tactics of the South Africans in occupying the pitch as long as possible become understandable.

Even if the pitch rolls out well England's task is a huge one, especially as the South Africans, during their brief time in the field, showed magnificent fighting spirit.

South Africa's batting early in the day, after several hours of slight rain, was more lively than people thought it would be. Nourse, who made his second century of the series, and the slightly-built wicket-keeper, Grieveson, began confidently against the fast bowling of Farnes and Perks. Grieveson made some splendid drives off the back foot which speedy running by the outfielders, Hutton and Paynter, prevented becoming fours, and Nourse played strokes all round the wicket much better.

The early liveliness went out of the batting when Verity was brought on, though Nourse and Grieveson missed few safe scoring opportunities. Both were quick in getting to the pitch of the ball, and their seventh wicket stand reached three figures when they had been together 144 minutes.

A little later a delightful on-drive gave Nourse his 100, and the crowd cheered for minutes. Nourse, a very popular man in Durban, batted 356 minutes for his 100. He hit only six 4's, but his innings was a good one for his side.

When he had scored three more he lashed out with a cross bat and was bowled by the untiring Perks. South Africa's seventh partnership realised altogether 107, and soon after Nourse went, Grieveson, who for several seasons has been unable to gain the sympathies of Transvaal selectors because of his nervous batting, reached a sound 50 in 157 minutes. This innings showed that Grieveson has shaken off his handicap, and the fact that he made 75 before playing on to Perks stamps him as very useful.

Grieveson's innings lasted 205 minutes and when he left the remaining batsmen fell quickly. Newson hit a ball straight back to give Verity a simple "c and b" and Langton, after driving the left hander straight over the sight screen for six, tried to hit another in the same way and was caught on the boundary by Paynter.

13-HOURS INNINGS

Thus, after 13 hours, South Africa's innings ended.

England began batting cautiously. No one expected Hutton and Gibb to do otherwise, especially as Langton and Newson, the opening bowlers, maintained a fine off-stump attack.

Both bowled in-swingers, and the England batsmen would not look at those balls. Unfortunately Gibb did not draw away from one quickly enough and an "edger" carried into the gloves of Grieveson, whose triumphant appeal was amplified by the crowd.

One wicket for nine was a bad start for England, and when Gordon, a bowler similar to Tate at his best, took over from Newson, he bowled three maidens in succession.

At tea England were 14 for one, and afterwards Hutton made some skilful leg-side strokes and cuts off Gordon, Bruce Mitchell and Langton. When heavy clouds gathered over the ground the Yorkshireman made an unsuccessful appeal against the light, but a little later heavy rain, which lasted for more than half an hour, drove the players into the pavilion. The captains, after the rain ceased, just before half-past five, decided that no further play would be possible, so England resume to-morrow with one wicket down for 35.

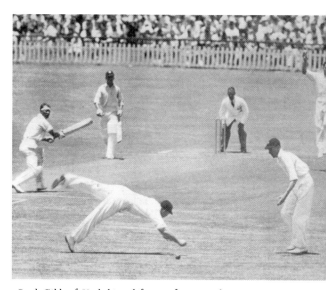

Paul Gibb of Yorkshire, left, out for 4 in the first innings.

SOUTH AFRICA	
P. G. Van Der Byl, b Perks	125
A. Melville, hit wkt, b Wright	78
E. A. Rowan, lbw, b Perks	33
B. Mitchell, b Wright	11
A. D. Nourse, b Perks	103
K. Viljoen, c Ames, b Perks	0
E. L. Dalton, c Ames, b Farnes	57
R. E. Grieveson, b Perks	75
A. B. C. Langton, c Paynter, b Verity	27
A. S. Newson, c and b Verity	1
N. Gordon, not out	0
Extras	20
Total	**530**

ENGLAND	
Hutton, not out	24
P. A. Gibb, c Grieveson, b Newson	4
Paynter, not out	6
Extra	1
Total (1 wkt)	**35**

W. R. Hammond, Ames, Edrich, B. H. Valentine, Verity, Wright, K. Farnes and Perks to bat.

Day Four

The Daily Mail
9/3/39

Running Out of Hutton Meant Defeat for England in Test

From R. J. CRISP, Famous South African Bowler and Daily Mail Special Correspondent

DURBAN, Tuesday.

England are still holding out, but their fall is imminent. Even allowing for all the traditional uncertainties of cricket it seems impossible that they can extricate themselves from their difficult position.

Doubtless, the majority of you reading

B. H. Valentine. During a conversation with Les Ames, it was decided to play a natural game.

of the poor display by the England batsmen assume that the wicket must have been rain-affected. Nothing of the kind. The wicket was damp but rolled out easy. The ball turned, but so slowly that no international bat should have experienced any difficulty in playing it.

Instead of blaming the wicket, I repeat my conviction that the majority of the England and Australian batsmen are unable to play on a turning wicket, and that South African superiority in that respect is due to training on matting wickets.

Looking back on the day's cricket, it is not easy to see why England wickets went so cheaply, but to me there were two significant points in the day's play.

THE TURNING POINT

First was Hutton's run-out. I said when it happened that it might well cost England the match, and though nobody could ever prove it, that is pretty near the truth.

Late in the afternoon, when Valentine went in, he and Ames had a conversation, during which it was obviously decided to drop negative tactics and play a natural game in an effort to get on top of the bowling. They nearly succeeded, and I have no doubt that had England played thus from the start, they would have been in a very different position at the end of the day.

Ames definitely saved England for

Eddie Paynter of Lancashire made a battling 62 in the first innings and 75 in the second.

another day, but for nothing more, and never was there a better man in a crisis. His innings to-day was the outstanding effort of the match.

Edrich remains the enigma. Can we wipe him off the Test slate yet? Don't ask me, ask Hammond.

South Africa owe their strong position to the canny bowling of Langton and Dalton on a wicket too slow paced for Newson and T. Gordon, plus England's mistaken policy of not going for the runs.

Nobody knows yet when the game will end, for there is not the slightest reason to suppose that Melville will enforce the follow-on if in a position to do so.

That would be foolish except on a sticky wicket. But if we cannot tell you when it will end, we can tell you how it will end in the defeat of England.

Wearing Wicket, But Test May Not End Until To-morrow

From R. J. CRISP, Famous South African Bowler and Daily Mail Special Correspondent

Day Five

The Daily Mail 9/3/39

DURBAN, Wednesday.

South Africa are in an impregnable position, with seven good wickets yet to fall—there is no purpose in declaring as long as the wicket holds—and a lead of 407 runs.

The wicket has lasted amazingly, but there were signs late in the afternoon that it is beginning to wear, and that can mean only one thing: the speedier end to the match in South Africa's favour.

The perky way the England tail wagged showed the ease of the wicket, and it was due only to two excellent catches that the innings closed before lunch.

Mitchell opened South Africans' second innings with Van Der Byl. The score mounted steadily, and under the relentlessness of these two, the England attack began to look worn and tired. It looked as though the men were bowling under the conviction of defeat, however subconsciously and however manfully they strove.

UNLUCKY VAN DER BYL

Van Der Byl provided the tragedy of the game when he missed by three runs the distinction of being the first South African to score a hundred in each innings in a Test.

Three quick wickets gave the attack much-needed encouragement, and Hammond immediately clustered the fielders round the bats of Nourse and Viljoen, but there was a touch of despair in the move or else he had seen the signs of wear on the wicket.

The sixth day cannot do otherwise than break gloomily for England. It is possible that it well mean for them another day in the field, and it now looks as though the game will not end before Friday evening.

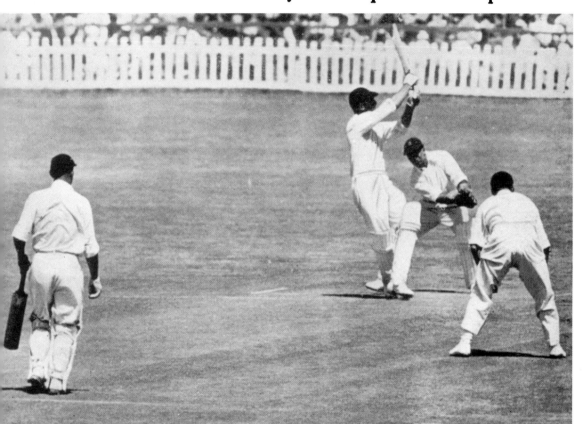

Van der Byl missed out on history by three runs. A hundred in the second innings would have secured for him the distinction of being the first South African to score a century in each innings of a Test.

Day
Six

Daily
Telegraph
& Morning
Post

10/3/39

ENGLAND NEED 696 TO WIN MARATHON TEST

South African Captain Scores His First Test Century Despite Injury

DURBAN, Thursday.

England require 696 runs to win the last Test match here, more runs than have ever been scored in the last innings of a first-class match before.

To-day South Africa carried their overnight score of 193 for three to 481 in their second innings on a pitch that improved after showers during the night, and their batting against tired and dispirited bowlers was just the type expected.

All down the line the Springboks tortured England, and their joy knew no bounds when their inspiring and popular captain, Alan Melville, in spite of an injured thigh, made his first century in Test cricket. Three thousand spectators cheered themselves hoarse.

Melville could not get to the ball quickly enough to play his usual cover-drives and late cuts, yet the terrific strength in his wrists enabled him to force the ball to leg and to the on in a masterly style.

During his stand with K. Viljoen, which produced 104 runs, and afterwards, England fought with a bitter grimness. They never gave up, not even the weary bowlers.

Ames, behind the stumps, was magnificent. Up to tea-time, after which P. A. Gibb took over, he conceded only six byes while more than 900 runs were scored. Yes, England fought well, and even at the close of this sixth day, with those disheartening figures glaring down at them from the score-board, they grinned and said, "We will win yet."

South Africa, from the first ball of this match, the end of which will be a relief to everyone concerned, have shown a determination which has to be admired, and none will say that they do not deserve the position in which they now find themselves. Last night, in the closing overs, Nourse and Viljoen looked the unhappiest of batsmen, but when they resumed in hot weather this morning they played with the greatest confidence against Wright and Verity.

Nourse quickly square cut and hooked Wright for successive boundaries to send up the 200 in 246 minutes. He and Viljoen played Verity with equal confidence and when England took the new ball at 209 and Farnes and Perks attacked runs still came at a good rate.

ANOTHER RECORD BEATEN

When the total reached 234 South Africa had scored their record total in a Test, their previous best being 763 (476 and 287) at the Oval in 1935.

The partnership ended at 242, when Nourse mistimed a hook and was out to a good running catch by Hutton.

So that his bowlers might exploit any possible wear on the pitch, Hammond gave Wright and Verity a lengthy spell as the partnership of Viljoen and Melville developed.

Nearing lunchtime Viljoen seemed to tire and Melville took a bigger part in the proceedings. He off-drove Verity to the boundary, pulled Wright for another 4, and enabled South Africa to go to lunch with the aperitif of a lead of 506 runs with six wickets still intact.

For a time after the interval the scoring was dead slow, only eight runs, including six extras, coming in half an hour. After the 300 had been reached in 366 minutes and Viljoen had completed his 50 in 2hrs 18min, however, the game became brisk again.

Never at any time really aggressive, Viljoen and Melville relentlessly piled on the runs. When 66 Viljoen was almost caught by Ames, who made a spectacular dive to the leg side, but apart from that neither batsmen ever looked like getting out.

The 100 for the partnership was reached when Viljoen and Melville had been together slightly under two hours, and a few moments later Viljoen, whose outstanding strokes were seven 4's, played-on to Perks. He had batted 3 hours and 3 minutes, and Dalton, who came in next, after a slow start, slammed the tired bowlers.

Melville completed his 50 in 139 minutes and then Dalton smashed three balls from Wright to the leg boundary. Hammond made his 25th bowling change when he put Hutton on, and the Yorkshireman was hit for 10 runs in his only over. Dalton on-drove a ball from Wright to the roof of the grandstand for 6.

BRILLIANT "C. & B."

Shortly afterwards, however, Wright made a wonderful catch off his own bowling, taking a fierce drive from Dalton down at his ankles; and Grieveson, who then joined Melville, narrowly escaped a similar fate.

Immediately after tea Melville on-drove Wright for three successive fours, to raise the 400 in 468 minutes, and a little later completed his century in 199 minutes, to a storm of cheering.

Farnes, however, bowled him with an outswinger which grazed the off stump when he had scored 103, and he walked back to the pavilion to the accompaniment of more deafening cheers. His innings contained 10 boundary shots.

South Africa's remaining batsmen were disposed of fairly cheaply. Langton was caught head-high by Hammond at deep first slip off Farnes, Newson was bowled by a leg-break, and Grieveson, who has had a good match in every way, was last out when he made a wild swipe and was bowled leg stump.

By the time attention had been paid to the pitch, England were left with five minutes' batting. As soon as Newson had bowled the first ball, Hutton and P. A. Gibb appealed against the light and the umpires upheld their claim.

Day Seven

Daily Tribune

11/3/39

SPRINGBOKS LOSING STRANGLE HOLD ON TEST MATCH

Fighting Rally By M.C.C.

Edrich's Happy Century

By JACK GAGE

Well played, England! What more can we say about the magnificent performance put up by the M.C.C. in scoring 253 runs for the loss of only one wicket on the seventh day of the marathon Test match?

Just as all the honours went to South Africa on the first five days of the game, so have England taken them on the last two days.

On Thursday their bowling and fielding were maintained at a wonderfully high level throughout the day and yesterday the three men who batted were always on top of the Springbok attack.

For almost the first time in the match South Africa are beginning to lose their grip, and although the odds are still very much on the Springboks winning the game, particularly in view of last night's rain, the M.C.C., thanks to their refusal to give in, have given themselves an outside chance of pulling off what would be the most sensational Test win in cricket history.

On each of the seven days of play there has been one outstanding feat of personal brilliance which has overshadowed everything else.

Yesterday was no exception to this rule. Bill Edrich's brilliant century coming after his failure in ten successive Test match innings, was perhaps the greatest personal triumph of the game.

The crowd rose to him to a man as he stole his short single to reach the coveted 100 runs. The ovation could not have been more warm hearted had he been batting at Lord's.

JUSTIFIABLE GAMBLE

Many were surprised to see Edrich walking to the wicket after Hutton's unexpected dismissal. But I can imagine that after Edrich's brilliant batting at number three in the Natal match last week and his failure at number seven in the first innings of the present Test, Hammond thought it worth while taking a chance and promoting him in the order.

After all, there was nothing to lose if he failed and everything to gain if he came off. It was one of those very justifiable gambles which every thinking captain must take, and in this instance it has succeeded beyond what must have been Hammond's wildest dream.

From the first ball he received Edrich looked a different player to the man who had failed in the earlier Test matches. He cracked a boundary off Mitchell and never looked back. True he had one or two narrow escapes but every batsman needs a little luck now and then and Edrich was certainly due his fair share.

At times his batting was delightfully aggressive and he was particularly strong on the leg side. At others, notably for the first hour after tea, he slowed down and played with the greatest caution, even being outpaced in scoring by Gibb. His innings has helped to place the M.C.C. in a very much better position than they might have been.

VALUE OF GIBB

While praising Edrich for his brilliant innings, however, we must not overlook the important part played by Gibb in staying at the wicket all day and scoring 78

runs. From a team point of view Gibb's effort was perhaps even more meritorious than Edrich's.

Never an attractive batsman to watch, Gibb is a great man to have on your side in a timeless Test match or when playing for a draw. He simply refused to take the slightest vestige of a risk yesterday and helped to break the hearts of the Springbok bowlers. His scoring was even slower than that of Nourse and Van der Byl in the Springbok first innings. But every run was invaluable to England.

We were naturally delighted from a South African view point to see Hutton go with the M.C.C. total well short of 100 runs yesterday, but he had batted so attractively up till then that we found it in our hearts to wish that he might perhaps have stayed another hour to entertain us with his glorious batsmanship. It will be many years before most of us will see the great Yorkshireman again, but we will carry many happy memories of the innings he has played in this country.

Perhaps I have rather carried away by the wonderful fight the Englishmen have put up in this Test match and failed in the last two days to give the Springboks their due. We must remember that early in the game the South Africans batted and bowled in winning form and were in a seemingly impregnable position on Thursday night. For the first time during the match, however, they were outplayed yesterday.

PSYCHOLOGICAL EFFECT

It may have been the psychological effect of having made such an enormous lead which made the Springboks slack off without ever meaning to do so to-day, or they may just have been outplayed.

It is remarkable to recall that the South African bowlers dismissed the full strength of the M.C.C. batting in less than two days for 316 runs under less favourable conditions (the wicket is not quite as good as it was four days ago, although still standing up wonderfully well) in the first innings and then only managed to dismiss one batsman yesterday.

But there it is. The Springbok bowlers were properly mastered yesterday and they must make a superhuman effort to recapture lost ground to-day.

If the two not out batsmen get set again this morning, South Africa will be in a very awkward position. There is very little hope of the visitors scoring the 451 runs needed to win the game to-day, and unless the Springboks dismiss the whole side before the close of play, the present match will break all previous records by lasting into nine days.

PLAY IN DETAIL

About 1,000 people were present when play started on the seventh day of the final Test match. Hutton had played one ball from Newson the previous evening before appealing against the light, and this morning Newson completed a maiden to the Yorkshireman. Gordon took the new ball from the other end.

A strongish wind blew down the wicket from the town end and the weather was rather warmer than it had been on the other six days. Gibb opened the English score with a neat leg shot for two off Gordon, but otherwise the Englishmen just took stock of the bowling. The wicket was still standing up to the strain remarkably well, although there was an ugly looking spot at the Umgeni end which threatened to crumble later in the day.

Newson only bowled one over before being switched to the town end in place of Gordon, Langton coming on against the wind. Hutton straight drove the fourth ball of the over for a perfect four. We soon saw that the Englishmen were full of fight and did not intend giving in without a struggle. Newson came on again with the wind from the town end.

Against Langton, Hutton played a perfect drive through the covers for four. The batsmen scored 23 in half an hour, Hutton having scored 17 and Gibb six. For twenty minutes the cricket was

Bill Edrich cuts for four in his double-century. The Middlesex man's 219 atoned for past failures.

uneventful. Hutton took ones and twos when he could, but Gibb did little other than play the ball straight down and about the wicket.

Dalton bowled against the wind at 29 and Hutton took three and Gibb two in his first over. After an hour's batting 38 runs had been scored. One over from Gordon costing six runs, Hutton and Gibb both taking three. The first 50 was scored in 80 minutes, Hutton at that stage having 37 and Gibb 12.

Neither batsman took any risks with the bowling. Hutton was the more enterprising and scored considerably faster than his partner. The South African fielding was good and no runs were given away. Gibb scored four to the leg boundary when he jabbed his bat at a well-pitched delivery from Gordon.

When the score was 65, England had scored their highest partnership for the first wicket in the series. Hutton reached his 50 by gliding Langton to fine leg for two. He had batted for 90 minutes and hit five fours.

During the previous half-hour the

batsmen had batted enterprisingly and doubled the total, which now stood at 76. Just after one o'clock Mitchell bowled in place of Gordon from the town end and in his first over he dismissed Hutton. Hutton made a vicious cut at the ball, which was pitched very short, and deflected it on to his wicket. England's sheet anchor openly showed his disgust for the shot as he left his crease. He had batted most enterprisingly.

Hammond sent Edrich in next and the Cinderella of the English team hooked the first ball he received beautifully to the boundary.

Langton bowled the last over before lunch and Edrich, who showed much determination, took a single off it. The lunch score was 88, Gibb having 22 and Edrich 10.

EDRICH SETTLES DOWN

The 100 was reached soon after lunch. Gordon bowled a ball wide of the wicket on the leg side and it went for four byes. The century was reached after 122 minutes' batting.

Leonard Hutton,
England's young
titan.

The batsmen built up the score at a good rate after lunch. Mitchell and Gordon bowled and although Gibb continued his cautious tactics Edrich made efforts to score as often as he could.

Twenty-six runs were added in the first half-hour, Edrich taking 13 of them and Gibb seven. Edrich played many forceful shots on the leg side. Edrich became more watchful as the minutes passed, but he continued to collect runs, mainly singles.

Gordon trundled away from the Umgeni end and Edrich reached his highest score in Test Match cricket, 29, with a lucky snick for four off Gordon.

Gibb meanwhile was batting with monumental patience. He played all bowlers with extreme caution and scoring shots from him were infrequent.

Gordon bowled many overs and when he was tired Melville brought on Langton. In his first over, Edrich made a stroke which signified that he was thoroughly comfortable, a straight drive for four. This brought his total two runs past that of Gibb, who was labouring on 34. The total was 136.

Edrich made several nice strokes after he had settled down. Once he hooked Langton to the boundary with terrific force.

He scored another boundary off Langton shortly afterwards to make the score 153, scored in 195 minutes. Playing Mitchell, Edrich hit the ball with such force that it knocked one stump at the other crease out of the ground. Playing a similar stroke off the next ball he scored four to reach his 50. He had scored seven fours and had batted for 90 minutes.

His effort was loudly cheered by the crowd, who sympathised with him for his recent failures in Test Match cricket. Then he became recklessly bold. Facing Langton he played a vigorous cross bat stroke to a ball pitched on the wicket and banged it straight to the screen. Gibb meanwhile was pottering around on 41.

At 3.45 p.m. there was a light drizzle and Gibb told Melville that water was collecting on his spectacles and obstructing his view. But the game went on and shortly afterwards the rain stopped and

Bill Edrich. His magnificent innings took England to the brink of victory

made Gibb's task easier.

Edrich took two more fours and then Gibb stole a single to reach his 50, which had taken 220 minutes and included two fours. Gibb scored one run off the last over before tea from Mitchell, and the score at the interval was 197, Gibb having 53 and Edrich 77.

NEW BALL AFTER TEA

With a three to fine leg off Langton Gibb made the score 200. The innings had been in progress for 228 minutes. Four thousand people watched a period of quiet cricket after tea. Edrich stood at 77 for about 20 minutes and Gibb continued to play patiently. Langton and Newson bowled with the new ball but they did not make use of it except to keep down the rate of scoring.

Off Newson Gibb played a nice late cut for two and then as Langton began to tire both batsmen played neat leg glides off him and the total reached 214, Gibb having 65 and Edrich 81. In 40 minutes after tea Gibb scored 14 to Edrich's five.

Rain began to fall at one stage, but the game continued. Gordon came on in place

of Langton at the Umgeni end of the ground, and was applauded for a maiden over, bowled to Gibb. Edrich was strangely subdued at one period, but he played some neat leg strokes off both Gordon and Newson later. Gibb stole a short single to cover to reach 70.

Langton had a turn in Newson's place from the town end and Edrich reached 90 by hitting him vigorously down to the long-on rails. The batsmen scored 32 runs in an hour after tea.

As Edrich began to approach his century the crowd cheered him whenever he scored a run. He reached 99 with a powerful drive off his back foot for two and then a riot of cheering, whistling and clapping broke out as Langton misfielded another drive off his own bowling and Edrich got the coveted run.

Edrich got an ovation yesterday which was as good, if not better, than that which Van der Byl got on Wednesday when he returned to the pavilion after scoring 97 and missing the distinction of being the first South African to score two centuries in a Test match by two runs.

Edrich had played a great innings, which was full of powerful drives and hooks. People will long remember the innings which gave Edrich his first Test match century.

Soon afterwards there was a successful appeal against the light. The score was 253 for one, Edrich 107 and Gibb 78.

SCORE SHEET

M.C.C.—Second Innings

Hutton, b Mitchell	55
Edrich, not out	107
Gibb, not out	77
Extras (8 byes, 3 leg byes, 1 wide 1 no ball)	13
Total (for one wicket) ..	253

Fall of wicket: 1-78.

Bowling Analysis

	O	M	R	W
Newson	17	2	28	0
Gordon	19	2	58	0
Langton	21	3	67	0
Dalton	9	0	41	0
Mitchell	15	2	46	1

Day Eight

Daily Tribune

14/3/39

ENGLAND TURNS THE TABLES ON SOUTH AFRICA

Springboks In Danger Of Defeat

DRAMATIC FINISH LIKELY TO-DAY

BY JACK GAGE

Was there ever such a Test match? To think that England were within a meagre 200 runs of victory at the close of play last night after being set 696 runs to win on the fourth innings, and still have seven wickets in hand.

Even the most ardent English supporters only hoped that England would put up a good show and perhaps score 500 runs in this fourth innings. But to collect 496 runs for the loss of only three wickets, must rank as one of the most amazing efforts which has ever been made or is likely to be made again.

The tables have been completely turned on South Africa although the Springboks still have an excellent chance of winning if only they can get rid of two more batsmen reasonably cheaply this morning. But once the batsmen get on top of the bowlers, as they did yesterday, the M.C.C. appear certain to win this historic game.

We have been treated to many exciting and dramatic moments in this Test match, but to-day, the twelfth since play started on March 3, promises to exceed them all as each side pulls out every ounce of vitality in a final desperate effort to win.

The players have played the game in a wonderful spirit of sportsmanship despite the tenseness and earnestness of the struggle. No unfair advantage has been taken by either side throughout the match.

Yesterday we had one little incident which illustrated the spirit in which the game has been played.

Van der Byl, fielding in the country, threw a rather wild return to Grieveson. Gibb just baulked the wicketkeeper as he was completing his run, the ball going loose. Instead of taking another run, which they could easily have done, Gibb and Edrich preferred not to take advantage of the mishap and stayed where they were.

Only a small point but, considering the tenseness of the struggle, worthy of note.

If play continues on the same lines as it has done, everything points to a decision being arrived at between four and five o'clock this afternoon. The whole of Durban should be there to see it.

Edrich was again the centre of attraction as far as spectators were concerned. He has broken his Test match hoodoo with a vengeance, and yesterday was the personification of confidence. All the bowlers came alike to him, and his huge innings included a hundred in boundary hits.

England must be very pleased that they persevered with the small Middlesex batsman as long as they did. He has made up for all his failures in this one innings and should be a different player when the next series of Tests against Australia are played.

Gibb batted on in his old stolid way, helping to break the bowlers' hearts and scoring occasional runs as the opportunity offered. He is another player who should have made his place secure in the M.C.C. side for many years. His painstaking knock had a lot to do with England's phenomenal success.

Hammond was not his usual confident self by any means. Early in his innings he was very shaky indeed, but towards the end he began to see the ball better and scored several pretty shots.

By that time the Springbok bowlers were tired out, however, and Paynter was his usual aggressive self and may cause a lot of trouble to-day.

The fielding of the South Africans was not up to the high standard we have come to expect in this Test series. There were several bad lapses in the field during the day, especially when the Gibb-Edrich partnership was at its height. Towards the close, when a couple of wickets had fallen, the South Africans improved a lot.

The bowlers stuck to their job on a wicket which favoured the batsmen for most of the day. On odd occasions the ball would pop up slightly, but on the whole the wicket played dead easy and the bowlers had an unenviable task.

Play In Detail

Anticipating an interesting day's cricket, a few hundred people were present at Kingsmead yesterday when play began. Newson bowled the first over to Edrich, who took two off the fifth ball. Newson and others made a loud appeal for lbw at the end of the over, but it was not successful. Langton bowled an uneventful over to Gibb from the Umgeni end of the ground.

A strong wind blew diagonally across the wicket and assisted Langton more than it did Newson. The wicket appeared to be in splendid condition, but both Edrich and Gibb watched the ball warily for the first few overs. Only seven runs were scored in the first half-hour. Newson bowled three overs and then Gordon made an appearance in his place at the town end of the ground.

Gibb batted most enterprisingly in Gordon's first over, cutting him nicely through the slips for two twos in succession. Van der Byl fielded one of these shots at third man and as he threw the ball in, Gibb unintentionally obstructed Grieveson and the ball travelled into the outfield. But the batsmen sportingly did not run.

200 PARTNERSHIP

Langton bowled to an attacking field and had Newson, Gordon and Melville close up to the batsmen on the leg side. The batsmen scored freely through Gordon's slip field and the score was built up gradually. When Edrich lofted a ball from Mitchell, who had come on in place of Langton, to leg for four, the 200 for the partnership had been reached.

Edrich, at this stage, had 119 and Gibb 93. Both seemed thoroughly comfortable. The South Africans were ragged in the field and Van der Byl once threw the ball well over Grieveson's head to give Gibb four extra runs. Mitchell conceded quite a number of runs to Edrich.

GIBB'S CENTURY

Then Gibb reached his 100. Facing Gordon, he forced the ball to long-on for two, which gave him his second Test century. His innings was more patient than those of either Van der Byl or Nourse and up to this stage had lasted 362 minutes and included only two fours.

Against Gordon, Gibb played a nice stroke past Nourse at cover for three, sending up the 300 in 372 minutes.

Because Mitchell was proving expensive and making little impression on the batsmen, Melville gave Dalton a turn and the new bowler started well; his first two overs being maidens.

Langton was switched round to bowl from the town end and once he was unlucky not to bowl Edrich. The batsman made a swing at the ball and snicked it just outside his leg stump. When the score was 309, the highest second wicket partnership between England and South Africa, that between Sutcliffe and Tyldesley at Johannesburg in the 1927-28 series, had been equalled.

Now the batsmen were the masters. They took opportunities to score off anything loose and although Dalton and Langton varied their deliveries in a desperate effort to effect a separation, their efforts seemed to gradually fizzle away as Edrich and sometimes Gibb made powerful hooks and drives on the leg side.

Although South Africa were still in a

RECORDS BROKEN DURING FIFTH TEST

LONGEST Test match ever played. To-day is the ninth playing day.

First time South Africa has ever scored over 400 in each innings of a Test.

South Africa has scored her highest total in a Test innings, 530

South Africa has scored her highest aggregate in a Test match, 1,011.

Combined scores total more than ever scored previously in any Test match (excluding West Indies). 1,823 runs have already been scored. Previous highest aggregate between South Africa and England, in England, is 1,297; highest in South Africa, 1,272; highest ever (in Australia), 1,753.

England has scored the highest second wicket partnership between the countries (Edrich and Gibb) 280.

This figure also represents the highest score for any wicket in Tests between the countries.

Paynter has scored highest individual aggregate of runs in a series with 602 and is still batting. Previous highest aggregates were Hobbs' 539 and Taylor's 582.

Edrich is the first batsman ever to score over 200 runs in the fourth innings of a Test match.

The previous highest score in the fourth innings of a Test match was 411. England now has 496 for three wickets.

good position the partnership was fast turning the scales in favour of England. Edrich was even courageous enough to take risks. Repeatedly he bent down on one knee and swept Langton round to leg. He made a lot of runs with this unorthodox stroke.

Meanwhile, Gibb, not quite as stolid as usual, was keeping up his end. Gibb is not an entertaining batsman to watch; if he ever is it will be a remarkable defence and phenomenal patience that will have put him in that flight.

As the score increased, Edrich reached 150. He batted for 208 minutes and hit 18 fours.

Melville gave Gordon a turn from the Umgeni end ten minutes before lunch. But Gordon did little other than slow down the rate of scoring; both Edrich and Gibb were thoroughly comfortable. Mitchell bowled the last over before lunch and Edrich played out a maiden. The lunch score was 333, Gibb having 112 and Edrich 152. The M.C.C. were 345 runs short of their objective.

INTERESTING CRICKET AFTER LUNCH

Gordon bowled round the wicket after lunch, but Gibb, who faced him for most of the time, was as stubborn as ever. Against Mitchell, Edrich drove a straight four.

Then for a period there was some interesting cricket. Bowling from the town end, Mitchell made use of a treacherous spot, and once or twice the batsmen had difficulty in playing the ball. One ball that Mitchell bowled to Gibb appeared to break right across the wicket.

When the score was 347 the partnership was the greatest ever recorded in Test matches between South Africa and England. The previous best was 268, scored by Sutcliffe and Hobbs at Lord's in 1924.

The wicket looked as if it was beginning to wear at last, for Mitchell turned the ball appreciably and both Edrich and Gibb scrutinised it after every over, patting down spots here and there. Mitchell beat Edrich twice in one over.

However, a good rate of scoring was maintained and when the total was 350, Edrich had 163 and Gibb 118. Sixteen runs were scored in the first half hour after lunch. But still a wicket did not fall.

As time went on the crowd became more and more anxious, making appeals of "Come on, South Africa. What about a wicket?" The Springboks were careless in the field, too, which did not improve matters.

When Mitchell was tired, Melville gave Dalton a turn in his place to exploit the bad patch at the Umegeni end. Dalton received encouraging shouts from his

Paul Gibb of
Cambridge
University, Yorkshire
and England. This
was his finest innings
for his country.

home crowd as he prepared to bowl.

Then in his first over, Dalton, as
though responding to the appeals of the
crowd, struck a vital blow for South
Africa.

He pitched down a good-length ball,
faster than usual, and the leg turn
completely beat and bowled Gibb. For a
moment there was silence. The crowd
could not believe that the highest
partnership in Test matches between
England and South Africa had at last been
broken. Then the cheering broke.

Gibb had batted 453 minutes and hit

only two fours. The score was 363. The
partnership added 280 runs.

Hammond was uncomfortable against
both Dalton and Gordon. Once Gordon
clutched his trousers at the knees, turned
round with deliberation and made a very
confident appeal for l.b.w., but umpire
Ashman did not flinch.

Gibb's wicket had given the Springboks
more thrust and even Edrich was not too
comfortable.

Hammond gradually became more
confident and Edrich played many
beautiful shots. Once he drove the ball

with terrific force to the screen off
Gordon, and Melville brought on Mitchell.
Dalton and Mitchell gradually became less
effective and the rate of scoring increased
accordingly.

The batsmen took many runs on the
leg side and Nourse on the rails was
frequently applauded for stopping hard
drives from reaching the boundary.

When Edrich vigorously hit a full toss
to the square-leg boundary the total on
the scoreboard rolled round to 400. The
innings had been in progress 500 minutes.
Edrich hit another four, off Mitchell this

time, making his score 195 and the total 410. Hammond had 25. Then Edrich cracked another boundary off Mitchell and two balls later took a single to square-leg to reach his double century. The crowd gave him a tremendous ovation. He had batted delightfully for 395 minutes and hit 23 fours.

Melville took a new ball then and Newson came on for his second spell of the day. When the total was 412, the previous highest fourth innings score in a Test match had been passed.

Langton bowled with the new ball from the Umgeni end and a quiet period followed while the batsmen settled down to take the shine off. Newson did not bowl for long and Melville brought on Gordon in the hopes that he would be able to use the new ball effectively. He nearly had Edrich caught in the slips, the ball once going just over gully's head.

Langton, too, was taken off after bowling only a short spell and Newson was brought on in his place to bowl with the wind.

Melville was using his bowlers in short spells in a desperate effort to effect a separation, and Langton came on to bowl against the wind in Gordon's place.

Gordon bowled the last over before tea and Hammond reached 34 by driving him for four. Tea was taken with the score 442 for two wickets, Edrich having 215 and Hammond 34.

CROWD INCREASES AFTER TEA

The crowd had grown considerably by the time play started after tea. The news of England's amazing resistance had spread through the town like wildfire and office workers donned their coats and hurried out to the ground.

There was a quiet period after tea. Newson and Langton bowled a good length, and neither Hammond nor Edrich forced the pace. Six runs were scored in 15 minutes.

Then the tranquility of the afternoon was broken by the suddenness of Edrich's dismissal. Playing carefully to a ball from Langton, which was pitched just outside the leg stump, he cocked the ball up slightly, and Gordon, fielding at short leg

five yards from the bat, took a neat surprise catch a couple of inches off the ground. Edrich batted for 440 minutes and hit 25 4's. He scored the vast majority of his runs on the leg side.

Paynter came in to partner Hammond, and the crowd hoped fervently for more wickets. England now had an excellent chance of winning the Test. Hammond

once played the ball high in the air on the leg side, and as Van der Byl ran towards it with hands outstretched everybody in the ground screamed with excitement, but the ball landed a yard short of Van der Byl. It was one of the most exciting incidents of the day.

Newson was now bowling with much more fire, and this narrow escape by Paynter off his bowling spurred him to greater efforts. Repeatedly both batsmen played doubtful strokes to his bowling. Against Paynter he made a very confident but unsuccessful appeal for l.b.w., and then he nearly had the same batsman caught on the leg side.

It seemed that Melville had rested him

during the morning, and for the early part of the afternoon so that he could reserve his energy to keep down the rate of scoring late in the afternoon. Langton, too, bowled well.

Newson bowled a long spell, and not many runs were scored off him. Hammond reached 50 by gliding him to fine leg for two. He had batted for 135

minutes and hit three 4's up to this stage.

As dark ominous clouds gathered overhead the light became worse and worse. The crowd, which had now grown to 5,000, became lively and restless, appealing to the Springboks to take a wicket. After the players had had drinks Dalton bowled from the town end.

The batsmen played very confidently as the evening grew on. When the total was 495, Hammond had 58 and Paynter 23. Neither Dalton nor Gordon, who replaced Newson, and Langton, looked like taking a wicket. At 5.35 the batsmen made a successful appeal against the light. The score was 496, Hammond having 58 and Paynter 24.

HOW THEIR RUNS WERE SCORED

EDRICH		GIBB	
Snicks behind the wicket	17	Snicks behind the wicket	17
Short singles (off side)	7	Short singles (off side)	10
Short singles (on side)	23	Short singles (on side)	16
Late cuts	10	Late cuts	13
Cuts behind point (gully)	6	Cuts behind point (gully)	5
Square cuts	3	Square cuts	5
Off drives	10	Off drives	5
Cover drives	8	Cover drives	8
Straight drives	13	Straight drives	0
On drives	39	On drives	9
Leg hits	30	Leg hits	6
Pulls to square leg	46	Pulls to square leg	7
Glides to fine leg	7	Glides to fine leg	19
Total	**219**	**Total**	**120**

Balls bowled to batsmen, 576.
Balls scored off, 101.
No chances.

Balls bowled to batsman, 471.
Balls scored off, 79.
No chances.

Test Abandoned As Victory Smiles On England

By
JACK
GAGE

SPRINGBOKS LEAD BY 42 RUNS: RAIN SWAMPS PITCH

HAMMOND SHINES

The timeless Test has become timeless in actual fact.

Late yesterday afternoon after rain had stopped play at four o'clock, it was announced that the South African Cricket Board had decided that the M.C.C. team must leave that night in order to give themselves time to make final arrangements before sailing from Capetown on Friday.

As rain poured down after tea yesterday afternoon the faithful 5,000 who had attended every one of the nine afternoons of play of the fifth and final Test waited anxiously while those in authority held a long consultation as to whether the M.C.C. could stay over until this morning.

It all seemed so obvious to the average layman that at least the five M.C.C. batsmen who might have to bat should wait over until this afternoon's train or even fly to Capetown.

It seemed such a pity that this remarkable game should have been brought to an unsatisfactory and unnecessary conclusion when an hour, at at the most an hour and a half's play, would have sufficed to bring a definite result.

As the game stood at the conclusion of play the odds were still on the M.C.C. winning, but the Springboks had made a last-minute bid for final victory by dismissing Paynter and Hammond within half an hour of one another, and from being in a hopeless position South Africa

The "timeless" wicket being made ready for the tenth and final day.

at least had an outside chance of pulling the match out of the fire.

Conditions throughout the match had remained so very fair to both sides that we all felt sorry when rain began to interfere with play at 3.10.

The general feeling amongst the crowd seemed to be that it did not matter which side won as long as a definite decision could be arrived at.

Both teams had in turn made tremendous recoveries when the position looked very black. Both winners and losers would have come out of the game with equal credit. In the fourth innings England had looked like pulling off the impossible all along the line until the dramatic half hour yesterday afternoon when the Springboks made their last desperate bid.

Hammond and Paynter had appeared quite capable of scoring the required runs without any assistance from the remaining batsmen, and just as we were beginning to

resign ourselves to a tame finish Paynter was caught behind the wicket off Gordon.

This sudden and unexpected wicket made all the difference to the weary Springbok bowlers. They went at their task with renewed energy, the fielders responding with several spectacular saves.

We all knew that if Hammond went the Springboks still had a faint hope. And then Eric Dalton, as he has done so often before, tempted Hammond out of his crease, and in a twinkling Grieveson had the bails off.

It was all very dramatic. Valentine had a narrow escape before rain drove the players from the ground for the last time at 3.55.

DALTON MIGHT HAVE BEEN BOWLED MORE

For some reason Melville refused to risk bowling Dalton yesterday, only giving him two overs in the morning. Quite possibly Melville felt that he could not risk the slow bowler giving away runs. But this policy, as it turned out, was a mistake. As it was Dalton took a wicket with the first ball of his over in the afternoon.

But it is easy to criticise sitting in the stands, and it is not difficult to understand that Melville had a very difficult job in trying to dismiss these M.C.C. batsmen who had determined to get the runs needed to win.

To my mind Hammond's innings was one of the highlights of the match. When he first went in on Monday afternoon he was far from comfortable, but once he had got over his initial shakiness he batted with consummate ease and skill.

Runs made no difference to him. He gave one the impression that he felt that as long as he was at the wickets he was quite capable of scoring any runs which England might require. His short singles between the wickets were an object lesson in certainty and precision.

Melville had placed a defensive field, and Hammond took advantage of this to hit the ball to vacant parts of the field close to the wicket. Paynter always backing his captain to the hilt.

Paynter himself was not in his usual aggressive form, being content to leave the scoring to his captain. Ames, during his short knock, looked as if he might have caused a lot of trouble before the end.

And now it all over. What an anticlimax after all these days of determined and at times exciting cricket.

The M.C.C. sail with the rubber in their pockets, and South Africa are left with the unsatisfied feeling that they might just possibly have pulled off this last game to square the account.

But we must be honest and agree that the odds were very much on England when stumps were finally drawn yesterday afternoon.

Play In Detail

The prospect of an eventful day's cricket brought hundreds of spectators to Kingsmead. When Gordon completed his interrupted over, there was a crowd of 2,500 present and the turnstiles were clicking merrily.

The odds were on the M.C.C., but there was a distinct possibility of rain when play started, the sky being black and overcast in parts.

The first run that Paynter scored nearly led to Hammond's dismissal; he played the ball to shallow fine leg and Hammond just reached his crease before Grieveson took Dalton's smart throw-in. Newson bowled from the town end. There was little wind.

Hammond played two nice drives through the covers and the score reached 500. The innings had been in progress for 618 minutes.

Newson was less effective than Gordon, Hammond scoring frequently off him on the leg side. The Springbok fielding was good. Gordon bowled vigorously in an effort to gain an early wicket, but the batsmen, except for the fact that they could not score off him, were quite comfortable. At 517 Mitchell bowled in Newson's place from the town end and Hammond, pulling him to leg, scored two.

Paynter hits Dalton to leg during his third wicket partnership with Hammond which produced 242 second innings runs. Hammond's 120 followed his century in the second Test.

Later in the over the batsmen stole a single, dangerously. Hammond drove the ball to Melville, who was standing next to the bowler, and as it rolled off the Springbok captain's foot Hammond called a run. Paynter just reached the batting crease before Grieveson whipped off the bails.

Gordon bowled for 50 minutes before Melville brought on Langton in his place. Gordon's analysis was 7-3-10-0. The running between the wickets of the batsmen was admirable. Melville's field

was mainly a defensive one, so both Hammond and Paynter casually tapped the ball here and there on either side of the wicket and ran comfortable singles while the fielders hastily ran in to meet the ball.

The first hour of play yielded 38 runs. When the total was 535 Hammond had 80 and Paynter 38.

After Mitchell had bowled a short spell Gordon came back. The wicket was wearing fast and occasionally the ball popped.

HAMMOND'S MACHINE-LIKE ACCURACY

Off both Langton and Gordon the batsmen scored at a good rate. Hammond batted like a machine. He seemed to look round the field before each ball, cast his eye on a vacant spot, and say, "Yes, I think I'll take a single there."

Paynter was stolid and he was not quite as fluent as Hammond, but he got runs just the same.

Hammond's second innings 140 provided valuable support for Edrich.

Gordon's second spell was only a short one and Newson displaced him at 546. Paynter cut his first ball down to third man to record the 100 partnership. Later in the over Paynter played the ball rhythmically through the covers to the boundary to make the total 552, and his own score 52. He had batted for 140 minutes.

Then, 15 minutes before lunch, Melville threw the ball to Dalton, whose penchant for breaking up partnerships is widely known.

But Dalton's first over yielded 11 runs, Paynter taking two boundaries off it.

South Africa's efforts to keep down the score were proving useless. It was like a small boy trying frantically to stop the water from gushing out of a tap after he had mischievously unscrewed the washer.

Four byes off Newson's bowling augmented the total. It seemed that England were to pass South Africa's total without the loss of a further wicket. The experience of Hammond and Paynter was rapidly extinguishing the glimmer of hope which flickered in the eyes of the South African enthusiasts who sat on the bank and hoped fervently for the fall of a wicket before lunch.

Hammond played many of his strokes in croquet fashion, tapping the ball insolently on either side of the wicket. The prospects of rain diminished as the black clouds passed over the ground and the sun shone brightly. Langton bowled the last over before lunch to Hammond. He had been switched round to bowl in Newson's place from the town end.

Melville lapsed in the field and Hammond took three off the last ball of the over. The score at lunch was 578. Hammond having 93 and Paynter 68. England then required only 129 runs for victory.

VAN DER BYL OFF AFTER LUNCH

Howard Foss, twelfth man, fielded in place of Van der Byl after lunch, the latter having strained his arm badly during the morning. The first three overs yielded only one run, Mitchell and Langton, who operated from the town end, bowling maidens.

Hammond reached his century with a powerful drive off Mitchell towards the screen. He had batted for 273 minutes and hit three boundaries. Much of the benefit which Hammond has gained from his vast experience was displayed in his innings.

After Hammond had reached his century, his third of the series, the scoring slowed down while Langton and Mitchell bowled a good length. Langton sent down a good over to Paynter, beating him once with a ball that went just outside the off stump. Fifteen runs were added in the first half hour after lunch.

BATSMEN OPEN UP

Hammond took the score to 602 by driving Langton beautifully past Nourse at mid-off for three. The innings had been in progress for 748 minutes. Both batsmen were now beginning to play with abandon, and after Paynter had hooked Mitchell for a single, Hammond made a terrific stroke through the covers for four. No fielder attempted to stop the ball, it travelled so swiftly.

South Africa's hopes soared when Umpire Ashman gave Paynter out at 611. Melville had brought Gordon on in place of Mitchell at the Umgeni end and in Gordon's first over the ball appeared to kick and Grieveson took a catch behind the wicket head high. Paynter look surprised when he was given out. He had battled in stodgy fashion for his 75 runs, which took 213 minutes to compile and included five boundaries.

Ames carried on where Paynter had left off. He was soon into his stride, square-cutting Newson aggressively for two. Gordon bowled with the new ball at 619 and Hammond snicked the ball high between Newson and Melville in the slips. As Newson was ineffective, Melville gave Langton a turn from the town end. About 3.10 p.m. an ominous black cloud which suggested certain rain began to blow over the ground. The wind began to blow with more force, and as the introductory spots of rain fell the crowd scampered for shelter. Hammond looked up at the black sky and seemed to say: "So you've saved their bacon after all."

But the rain did not last, and the umpires walked back on to the field with England needing 64 runs for victory. The batsmen added three runs before another shower sent them scuttling back to the pavilion for the second time. This time the delay lasted for 20 minutes.

Then Hammond lost his wicket with England still 56 runs short of their objective. Again it was Dalton who broke

The final scoreboard shows England 42 runs short of a memorable victory when the match was abandoned.

the partnership. Melville brought him on in place of Langton, and in his first over Hammond jumped well out of his crease, missed a big leg turn and Grieveson stumped him.

When Valentine came in and was nearly stumped off Dalton's next ball the crowd shook with excitement. South Africa still had a fighting chance.

Three minutes before tea a shower of rain sent the players into the pavilion. The total was 654, Ames having 17 and Valentine 4.

A GREAT INNINGS

Hammond's innings was magnificent. England's captain will probably play many more Test match centuries, but the one which helped to put England on the road to victory in this match will be remembered as one of his best if not his very best. He batted for 349 minutes and hit seven fours.

FINAL · SCORES

SOUTH AFRICA — First Innings

P. G. van der Byl, b Perks	125
A. Melville, b Wright	78
E. A. B. Rowan, lbw, b Perks	33
B. Mitchell, b Wright	11
A. D. Nourse, b Perks	103
K. G. Viljoen, c Ames, b Perks	0
E. L. Dalton, c Ames, b Farnes	57
R. Grieveson, b Perks	75
A. B. Langton, c Paynter, b Verity	27
R. S. Newson, c & b Verity	1
N. Gordon, not out	0
Extras (b 2, lb 12, nb 6)	20
Total	530

Fall of wickets: 1-131, 2-219, 3-236, 4-274, 5-278, 6-368, 7-475, 8-522, 9-523, 10-530
Bowling: Farnes 46-9-108-1, Perks 41-3-100-5, Wright 37-5-142-2, Verity 55.6-10-97-2, Hammond 14-4-34-0, Edrich 9-2-29-0

ENGLAND — First Innings

L. Hutton, run out	38
P. A. Gibb, c Grieveson, b Newson	4
E. Paynter, lbw, b Langton	62
W. R. Hammond, st Grieveson, b Dalton	24
L. E. G. Ames, c Dalton, b Langton	84
W. J. Edrich, c Rowan, b Langton	1
B. A. Valentine, st Grieveson, b Dalton	26
H. Verity, b Dalton	3
D. V. P. Wright, c Langton, b Dalton	26
K. Farnes, b Newson	20
R. T. D. Perks, not out	2
Extras (b 7, lb 17, w 1, nb 1)	26
Total	316

Fall of wickets: 1-9, 2-64, 3-125, 4-169, 5-171, 6-229, 7-245, 8-276, 9-305, 10-316
Bowling: Newson 25.6-5-58-2, Langton 35-12-71-3, Gordon 37-7-82-0, Mitchell 7-0-20-0, Dalton 13-1-59-4

SOUTH AFRICA — Second Innings

B. Mitchell, hit wkt, b Verity	89
P. G. van der Byl, c Paynter, b Wright	97
E. A. B. Rowan, c Edrich, b Verity	0
A. D. Nourse, c Hutton, b Farnes	25
K. G. Viljoen, b Perks	74
A. Melville, b Farnes	103
E. L. Dalton, c & b Wright	21
R. Grieveson, b Farnes	39
A. B. Langton, c Hammond, b Farnes	6
E. S. Newson, b Wright	3
N. Gordon, not out	7
Extras (b 5, lb 8, nb 4)	17
Total	481

Fall of wickets: 1-191, 2-191, 3-191, 4-242, 5-346, 6-382, 7-434, 8-450, 9-462
Bowling: Farnes 22.1-2-74-4, Perks 32-6-99-1, Verity 40-9-87-2, Wright 32-7-146-3, Hammond 9-1-30-0, Edrich 6-1-18-0, Hutton 1-0-10-0

ENGLAND — Second Innings

L. Hutton, b Mitchell	55
P. A. Gibb, b Dalton	120
W. J. Edrich, c Gordon, b Langton	219
Hammond, st Grieveson, b Dalton	140
Paynter, c Grieveson, b Gordon	75
Ames, not out	17
Valentine, not out	4
Extras (b 8, lb 12, w 1, nb 3)	24
Total (5 wkts)	654

Fall of wickets: 1-78, 2-358, 3-447, 4-611, 5-640
Bowling: Newson 43-4-91-0, Gordon 55.2-10-174-1, Langton 56-12-132-1, Dalton 27-3-100-2, Mitchell 37-4-133-1

·1948·

RECORDS TUMBLED AT LEEDS, in the fourth Test of Australia's first tour since the second World War. It began with Len Hutton (81), Cyril Washbrook (143), Bill Edrich (111) and Alec Bedser (79) helping England to 423 for two but with eight wickets falling for 73 runs, much of that good work was undone. Neil Harvey then became the first Australian left-hander to score a century in his first Test against England, going on to make 112. The real star, though, was swashbuckling Sam Loxton who hit five sixes in his 93 before being bowled going for his sixth. Australia were all out for 458 and England's second innings was all about quick runs. Hutton (57), Washbrook (65), Edrich (54) and Denis Compton (66) enabled England to declare at 365 for eight, setting Australia 404 to win. Arthur Morris began the reply in immaculate fashion, making 182 before he fell to Norman Yardley. Then Don Bradman, *left*, took up the gauntlet, scoring 173 not out, the last of his 29 Test hundreds. Australia won with 12 minutes left on the final day with the highest fourth innings total to win a Test match until 1976.

Neil Harvey, aged 19, returns to the pavilion having scored 112 in his first Test against England.

Day One

The Times
23/7/48

THE FOURTH TEST MATCH

ENGLAND'S SPLENDID START

CENTURY BY WASHBROOK

FROM OUR CRICKET CORRESPONDENT

England made a good start against Australia in the fourth Test match at Leeds yesterday, Hutton and Washbrook scoring 168 runs for the first wicket. At the close of play the score stood at 268 for two wickets.

The first information to be gained was that Young was the unlucky man to be discarded from England's team, with Emmett, the traveller from Torquay, officially established as twelfth, and that neither Barnes nor Tallon was sufficiently recovered from injuries to play for Australia. Also one noticed that there was no sight-screen at either end.

Yardley won the toss, and the huge crowd having settled themselves down to some measure of comfort and composure, England started off on a pitch quiet enough and without any suggestion of that greenery which is so frequently referred to. Lindwall bowled the first ball of the match to Hutton, and Miller started sedately at the other end. It was a normal start to a five-day Test match, no hurry, no flurry, with a drive by Hutton off Miller thrown in just to give it a touch of class. A few overs were expended before Johnston came on in place of Miller and a suggestion that Lindwall was speeding up. When Miller came on again, only one of many changes which were tried in the bowling, he made one ball rise sufficiently to reach the wicketkeeper's head but, curiously enough, it was his slower ball.

The bowling did not look particularly good, except that of Toshack, who kept a length while varying his pace and flight, and once he persuaded Hutton to a false stroke intended to go through the slips. Loxton was inclined to bowl too much on the leg side, but he was desperately unlucky when Hutton, with his score at 25, was missed off him at short leg. The preliminaries of pace, with the variety of Toshack's spin, having been overcome Hutton and Washbrook settled down to a partnership which seemed to offer the whole day before them. In this type of cricket outstanding strokes are few and far between but before luncheon Hutton had

Cyril Washbrook: "advanced to play stroke after stroke of grandeur."

made one beautiful cover drive off Toshack and Washbrook had chopped a ball with perfect timing off Loxton to the boundary, fine of third man. So at the interval the score stood at 88, Hutton then having made 46 and Washbrook 41.

CONFIDENT BATTING

When they started again both batsmen played as if some time lost in the morning had to be recovered, attacking the bowling of Toshack and Johnston with some degree of confidence. Runs were coming comfortably at the rate of one a minute when rain clouds blew up followed by the tiresome period which occurs even in the smartest cricket matches when players dodge in and out of the pavilion. Hutton was once hard pressed to keep a ball from Toshack out of his wicket and, to reassure

himself, he cut the next with a roll of the wrists to the boundary. More rain was succeeded by Hutton gaining five runs thanks to an overthrow by the ambitious Toshack. The first full-blooded burst of applause came when Loxton darted round by the long-leg boundary to intercept a glide by Washbrook, who immediately afterwards drove Miller to long on for 4.

Miller, who bowled a few balls a shade short of a length, once surprised Washbrook and all the crowd as well with a ball which whistled only a hair's breadth over the bails. In his next over he treated Washbrook to a full pitch, which went to the off boundary. With the score at 150, after a bewildering amount of bowling changes, Johnston came on with no slip and an alignment of off-side fieldsmen, not close enough, however, to prevent Washbrook from finding a fairway to the boundary. Nothing that Bradman could evolve had the least effect on Hutton, who, without showing the full range of stroke play which one has so often admired, was utterly master of the situation. The new ball was given to Lindwall at 164, some time after it could have been asked for. Hutton greeted it with a drive to the boundary past extra-cover, but to the next he was not quite across and had his off stump knocked back. He had batted admirably for a little over three hours, and this opening stand is the highest that has been made for England against Australia since Hutton and Barnett made 219 in the first Test match at Trent Bridge in 1938.

Washbrook, having reached his century out of 189 on the board, advanced to play stroke after stroke of grandeur. He had to pay constant attention to the accuracy of Johnson, but he found opportunity in his own time to make a succession of strokes to the off side not normally of his pattern. Into this had advanced Edrich, with a not very enviable duty of carrying on with an affair which was so well started. He played carefully enough to start with and then took his fair share of any loose balls, and there were not a few offered him. His innings in the circumstances was worth a deal to England, but in the very last over of the day Washbrook was caught in the slips.

Day Two

Daily
Telegraph
& Morning
Post

24/7/48

ENGLAND SCORE CREEPS TO 496

AUSTRALIA LOSE MORRIS FOR 6

From E. W. SWANTON

LEEDS, Friday

England are out, Australia are in, and, wonderful to relate, we are beginning to wonder whether our 496 is enough.

As the match stands Australia are 433 behind, having lost the vital wicket of Morris, but with Bradman, greeted like an emperor by the crowd which has seen him play Test innings of 334, 304 and 103, very much not out.

If ever the fact needed emphasis that the pitch is the key to a cricket-match the doings of the last two days have provided it. This pitch so far has been a survival from the early thirties, very like those on which Bradman forged his reputation. And if anyone may be inclined to compare Larwood and other English fast bowlers of his time unfavourably with Lindwall and Miller on the strength of their respective performances in England, the relative impotence of these two here may help to revise such a view.

On so comfortable a surface as this spin and flight must be the basis of any attack, however frequently new balls become due, and neither team in this match has a leg-break bowler. I can see no sign whatever of the pitch becoming loose or rough, and if the English bowlers, in the absence of rain, get out Australia tomorrow they will have done a great thing.

SIXES BY BEDSER

Our batting today was a grievous disappointment. It goes against the grain to blame Edrich after his brave effort in the third Test, which was one of the chief factors that have changed the moral balance of this series, but five and a

quarter hours, considering the position and the exceptional speed of the outfield, was an inordinate time to spend on 111 runs, and the truth is his innings was worth vastly less than his splendid one at Old Trafford. Only as an essay in concentration and will-power, and they are virtues indeed in these battles, was it of Test quality.

The beginning was dreadfully slow, seven runs in the first 35 minutes before the next new ball became due, 23 in the hour. Bedser existed precariously while Edrich gave the impression that possession was an end in itself.

The second hour was much more fruitful, for the increase was 70. Bedser, in two bursts of violence, hit Toshack and Johnson each for 14 in an over, mostly by strong true hits, including a soaring six wide of long-on off Johnson.

Once his new-ball bowlers had failed to penetrate, Bradman was happy to keep the rate down by a deep-set field. This was made easier by the fact that neither batsman sought to draw the fielders in by short pushes. Hobbs and Sutcliffe must have looked on with twitching feet, while the famous Australian spin bowlers in the Press box were probably cracking their fingers beneath the desk.

After lunch Bradman thought of Morris, whose left-arm bowling is on the lines of Leyland or Compton, and it was noticeable that he seemed more likely to dispose of Bedser that anyone because he spun the ball and gave it air. It was at the other end that Johnson, who does the same things, did break the partnership soon after Edrich had reached his 100.

That, as it proved, was the turn of the innings.

EDRICH CAUGHT

At last Edrich hit the ball into the air, pretty hard, too, but straight to Morris, fielding at short mid-wicket, a pitch's length from the bat.

Compton began almost surprisingly well, for he has hardly ever come in with this sort of score on the board and batted as well as he can. But when Crapp fell to a yorker, the time for another new ball had come round, and this quietened Compton more than Yardley, who hit both Lindwall and Johnston to the square-leg boundary and was always making strokes.

Just after 4 o'clock Compton snicked Lindwall too finely to leg, Saggers making ground quickly enough to hold the catch easily. That was 473 for six, and the first intimation to most that they might have to be satisfied with something below 600.

The remaining batting was highly un-Bedserish, and when, at five o'clock Yardley found himself with Pollard for company he aimed a forcing blow and missed, and that was that. The really disappointing innings was that of Cranston, who, before he was bowled, several times projected strokes through the covers that sent the ball to short-leg.

The last seven English wickets had fallen for 73, and once again it had been shown how hard it is to shake an innings into life once it has become set in a groove. Our scoring rate over the whole effort worked out at 45 an hour. A word more for Bedser: after his lucky start he batted sensibly and well, and some of his driving was really admirable.

In an hour and a quarter Australia have made 63 for one, Hassett's share being 13 and his intentions manifest. Morris, who sometimes plays uppishly off his front foot, on-drove Bedser to a straightish short-leg at 13, which, of course, was a great start for England. Bradman had a narrow squeeze or two against both Pollard and Bedser, who strove hard to get some response out of the pitch and once or twice succeeded. Whether Laker will turn the ball one does not know for he has not yet been given the chance to try.

Day Three

The Sunday Times

25/7/48

SUPERB BATTING SAVES AUSTRALIA IN CRISIS

Australia's tenth-wicket pair, Lindwall and Toshack, are still defying England at the end of a splendid batting recovery in the Fourth Test Match at Headingley, Leeds. After being at one time 355 for 8, the Australians ended with 457 for 9, only 39 short of England's first-innings total.

From NEVILLE CARDUS—Leeds, Saturday

Australia's tenth-wicket pair, Lindwall and Toshack, are still defying England at the end of a splendid batting recovery in the Fourth Test Match at Headingley, Leeds. After being at one time 355 for 8, the Australians ended with 457 for 9, only 39 short of England's first-innings total.

From NEVILLE CARDUS—Leeds, Saturday

The wicket subsided to docility after a brief period at the day's beginning, during which rain in the night enabled a ball here and there to bounce a little and come off the turf with alacrity. In this time there were alarums and excursions. Bradman and Hassett both succumbed. England caught a glimpse of victory, and the crowd was loud and voracious.

As a fact, Miller and Harvey waved crisis aside, almost condescendingly and not only held back the advancing bowlers, but scored 121 together in an hour and a half.

A fortuitous ending of Miller's innings probably robbed us of a most inflammatory display of batsmanship, for he was obviously happy, and in the mood to apply the sword all over the field and out of the field.

HARVEY'S HUNDRED

His cricket had savagery, litheness and rapid power, and Harvey, a mere youth, scored a century in his first Test Match against England, even as not long ago he scored a century in his second Test against India.

Loxton failed by seven only to make a magnificent century, and he smote so many sixes that they were becoming quite vulgar in a Test Match.

When Harvey was bowled Australia were 294 for five and 344 for six when Loxton lost his wicket going for another six. His downfall was providential for England, who may be said to have had a narrow escape.

Yardley, by putting on Laker after tea, frittered runs away and Lindwall was able to enjoy a few encouraging and easy hits.

I imagined for a while that Pollard and Bedser were beng held in reserve to dispose of Toshack with the new ball. When Toshack did come in, crippled somewhat and needing a runner, he

Don Bradman. Cardus found it: "difficult to describe how he faltered."

defended exasperatingly, and he and Lindwall held the tenth wicket so long that thousands turned away before the end of a long and, for England, trying afternoon of disappointment at the pinch.

BRADMAN GOES

The morning began eventfully. After Bradman had struck a no-ball from Bedser for two to square leg rather hungrily, like an urchin snatching a thrown coin, he was hit between wind and water. Pollard then bowled, and from a good length ball that popped up to the shoulder of the bat, Hassett was caught easily in the slips.

Miller drove his first ball for three and now, before the crowd had recovered after one complete exhaustion of breath, Pollard clean bowled Bradman, the off stump falling to earth with an inertness really awful.

The sight of it, this sudden removal of Bradman from a position threatening restoration of old power caused a roar of exultation such as is heard nowhere except in Yorkshire, at cricket or football matches.

From my position in the Press Box it was difficult to describe how Bradman faltered: he played rather late, and maybe the ball came across sharply, a little low. He missed, as a man misses his footing on the safest stairs, and he came back to the pavilion deep in thought.

On Friday he had made the blueprint for a century. Pollard's over, fatal to two batsmen of their eminence, will go down in the game's history as one of the most momentous ever achieved by an Englishman born in Lancashire.

In an hour of severe challenge young Harvey began his first innings in a Test match against England as coolly as a veteran, with perfect footwork. Miller, his companion, showed fight and pulled a great six as soon as Laker came on.

Harvey's strokes were thoroughly cultivated on the whole, though Laker quickly beat him with a superb off-spinner; very nasty for a left-hander. Though Pollard also beat Harvey, the boy was not at all downcast.

Here is a great and beautiful batsman in the making. He watched Laker carefully, and at the first chance pulled him three times for fours, each stroke invested with some grandeur. But when an off-spin bowler permits a left-handed batsman to hit him square to the on, the offence is more than offence—it is anathema.

Miller, who has been out of form, now was nearly at his best. Nobody drives a six like him: he swings all his tall, supple strength vehemently, yet there is a thrilling grace as well as elemental punitive power in his drive.

He seems to try to send a ball as far as cricket ball can ever travel, and still there is ease in the glorious swing of his bat.

MILLER'S BAD LUCK

He sent a half-volley from Laker soaring straight for six, and when Yardley came on he drove for four to the off and four to the on. A leonine blow. Then, as he tried a mighty sweep to leg, he only just touched a bad ball and it somehow collided with Evans's or his own pads whence it bounced into the air, and Edrich held a grand catch near the wicket, full stretch on the grass.

Lucky for England, and an irreparable loss to the glamour of the match. Australia were now 189 for four, and Harvey had reached 50 in 80 minutes. In one over from Cranston he cut and pulled two fours and a three.

Like all Australian batsmen he is strong on the on-side, but has a pretty square cut, and when he was 88 he had made 32 by means of this neglected stroke.

Harvey reached one of the most valiant centuries in all the history of Test cricket at 25 minutes past three, after three hours' extraordinarily resolute play for one so young. The Leeds crowd cheered him long and generously, and Loxton ran down the pitch to shake him by the hand.

This same Loxton had not been negligent: he punished a loose ball at sight, as though livid with scorn. He mistimed once or twice, while going forward, but he had immense confidence, and completed his 50 with a gigantic straight six off Cranston; the ball went so high that I got a crick in the neck watching its course.

The Australian batting, in spite of the early catastrophe of Bradman and Hassett, caused England's effort on Thursday and Friday to appear, in retrospect, laborious and acquisitive.

SIXES BY LOXTON

Harvey was bowled by Laker at 294, and was fifth out, he and Loxton adding 105 in an hour and a half.

Another six by Loxton off Laker, over

Australia's Sam Loxton hit five sixes in his 93 and was bowled attempting a sixth.

the square-leg boundary, was massive. And in Laker's next over Loxton drove yet another six to the on. The Australian is a very naughty animal: when it is attacked it defends itself.

Yardley, who is always breaking a partnership when he puts himself on belatedly, bowled Loxton just when the game was eluding England's grasp altogether.

Loxton lambasted his 93 in some two hours and a quarter. On the stroke of tea, Saggers was stumped, eighth out for 355,

and so England could breathe again. After tea the Australian Lindwall enjoyed one or two excellent and free fours from Laker, so Pollard was put on possibly as a protest against levity at a moment when England's lead was coming down, as Montague Tigg might say, to the ridiculous sum of less than 50.

For an hour Lindwall and Johnston held the ninth wicket, a most irritating resistance to the rather impatient multitude: and when Johnston was caught at 403 and did not leave the field, everybody got excited and outraged. But Johnston was merely remaining there to run for lame Toshack; so sensation, having smacked its lips, subsided regretfully.

Lindwall, by diversified cricket, compiled 50 and more. Toshack, limping badly, could not do justice to his strokes.

Still, in the end and after all, Australia were only a mere bagatelle behind, and the crowd went home disillusioned and dusty.

Day Four

The Manchester Guardian 27/7/48

Fourth Test Match

ENGLAND AHEAD BY 400 RUNS

Great Day's Play

EVANS CROWNS A FINE INNINGS

ENGLAND, 496 and 362 for eight wickets; AUSTRALIA (first innings), 458.

TO-DAY'S WEATHER: Fair or fine; warm.

From our Cricket Correspondent

HEADINGLEY, Monday

There has been another great day's cricket in the fourth Test match here to-day, and there should be a glorious finish to the match to-morrow. England's batting was perhaps not so well organised as was Australia's on Saturday, but Hutton, Washbrook, Compton, and Evans each did magnificently and only Cranston failed unfortunately and lamentably.

England began the second innings at a quarter to twelve, after Lindwall had been caught brilliantly by Crapp at second slip for the addition of only one run to Australia's overnight total. In five and three quarter hours England made 362 runs for the loss of eight wickets and led by 400 runs at the close. Australia still has a good chance of winning to-morrow, but will have to bat aggressively to do so, and if Yardley does not declare at to-night's total the Australian batsmen will have to take considerable risks.

Washbrook and Hutton again served England nobly. They put on 129 runs for the first wicket and gave only one chance as they did so. This was when Hutton was 28 and Johnston missed a low drive just to his left at mid-on. It was an exceptionally

hard shot, and though Johnston half held the catch the ball then travelled so far behind him that the batsmen took two runs.

IN BRILLIANT FORM

For the rest, both batsmen batted with the same assurance that they showed on Thursday. They were keen for every run and aggressive in their aspect. Washbrook

Edrich and Compton had to re-establish England's innings.

turned Lindwall beautifully to square leg in his third over, then drove him handsomely through the covers. Hutton drove him past mid-off with the same unconditional authority and it was at once patent that both batsmen were in their most brilliant form.

Their defence proclaimed it no less. They were beautifully behind and over every ball they played, and their leaning in to their leg glances was a delight to see. No rising balls could perturb them, though both were hit on hands and body. Yet aggression was always tempered by restraint, and only when Johnston replaced Miller did Washbrook and Hutton each make risky late cuts to slower well-flighted balls outside the off stump. They

scored 40 in the first hour. After lunch both men attacked. They drove, swept, and hooked high over Bradman's half-deep field, and so commanding now was Washbrook that he lay back and square cut Lindwall as he frequently does slow spin bowlers. These were vivid shots and contemptuous ones. Inevitably each batsman was caught as he tried to score still more quickly—Washbrook from a hook shot for which Harvey had to run forward many yards, and Hutton at mid-on as he tried to drive one of Johnston's slower good-length balls.

ONSLAUGHT CONTINUED

It was unfortunate, however, that both men were out at once. Edrich and Compton had now to re-establish England's innings against bowling which, in spite of the day's moist heat, discovered new leases of energy and half an hour later took the new ball.

They did so with a coolness of judgment which could still drive Johnson high over mid-off and to mid-wicket for fours, and which allowed Compton to cut the same bowler with a lateness which was almost impertinent.

The fast bowlers and the new ball troubled them no more. Compton square drove and square cut Miller unmercifully and Edrich drove him past mid-off. Bumpers were now hooked violently, and after half an hour Miller reduced his pace to medium and a quarter of an hour later Lindwall was replaced by Johnston. Compton leapt to attack the latter at once and then swept him to the leg side when he shortened his length. At tea England had reached over 200 and Australia's bowlers had been mastered again. Edrich and Compton had survived a most dangerous 85 minutes without stress or anxiety and had scored 80 runs while they did so.

It was a splendid stand, remarkable for its shrewd judgment and watchful concentration, and after tea both batsmen reaped their rewards for it. Something moved Edrich to unexpected violence. In one over he swept and drove Johnson for three fours and a six, reached a great fifty, and almost immediately afterwards was

Godfrey Evans: "friskier than ever", but he later gave one of his rare poor performances behind the stumps.

lbw as he tried to turn Lindwall to the leg side. The excitement of his hitting was infectious. Crapp began to imitate him at once, and though Bradman now deepened his field and Lindwall had no slip, England's fourth wicket put on 28 in 25 minutes before Crapp was bowled off his pads by a ball which swung into him.

Yardley hit merrily, and then too merrily, Cranston was deceived by the length of his first ball and was caught at the wicket as he was drawn forward, and then Compton was caught at extra cover as he also tried to drive a good-length ball. This seemed like rashness carried too far. England were 293 for seven wickets, and Australia's fielding was tense with expectancy. It looked hungrily for chances, and when Bedser began to hit out lustily it seemed likely to receive them. Very soon it did, and though England's score was 330 two quick wickets might have made Australia's task tomorrow an easy one.

EVANS IN FRISKY MOOD

Once again it was Evans who frustrated his opponents. He was friskier than ever. He stole more cheeky singles than even normally he does, suggested that he might steal many more, and made shots that were daring to the point of impudence. Twice he late-cut Miller off his middle stump and offside balls he chopped impishly. Long hops he square cut no less brazenly than did Washbrook, with an added flourish of his own. He leapt down the wicket to half-volleys and sometimes hit length balls inexplicably to square leg. For the first time in the match Australia's brilliant fieldsmen looked tired, and at last there was something near confusion.

It is Evans's genius and enjoyment to break laws and breed chaos out of well-ordered planning. In the game's last hour he did so once more and grinned happily at the sight of it. For Evans all things are possible, and he will doubtless dream to-night of England's victory to-morrow and sleep the deep peaceful sleep of a schoolboy.

ENGLAND'S TEST CHANCE LOST—FOR LACK OF LEG-SPINNER

Bradman-Morris 301 stand in 7-wicket win

COSTLY ERRORS IN FIELDING

By ALEX BANNISTER

Australia's seven-wicket victory in the Fourth Test at Headingley, Leeds, yesterday will go down in cricket history as one of the most sensational of all time.

It was particularly remarkable for the second-wicket stand of 301 between Morris and Bradman and tragic for the manner in which England threw away a golden chance.

Acutely disappointing as the result is to England, bitter though the criticisms will be of poor bowling and fielding lapses, Australia's achievement glittered with brilliance.

The winning hit was made by Neil Harvey, youngest player of the match, with Bradman undefeated for 173, running down the wicket and putting his arm affectionately on his partner's shoulder. And Bradman ended his last appearance on the ground, where he has scored the amazing total of 963 runs in six innings with a sprint to the pavilion as the crowd moved in to mob him.

It was a great triumph for Bradman, Morris and Australia—a tale of ifs and buts for England who were left only with the doubtful consolation of being gallant losers.

No team had scored 350 on the final day in England previously, yet Morris and Bradman hit 301 in three hours, 58 minutes, and Australia, set the "safe" task of getting 404 to win on a suspect wicket in five hours and 45 minutes, got the runs with 13 minutes to spare.

This was Australia's beat-the-clock

Arthur Morris: 182 out of a second wicket record stand of 307 with Don Bradman.

timetable: 100 in 95 minutes: 200 in 158 minutes: 300 in 344 minutes: 400 in 327 minutes.

THREE GOOD REASONS

You cannot begrudge a success of this sort. All the drama of a dozen Tests has been crowded into this wonderful match, which has produced record after record—more runs than any match in

England, more spectators, and more thrills.

England lost because:

(1) Yardley was left without a leg-spinner. It was a first-class blunder to leave out Young, the slow left-hander. To say the least, I believe England would have gone very close to winning if Young had been there yesterday.

(2) England's bowling, stumping, and catching have seldom been of poorer standard.

(3) Australia had the ability to take advantage of England's lapses.

It was in the critical hour before lunch that the Test was won and lost. After Hassett had been superbly caught and bowled by Compton England had a victory vision. But with Compton turning the ball sharply, and Bradman groping like a novice, England could not take the catches.

With a competent leg-spinner Australia would have been in real trouble. As it was, England's bowling, never fully supported in the field, could not take advantage of a wicket which accepted spin. The simple fact does not detract one iota from the magnificence of Bradman (29 boundaries) and Morris (33 boundaries).

THE HUTTON BLUNDER

Yardley made one major tactical blunder in giving Hutton four overs, which cost 30 runs, a fateful and doubtful experiment, which put Australians on terms with the clock. With Compton at one end, Yardley should have concentrated on closing the other.

Australia would probably have won in any case.

All that remains is to congratulate the holders of the Ashes. They have shown England a standard of cricket which will be hard to emulate.

The Don in full flow.

FINAL · SCORES

ENGLAND — First Innings

Hutton, b Lindwall	81
Washbrook, c Lindwall, b Johnston	143
W. J. Edrich, c Morris, b Johnson	111
Bedser, c & b Johnson	79
Compton, c Saggers, b Lindwall	23
Crapp, b Toshack	5
N. W. D. Yardley, b Miller	25
K. Cranston, b Loxton	10
Evans, c Hassett, b Loxton	3
Laker, c Saggers, b Loxton	4
Pollard, not out	0
Extras (b 2, lb 8, w 1, nb 1)	12
Total	496

Fall of wickets: 1-168, 2-268, 3-423, 4-426, 5-447, 6-473, 7-468, 8-490, 9-496, 10-496
Bowling: Lindwall 38-10-79-2, Miller 17.1-2-43-1, Johnston 38-13-86-1, Toshack 35-6-112-1, Loxton 26-4-55-3, Johnson 33-9-89-2, Morris 5-0-20-0

AUSTRALIA — First Innings

A. R. Morris, c Cranston, b Bedser	6
A. L. Hassett, c Crapp, b Pollard	13
D. G. Bradman, b Pollard	33
K. Miller, c Edrich, b Yardley	58
R. N. Harvey, b Laker	112
S. Loxton, b Yardley	93
I. Johnson, c Cranston, b Laker	10
R. Lindwall, c Crapp, b Bedser	77
R. Saggers, st Evans, b Laker	5
W. A. Johnston, c Edrich, b Bedser	13
E. Toshack, not out	12
Extras (b 9, lb 14, nb 13)	26
Total	458

Fall of wickets: 1-13, 2-63, 3-68, 4-189, 5-294, 6-329, 7-344, 8-355, 9-403, 10-458
Bowling: Bedser 31.2-4-92-3, Pollard 38-6-104-2, Cranston 14-1-51-0, Edrich 3-0-19-0, Laker 30-8-113-3, Yardley 17-6-38-2, Compton 3-0-15-0

ENGLAND — Second Innings

Hutton, c Bradman, b Johnson	57
Washbrook, c Harvey, b Johnston	65
W. J. Edrich, lbw, b Lindwall	54
Compton, c Miller, b Johnston	66
Crapp, b Lindwall	18
N. W. D. Yardley, c Harvey, b Johnston	7
K. Cranston, c Saggers, b Johnston	0
Evans, not out	47
Bedser, c Hassett, b Miller	17
Laker, not out	15
Extras (b 4, lb 12, nb 3)	19
Total (8 wkts dec.)	365

Fall of wickets: 1-129, 2-129, 3-232, 4-260, 5-277, 6-278, 7-293, 8-330
Bowling: Lindwall 26-6-84-2, Miller 21-5-53-1, Johnston 29-5-95-4, Loxton 10-2-29-0, Johnson 21-2-85-1

AUSTRALIA — Second Innings

A. R. Morris, c Pollard, b Yardley	182
A. L. Hassett, c & b Compton	17
D. G. Bradman, not out	173
K. R. Miller, lbw, b Cranston	12
R. N. Harvey, not out	4
Extras (b 6, lb 9, nb 1)	16
Total (3 wkts)	404

Fall of wickets: 1-57, 2-358, 3-396
Bowling: Bedser 21-2-56-0, Pollard 22-6-55-0, Laker 32-11-93-0, Compton 15-3-82-1, Hutton 4-1-30-0, Yardley 13-1-44-1, Cranston 7.1-0-28-1

THE CALYPSO ATMOSPHERE generated by West Indies supporters was brought to Lord's in June, 1950, as the visitors swept to their first ever Test win in England. Frank Worrell, *right*, (52) and Everton Weekes (63) put on 105 for the third wicket following Allan Rae's century in a West Indies first innings total of 326. England then discovered that besides flamboyant batsmen, the West Indies also possessed the deadliest of spin twins in Ramadhin (five for 66) and Valentine (four for 48). England were bowled out for only 151. There seemed no sign of such a poor

performance as Len Hutton and Cyril Washbrook made a 62 run opening stand. The West Indies batsmen then put victory beyond England scoring 425 for six declared in their second innings. Clyde Walcott, made 168 not out with valuable support from Gerry Gomez (70) and Weekes (63). Cyril Washbrook led England's valiant attempt to hang on for a draw with 114 but Ramadhin had the final say, adding to his five first innings wickets with six for 86. Valentine took another three wickets and West Indies were the victors by 326 runs.

Calypso cricket arrives at Lord's. West Indies supporters celebrate their first Test win in England.

Day
One

The
Observer
25/6/50

Second Test Match

ENGLAND KEPT IN THE FIELD

By R. C. ROBERTSON-GLASGOW

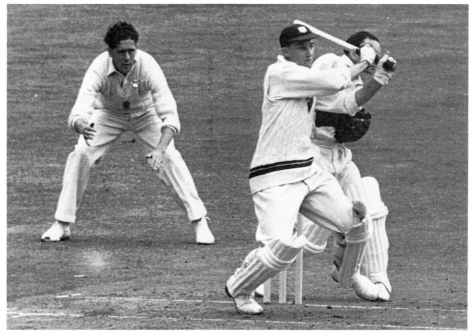

Jeff Stollmeyer hits out during his first innings 20. Later he became Johnny Wardle's first Test victim, lbw.

The crowd at Lord's were 12 deep on the grass when, a quarter of an hour before the start of the second Test match between England and the West Indies, they rose in honour of the King, who walked out on to the field with Sir Pelham Warner. The teams and spare men were then introduced to His Majesty, and soon, Goddard having beaten Yardley in the toss, Stollmeyer and Rae were facing the bowling of A. V. Bedser (nursery end) and Edrich. The pitch, that versatile villain, satisfied the most scientific prophets by being, like a muscular Philistine, hard underneath and a trifle soft on top.

The West Indies batted all day and scored 320 for seven wickets. Week-end rain followed by sun could make this a winning total. Happy were we 30,000 who saw the brilliance of Worrell and Weekes set off by the persistence of Rae, who made a century. Lucky, too, were England to have, in A. V. Bedser, a man with the skill to end Worrell and Weekes, when in full and warm exercise of their art, and to have, in Jenkins, a slow-spinner who could "come again" after early failure.

The West Indies position is commanding. It might have been almost impregnable. England may thank Yardley, too, for his adroit handling of an attack which, containing two slow left-handers, was not completely suited to a true and fastish pitch.

BEDSER AT HIS BEST

The start was quiet; which was natural enough, for Bedser bowled just about at his best. Stollmeyer, all grace, three times played him away for runs to leg, but three times he was beaten. At the other end the left-handed Rae was solid. Edrich was adequate. Once Stollmeyer stroked him to the Tavern boundary with perfect timing. Then, after 40 minutes, 22 being on the board, the slow spinning Jenkins came on for Bedser, who changed ends.

Jenkins must surely be the world's most eager bowler. He looks as if he'd like to snatch the striker's bat and play the ball he's just bowled. In trying to stop a drive that was going to mid-off he fell and seemed to hurt his bowling hand. The next ball was very short, and Rae chopped it in the air only just wide of Edrich at short slip.

But the West Indies seemed to be advancing from exploration to moderate comfort when the left-handed Wardle came on for Bedser, and with his first ball in a Test in England, had Stollmeyer l.b.w. So the fluent Worrell joined Rae.

Worrell is one who starts as if he were in the middle of a long and prosperous innings. He is fierce noon without dawn. Very soon he cracked Wardle and Jenkins each to the leg boundary; so Bedser came back for Wardle, and Berry replaced Jenkins. But changes meant little to Worrell, and he scored all round with the ease of the master. Rae, who did the appointed job, broke out once or twice under Worrell's influence, and at lunch West Indies were 102 for 1, Worrell 44, Rae 33.

Soon after lunch Rae began knocking Jenkins round the field and Bedser had to be called in. On Bedser, enduring and accurate, a heavy burden lay: for of fast bowling there was none, and spin just now was availing little. Worrell, then Rae, went to 50 in one over from Wardle. It seemed that only some vast negligence could part the batsmen. Then Worrell, who had once or twice shown slight uncertainty in defending on the leg stump, missed a ball from Bedser and it rolled on to the leg stump. Only 52, but it was a great innings, glorious to see.

Weekes studied the attack now of Berry and Wardle, with care. He had some trouble at first with Wardle, once snicking him past the leg stump but three fours in an over put him right. To Rae, the all-left attack was not inconvenient. Then Weekes decided that he could safely hurry, and he rattled the boundaries with fierce precision.

The 200 went up, and hopes of a run out were being canvassed. It nearly happened to Rae when a brilliant pick-up at mid-on by Yardley just missed the stumps. Yardley gave himself the last of the old ball, and once beat Rae; Weekes reached 50; then back came Bedser with the new ball and the tone of the attack stepped up. At the other end, Edrich.

THUNDERING SKILL

Both Bedser and Edrich beat Weekes, and Rae gave a chance to second slip off Bedser. But we were making wickets when Weekes played on to Bedser, who was bowling like the Maurice Tate of 25 years ago and appealed for caught wicket against the newcomer Walcott. Weekes, by the way, hit 10 fours in his 63. So to tea, 237 for 3, and the stalwart Rae 82.

After tea Bedser continued with thundering skill, aided by Jenkins. Rae, too, went on collecting and collecting. At 262 he lost Walcott, whom Jenkins drew out with a leg-break. It was wide-ish, and Evans had to "bring 'er," as they say in the North. Rae went to his 100 by driving Jenkins against the pavilion rails, then, mistiming a hook, was neatly caught and bowled. His innings lasted 4 and a half hours, and Hector might have admired it. Twelve runs later Jenkins bamboozled Gomez with another leg-break, and the West Indies were almost slipping.

With an hour to go, Christiani and Goddard batting, Bedser had to be rested. Goddard defended while Christiani scored, mostly by well-timed off drives; an innings of courage and quality.

Jenkins had a try at the Nursery end. Bedser drew again on his almost limitless resources, and Wardle, coming on for the last over, bowled Goddard, when hooking, off his pads. Jones sustained the last balls on his pads.

THE SECOND TEST MATCH

◆

ENGLAND COLLAPSE

―――

WEST INDIES STRONGLY PLACED

FROM OUR CRICKET CORRESPONDENT

The West Indies gained a lead of 175 runs on the first innings over England in the second Test Match at Lord's yesterday, a lead, after all due respect is paid to the bowling of Ramadhin and Valentine, which was in the main due to the preposterously bad batting of England. Surely never can a series of batsmen representing England have allowed themselves to be dismissed with such unworthy strokes. At the close of play the West Indies, with their opening pair Rae and Stollmeyer still together, were 220 runs ahead.

The West Indies first innings finished quickly in the morning. Christiani, who might have protracted the innings, being out to the third ball bowled by Bedser and the other two wickets falling with formality. It had already been seen that the pitch was playing faster than it had done on Saturday and it was no surprise when at the beginning of England's innings both Worrell and Jones began to get the ball past the bat and on to the pads. Neither Hutton nor Washbrook were at ease, being forced to hurry their strokes, and there was a succession of appeals for l.b.w. Hutton, in fact, cocked the first ball he received from Jones dangerously to the leg side and Worrell later twice beat him when he offered a stroke to a ball outside the off stump.

It was a shakey start, indeed, yet the large crowd felt that surely two such distinguished batsmen would soon overcome their early troubles. They had laboriously collected 27 runs between them when on came Valentine at the Nursery end and Ramadhin at the other,

henceforth, as it was shown, to control the run of the play. Ramadhin allowed the batsmen a chance of seeing the ball by twice overpitching it, but he was never discouraged and kept the ball well up to the batsmen. There were signs that England's opening pair were beginning to settle down, when suddenly Hutton chased a ball away to the off side to be stumped with the score only 62.

Even so, that was not a calamitous start, certainly not so fearful as to justify Edrich's attitude. Utterly refusing to offer any stroke but a smothering dab he allowed Valentine to bowl to two silly mid-offs, two slips, with no third man and no one in the region of extra cover. The West Indies responded to this type of batting and, with Washbrook almost equally obdurate, stubbornly ineffective batting allowed the bowlers maiden over after maiden over.

In 95 minutes before luncheon England were well on their way to allowing the West Indies to dictate the rate of scoring, which was small indeed.

A TIME OF TRIBULATION

The second wicket fell, almost as a relief, when Washbrook, going out to a ball outside the off stump, was beaten by Ramadhin's spin and stumped. There followed a time of tribulation for England and joy for the West Indies. Doggart, having once tried a sweep to leg off Ramadhin which he missed, repeated the stroke and was this time l.b.w., having ignored the clear warning. Parkhouse, playing a cow shot, missed the ball both in time and space and was bowled—an inglorious entry to Test Match cricket. Four wickets were now down for 75 runs. Edrich having batted for an hour and a half for 8 runs, four of which came from one blow, was caught at the wicket when stretching out to a ball of good length. Edrich has frequently glued the faltering batting side together, yet one could not but feel that yesterday his was not the innings of a number three batsman playing for England.

Half the side was then out for 86 and it was left to Yardley to explain that the bowling on so easy a wicket was not unplayable. In one over from Valentine, who from the Nursery end was bowling on the off stump or wide of it, Yardley drove him straight to the boundary and then forced the ball square to the off for 4. Good strokes were made regularly and, with Evans now in—so low had England's batting order descended—and hitting a ball from Ramadhin away to leg for 4, the hundred went up. The cheers that greeted this were of the kind that implied that even a mere 100 runs was something to be grateful for; but Evans spoilt it all by playing an atrocious stroke with his eye far distant from the ball, to be bowled by Ramadhin.

So came Jenkins's turn to allow his captain some opportunity of revival. Yardley, in truth, looked to be the man, but with score at 110 he was out to a really good ball, and three runs later Jenkins, after continually playing back to well pitched-up balls, was snapped at the wicket off Valentine. Bedser hit one wholehearted drive off Ramadhin before he showed a crooked bat to a straight ball, and then at long last Wardle provided the attacking strokes one had been waiting for since the beginning of the innings. He played two perfectly timed off-drives off Ramadhin and gave the crowd something truly to cheer when he swept that bowler

twice in one over to the leg boundary. Some adroit strokes to the last ball of each over and some good running between the wickets kept Berry away from the new ball, which Goddard at last was constrained to use. In the end, however, Berry had to face up to it. He is not quite qualified as a batsman for such an occasion.

So an innings, dismal to watch, came to an end and the West Indies went in once more with a most heartening lead. Rae, when he had made only three, should have been caught at short-leg off Edrich, but for the rest England's bowlers received little encouragement or hope.

Day Three

Daily Express

28/6/50

Dropped catches wreck England's last hopes
ONE SUCCESS—JENKINS
West Indies set up new Test record
By PAT MARSHALL

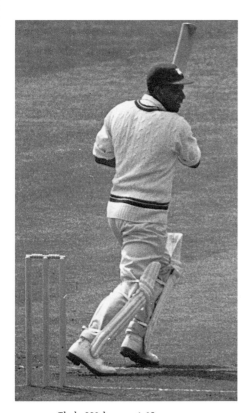

Clyde Walcott - 168 not out.

Only hard-working, never-give-up Roley Jenkins looked really dangerous as a bowler; only skipper Norman Yardley and jack-in-the-box wicketkeeper Godfrey Evans fielded like England cricketers.

That, my friends, is the sad summing-up of the third day's play in this heart-burning Test match at Lord's. West Indies are 561 runs on, and what are we going to do about it?

Way back in 1939, on a sun-drenched wicket at Durban, England scored 654 for the loss of five wickets in the fourth innings of a Test match against South Africa. If we hope to win this second Test it looks as though we will have to score just about the same number of runs.

In that timeless Test at Durban were two members of the present England side—Len Hutton and Bill Edrich. Len hit 55 and Bill 219.

If they can do it again England have a chance. If they fail, England's 13th man—rain—is the only hope. And that would be a terrible travesty of justice.

Just as our batting failed on Monday, our bowling wilted yesterday. For a few brief overs Jenkins gave us hope.

TRICKY BOWLING

Jenkins, toiling and spinning, using every trick and artifice in the spin-bowler's handbook, almost had the West Indians on their knees.

He bowled both the opening batsmen, Jeff Stollmeyer and Alan Rae, at 48 and 75 respectively. Than he had danger man Frank Worrell caught in the slips by Doggart and the West Indian skipper, John Goddard, taken at the wicket by Evans.

Four wickets were down for 146. England still had a decent chance. The West Indians at this stage had a lead of 321. A collapse now and the game was still very much alive.

Weekes was in and none too happy. He was joined by the jovial giant Clyde Walcott. Then came tragedy and a series of blunders.

Just after lunch Yardley claimed the new ball and put Bedser and Edrich on. Straight away Weekes slashed at a rising ball from Edrich and sent it hard past Doggart's left ear at first slip. He got a hand to it but merely deflected the ball for four runs.

Worse was to follow. Two overs later Edrich made another ball kick viciously off just short of a length.

It found the outside edge of Walcott's bat and again went to the unfortunate Doggart at first slip. And he dropped it. Walcott was then nine.

Though Weekes was brilliantly run out by Yardley for an enterprising 63—the same number as he scored in the first innings—England's big chance had gone.

STAND OF 187

"Jersey Joe" Walcott and Gerry Gomez smashed the West Indies sixth-wicket Test record of 118 set up against us by J. E. D. Sealey and Learie Constantine in Trinidad in 1934.

Then they passed the sixth-wicket record for the series (161) set up by Trevor Bailey and Godfrey Evans in the first Test.

So far they have added 187, and if Goddard decides to bat on today they will probably beat the all-time all-wicket record of the West Indies in Tests in this country—200 between George Headley and L. Barrow at Manchester in 1933.

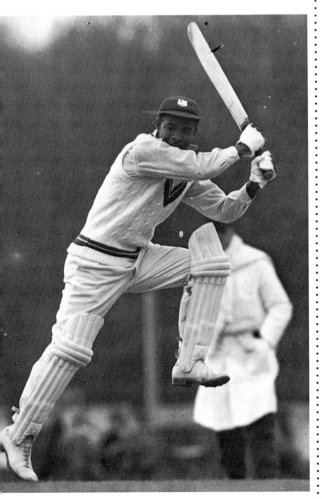

Everton Weekes scored 63 in both innings.

WASHBROOK STILL IN
But last over got Parkhouse

By ALEX BANNISTER

CYRIL WASHBROOK
—by ROSS

Set the stupendous task of making 601 to win the second Test match at Lord's in 11 hours ten minutes, England reached the creditable total of 218 for four wickets last evening.

This was due to a great effort by Cyril Washbrook, still undefeated in his fifth Test century (114), and splendid support, first by Doggart and then by Parkhouse.

But skipper John Goddard struck a blow for the West Indies by making a superb catch at silly mid-off to dismiss Parkhouse in the last over. It was a full toss from Valentine which Parkhouse hit well and truly in the middle of the bat.

Had Parkhouse survived I would have suggested England had an outside chance of saving the Test. Now, with 383 still needed, the outlook is desperate. The West Indies have six hours today in which to get the last six wickets.

A point in England's favour is that the wicket remains good. The task could be accomplished, but whatever happens, England have made a heartening fight-back, and the batsmen have done much to erase the blot of the first innings performance—and to destroy the myth that Ramadhin is unplayable.

Parkhouse, untroubled by nerves, has surely earned another chance in the third Test at Trent Bridge, and in a match of many disasters his second-innings performance was a strong redeeming factor. I predict he will be a strong candidate for the M.C.C. tour of Australia this winter.

Falling to Goddard, one of the finest and most daring close-to-the-bat fielders in the world, when only two short of his 50 was bad luck, but Parkhouse made a first-class impression.

There was not much encouragement for English hopes when, after Goddard had declared at 425 for six, Hutton was bowled by the left-handed Valentine without offering either bat or pad to the ball.

Just after lunch Edrich fell to a good slip catch by Jones. Then the wall of resistance was built.

Washbrook wisely shielded Doggart from the wiles of Ramadhin, and gradually the bowling lost much of its sting.

Doggart was as courageous as at Manchester, and his stand of 83 for the fourth wicket with Washbrook was a valuable example of defiance to the rest of the team.

Parkhouse began by taking seven off Ramadhin in one over and continued like a seasoned Test campaigner.

Washbrook has rarely played a better innings, either for England or Lancashire, and, despite signs of fatigue towards the end, he successfully concentrated on surviving for another day.

So far he has batted five hours ten minutes and has hit a six and 14 boundaries. This, his first century of the season, is an addition to the Test hundreds he has taken off Australia (two), South Africa and New Zealand.

Before Goddard declared Gomez and Walcott took their sixth-wicket partnership to 211, which is the best-ever stand by a West Indies pair in Tests in this country. Walcott, undefeated for 168, and 24 fours.

Day Five

Daily
Telegraph
& Morning
Post

30/6/50

TEAMWORK GAINED WEST INDIES WIN BY 326 RUNS

Great Bowling Feat By Two Men

By E. W. SWANTON

The spin twins who destroyed England, Sonny Ramadhin (11 for 152), left, and Alf Valentine (7 for 127).

LORD'S, Thursday

Soon after lunch to-day West Indies gained the victory that had seemed theirs from the time on Monday afternoon when England's batting failed against Ramadhin and Valentine. The difference was 326 runs.

Thus West Indies follow South Africa, who not only chose Lord's as the scene of their first and only success in a Test in England 15 years ago, but also won by a handsome and conclusive margin.

There could be no possible question of the justice of to-day's result.

The two young spin bowlers certainly were chiefly responsible, but Rae and Walcott, Worrell, Weekes and Gomez have distinguished deeds against their names in the score sheet. Indeed, every member of Goddard's team contributed, not least the captain himself, who made several shrewd assessments in the field as well as setting an admirable lead by his performance at silly mid-off and short-leg.

From first to last the England batting was thrown completely back on trepidant and unconvincing defence, whereas the West Indies, faced by spin bowlers whose performance certainly could be expected to lose little or nothing by contrast with their own, declined to be dictated to at the wicket.

The delightful innings of Worrell and Weekes on the first day had a significance not properly expressed in the score. When this game is looked back to it may always be used as the model illustration of the ancient axiom that bowlers bowl as well as they are allowed to.

RAMADHIN MAGNIFICENT

I would not seem to detract from the merit of Ramadhin and Valentine. The former, especially, bowled magnificently, using the arts and subtleties of a spinner in a way extraordinary in one who had had not a scrap of experience before this tour. But more than one wise critic hit the nail on the head when they said they would like to see those two bowling to Worrell and Weekes.

To find the ideal pair of batsmen among Englishmen of the last generation one need not go beyond Hendren and Ames. If they, or their like, had been playing it is quite certain that Valentine would not have bowled 116 overs without being hit over his head.

The most significant of all the statistics connected with the game, even making allowance for the fact that England were latterly playing for a draw, is that in the two innings West Indies received from England only 11 overs more than they bowled themselves and they scored 326 more runs.

LONG BOWLING FEATS

From the English angle it is fair to add that the side was considerably weakened beyond the expected absence of Compton, who has been the focal point of all our post-war Test teams, by the injuries to Simpson and Bailey.

The rubber is all square now, with two matches to come, and it would be a foolish prophet who plumped very strongly for either side finishing with a clear lead.

The analyses of Ramadhin and Valentine set many wondering what new "records" could be unearthed to underline their performances. Alfred Shaw inevitably came to mind and Geary and J. C. White.

In 1880 Shaw bowled 116 four-ball

overs against Gloucestershire and five years later W. G Grace, who never liked to be outdone, returned the compliment against Notts with 120 overs, which is the equivalent of 80 to-day.

Geary and White bowled 81 and 75.3 respectively of six balls each against Australia at Melbourne in 1929 and (this makes a gratifying memory) Fleetwood-Smith and O'Reilly bowled 87 and 85 against England at the Oval in 1938. Incidentally Fleetwood-Smith's analysis was one for 298.

So the 72 and 71 overs of Ramadhin and Valentine in this second innings are not beyond compare. Furthermore, White bowled 124.5 overs in all at Adelaide in the Fourth Test of 1929.

But it is safe to say that Valentine's 116 overs are the most that ever have been bowled in a match in England and that their combined score of 231 out of 298.1 is assuredly unique.

WASHBROOK'S DISMISSAL

No summing up of the game is complete without a special word about the wicket, which was as near ideal as could be imagined. In spite of the preceding rain it was reasonably quick, it always took a sensible amount of spin and it lasted just about as well as was needed. I hope

Valentine entertains curious onlookers.

Martin has many applications for the recipe. The onus of spinning out the game when it was restarted this morning rested really on Washbrook giving a repeat performance. He began by playing six maiden overs from Ramadhin, who mostly was attacking his legs with, of course, a close field.

Washbrook seemed to have got the measure of this when he apparently struck his boot and was bowled by a ball that pitched about leg-stump and hit the middle. He had been in for five and a half long hours, fighting bravely.

Yardley alternated moments of difficulty with some clean hits off Valentine into the covers, but he lost Evans after 25 minutes from a half-hit sweep which Rae caught at the second attempt about mid-way between square-leg and the Mound.

Then Yardley, who played Ramadhin better than anyone but Valentine rather more sketchily, snicked the ball hard to the wicket-keeper, off whose glove it bounced to slip.

ONE WICKET LEFT

It was now a matter of whether the end would be before lunch or afterwards. Thanks to Wardle, who seemed to find little difficulty in the two young heroes now both flagging slightly, one wicket remained at half past one. No sudden thunderstorm threatened to cloud the bright blue sky.

Wardle hit four rousing fours off Valentine which had the effect of causing the runs scored against him slightly to outnumber his overs, and it was Worrell who finally despatched him to the unbridled joy of his countrymen.

Some of them, armed with impromptu instruments, saluted the great occasion with strange noises, and a handful with their leader swayed round the field to give a faint reminder to those who know the West Indian Islands of the bands at carnival time.

One felt sorry that the august dignity of Lord's and perhaps the sight of many helmets and uniforms so subdued the rest. But, for them at least, it was a victory unforgettable.

FINAL · SCORES

WEST INDIES — First Innings

A. F. Rae, c & b Jenkins	106
J. B. Stollmeyer, lbw, b Wardle	20
F. M. Worrell, b Bedser	52
E. Weekes, b Bedser	63
C. L. Walcott, st Evans, b Jenkins	14
G. E. Gomez, st Evans, b Jenkins	1
R. J. Christiani, b Bedser	33
J. D. Goddard, b Wardle	14
P. E. Jones, c Evans, b Jenkins	0
S. Ramadhin, not out	1
A. Valentine, c Hutton, b Jenkins	5
Extras (b 10, lb 5, w 1, nb 1)	17
Total	326

Fall of wickets: 1-37, 2-128, 3-233, 4-262, 5-273, 6-274, 7-320, 8-320, 9-320, 10-326

Bowling: Bedser 40-14-60-3, Edrich 16-4-30-0, Jenkins 35.2-6-116-5, Wardle 17-6-46-2, Berry 19-7-45-0, Yardley 4-1-12-0

ENGLAND — First Innings

Hutton, st Walcott, b Valentine	35
Washbrook, st Walcott, b Ramadhin	36
W. J. Edrich, c Walcott, b Ramadhin	8
G. H. G. Doggart, lbw, b Ramadhin	0
Parkhouse, b Valentine	0
N. W. D. Yardley, b Valentine	16
Evans, b Ramadhin	8
Jenkins, c Walcott, b Valentine	4
Wardle, not out	33
Bedser, b Ramadhin	5
Berry, c Goddard, b Jones	2
Extras (b 2, lb 1, w 1)	4
Total	151

Fall of wickets: 1-62, 2-74, 3-74, 4-75, 5-86, 6-102, 7-110, 8-113, 9-122, 10-151

Bowling: Jones 8.4-2-13-1, Worrell 10-4-20-0, Valentine 45-28-48-4, Ramadhin 43-27-66-5

WEST INDIES — Second Innings

A. F. Rae, b Jenkins	24
J. B. Stollmeyer, b Jenkins	30
F. M. Worrell, c Doggart, b Jenkins	45
E. Weekes, run out	63
J. D. Goddard, c Evans, b Jenkins	11
C. L. Walcott, not out	168
G. E. Gomez, c Edrich, b Bedser	70
R. J. Christiani, not out	5
Extras (lb 8, nb 1)	9
Total (6 wkts dec.)	425

Fall of wickets: 1-48, 2-75, 3-108, 4-146, 5-199, 6-410

Bowling: Bedser 44-16-80-1, Edrich 13-2-37-0, Jenkins 59-13-174-4, Wardle 30-10-58-0, Berry 32-15-67-0

ENGLAND — Second Innings

Hutton, b Valentine	10
Washbrook, b Ramadhin	114
W. J. Edrich, c Jones, b Ramadhin	8
G. H. G. Doggart, b Ramadhin	25
Parkhouse, c Goddard, b Valentine	48
N. W. D. Yardley, c Weekes, b Valentine	19
Evans, c Rae, b Ramadhin	2
Jenkins, b Ramadhin	4
Wardle, lbw, b Worrell	21
Bedser, b Ramadhin	0
Berry, not out	0
Extras (b 16, lb 7)	23
Total	274

Fall of wickets: 1-28, 2-57, 3-140, 4-218, 5-228, 6-238, 7-245, 8-258, 9-258, 10-274

Bowling: Jones 7-1-22-0, Worrell 22.3-9-39-1, Valentine 71-47-79-3, Ramadhin 72-43-86-6, Gomez 13-1-25-0, Goddard 6-6-0-0

·1953·

THE 1953 ASHES SERIES had been a gripping affair. Both sides missed opportunities to win, the weather played its part and they went to the Oval with the series all-square. Alec Bedser, *right*, began well. When he had Ronald Archer caught and bowled, Bedser had taken his 39th wicket in the series, surpassing Maurice Tate's record against Australia. Fred Trueman, making his first appearance of the summer, took four for 86 as Australia slumped to 275 all out. England's reply was a measured effort. Captain Len Hutton led the way with

82, getting valuable support from Essex all-rounder Trevor Bailey (64). The first innings lead for England was only 31 but it began to look like an increasingly comfortable cushion as Tony Lock and Jim Laker rattled through the Australian order. Archer's 49 was the most resistance they encountered as Lock finished with five for 45, Laker claiming four for 75. The rest was a formality. England required 132 and, with Bill Edrich making 55 not out, Denis Compton made the winning hit. England thus regained the Ashes after 19 years.

Trevor Bailey cuts Ian Johnstone for four to reach 50 on his way to 64 in England's first innings.

Day
One

The
Sunday
Times

16/8/53

FLUCTUATING FORTUNES IN THE FINAL TEST

Australia's Tail Raises Total to 275

From IAN PEEBLES

THE OVAL, Saturday

Both England and Australia had a very in-and-out day, the latter in the literal sense. England may be said to have done fairly well to dismiss Australia for 275, but several chances went astray and the great opportunity of seeing Australia out for a small score was frittered away.

When half the side were out for 118, despite a fine innings from Hassett, a series of courageous stands snatched the early advantage from England. Lindwall again shone as a batsman with a splendid 62.

To England's credit was the bowling of Trueman, who took four wickets for 86, though not favoured by good luck.

England had batted for only two overs when bad light stopped play with the score at one run.

Today was a momentous one in cricket history, and one of much hope from an English point of view, although Hassett once again won the toss and thus equalled Sir Stanley Jackson's record of all five in 1905.

When Bedser opened from the Vauxhall end the sky was overcast and the atmosphere had that heavy humid quality dear to the heart of the seam bowler. As the wicket was surprisingly green in spite of the recent dry spell, there was reasonable expectation of an eventful first hour. It proved to be so.

Hassett immediately turned the ball to fine leg for four. Morris avoided a bouncer without difficulty, then flicked the ball down the leg side. It rose breast high and Compton dived desperately to his left but getting both hands to it shot it away like a goalkeeper making a spectacular save.

Despite this early disappointment Trueman soon started to bowl well and fast. He swung the ball considerably and on occasions made it dive into the left-handed Morris in a remarkable manner. His chief shortcoming was the old one of lack of consistent direction. At the other end Bedser, as ever, went rolling along like Ol' Man River.

The batsmen met these early hazards with intense watchfulness but with the commendable Australian habit of snatching every chance to score. Hassett once more showed himself as a player of the highest class against good bowling in responsive conditions.

The buoyant Morris showed a great readiness to carve at the wide ball to the off and a cheerful indifference to the gasps and sighs when he missed.

After 40 minutes, Bailey bowled for Trueman and also found the pitch to his liking, but it was the constantly threatening Bedser who struck the first blow. Morris, making no attempt to play a ball of good length outside the off stump, saw it whip back to strike his undefended pads. Thirty-eight for one.

Miller having scored one from a no-ball was lbw to a very good one from Bailey which came back quick and sharp. The first hour had undoubtedly been England's, but in the next Harvey played beautifully in helping his captain to take the score to 98 by lunchtime.

The hour after lunch again brought advantage to England. Nine runs had been added when Hassett, defending to a ball which pitched about the off-stump and ran away, was caught at the wicket. It was the first mistake he had made in an impressively sound yet attractive innings. His chief worry seemed to be the Oval pigeons, for whom he apparently exerts a St. Franciscan attraction.

Next over from the Pavilion end, Trueman bowled a long hop to Harvey who went to hook but skied the ball off the top edge at which Hutton made a good catch running back from short leg.

After a short interruption due to rain, de Courcy met the crisis by hitting Bedser's first ball straight and lustily for four. On gaining the other end, however, he was caught behind the wicket playing back to Trueman.

With five out for 118 the crisis was now acute. Hole and Archer tackled the situation characteristically by counter-attacking straight away. Hole cut, hooked and drove and Archer concentrated on the stolen short-single.

In view of the position runs came at an astonishing rate and when 42 had been added England's stranglehold seemed to be loosened. At that moment, however, Australia was floored again by another "one-two" punch. Hole playing a pushing-back shot off Trueman, got a slight tickle and also fell to the omnipresent Evans. Archer played a graceful forward stroke to return the ball to Bedser.

With the arrival of Lindwall the crowd enjoyed the spectacle of the rival fast bowlers at grips, like a couple of war lords

England's XII for the final and deciding Test against the Australians at the Oval in 1953.
Back row (left to right): Trevor Bailey, Peter May, Tom Graveney, Jim Laker, Tony Lock, Johnny Wardle and Fred Trueman.
Front row: Bill Edrich, Alec Bedser, Len Hutton (capt.), Denis Compton and Godfrey Evans.

pondering the advisability of using the atomic bomb in the shape of a bouncer.

There was just enough time before tea for Lindwall to hit a couple of magnificent smashing fours past cover, which revived uneasy memories of his 50 at Lord's. After tea things did not go according to English plans. Davidson, dropped at first slip, made a brisk 22 before being very well caught in the same position.

The wicket had added 47 invaluable runs and Langley at once revealed unsuspected powers as a batsman. When Trueman bowled a bouncer he hooked it square for four, a stroke worthy of Sir Donald Bradman. Lindwall was dropped just after his arrival off a skier owing to a misunderstanding between mid-off and extra. This proved costly and another 38 runs were added before Langley was caught in the slips. It seems that, as the nine of diamonds is the curse of Scotland, so ten of batters is the curse of England.

Bill Johnston arrived, amidst shouts of affectionate welcome, to show that the cricket bat can be the comedian's finest prop. Things got beyond a joke, however, when with Lindwall going magnificently, he started to hit fours on his own account. He also was dropped at second slip. Yet another stand of 30 runs brought Australia to 275 before Evans caught Lindwall, so bringing his bag to four. The England bowling had been good through the day.

Trueman certainly justified himself. Though he appeared to tire towards the end he bowled a good pace most of the day and made the ball move. Bedser, though not producing one of his more sensational spells, was always reliable and dangerous with the shine.

The fielding was less satisfactory, with several chances going down.

In the gloom of the evening, Lindwall bowled an over of great pace and hostility at Hutton but, apart from causing his hat to fall off, did no material damage. An over from Miller to Edrich confirmed a general idea that it was getting a bit dark for this type of play and at 6.15 the players retired for the day.

Day
Two

The
Manchester
Guardian
18/8/53

ENGLAND'S HOPES WENT ADRIFT

Bailey Casts Anchor and the Barnacles Grow

FROM NEVILLE CARDUS

Hutton survives a
run-out chance during
his first innings 82.

FORECAST FOR TO-DAY
Mainly dry though cloudy. Perhaps
rain late in the day.

THE OVAL, Monday

Yet again did England raise our hopes then depress them on this, the second day. At half-past two the score had gone beyond a hundred with only Edrich out and Hutton and May were playing commandingly, with brilliant strokes. All seemed set fair for a prosperous voyage along the sunny afternoon.

A peculiar mood came into England's innings when Johnston bowled at the Pavilion end and by actual and potential spin compelled the batsmen to alter gear. He certainly got enough out of the pitch to suggest that it was beginning to show willingness to respond to spin. The truth is that though Johnston's spin put the England innings out of joint, the wickets of importance fell to swing or pace: and not for the first time the passing of Hutton apparently elevated the spirits of the Australians as much as it lowered those of his colleagues. Compton and Graveney faltered sadly with much depending on them.

A QUICK START

The sun shone from a blue sky with white clouds in it when the match opened this morning. Against Lindwall and Miller in the fresh of this August morning Hutton and Edrich scored confidently, though both missed off-side balls from Lindwall, their forward lunges much too late for the speed: moreover, Hutton snicked fortuitously for two to leg in Lindwall's first over.

Edrich set a tempo of scoring which put more than thirty runs on the scoreboard in half an hour: he forced Lindwall to the on for three in Lindwall's third over, then hooked Miller contumaciously for four, and next ball swung him for four high over the leg trap. Lindwall by means of a Nijinsky leap got a finger to the ball, but the only chance presented was that of a contusion or a removed nail. The wicket so far was amiable to batsmen. So was the bowling.

Hutton played Miller to the leg boundary serenely, popped a ball from Lindwall which lifted a little, but the stroke was not in the field's danger zone, and drove the same bowler for two to the on so easily that the rhythm of the hit, easy as the pendulum of Big Ben, stole yards of pace from the ball.

Edrich's assurance dispersed mists of gloomy self-doubt which have hung over an England innings lately: possibly he was urged to go beyond the technical scope of any batsman facing a fast bowler in a Test match while the ball retained seam and polish, for he hit to the on across the line of a potential yorker from Lindwall and succumbed leg before. Still, his little innings contributed a moral value beyond the scorers' powers of estimation.

May, in next, was a cricketer much blessed not to have his off stump knocked flying first ball, a very fast one from Miller which shaved the wicket while May's bat thudded down by reflex action very late in the day, so to speak. Curiously and inexplicably Hassett allowed Lindwall only two balls with which to exploit May's natural unease at the outset of an already disconcerted innings, then took him off. I have known fast bowlers who would have declined their sweater at such a moment. May drove Miller for a sumptuous four to the off, but was surely nearly leg before to Miller's well-tempered square-armed skimmer.

For a while May looked less than a young batsman born to greatness: he checked his strokes dubiously and played forward with a short front leg. When he was only nine he was fortunate to miss an off-side ball from Davidson because he reached to it at arm's length almost. As May gradually modulated from a tentative chromatic key to one of a more diatonic resonance, Lindwall probably watched his progress with more than an academic interest. For the Australian attack waned to respectable industry every over that aged the ball.

Johnston was steady, more or less aiming at or outside the leg stump. Davidson's approximations to pace differed from Archer's mainly because Davidson is left-handed and Archer right. Some element of variety and surprise might have here been introduced into Australia's attack if Hassett had instructed Davidson to bowl right-handed and Archer left. On the easy wicket, Hassett was at a loss for real spin from the back of the hand. (If I had been told in Armstrong's and Mailey's and Grimmett's period that I would live to see the day when an Australian team would take the field at the Oval without a bowler commanding authentic finger spin, I could no more have believed the prophecy than I would one day have believed I would hear the Fifth Symphony of Beethoven played without 'cellos.) Johnston endeavoured to exploit his slower stuff, but all in all the batsmen were under no obligation to look for problems of flight or ask questions to the ball while it was in the air.

Lindwall bowled from the Pavilion end when England's score stood promisingly at 77 for one: his pace was now a shade quicker than E. A. Macdonald's, when that satanic prince of fast bowlers indulged his fancy to go on round the wicket with off-spin. These Australian bowlers of Coronation year put me in mind of remittance men I have known in their own country: they wait for the new ball to come periodically to relieve them from temporary embarrassments.

Ray Lindwall, England's old adversary.

At lunch England were 89 for one, Hutton not out 46, May not out 21, and May had then been batting 85 minutes. Hutton looked safe as Threadneedle Street: so many runs has he scored at the Oval in Test matches that I am sure the Australians would support any move to award him the Chiltern Hundreds.

After lunch the England innings was kindled to a temporary and really brilliant and consuming fire. Hutton drove Miller through the covers gloriously, a hit of sculpturesque rhythm and substance, a stroke poised classically as though on a pedestal.

In the same over he pulled to leg with a circling wing of the bat as lovely as the flight of the pigeons he disturbed in the long field. Then May drove Archer through the covers, another stroke handsome enough for the cricketer's Parthenon.

Two other quick fours by May, both off Johnston, one to the off, the other to the on, also thrilled the sense of speed and beauty. England passed the hundred mark at half past two, and no cloud of trouble, not one even as large as a man's hand, was to be seen in the English sky, excepting that Hutton would have been run out, sent back by May, if Hassett at the wicket, had gathered the ball.

SUDDEN CHANGE

Suddenly, as though some invisible agency had operated on the pitch, the atmosphere and technique of the batting changed. Johnston crossed over to the Pavilion end, and this time his slow medium bowling began to turn, though it was a ball that came with his arm that broke the splendid stand for England's second wicket after it had added one hundred runs in roughly two and a half hours.

Compton began in heavy weather and there was nearly a run out characteristic of Compton. The game's transformation became dramatic with England's total 154, for here the third wicket fell, and moreover it was Hutton's, clean bowled by Johnston, and he was not, I think beaten by spin: for the ball travelled, again, with Johnston's arm and was well pitched up to the crease. Hutton's stroke seemed a little relaxed, even careless.

It is not generally realised how great is the strain this rubber has subjected him to, psychologically if not technically. Few England batsmen have been asked to carry his responsibility, and at one and the same time contribute both to the spinal column and cerebellum of an England eleven. For the first time in the rubber, I believe, Hassett to-day did not at once claim the new ball, due when England were 154 for three: he continued to rely on the spinning potentiality of Johnston—which might appear to make nonsense of my remarks above about this Australian attack's dependability on the new ball: but I cannot withdraw them out of concern for the wit of them.

Compton scored only seven in 50 minutes and did nothing at all for nearly half an hour after Hutton departed. He could not trust Johnston out of his sight for the briefest moment and Johnston was not spinning all that much. this wicket is an angel at the moment compared with what it will be in England's second innings unless rain comes to bind it together. Now was it necessary for England to score runs from every ball the slightest loose.

After tea Compton was out to a culpably negligent half-glance at Lindwall swinging wide to leg; Langley caught him grandly as he fell to the left on the ground. England four out for 167 were thus once more precariously placed when Bailey came in—Bailey born to trouble (which he enjoys) as the sparks fly upward.

The new ball was claimed and Graveney snicked Lindwall convulsively and Miller held a magnificent catch in the slips. This was a flashing ball doing its work like aconitum or rash gunpowder. England 170 for five—and oh! the vanity of our pleasure and expectation only some

two hours ago. But Evans came in here perky and indecorous as Till Eulenspiegel himself and with a bat as busy as a man swatting wasps from his head, not defensively but aggressively, snicked, drove, and pulled the fast bowling and also played Miller once with his bottom. A pull by him off Lindwall was a thump of sheer gusto. So Lindwall retired again into his sweater.

Twenty-nine runs scampered over the field in 20 minutes because of Evans and his high-spirited distrust of science to cope with the crisis.

Meanwhile Bailey batted according to his Test match habit—blade to the ball which he met in the middle of it, statuesque in the manner of some monumental stonemason emulating Michelangelo.

Bad luck ended a gallant sixth-wicket stand worth 40. Evans turned a ball to leg, dashed impetuously for a single, was sent

back, slipped and fell, and was run out. Two stylish fours to the off reminded us of what Bailey can do when he is batting down at Southend-on-Sea. Both these strokes in the same over by Johnston urge me to correct a word in a sentence appearing above and exchange the name of Michelangelo for Phideas. Laker flicked fatally at an unusually fast one from Miller who celebrated his success with a gesture as triumphant as if he had overthrown Jack Hobbs himself.

A blow on the body swayed Bailey backward, but only as a blow by a direct hit at an Aunt Sally at a fair sways it: it comes back again without going over and you lose your money. Bailey remained intact at the close, if not invincible, after two hours of calm obstinacy. I wonder he had not driven Miller mad by this time. He is not only an anchor for England: he barnacles the good ship to the floor of the ocean.

Day Three

Daily Telegraph & Morning Post

19/8/53

ENGLAND'S FINE PROSPECT OF REGAINING "THE ASHES"
94 More to Make on Spinners Wicket

From E. W. SWANTON

OVAL, Tuesday

Sometime around luncheon to-morrow, just before or soon after, the Ashes will be lost and won. On the face of it, they should be won by England, who need 94 more with all wickets but their captain's left for the purpose.

However the game ends it must be remembered as one of the great ones and to-day's cricket will live in all our minds. Many things about this series in this hypercritical age have been accounted disappointing and the pressure of public opinion, the hope and fears, have perhaps magnified the weaknesses and obscured the merits.

But there has been some wonderful cricket and one will look back with

particular pleasure on to-day because it showed the players on both sides in the best light.

Each of the four phases was admirable in its own way; the skilful, sensible effort of the English bowlers which after all gave their side the precious lead: the bowling of Laker and of Lock, which first capsized the Australian second innings and threatened to sink it: the gallant counter-effort by the young Australians—especially that of Archer; and finally England's batting in their last 50 minutes when embarking on the 132 needed to win the first rubber against Australia in this country since 1926.

All, indeed, in the suburban garden of the Oval was lovely this matchless summer

evening except one utterly disappointing the thing, the extraordinary suicide of Hutton.

At 10 minutes past six England's score stood at 23 for no wicket, 23 runs scored, all circumstances considered, with extraordinary certainty and aplomb. If anyone seemed ice cool it was Hutton.

Then he pushed a ball from Miller through the field of three short legs, of whom De Courcy was the middle one. As the ball rolled towards Umpire Davies at square leg there always seemed one for the hit and never remotely a second run.

HUTTON RUN OUT

As De Courcy stooped to pick up the ball Hutton suddenly embarked on a long and from the outset completely hopeless second. De Courcy's throw to the stumps was taken over the bails by Langley and Hutton was out probably by the best part of two yards.

They say the greatest of all silences was that at Melbourne more than 20 years ago when Bradman was bowled first ball in the second of the body-line tests. I can only say that I have not known a similar moment of complete quiet, stupefaction.

It can be illustrated no better than by saying that the Australians, who are not slow to express their jubilation when they take any wicket, made no gesture of any kind as Hutton walked through their ranks to the pavilion.

So much for the pressure on the individual—and of course above all on the captain. May gave us never a moment of disquiet in the remaining time and Edrich matched May's on-drive for four off Miller with a fine stroke for four through the covers.

All one must add is that with Hutton gone Australia have a chance—just a chance.

The wicket this afternoon and evening helped the spin bowlers Laker and Lock, and Lock, especially, was most difficult to play. His pace, of course, is fully slow-medium and at that speed he was able not only to straighten the ball bowling round the wicket but to make it fizz and fly towards the slips. Laker, likewise bowling round the wicket, made a sharp angle and when the ball raised a whiff of dust it tended also to lift.

To use these conditions the Australians have Johnston at his slower pace and this fine bowler could never bowl other than extremely dangerously in such a crisis. At the same time he is not a spinner with quite the venom of a Lock and the Australians have no one well suited to bowl at the other end.

It has turned out as it seemed when their team was announced that they greatly missed one of the trinity: Hill, Benaud and Ring.

LOCK SOON GOES

In the calm and the cool of the morning Bailey set about manufacturing

A rare display of aggression from Bailey during his 64. According to Neville Cardus: "He is not only an anchor for England; he barnacles the good ship to the ocean floor."

something valuable out of the remains of the English innings. The beginning was inauspicious, for with the first ball of his second over Lindwall had Lock caught at backward short leg.

It was a particularly nasty ball that rose shoulder high and Lock fended it away as best he could in a gesture of instinctive protection. At the time one had harboured resentful thoughts against Lock, who had declined a call for an easy single off the previous ball, Bailey naturally running for the bowling.

The principle holds and it was a bad piece of cricket. Still, as the morning wore on and the precious runs ticked up one reflected supposing Bailey had had that ball and it had been too much for him: where would England's lead have been then?

Lindwall and Miller put all they knew into the opening spell, but Bailey was admirable both technically and in point of judgment. He is the coolest of all cool cards.

Young Trueman, too, acquitted himself very well. He schooled his batting, which, by nature, is forceful, to a sensible playing down the line—or at least playing down a line. He did not always choose the right one.

Trueman's troubles became fairly acute when at noon Johnston took over from the

pavilion end for a long spell that was to end only a couple of overs before luncheon. However, he persisted and runs accrued, some in singular directions, including one leg bye off his rump.

It was twenty past 12, and the ninth wicket had raised 25 runs, when Trueman made a fatal misjudgment and was bowled behind his legs.

It was Bedser and Bailey now, and a Bedser of much poise and confidence. Soon a handsome square cut by Bailey brought him to 50 and England to 271: five for the lead. Ten minutes now against Johnston and Lindwall yielded only a single, and then Johnston threw one up to Bedser fishing for the lofted hit to deep mid-off from which the Australians have often caught him.

This time Miller focused the hit late, and it "yorked" him as he ran in, Miller thinking the ball would reach the pavilion fence was slow to go after it, and as the batsmen ran to and fro the score revolved by four to the sort of noise that announces a goal at the Cup-final.

BAILEY'S HIGH CLAIM

This was by no means the end of it. For 40 minutes more right up to luncheon Bailey and Bedser batted on finding few chances to score off Johnston, in spite of the hard doing Hassett had given him

Bill Edrich turns Lindwall to leg following Hutton's suicidal run out. He was unbeaten overnight and the next day led England to victory.

yesterday. He came up almost as fresh as paint for a tally of 45 overs in all.

At the other end Miller, Hole and finally Archer relieved Lindwall and it was Archer who got between Bailey's bat and pad on the stroke of half-past one. In four tests Bailey has played four innings to suit four different situations and if the rubber is won no one except Hutton and Bedser will have as high a claim on English gratitude.

When Australia went in this afternoon Hutton brought on Laker after Trueman had bowled only two overs and Laker straightway brought a ball back and had Hassett lbw. Whether in any event Hutton would have called at once upon Lock cannot be said, but the evidence was enough and so Hole, promoted in Miller's place, with Morris fought the issue out.

It was soon plain that the batsmen were not prepared to be thrust back on their stumps and accordingly Hutton had to make some compromise in his field placing. He always and for both bowlers had sufficient fielders at hand for the short catch, slips for Lock to the right-hander, short legs for Laker and vice versa with the left-hander.

The general criticism that seems justified is that the off-side was largely

Alan Davidson is bowled by Lock.

ranged to save one and a good many hits got through that men on the fence square and at extra cover would have saved.

FOUR OUT FOR TWO RUNS

Australians in the main swing the bat from a fuller back lift and their strokes when timed leave the in-field standing. Morris and Hole made 36 in 40 minutes before Laker began an illustrious breath-

taking procession by having Hole lbw, as Hassett had been. Now in a quarter of an hour Australia lost the cream of their batting for two runs. Hole, Harvey, Miller, and then most formidable of all, Morris.

Harvey, after receiving only eight balls tried to force Lock past mid-on. It was well up, he hit over the ball and a great roar and a leap in the air by Lock announced he had been bowled.

Miller, at the other end, thrust out too firmly at an off-break and cocked it to short leg, retiring with the imperial dignity that it takes a big personality to summon who has been sent back in a crucial Test match for 1 and 0.

Last went Morris lbw to an off-break and as he passed the triumphant Lock one could clearly see him through the glasses giving him a smiling "well bowled." The Australians are tough cricketers but grim no, certainly not the post-war brand.

Australia were half out and only 30 to the good and all rested on the young contingent ranged from six to eight in that order. One can scarcely overpraise the 19-year-old Archer for his part in what followed. With the innings all but in ruins he sensed there might be no time for sober playing in. In any case Lock and Laker posed too dangerous a threat. Accordingly he attacked and naturally turned his attention to Laker, whom he could hit to the on with the spin.

DE COURCY RUN OUT

In one over from Laker he took 10 and 61 had rapidly become 85 when De Courcy set off on a dire impulse for a push by Archer to mid-wicket. Archer yelled "No," but De Courcy was far commited

Jim Laker; with Lock he turned the match for England.

and Bailey, cool as a cucumber, paused to make sure that Lock was back at the stumps, and gently tossed him a catch with De Courcy still out in the wilderness.

Archer, perhaps to relieve his feelings, greeted Davidson with a glorious six off Lock to long-on and Davidson likewise hit Laker for another. In a twinkling they scored 20, and with tea impending Hutton

quietened things by forsaking Laker for Bedser.

Tea did the trick for England and Davidson, bowled by an off-break, Archer and Langley caught at slip off balls that spun away were out within quarter of an hour and nine runs of one another. Archer had batted a few minutes over the hour for a 49 that included a six and seven fours, and for all the part he has before him in Australian cricket he may never do anything much better.

The last threat was made by Johnston and Lindwall. Hutton fearing Lindwall against Laker on Saturday's evidence and general principles switched to Bedser and 20 minutes went by while the batsmen collected quite coolly and rationally. Finally Hutton made the gamble and called back Laker to spin away from the left-hander. But he hooked the bigger fish and all was over.

Lindwall off drove Laker handsomely, straight and powerfully towards the ladies' stand. Compton was right on the fence and as the ball was soaring over he reached it and made a fine catch look simple, pinned by the ball against the woodwork. Thus the innings ended on a defiant note and it was in similar mood that England took up the last challenge.

Day Four

Daily Mail 20/3/53

Ashes win among greatest in cricket history

TRIUMPH FOR SKIPPER HUTTON

By ALEX BANNISTER

It has happened at last! England have won the Ashes for the first time in 19 years. Not since 1926, when Australia fell at the Oval after four draws, had England's cricketers emerged triumphant in a home series with Australia. Though Hassett's side cannot be compared with Bradman's of 1948 (still the only Australians to go through an English tour undefeated), Hutton's achievement in leading England to victory must rank as one of the greatest in the history of the game.

The balcony scene; Australian captain Lindsay Hassett congratulates Hutton, left, after jubilant spectators had invaded the pitch, above.

To lose the toss in all five Tests, to hold out in four, and then go on to win the fifth and last by the convincing margin of eight wickets, surely proves England slightly the better side over the series, which has been a tremendous struggle.

When, in the moment of supreme triumph, the crowd surged in front of the pavilion calling for the captains, hailing conquerors and conquered with equal enthusiasm, I could not help but think of

Compton makes the winning hit off Arthur Morris.

Willie Watson, saviour of that second desperate Test at Lord's.

But for him, now dropped from the side, there would have been no Ashes victory to celebrate.

Len Hutton, in an interview when it was all over, picked out three players for special praise from an England team "that has done well." Bedser he said "has done a magnificent job."

TRIBUTE TO BOWLERS

Bailey and Evans were the other two he congratulated.

As to Evans, I must confess I believe Langley to have been the better wicket-keeper over the series.

Of the England team for the future—they go to Australia in 1954-55—Hutton says: "Our side have still a long way to go, but is possible that in two or three years' time we shall have a really good team. The young players should take heart and encouragement, for they have a splendid chance now."

Hutton also paid gracious tribute to England's old adversaries, Ray Lindwall and Keith Miller ("the finest pair of opening bowlers I have ever faced") and to Lindsay Hassett as the opposing captain.

The first professional to captain England in modern times, Hutton has scored a resounding personal triumph by his leadership and batting.

HASSETT HOPES

Hassett said afterwards that he expects Australia to regain the Ashes in 1954-55.

"The players with us on this tour will find several youngsters at home bidding against them for Test places," he added. "I think our side played well. The biggest failing was in concentration."

Nobody at the Oval yesterday will forget the drama of those last hours—the superb Australian fielding, the runs squeezed slowly, the determination of Bill Edrich, the splendid temperament of May.

And not least, the offensive right up to the last of Bill Johnston, one of the best-loved players ever to tour England.

When he came off at last he was accorded the warmest ovation I have ever heard a bowler receive.

Lindwall was given almost the same tribute. He, too, was fast and menacing to the end.

It was left to Denis Compton to make the winning hit—a sweep to the boundary off Morris, who shared with Hassett the last two overs.

Then, within a few seconds, the ground was a surging mass of cheering people, with Edrich and Compton fighting their way through the crowds back to the pavilion.

Now for the West Indies—and the championship of the cricket world!

FINAL · SCORES

AUSTRALIA — First Innings

A. L. Hassett, c Evans, b Bedser	53
A. R. Morris, lbw, b Bedser	16
K. R. Miller, lbw, b Bailey	1
R. N. Harvey, c Hutton, b Trueman	36
G. B. Hole, c Evans, b Trueman	37
J. de Courcy, c Evans, b Trueman	5
R. Archer, c & b Bedser	10
A. K. Davidson, c Edrich, b Laker	22
R. R. Lindwall, c Evans, b Trueman	62
G. R. Langley, c Edrich, b Lock	18
W. A. Johnston, not out	9
Extras (b 4, nb 2)	6
Total	275

Fall of wicket: 1-38, 2-41, 3-107, 4-107, 5-118, 6-160, 7-160, 8-207, 9-245, 10-275
Bowling: Bedser 29-3-88-3, Trueman 24.3-3-86-4, Bailey 14-3-42-1, Lock 9-2-19-1, Laker 3-0-34-1

ENGLAND — First Innings

Hutton, b Johnston	82
W. J. Edrich, lbw, b Lindwall	21
P. B. H. May, c Archer, b Johnston	39
Compton, c Langley, b Lindwall	16
Graveney, c Miller, b Lindwall	4
T. E. Bailey, b Archer	64
Evans, run out	28
Laker, c Langley, b Miller	1
Lock, c Davidson, b Lindwall	4
Trueman, b Johnston	10
Bedser, not out	22
Extras (b 9, lb 5, w 1)	15
Total	306

Fall of wickets: 1-37, 2-137, 3-154, 4-167, 5-170, 6-210, 7-225, 8-237, 9-262, 10-306
Bowling: Lindwall 32-7-70-4, Miller 34-12-65-1, Johnston 45-16-94-3, Davidson 10-1-26-0, Archer 10.3-2-25-1, Hole 11-6-11-0

AUSTRALIA — Second Innings

Hassett, lbw, b Laker	10
Morris, lbw, b Lock	26
Hole, lbw, b Laker	17
Harvey, b Lock	1
Miller, c Trueman, b Laker	0
De Courcy, run out	4
Archer, c Edrich, b Lock	49
Davidson, b Lock	21
Lindwall, c Compton, b Laker	12
Langley, c Trueman, b Lock	2
Johnston, not out	6
Extras (b 11, lb 3)	14
Total	162

Fall of wickets: 1-23, 2-59, 3-60, 4-61, 5-61, 6-85, 7-135, 8-140, 9-144, 10-162
Bowling: Bedser 11-2-24-0, Trueman 2-1-4-0, Laker 16.5-2-75-4, Lock 21-9-45-5

ENGLAND — Second Innings

Hutton, run out	17
W. J. Edrich, not out	55
P. B. H. May, c Davidson, b Miller	37
Compton, not out	22
Extras (lb 1)	1
Total (2 wkts)	132

Fall of wickets: 1-24, 2-88
Bowling: Lindwall 21-5-46-0, Miller 11-3-24-1, Johnston 29-14-52-0, Archer 1-1-0-0, Hassett 1-0-4-0, Morris 0.5-0-5-0.

PAKISTAN STUNNED THE cricketing world by winning at the Oval and so squaring the series, on their first visit to England. Their early efforts were inauspicious. They were 51 for seven in their first innings before a brave fight back helped them reach 133. Then, on a drying pitch, England, Denis Compton (53) apart, also struggled against the accuracy of medium pace bowler Fazal Mahmood, *right*. He took six for 53 leaving England three runs in arrears. When Pakistan slumped to 82 for 8 in their second innings, England, for whom Johnny Wardle

produced figures of seven for 56, appeared in control. Then Zulfiqar and Wazir Mohammed added 58, leaving England 168 to win. In the light of what had happened over the previous three days, however, this looked anything but a formality. England cruised to 109 for two before Peter May was out for 53. Then Fazal struck again. He repeated his six-wicket first innings haul, this time at a cost of 46 runs, as England collapsed, their last seven batsmen managing just 24 runs. Thus Pakistan achieved a sensational win by a margin of 24 runs.

Victorious Pakistan players indulge in a dance of delight after England's last wicket had fallen, giving them victory by 24 runs to square the series. Pakistan's win made them the first nation to win a Test match on their first visit to England.

Day
One

The
Manchester
Guardian
13/8/54

PAKISTAN'S POOR BATTING

Good Fast Bowling on Dead Wicket

FROM DENYS ROWBOTHAM

THE OVAL, Thursday

Two innings of some watchfulness and hint of stroke play by Imtiaz and Kardar and two stubborn stands of 29 and 27 for the last two wickets saved the Pakistanis from complete ignominy in their fourth and final Test match with England here to-day. In the end they were dismissed for 133 after morning rain, which affected the immediate surroundings of the covered wicket and delayed the start until half past two. Hutton and Simpson survived the day's last five minutes without alarm and England should be in a commanding position to-morrow night unless further rain affects the wicket adversely.

To-day the wicket hardly could have been easier. It looked slightly green but did not behave like a green top. It was soft enough underneath to take most of the dangerous pace from England's three fast bowlers and firm enough on top to deny visible assistance to spin. Hutton indeed did not bowl McConnon until half an hour after tea, after some two hours and 25 minutes' play, and did not use Wardle at all. How little McConnon was able to spin the ball was shown clearly by Zulfiqar and Mahmood Hussain. The former twice drove him against the intended spin past point for fours and once swept him imperiously to long leg while Mahmood, who used his feet quickly to any ball slightly over-pitched, twice off-drove him for handsome fours along the ground as well as lofting him without danger straight and to long-on.

HANIF'S MISTAKE

It was the pace-bowlers in fact who took all Pakistan's wickets apart from a single run out, though it was the Pakistanis who got themselves out rather than the

Frank Tyson bowls Alimuddin for 10 to leave Pakistan 10 for 2. After the Northamptonshire fast bowler's next delivery, to Maqsood Ahmed, Pakistan were 10 for 3.

bowlers who overwhelmed them. Hanif for instance did not survive Statham's first over. He tried to hook an in-swinging long hop which did not lift, missed it and was l.b.w. Then after a most erratic, mainly short, first over Tyson found an accurate length and direction and with the third and fourth balls of his third over bowled Alimuddin and Maqsood. The former played half cock too and missed a fast good length inswinger, and the latter was much too slow in playing forward to a fast straight ball of full length. Waquar was deceived by a slow yorker, which he tried to drive fatally off the back foot, some ten minutes after Loader had replaced Tyson and the Pakistanis were 26 for four wickets after being none for 1 and 10-3.

Even Imtiaz, much more watchfully though he defended and crisply though he hooked any ball palpably short, lost his

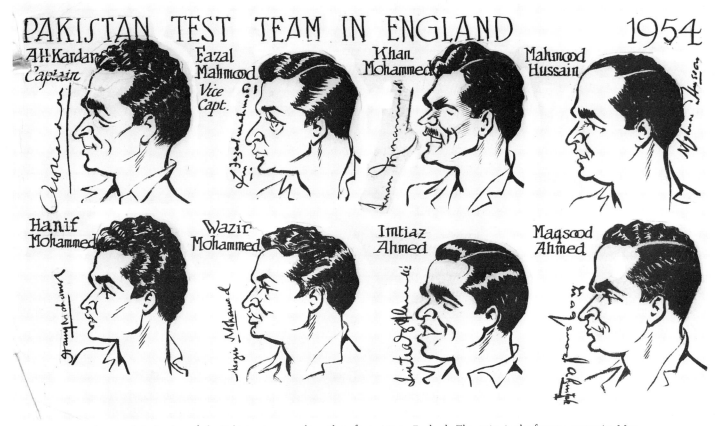

Autographed sketches of the Pakistan team making their first visit to England. The artist is the famous cartoonist Mac.

wicket through a moment's mental aberration. He tried to hook an inswinging bumper twenty minutes after Tyson returned in place of Statham, only just deflected it, and was brilliantly caught on the leg-side by Evans. To make matters worse Wazir Mohammad was run out before he had received a ball and Fazal unbelievably hung out his bat to an innocuous, wildly pitched inswinger from Loader and was caught at the wicket. At tea the Pakistanis were 59 for seven wickets.

So far only Kardar had looked thoroughly a business-like, organised player. He had defended carefully off his back foot, driven anything overpitched in forthright fashion, if not always with a bat academically straight, and had played some beautiful turn shots off his body to square leg. It was his misfortune to receive from Slatham, some twenty minutes after tea, the one really nasty ball of the day. It

swung away late from a nearly perfect length: Kardar could not check his half-cock shot and somewhat cruelly was caught at the wicket.

FAVOURABLE OMENS

For the remaining 85 minutes of Pakistan's innings Shujaddin, Zulfiqar, and Mahmood Hussain showed how little malice the pitch held. They resisted Statham, Tyson, and Loader from the pavilion end as if unaware of those hidden menaces that had overcome their more qualified colleagues and Zulfiquar and Mahmood in particular, treated McConnon much as they might have done an earnest but less accurate club bowler. A rash hook rather than a good ball, brought about Zulfiqar's downfall and only when Tyson at the last replaced McConnon at the always faster-looking Vauxhall end did his pace prove too much for Mahmood.

These last two partnerships would have

put the earlier Pakistan batting into proper perspective even had critical observation not done so at the time. England's pace-bowling none the less augured well for Australia. When a wicket is unhelpful it is necessary above all to be accurate. Tyson, after his first bad over, Statham, and Loader were accurate—in direction as well as in length, Tyson's general length—perhaps slightly short for the day—should be even more dangerous in Australia, and from a wicket on which Statham could bounce a short ball only just above the stumps, he more than once lifted one head high. Tyson also was consistently fast until he tired after tea. Loader again varied his pace intelligently as did Statham. These were the right omens. Though three possible difficult chances were missed England's fielding generally was alert and could become first-class with concentrated practice in Australia. Hutton probably was pleased with the day.

Day Two

Daily
Telegraph
& Morning
Post

14/8/54

ANOTHER BLANK TEST DAY

DOWNPOUR LEAVES OVAL FLOODED

From E. W. SWANTON

THE OVAL, Friday

If further proof of the malevolence of nature towards this Test series were needed it was provided in the course of ten drenching minutes here this morning.

The prospect just before noon was of an immediate wicket inspection by the umpires (the captains having disagreed) and a probable start by 12.30 at the latest.

The groundsman, chiefly by use of the patent "Duck" machine, reckoned that since dawn he had removed 650 gallons of the night's rainfall from the square.

The sun shone, there was the likelihood of the England batsmen's having to struggle at some stage of the play on a drying wicket, and there were, perhaps, anything up to 15,000 queuing around the Oval waiting for the word to enter.

Suddenly out of the west came a storm of such ferocity that within a few moments everyone was soaked through, and the whole field was flooded. The crease covers looked like rafts at sea. TV viewers at places within a few miles, such as Richmond saw the devastation on their screens, while their own gardens remained bathed in sunshine. This was the 16th day of the Test series, and the seventh blank one. On six days play has been interrupted by the weather. Three only have escaped, including the last day at Lord's, where the game had not been begun until the fourth afternoon.

FINAL TEST EVENLY POISED

From ALAN ROSS

KENNINGTON OVAL, Saturday

The luck changed with the weather here to-day and Pakistan, who took a lead of three runs over England on the first innings, ended the day 66 ahead with six wickets in hand. England batted with no great resolution on a drying pitch, largely preferring to trade wickets rather than time for their runs. As a result their technique was scarcely put to any test, though Compton and May both played with the discrimination one hopes for, if now seldom gets, from batsmen of their class. Otherwise the wicket was as subtly flattered as a declining dowager.

As things stand the match is nicely balanced; but had Pakistan been surer in their catching and less free with their wickets when they batted again, Hutton would have had reason for a thoughtful week-end.

Three-quarters of an hour was lost this morning, though the sun had shone since dawn more sweetly than it has all summer. There was so much pottering about, inspecting, prodding and conferring between captains, then umpires and finally groundsmen that it began to appear likely that the whole matter would have to be referred to the Upper House.

However, at 12.15 a capless Hutton and Simpson set about the English innings before a large, swelling crowd, mostly in shirt sleeves and with even a few cocked hats made of newspaper about. It was immediately apparent that the pitch was a good deal wetter than appeared, for every ball for some time produced a sizable bruise.

UNCERTAIN WICKET

Hutton, after being beaten the ball before by Fazal, edged him shakily past slip for four and then played the ball quite hard down, so that it rolled back against the stumps. Expressionless, Hutton pushed a stray lock of hair back and blandly paid no attention to the ball nesting between the middle and leg stumps. Simpson departed in Mahmood Hussain's second over, being easily caught by Kardar at gully off the shoulder of his bat. The ball was shortish, lifted sharply, and Simpson perhaps was not quite behind it.

Both bowlers now summoned up four men close in on the leg side and on a wicket that was uncertain in pace rather than vicious by nature they bowled extremely well. May began with a thoroughly bad shot, airy and indeterminate outside the off stump—just such a one as Lindwall had him out with when the Australians first played Surrey here last year—and then made two handsome drives, one to the off and one lofted to mid-wicket, which restored decency of a sort.

Hutton, seeming to fancy the sound of these shots more than the troubled dead bat strokes of the opening minutes, next lifted his head to two balls from Fazal in succession, scoring four to extra cover and two vertically over the bowler. May slashed Mahmood Hussain for four just over Kardar's hands at gully and when this frolic was becoming agreeable but rather less necessary Hutton skied a good length ball from Fazal and Imtiaz, running back, held a nice catch in the region of short third man.

Fazal and Mahmood Hussain, each bowling with splendid concentration and economy, kept May and Compton quiet for a longish period, the taut stillness of which was broken only by a perfect off-drive by May.

Compton was all but caught by Kardar in the gully when four, the ball coming slow and high off a forward stroke. Two more gullies joined Kardar and when

lunch was thankfully taken England had managed 35 runs in an hour and a quarter for their two wickets. Zulfiqar bowled two excellent maidens to Compton, the last but one ball of which stood up straight. It was something to ponder on over the cold chicken and ham.

COMPTON MISSED

A few clouds only trailed the sky after lunch when the ground was as full and happy and speckled with colour as a painting by Frith. One had quite forgotten what a Test match looked like in the sunlight. May's batting now looked full of breeding, clean and austere in outline, the flesh of the bat put fully to anything at all overpitched.

The sun had at last developed a true hunger for the top of this pitch and May, after 20 minutes of unconcern, played forward to Fazal and Kardar took a sharp catch, low and right-handed, at point. The ball was of good length and kicked the merest shade, but enough.

Graveney came in to an over in which Fazal shot one ball after another past his bat at a series of comically steep angles. The second over was worse for Graveney got the splice to one that curled the ball gently to second slip. Evans, at the head of probably the longest tail to wag or otherwise for England, hooked too soon at Mahmood Hussain and Maqsood caught him at square leg. 69 for five.

It was now more or less hit or miss, so spritely and various had become the sun's effect, and Wardle mostly missed while Compton hit. At 92 Wardle did hit and was taken at the wicket. Tyson made sensible enough strokes but without getting his feet close to the ball, a fault which cost him his wicket, caught by Imtiaz off Fazal.

Compton hereabouts, his score 31, was missed three times in as many minutes off Fazal. His habit had become to advance down the pitch and then drive, carve or pull as length dictated. First he hit Fazal straight and high over his head, an easy catch for anyone but the bowler. Fazal ran back, held it, sat down with a bump, and dropped it. Next ball Compton hit hard and wide of Wazir at mid-wicket, a stroke

Compton's innings of 53 out of 130, "as full of jokes and sudden melodies as a Haydn symphony" comes to an end as he is caught by wicket-keeper Imtiaz Ahmed off Fazal Mahmood.

he repeated soon after. Both catches went extremely high, and Wazir had plenty of time to get under them. Both spun agonisingly out.

At 115 Compton, prancing forward, gave Fazal his sixth wicket, Imtiaz his fourth catch. Compton's innings was one only a great batsman and an original character could have played. It was not quite a great innings, though as full of jokes and sudden melodies as a Haydn symphony.

SENSIBLE BATTING

Statham was out one run later, which left McConnon and Loader 18 runs to get to pass the Pakistan score. They got all but three of them, McConnon by means of the smoothest of leg glides and Loader with some happy off-drives. At exactly tea-time McConnon was taken at first slip by

Fazal, who himself had bowled throughout the innings. He is a bowler of genuine arts, and on this summer he has richly deserved the fortune of to-day's wicket.

Loader, not Tyson, opened the English bowling with Statham, who was struck to leg for 15 runs off the middle of the bat by Hanif. Hanif was crouching so low he was little more than stump high, but his hooking was quick and powerful, the arm moving no more than for the closest of upper-cuts. Shujauddin, who went in with him instead of Alimuddin, has scored a hundred recently at No. 2, but he was quickly dropped by Hutton at slip.

Statham and Loader were not much more than formalities, however, for after sharing five overs Wardle, from the Vauxhall end, and McConnon took over. The last ball of Wardle's second over spun away abruptly from a length, Hanif had no

chance of altering his forward stroke and Graveney took a comfortable catch off the edge at first slip. Hanif had made all the 19 runs for the opening partnership.

Shujauddin, a genial and uninhibited player, who indulges his fancy to the full at the wicket in a wide variety of imaginary shots, batted with much sense until Wardle spun another, in identical manner as to Hanif, and May snapped the ball up at second slip. Maqsood, impatient as ever, lashed McConnon high to mid-wicket where Wardle, after several attempts, held a difficult catch. It was a wicket too willingly sacrificed.

Just when it seemed that Waqar and Imtiaz had got the hang of things on a pitch much quietened, Waqar was quite pointlessly run out, Hutton throwing down the wicket from short leg after some doubtful calling.

Day
Four

Daily
Telegraph
& Morning
Post

17/8/54

ENGLAND NEED 43 WITH FOUR WICKETS TO FALL

Pakistan's Chance to Win Test

By E. W. SWANTON

THE OVAL, Monday

The general uncertainty and dramatic possibilities that are inherent in cricket were expressed here to-day in the most remarkable way: intriguing, one might say, or merely exasperating, according to the point of view.

Just before half-past 12 one felt that the great crowd basking in the unaccustomed luxury of sun, shirt-sleeved and loquacious, were going to be deprived of a full measure of play. For Pakistan were 82 for 8, with only inconsiderable batting left. One imagined them streaming away some time around four o'clock, if no earlier.

Inconsiderable or not, so far as reputation was concerned, Zulfiqar and Wazir in two hours grafted gamely away to score 58.

And when England broke their stand, Mahmood stayed long enough to enable Wazir to make some thoroughly effective strokes on the off-side. In the end the last two wickets exactly doubled the score and England went in to make 168 to win.

The wicket had recovered well from earlier inundations, and it was a matter of whether Fazal, who in this critic's opinion is a considerably better bowler than is widely supposed, could make a dent in the England innings early enough to expose that frighteningly long tail.

LANDSLIDE

He had the illustrious scalp of Hutton, as in the first innings, but then England for the further loss only of Simpson progressed well over half-way towards their goal.

Shortly before six England were coasting pleasantly along, May and

Johnny Wardle took seven for 56 in Pakistan's second innings.

Compton in occupation, and with three figures showing on the board. At 109 May was out. Evans was sent next, presumably to save the more valuable wicket of Graveney until the morning. But Evans lasted only 10 minutes, and when Graveney, perforce, appeared he was out practically at once.

The last thrust was the worst of all, for Compton ended a somewhat undistinguished innings by being caught behind the wicket, and at the end Wardle and Tyson were defending with all their wits, and with Pakistanis bristling round the bat.

England in the morning need 43 to win, and there are Wardle and Tyson, Statham, McConnon and Loader to get them. It is hardly necessary to emphasise the part that Wardle is likely to have to play if the game is to be won.

No side can be other than vulnerable whose tail begins as early as England's. That is the predominant thought at the moment of crisis. Further moralisings can be left until to-morrow.

PAKISTAN UNCERTAINTY
Wickets Soon Fall

The Pakistani batting has always been uncertain, and this morning's play illustrated the fact to the despair of their friends in the Visitor's stand. When the game was continued on a wicket that had quite dried out Pakistan were 63 for four: 50 minutes later at 82 for 8 the affair looked more or less over.

For this landslide in their fortunes Pakistan had only themselves to blame. Hutton unleashed the fastest of his fast bowlers, Tyson for the first over, and Imtiaz could not avoid scooping up the last ball to backward short-leg. Kardar watched Alim survive one or two perilous moments against Statham, himself subscribing a number of good strokes and a general air of competence and purpose.

The England bowlers, on a wicket of easy pace, became disconcertingly bereft of both hostility and ideas. They did not include McConnon, for he had retired with a dislocated finger.

WICKETS FOR WARDLE

Wardle changed the situation as soon as he appeared. In his first over he had Alim lbw with a ball that seemed to drift in a little with the arm, and next Kardar, driving straight, hit the ball low on the bat, and Wardle held on to the ball half-shin high. Fazal produced two strokes of quality for 4 and 2, and then a dreadful hoick against the spin.

This was the nadir of Pakistan's fortunes, though Wazir's beginning held little hope of his surviving long. However he did, while Zulfiqar's batting was always characterised by a certain modest confidence.

ZULFIQAR MISSED

When luncheon arrived Pakistan were 111 for eight, an increase for the ninth wicket of 29. Hutton again began with Tyson, and presently Zulfiqar snicked him to second slip. May almost had it, but the ball dropped to the ground just before he could scoop it up on the half-volley. The score was 140 before the next chance came, and this time May made a very good catch, two-handed, and low at second slip off Wardle. Pakistan were not yet done with and the patient Wazir had the chance to make some telling strokes through the covers before Mahmood's discretion proved unequal to the strain.

Thus Wardle had his seventh wicket and his flight and guile had been among the few merits of the English attack.

HUTTON SOON GOES
Wicket Still Easy

England ordered the heavy roller for the fourth innings, and the wicket's behaviour continued to be remarkably trustworthy, considering how the top had been knocked about on Saturday.

But Fazal and Mahmood could not be dealt with lightly. Hutton was in some trouble in Fazal's first over, and the score was only 15 when he touched to the wicket-keeper a good ball that went away after pitching.

May began luckily against Mahmood, for in the same over he snicked him to the boundary twixt legs and wicket, and mis-hooked a short ball off the splice only just clear of short-leg.

A proper hook for four in the same over was a better stroke, and thereafter he was in firmer command, without quite showing the sureness of touch that one expects from him at his best. May has been living a long time on a diet of low scores.

Simpson and May were unscathed at tea (49 for one), and it was five o'clock

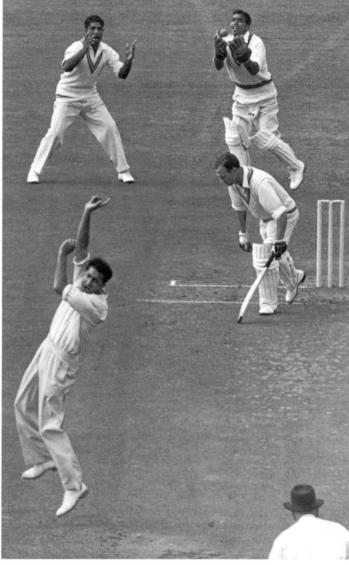

Hutton is caught at the wicket off Fazal. England were 15 for one, chasing 168, but there was still no hint of the drama to come.

when Simpson drove a ball back to Zulfiqar very hard and very straight.

COMPTON UNEASY

Compton began uneasily, frequently mistiming his strokes on the leg-side, and actually playing several sweeps without connecting. When he is on terms with himself his sweep is a thing of joy and profit: if some cog in the machinery fails spectators look on with apprehension.

Gradually, however, England's score jerked up. Fazal had to be rested, and the situation looked to be well in hand. Then came the last disastrous half-hour. Evans

went... Graveney... and finally Compton, the latter from another of what the older generation will, I hope, excuse my describing as a leg-cutter.

In Fazal's last over there was a great shout for lbw against Tyson that he cannot have survived with much to spare. A different answer to that appeal would surely have put the lid on it. As it is, the Pakistanis will still be scratching their heads and wondering whether at the first time of asking they are to be numbered with Australians, the South Africans and the West Indians, who alone have ever won a Test against England in this country.

Day Five

The Times
18/8/54

COMPLACENT MASTERS BEATEN BY THEIR PUPILS

PAKISTAN'S WELL DESERVED WIN BY 24 RUNS AT THE OVAL

From Our Cricket Correspondent

The young cricketers from Pakistan had their finest hour, and England one of their most inglorious, at the Oval yesterday when the fourth and final Test match was won and lost there by 24 runs. Pakistan gained a victory which carried with it a sharing of the rubber and England suffered a defeat which came as an unwelcome awakening within a month of sailing for Australia.

Some may say that the full strength of England was not in the field, some may claim that the losers had the worst of the wicket, but first and foremost all should acknowledge a performance of great merit by Pakistan, and one upon which they are to be congratulated most warmly. As the Goliaths and by the Davids of cricket were England slain, and by seizing their chance with both hands and winning this Test match on England soil on their first tour Pakistan achieved in less than four months what it took Australia two years, South Africa 28 years, and West Indies 22 years to achieve and what to this day has eluded New Zealand and India.

Pakistan's particular hero was Fazal, who brought his tally of wickets in the match to 12, and who throughout the series has established himself as a bowler of medium pace fit to rank near our own Bedser. Next to Fazal one would put Wazir and Zulfiqar, whose ninth wicket partnership of 58, when all seemed lost, gave birth to the recovery from which victory sprang. Kardar, when suddenly he saw the heel of Achilles naked and exposed, captained his side in every respect as astutely as he has done all summer, and there was an alert response from those under him.

A. H. Kardar, the victorious Pakistan captain.

LACKADAISICAL

Much of England's play, from the moment that Wazir and Zulfiqar came together on Monday morning, was almost too bad to be true. The bowling of Loader and Tyson became lifeless and inaccurate; the fielding became casual; and the inadequacy of the batting on a good wicket is reflected in the scorebook. May and Simpson played well, but they got themselves out, and Compton's 29 would have been nearly 50 had he made the most of the loose balls he received. Graveney failed in the crisis, as he had in the first innings, and the tail proved to be no shorter than one had feared. Nor, should T. E. Bailey by some mischance be out of action, and if five bowlers are played as they surely must be, will it be of any less horrifying a length in Australia.

The odds, when play started yesterday with England's last four wickets needing 43 runs, seemed to be slightly in Pakistan's favour, and one simply hoped that England would put up a fight. Their main chance rested with Wardle, who has made a good many runs against Pakistan this year. Given the opportunity he could have won the match off his own bat in 10 minutes, but Kardar sensibly chose Mahmud to bowl with Fazal, and speed does not suit Wardle's book so well as spin. The result was that Wardle was prevented from using the long handle and never flourished.

There was an impartial cheer for anything of note from the small crowd, and the sense of strain in the middle was soon shown in an injudicious single. Then at 129 Wardle was dropped at second slip off Mahmud, a none too difficult catch as slip catches go, and presently the same batsman survived two leg-before appeals from Fazal. After 25 minutes only six had been scored, but by then Tyson seemed to be finding his feet,and Pakistan's need of a wicket was great. It came just on noon, when Tyson felt speculatively for an out-swinger from Fazal and gave Imtiaz his seventh catch of the match. Loader now came in ninth and at once forced a 4 to long-on, followed by a quick single which took the score to 138.

FATAL 15 MINUTES

With 30 needed from three wickets it was anyone's game, and yet within a quarter of an hour the end had come. At 138 Wardle was caught round the corner turning Fazal off his legs, and Loader, hitting out desperately, immediately sent a steepling catch to cover-point, where Warqar, after an agony of suspense, held it and threw it aloft. There remained only some missing and snicking, a run out

McConnon is run out by Hanif Mohammed's throw and Pakistan have won by 24 runs. Far right: Pakistan players are warmly applauded by the Oval crowd.

FINAL · SCORES

PAKISTAN — First Innings

Hanif Mohammad, lbw, b Statham	0
Alimuddin, b Tyson	10
Waqar Hassan, b Loader	7
Maqsood Ahmed, b Tyson	0
Imtiaz Ahmed, c Evans, b Tyson	23
A. H. Kardar, c Evans, b Statham	36
Wazir Mohammad, run out	0
Fazal Mahmood, c Evans, b Loader	0
Shujauddin, not out	16
Zulfiqar Ahmed, c Compton, b Loader	16
Mahmood Hussain, b Tyson	23
Extras (nb 2)	2
Total	**133**

Fall of wickets: 1-0, 2-10, 3-10, 4-26, 5-51, 6-51, 7-51, 8-77, 9-106, 10-133
Bowling: Statham 11-5-26-2, Tyson 13.4-3-35-4, Loader 18-5-35-3, McConnon 9-2-35-0

ENGLAND — First Innings

Hutton, c Imtiaz Ahmed, b Fazal Mahmood	14
R. T. Simpson, c Kardar, b Mahmood Hussain	2
P. B. H. May, c Kardar, b Fazal Mahmood	26
Compton, c Imtiaz Ahmed, b Fazal Mahmood	53
Graveney, c Hanif Mohammad, b Fazal Mahmood	1
Evans, c Maqsood Ahmed, b Mahmood Hussain	0
Wardle, c Imtiaz Ahmed, b Fazal Mahmood	8
Tyson, c Imtiaz Ahmed, b Fazal Mahmood	3
McConnon, c Fazal Mahmood, b Mahmood Hussain	11
Statham, c Shujauddin, b Mahmood Hussain	1
Loader, not out	8
Extras (lb 1, w 1, nb 1)	3
Total	**130**

Fall of wickets: 1-6, 2-26, 3-56, 4-63, 5-69, 6-92, 7-106, 8-115, 9-116, 10-130
Bowling: Fazal Mahmood 30-16-53-6, Mahmood Hussain 21.3-6-58-4, Zulfiqar Ahmed 5-2-8-0, Shujauddin 3-0-8-0

PAKISTAN — Second Innings

Hanif Mohammad, c Graveney, b Wardle	19
Alimuddin, lbw, b Wardle	0
Waqar Hassan, run out	9
Maqsood Ahmed, c Wardle, b McConnon	4
Imtiaz Ahmed, c Wardle, b Tyson	12
A. H. Kardar, c & b Wardle	17
Wazir Mohammad, not out	42
Fazal Mahmood, b Wardle	6
Shujauddin, c May, b Wardle	12
Zulfiqar Ahmed, c May, b Wardle	34
Mahmood Hussain, c Statham, b Wardle	6
Extras (b 3)	3
Total	**164**

Fall of wickets: 1-19, 2-38, 3-43, 4-52, 5-63, 6-73, 7-76, 8-82, 9-140, 10-164
Bowling: Statham 18-7-37-0, Loader 16-8-26-0, Wardle 33-16-56-7, McConnon 14-5-20-1, Tyson 9-2-22-1

ENGLAND — Second Innings

Hutton, c Imtiaz Ahmed, b Fazal Mahmood	5
R. T. Simpson, c & b Zulfiqar Ahmed	27
P. B. H. May, c Kardar, b Fazal Mahmood	53
Compton, c Imtiaz Ahmed, b Fazal Mahmood	29
Graveney, lbw, b Shujauddin	0
Evans, b Fazal Mahmood	3
Wardle, c Shujauddin, b Fazal Mahmood	9
Tyson, c Imtiaz Ahmed, b Fazal Mahmood	3
McConnon, run out	2
Statham, not out	2
Loader, c Waqar Hassan, b Mahmood Hussain	5
Extras (lb 2, nb 3)	5
Total	**143**

Fall of wickets: 1-15, 2-66, 3-109, 4-115, 5-116, 6-121, 7-131, 8-138, 9-138, 10-143
Bowling: Fazal Mahmood 30-11-46-6, Mahmood Hussain 14-4-32-1, Zulfiqar Ahmed 14-2-35-1, Shujauddin 10-1-25-1

escape, and then a fatal call by McConnon, who underestimated Hanif's quickness and accuracy of throw from cover-point to the bowler's end. Hanif hit the stumps, umpire Davies adjudicated, and Pakistan, who had come to learn, had come and conquered.

Perhaps a run-out was a suitable end to England's humiliating display. At any rate, it meant that the last eight England wickets had fallen while 34 runs were being scored. Twelve months ago in the corresponding innings of the corresponding Test match the last eight Australian wickets tumbled for 98: now the boot was on a very different foot, and it was Pakistan who were being serenaded on their balcony. The over-confidence from which England seemed to have suffered had proved a dangerous anodyne. In the hour of need the will and skill had not been there, and the first defeat at home for three years had been suffered.

•1954•

THE SECOND TEST was the turning point in a series which had begun disastrously for England with Australia winning by an innings in Brisbane. At Sydney, England were again disappointing in the first innings and it looked as though a second consecutive defeat was inevitable. They were whipped out for only 154 but Australia took only modest advantage in replying with 228 — Ronald Archer top scoring with 49. England needed to set a target and did so courtesy of Peter May's 104 and Colin Cowdrey's 54. Bob Appleyard (19) and Brian Statham (25) added 46

for the last wicket, in what proved to be an invaluable partnership. Australia needed 223 runs to win but Frank Tyson was inspired. The Northamptonshire fast bowler had been laid unconscious by a Ray Lindwall bouncer, *left*, and was determined to take his revenge. Lindwall eventually became one of Tyson's six victims at a cost of 85 runs for a 10-wicket match haul and as always he received invaluable support from Statham. Neil Harvey made a magnificent 92 not out but to no avail. England won by 88 runs and eventually won the series 3-1.

Frank Tyson gains revenge over Ray Lindwall who earlier had rendered him unconscious with a bouncer.

Day One

The Sydney
Morning
Herald

18/12/54

English Collapse
On Tricky Wicket

OPENING SCENES IN
SECOND TEST
MATCH AT SYDNEY
CRICKET GROUND

By Lindsey Browne

Trevor Bailey,
pressed into service as
Len Hutton's opening
partner, loses his
middle stump to Ray
Lindwall for nought.

England's captain Len Hutton, sent in to bat on just the sort of temperamental pitch he had misguidedly expected in Brisbane, saw his perplexed batsmen crash before Australia's prancing pace bowlers in the Second Test in Sydney yesterday. But if it was a galling irony for him, he did get the minor pleasure of the last laugh.

For on the last ball of the day, with the Australian batsmen briskly chasing after England's near-bankrupt first innings total of 154, Australian captain Arthur Morris himself made an embarrassed one-hand stroke at a sharp-rising ball from Bailey, and Hutton, at leg-slip, was ready and willing to pocket the catch.

At one wicket for 18, the Australians still have the task of showing whether they can tame pace bowling any better than England's batsmen did yesterday—and the hilarious carpet-beater's wallops that won top score (35) for tail-ender Wardle in England's innings could hardly be reckoned as a technique to be successfully imitated by anybody but a hawk-eyed jester with wrists of iron, and a baseballer's gift for reckless mistiming. Poor Hutton! Who could have thought that a toss-winning captain would risk sending an opponent to bat first after the cautionary disaster that befell toss-winning Hutton in Brisbane?

Yet Australia's Morris—"conservative Morris" they used to say—was quick to try it, and was soon rubbing salt in with the irony as opening bowlers, Lindwall and Archer, found conditions ideal for veering swing and sharp lift.

Morris was right, of course, and Hutton and his opening partner Bailey, new in the job, were left in no doubt of it. One well-pitched ball reared up sharply to jam Hutton's fingers painfully against bat handle.

THE SLIPS WERE WAITING

Several times the Lindwall out-swinger, with a wider curve than ever, hissed venomously at the edge of Hutton's questioning bat, and had the five slips watering at the mouth like wolves barely beyond the ring of a campfire's glow.

Bailey, obstinate and vigilant for half an hour or so, had no answer for the in-swinging Lindwall yorker that uprooted his middle stump.

But Hutton himself batted as if determined to let Morris get away with his jest—watchful, cautious, resourceful, he stayed on 14 for 40 minutes, and on 19 for 25 minutes, and the total at lunch was merely 34. Surely the smallest pre-lunch total ever!

But as long as Hutton stayed England had hope—and the growing crowd was always alive to the tension which animated the play while he fought for runs.

Then just when the main hazards of

the day seemed to have been safely navigated, he fell to a sensational diving catch at leg-slip by Davidson. There the innings began to come open at the seams.

BATSMEN IN PROCESSION

The bowler Bill Johnston, who became a father earlier in the week, had bowled until then in a spirit of fatherly kindness, but within a few minutes he found Graveney after a solid and judicious innings, indiscreetly feeling a catch to wideawake slips.

Batsmen came and went like voters at a polling booth—a few brief assertions of their democratic right, then back to base.

Hutton (30 in 132 minutes) went at 2.23, Graveney at 2.31 Edrich at 2.55, Tyson at 3.10, Evans at 3.14, five wickets in less than an hour on a pitch that was by no means that bad.

Cowdrey, with only tail-enders left for company lost his wicket in trying to force the pace after tea.

And then came Wardle, who, in seven balls from Johnston, sliced, winnowed and thrashed 4, 2, 2, 4, 4, 0, 1—17 runs, half as many as England had made in the whole

of that miserly prelunch session of pats, prods, nudges and stabs.

ARCHER'S THREE FOR 12

The soft light of the grey day and the lush greenness of the ground could well have given a special cheer and encouragement to English prowess—and yet it was Queenslander Ron Archer, just down from the heat and the harsh light, who seemed most to revel in the conditions.

Limber, springy, aggressive, his fast bowling earned him three wickets for 12 off a dozen overs, and eight of the runs were from desperate fours.

Fours? They were scarce all day. Until Wardle plundered five, England's innings had included only five boundaries all told—a result partly of fine bowling, and relentlessly tight fielding and partly because of unadventurous batting.

Rain caused an adjournment of half an hour at the end of England's innings.

The little moisture which reached the pitch before the covers may well have helped to liven it up a little for to-day's encounter.

Inspired Speed Bowling In England's Hard Fight-back

AUSTRALIA LEADS BY 74

By TOM GOODMAN

Inspired bowling by England's pace bowlers, coupled with some indifferent Australian batting, allowed the touring team to make a magnificent fight back in the second Test at the Sydney Cricket Ground yesterday.

England shattered Australia's defences, and despite a strong rearguard action led by 21-year-old Ron Archer, the home side was dismissed for 228 runs — a first-innings lead of 74.

Archer top-scored with his gallant innings for 49.

He and left-hander Alan Davidson saved Australia a lot of embarrassment by holding up England's hostile attack for an hour.

They put on 52 runs for the seventh wicket.

But the main honours, from one of the best days of cricket seen at the ground in years, go to England's bowlers, Trevor Bailey, Frank Tyson, and Brian Statham.

The biggest crowd of the tour, 44,879, was animated throughout the day.

The spectators showed full appreciation

of the grand manner in which the Englishmen lifted up their attack and maintained pressure.

After two days' play the match is "open".

Is Australia's first innings lead of 74 runs big enough?

It used to be estimated that a team having fourth innings of a six-day Test required a compensation lead of 150 runs.

But batting standards have altered, and this match might last less than five days. To-morrow's play will help supply the answer.

Australia is to have last use of a pitch that yesterday afternoon indicated that it would give spin bowlers some help. England's medium-pacer, Bob Appleyard, who "cuts" rather than spins the ball, caused several balls to turn.

This suggested that he could be a danger man in the fourth innings of the match.

The pitch yesterday behaved very much as it did on the first day.

There was some variation in "lift".

Frank Tyson, the "Typhoon" from Northamptonshire. Trevor Bailey reckoned that, for two years, Tyson bowled as fast as any man had ever done.

Fast bowlers Statham and Tyson both caused the ball to rear startlingly at times.

Off one such ball from Tyson, left-hander Neil Harvey was caught.

It was not at all a bad wicket — it was just that the element of surprise caused by slight variations helped to unsettle batsmen, whose technical faults were exposed.

There was a lot of streaky batting yesterday.

It all boiled down to confirmation that Australia's batting generally, if not as

unsatisfactory as England's, is far from stable.

However, there was one lesson rammed home to England's batsmen.

That was that the Australians, and especially the younger players like Ron Archer, were prepared to hit a ball hard if it deserved to be hit.

This Australian innings required only one more ball than was bowled in England's innings, yet 74 more runs were scored.

And now we must await England's second turn at the wickets.

Can Len Hutton and his supports continue the fight back begun so splendidly by Bailey, Tyson and Statham yesterday?

They again have Ray Lindwall to overcome.

And it could be that Bill Johnston, bowling medium paced leg-spinners and perhaps Richie Benaud will cause batsmen

some concern on the three-day pitch.

Hutton and Tyson combined to prevent Australia's last wicket from falling in such time that England would have to bat.

It was a sensible plan, but some spectators "barracked" Hutton for what they thought was deliberate waste of time.

Tyson, about to bowl to last man Bill Johnston, with a quarter of an hour left for play, was approached by Hutton for a consultation.

Then Tyson bowled an over almost entirely off the pitch, to ensure that the last wicket would not fall.

Bailey from the other end bowled Gil Langley.

The umpires time showed 5.21 p.m.

There was not enough time for the required 10 minutes between innings, and so play for the day ended.

"BIG THREE" TOOK TEN WICKETS

England's "big three" of bowlers yesterday all played grand parts.

Bailey and Tyson each took four wickets, Statham the other two.

Statham early in the day had bowled well, especially when he changed round to the Paddington end to have the cross-breeze help him.

Tyson after two very erratic overs in the opening session answered the call after lunch and was decidedly hostile.

He showed the crowd that what they had heard of his improvement since he last played here, against N.S.W., was true.

Tyson using his shortened run to the bowling crease, was very fast. He controlled length and direction well. He was a keen, venomous, attacking bowler.

But to that more-than-useful player, Trevor Bailey, must go the greatest credit for influencing Australia's batting failure.

It was Bailey who first began to exploit the glaring weakness in the home batsmen — their inclination to "nibble" at good-length swinging balls pitched on or just outside the off-stump.

Bailey before lunch had opening batsmen Les Flavell caught off such a "stroke", at second slip.

Then he had Jim Burke, at 31, missed in the same position.

After lunch Bailey persevered with this

shrewd and nagging attack. He continually "baited" batsmen, and there were many times when an attempted drive all but resulted in an edged shot to the waiting slip men.

Rarely did Bailey waste a ball outside the leg stump.

He varied his swing — the breeze and the heavy atmosphere again helped swing — and his length was unfalteringly good.

He had Burke (44) caught just where he had been missed before: at second slip, by Tom Graveney.

The 110-minute session between lunch and tea was intensely absorbing and the big crowd which packed the "Hill" buzzed with excitement.

During that session, which marked the peak of England's fight back, inspired then by Bailey and Tyson, Australia lost four wickets for 70 runs.

The score swung from the lunchtime 88 for two wickets (Morris and Favell) to the tea-time 168 for six.

But the sixth wicket (Benaud) had actually fallen at 141 — still 13 runs short of England's score.

The upright Bailey's purposeful fast-medium sniping, and the balding Tyson's hunched-up, plunging barrage of heavy fire kept the batsmen quiet.

Tyson, from being a "wild bull" bowler before lunch, when his "no-balls" and full tosses forced Hutton hurriedly to take him off, became something of a terror.

The pressure was on, and Tyson responded to it in true Test tradition.

Statham chimed in, as relief to Tyson, and he also had batsmen disturbed by the manner in which he lifted from the pitch and occasionally swung off it.

Burke and Neil Harvey, caught off a "kicker" from Tyson from which he could not completely withdraw his bat, were both dismissed within 25 minutes after lunch, with the addition of only 16 runs.

Harvey had batted 69 minutes for 12 runs and had not hit a four.

He had not looked like taking charge of the attack.

With his departure, the English pressure became ever stronger.

Bailey had bowled from noon to the 1 p.m. luncheon adjournment.

Brian Statham gave Tyson invaluable support

He and Tyson were unchanged for the first 70 minutes after lunch.

When Bailey at last received the signal from Hutton to spell and adjusted his sweater the crowd gave him a round of applause.

Bailey then had bowled 14 overs for three wickets and 43 runs, his stretch after lunch having been 6-2-13-1.

Tyson also rested with his figures 2-36 including 6-0-23-2 since lunch.

Tyson had bowled Hole leg stump, with a fierce swinger, after Hole had played some nice shots and looked much better than his fifth-wicket partner Richie Benaud.

Benaud, when three, blazed desperately at Tyson and mishit him over the wicket-keeper for four.

Two balls late, when seven, he was dropped by Graveney at backward short-leg.

Benaud, in all sorts of trouble, struggled on to 20, and then went lbw to Statham.

Ron Archer and Alan Davidson began their vital and spectacular stand 20 minutes before tea.

Appleyard, called on as the fourth bowler, had demanded respect but just before tea young Archer decided that some aggression was called for.

After making an uppish off-drive to the fence, he pulled a short ball for a six into the crowd in front of the "outer" stand.

This big hit took the score to 155, and one run past England.

There was some exhilarating play immediately after tea, with both Archer and Davidson making splendid shots off Bailey and Statham.

Here was a demonstration of how fortunate is Australia, compared with England, in its array of players with "all-round" ability.

Their partnership realised 52 runs in an hour before left-hander Davidson was forced by Statham to play on.

Ray Lindwall, who was given a great welcome back in Sydney, made a delightful glance to the fence off Appleyard. But when the new ball was taken at 207 Archer fell to it.

Tyson missed his off-stump with one that really whizzed by.

The next ball was mis-timed by Archer and it flew to third slip where Hutton

easily caught it. Archer's 29 equalled the score he made in his fighting stand for Australia in the second innings of the test at The Oval last year.

He had some narrow squeaks yesterday, but his batting was determined and he gave a lead to his fellow Australians in hitting hard.

England's fielding was extremely keen, and showed improvement.

Tom Graveney close to the wicket had two catches — and missed two.

Day Three

The Manchester Guardian

21/12/54

ENGLAND AVOIDS THE PIT
Australia's Dose of Her Own Medicine
FROM DENYS ROWBOTHAM

SYDNEY, Monday

It is a pleasure to report that the old universities served England proudly in her second Test match with Australia here.

Cowdrey joined May eight minutes before lunch, after England had lost Hutton and Graveney disastrously in a single over from Johnston and became 55 for three. When Cowdrey made the first misjudgment of his innings and was caught in the deep off Benaud England was 171 for four. He and May had not only added 116 for the fourth wicket, but had so mastered Australia's bowling in the process that in the day's last 25 minutes May and Edrich were able to drive, hook and pull 33 vivid runs and bring England a lead of 130. If Edrich and May can survive the new ball to-morrow morning and the side adds another 150 runs to its present total England's chances of victory will be good on a wicket which by then must be showing signs of wear.

Just before lunch these chances hardly could have looked bleaker, for England had suffered three stunning blows, two of them the heavier because England had looked in command when they occurred. From the start, for instance, though the wicket still looked too green for comfort neither Archer nor Lindwall gave hint of that devil which so undid England on Friday. Archer was extremely steady at medium-fast pace,

but not more. Lindwall's length first was too full and then too short, and not only did he never settle to his right form of accuracy, but only twice in the morning did he bowl a dangerous outswinger. England, it seemed had only to take no risks. Hutton and Bailey took none, and though after half an hour the score was only 12 neither batsman had been presented with a problem.

BAILEY TRAPPED

Then the first blow fell without warning. Archer caused a ball of excellent length to move slightly away from the bat off the pitch. Bailey, who had once more pushed forward, was caught at the wicket, and England was 18 for one. With such eager, cool incisiveness did May begin that England might have been 80. He turned Archer square again for four. Hutton also had turned Archer off his legs for three with the same lovely inclination of body and supple flex of wrist, and though each batsman in turn was nearly drawn forward fatally by Lindwall's two outswingers the controlled temper of their clean, confident attack only quickened. As soon as Johnston replaced Archer May straight-drove him to the boundary and turned him square for three. Hutton greeted Davidson with a glorious flowing off-drive and England was 55 and on top.

Peter May. With this century, according to Swanton, "he reached a new stature."

Within a single over she was facing possible defeat. The first blow fell when the strong morning wind had blown all cloud away and the ground was golden with sunlight. Hutton put his left foot down the wicket, presumably to drive the wide half-volley Johnston bowled to him square of backward point. The ball moved away from his bat and he was caught in the gully. This error at least was understandable. It was the error of a man who was in form and knew it. Graveney's was reducible to no sort of reason. He tried to drive an outswinger that pitched at least a foot outside his off stump, inevitably edged it, and was caught at the wicket. This was the sort of shot that loses Test matches and thoroughly deserves to.

PATIENCE TEMPERS ZEST

Fortunately May and Cowdrey now brought to England's batting calculating thoughtfulness, clear determined purpose, and the patience needed to play the good ball defensively without loss of ability to recognise the bad one and hit it zestfully: qualities her batsmen too often have lacked, apart from Hutton and Compton. Theirs, indeed, was batting made to Australian measure, quick and unerring in its judgment, dogged in its defence, and resourceful enough in range of shot to cover every angle of the field. The crowd of over thirty thousand approved every stroke the two made. It was watching batting, not the scoreboard.

That the scoreboard moved somewhat slowly—only 71 runs came in 110 minutes between lunch and tea and only 42 in the first 75 minutes afterwards—was part of the two players' plan. They appraised the situation quickly, saw that the wicket's treacherous greenness now had gone and with it all menace of dangerous swing and variable pace and lift. They knew Lindwall's changes of pace would need watching, as would Johnston's mixture of attack on the leg stump and balls floated with his arm to the slips. Archer now was only steady to a length, and Davidson to just short of one. Only Benaud's rich flight would present a crucial problem of judgment. So since time was England's ally in terms of increasing wear on the wicket for Australia's second innings they rightly took no risks whatsoever. They watched, they concentrated, they stunned every good ball on the wicket, and they disregarded everything short of a palpably bad ball off the wicket.

So much has been done for England before now, with the loss of Test matches in its wake. What was different in this stand was the schoolboy relish with which each batsman thumped every bad ball that

was bowled to him. There were not many of these. But there were enough to bring cover-drives and sweeps from Cowdrey, broad and spacious as Hammond's, and one majestic off-drive and one straight drive with follow throughs that would have done Sir Thomas Beecham credit. May scored a greater number of his runs off the back foot from crisp turned shots and glances and square cuts made clean as a woodman's axe blows. When he drove

it was more often straight and firm-footed or off his toes to the on side.

The two achieved a unity of domination perhaps greater even than they knew. But Edrich knew. And when Cowdrey at last lofted Benaud and was caught, Edrich even forgot about to-morrow and enjoyed himself immensely and immediately to-day. If such heart and sense can live to-morrow England indeed may have a happy Christmas.

LINDWALL WRECKS TEST RECOVERY EFFORT

Tyson, Hurt, Leads Fight-back
From E. W. SWANTON

Day Four

Daily Telegraph & Morning Post
22/12/54

SYDNEY, Tuesday

There is a famous golf writer whose idea of a really good game is to win by eight and seven. He likes very much to win the bye, too, but admits to relenting sometimes on the "bye bye." The watching of many Test matches induces a

similar state of mind: it would be nice to see England bowl out Australia for about 50 and then make 500 and get them out again for the same score as before.

To-day the play before lunch filled one with gloom. The continuation of the collapse afterwards was as bad and then

Tyson is helped from the field after being knocked out by Lindwall during England's second innings.

came an exhilarating partnership by Statham and Appleyard (yes, those are the names) which put on 46 priceless runs for the last wicket and gave Australia 223 to chase in the fourth innings.

A dropped catch before a run was scored and an almost incredible amount of playing and missing preceded the fall of the first Australian wicket at 27. Two were down for 34 and Harvey died several deaths before he at last got off the mark.

But there England's successes ended and by the close Australia had reduced the number still needed to 151.

All of which fluctuation and excitement adds up, of course, to what is generally called "a good day". And of course there may well be still more drama to come.

England to-day were undone once again chiefly by Lindwall, who during the course of play achieved a distinction which I suppose may possibly have eluded the figure experts. Tom Richardson took 88 Australian wickets in his time and Spofforth, that stark figure of hostility, 94 of England's. To-day Lindwall brought his number against England to 96, the most ever reached by a fast bowler in Tests between England and Australia.

It is droll to recall that he was written off as finished on the Australian tour of South Africa as long ago as 1949.

Lindwall it was who prevented May from again taking root and that was the final turning point of the inning. However, May with this performance has reached a new stature.

TIGERISH ASSAULT
Statham and Tyson

The England fast bowlers Statham and Tyson went at the Australians like tigers when Morris and Favell came out to begin the last innings.

Statham might have had Favell twice and Morris four or five times in his first three overs: but a special merit attached to Tyson, who had been struck down with a blow on the head by Lindwall earlier in the day.

There is a fine rugged tenacity about Tyson that reflects well the spirit of his native Lancashire.

Lindwall, pace and grace.

MISERABLE MORNING
Drizzle and Disaster

May and Edrich continued England's innings at 204 for four and a more miserable morning's watching for English eyes could hardly be imagined. After one over from Lindwall, in which May scored the two needed for his 100, a thick drizzle held up the game for 20 minutes.

The wicket, having been covered, had not been affected, but Morris waited until the outfield had had a chance to dry before taking the new ball. This was a period of quiet play in which Edrich had most of the bowling of Johnston and Davidson and seemed to have settled in nicely.

May was getting acclimatised waiting for the challenge that Lindwall would fling down at any moment. It was almost half an hour before it came, the score being 222. In his first over Lindwall insinuated yet another swinging yorker under an enemy bat.

With May there departed any real hope of a comfortable score and it became a matter of what the rest would be able to scratch together. For several overs with Tyson and Edrich in partnership virtually nothing came at all.

Lindwall, who had fallen to a bumper from Tyson in the first innings, with the last ball of an over, suddenly returned the compliment. Tyson seemed at first inclined to duck then backed and straightened, and was hit full on the back of the head. The description, of course, will take much longer to read than the thing took to happen.

Tyson tottered and fell with a thud while the ball made most of the distance to the leg boundary.

For a moment he was quite "out". Then he was helped off and taken for an X-ray, returning after a favourable verdict in time to bat as soon as the first wicket fell after lunch.

But the morning was not over yet.

With only two balls to go, Edrich elected to make no stroke at a ball from Archer outside the off-stump, withdrew the bat late and the ball, nicking the bottom edge, cannoned on to the stumps.

Thus May and Edrich fell and Tyson was knocked out while the score was advanced by 88.

The sorry chapter continued well into the afternoon. Evans, who averages only eight with bat on this tour, soon played the stroke that usually cost him his wicket—the off-side poke or slash that snicks the ball into slips.

Tyson emerged to long applause, which was renewed when he straight-drove Archer violently for four.

But Lindwall quickly had both Wardle and Tyson and England were 250 for nine. Since the new ball five wickets had fallen for 28, which even by the standards of this tour is cheap going.

SURPRISE FINISH
Raising the Target

The pattern of the English batting suggested nothing less probable than a last-wicket stand.

Yet it did not look so fantastic as soon as it got under way, for Appleyard at least played straight and Statham, though he generally gives the ball room, had a good eye and when he connects hits the ball extremely hard and from somewhere in the leg stump area pushes the ball shrewdly past point. In particular he is a good straight driver.

Appleyard progressed more by deflections, in particular a sort of off-glide with which he safely penetrated the slips. Statham needed a few near misses (but nothing more than the number he is entitled to) and in the mounting excitement with which a crowd always acknowledges a last-wicket stand the target for Australia rose from 175, when they came together, to 200 and finally, after nearly an hour's partnership, to 223.

Langley made his fifth catch of the match when he caught Statham and he did not give a bye in either innings. He is not one of those wicket-keepers who take the eye. But he does take his chances and except for Evans at his best (which he has

not quite reached in this match so far) there is no one better.

MORRIS LBW
Favell Starts Shakily

In Australia's second innings Statham began into the breeze to allow Tyson the use of it but Favell nevertheless received a fast and fateful over. He was first appealed against loudly by both bowler and wicket-keeper for lbw and I imagine will have got the benefit of the doubt. Then he snicked high to first slip where the ball ricochetted off Edrich's upstretched hands for two runs.

At the other end Tyson worked up an excellent pace—I hope he will suffer no reaction from his efforts to-morrow. Favell after his first adventures batted well but we now saw a most extraordinary innings from Morris.

It was hard to believe this was the same rejuvenated Morris, impeccable in judgment and technique, whom we had seen at Brisbane. It seemed as though he must have a pressing appointment for tea.

If he flashed outside the off stump once he must have done it six times, was nearly lbw and finally did depart lbw trying to hook the only ball of the day that kept unfairly low.

The wicket altogether has played admirably. Morris was out to the last ball before tea and Favell shortly followed him, caught this time by Edrich from a snick not dissimilar from the earlier one.

Tyson greeted Harvey (whom he had got out on their last two meetings) with two of the fastest balls of the match.

Harvey aimed at both and missed each time. Neither he nor Burke was comfortable and Burke was slow enough to rouse the crowd to speech, yet England could not again break through.

Hutton used all his five bowlers this time, giving them short spasms of work. Appleyard hit the edge more than once and Wardle kept Burke pushing quietly forward though he seemed to hold little difficulty for Harvey.

In the last 80 minutes Australia scored 38. If that is to be their pace to-morrow the end, whatever it is, will be a long time coming.

TYSON LEVELS TEST SERIES FOR ENGLAND

◆

HARVEY ALONE HIS EQUAL

From Our Cricket Correspondent

Neil Harvey's unbeaten 92 was Australia's only resistance.

SYDNEY, Wednesday

At Brisbane, tragedy; at Sydney, triumph. Here this afternoon England won a memorable victory by 38 runs after one of the most exciting Test matches for many years. At 10 minutes past three Tyson and Statham, heroes at the head of England's team, were cheered from sight through one pavilion gate, and through the other went little Harvey, undefeated after a masterly effort to steer Australia home.

There have been many Test matches in which the technical standard has been higher, and for that matter, several in which the margin of victory has been smaller. But few can have followed a more winding course or reached so great a climax as did this one. And in few can there have been so courageous and sustained a piece of fast bowling as Tyson's to-day. For four days England's cricket alternated between the pit of depression and, very occasionally, the heights of expectation, until this morning it seemed that Australia would most likely win.

Indeed it had seemed that way since England were bowled out for 154 in their first innings. But Tyson, with a bump on the back of his head the size of an egg, swung the balance after 15 minutes to-day with two shattering yorkers in an over. Thereafter England fought like lions, paralysing all Australia's batsmen except Harvey. Statham supported Tyson with great heart and determination, Appleyard got a valuable wicket, and Evans took a staggering catch. Nor must one forget the batting of May and Cowdrey or England's last wicket partners. Yet one feels that the match should be remembered more than anything for Tyson's fast bowling to-day on an easy wicket.

LEARNING FROM LINDWALL

Only last week at Melbourne he changed to a shorter, more controlled, run. Now he has also learnt the value of a full length by watching Lindwall, and 10 wickets in a Test match is the result. He is strong, and it is difficult to see how a man can bowl much faster than he did at times to-day. Within a fortnight he has acquired for himself a considerable ascendancy over Australia's leading batsmen through being genuinely too good for them.

M.C.C., too, can thank him for being able to spend Christmas with happy hearts, and England are in the elevating psychological position in which Australia found themselves after Brisbane. Had this match gone the other way, however, as it came within an ace of doing, much of the interest might have gone from the series. Now it is ablaze with possibilities, with

Hutton's side restored to confidence and their doubters faithful again. Hutton captained calmly and with judgment to-day. It was not easy for him with runs so precious and with Tyson and Statham to be conserved and yet released.

Nor is Harvey an easy man to keep down. This innings of his was altogether better than his century at Brisbane, and it would have gone down to posterity had he

The "Typhoon"

somehow won the match for Australia, as there was a chance he was going to during a, to English eyes, torturing last-wicket partnership of 39 with Johnston. For the first time on this tour Harvey looked a great player. Never before has one seen him so scrupulously behind the line of the ball, and never has one seen his bat have fewer edges. Almost always before when playing against England he has looked brilliant but unsound; to-day he played hardly a false stroke.

REMARKABLE START

When Harvey and Burke made their way to the wicket in cool and sunny weather this morning it needed only an over apiece from Statham and Tyson to reveal that the pitch was dead and remarkable things would have to happen if England were to win. Remarkable things did happen in Tyson's second over, for off the third ball the obdurate Burke was yorked, and off the seventh Hole met a similar fate. Benaud was struggling, Harvey was hemmed in, the bowlers'

length was checking many drives, and for almost an hour the battle went slowly yet tensely on with 29 runs being scored. Hutton soon had Bailey on from the M. A. Noble stand end, with Tyson and Statham in short bursts from the other, but it was Appleyard who made the next vital contribution to England's day when he replaced Bailey. Appleyard is forever likely to beat in the air someone to whom he has not bowled before with the ball he holds back, and sure enough in his second over he caused Benaud to sweep too soon and send a high swirling catch to Tyson off the top edge of the bat. Tyson was at backward square leg half-way to the boundary, and he caught the ball so far from his body that for an awful moment one feared the catch might go to ground.

Australia's innings, if not now open as England's would have been, was at least ajar and Archer survived until luncheon, when Harvey had passed his 50 in 165 minutes. During the interval nobody could make up his mind who was going to win. Some said two to one against England, some said even money, few yet favoured England, but the first half-hour of the afternoon virtually settled the issue. Tyson and Statham began the bowling and the former bowled Archer in his second over. The ball fairly whipped back off the pitch and Australia, with four wickets to go, still needed 101 to win. One had lurking fears of Davidson and Lindwall, both of whom are highly inflammable drivers, and yet before Harvey could get at the bowling to shield and prepare them they had gone. Davidson was the victim of Evans's resilience, for he flicked at an outswinger and there was Evans throwing himself at the ball in front of first slip.

The crowd savoured the meeting of Tyson and Lindwall after Tuesday's accident and at 136 Tyson got ample revenge with his one stroke of luck to-day. He pitched one well up outside the off-stump and Lindwall, trying to chop it, dragged it on. Four times had Tyson hit the wickets and he deserved all the praise his colleagues gave him. But the game was by no means over yet, for it was now that Harvey began to rule it while he had the chance. He pulled Statham for four and hooked Tyson for three before losing Langley, bowled by Statham in trying to keep a half-volley out of his stumps with a shot of his own.

Surely all was as good as over and, one felt, Hutton thought so too when he called for drinks to let victory linger on the palate. Nor did Johnston do anything to destroy the feeling of exultation when he missed his first three balls and escaped an l.b.w. appeal off his fourth. These were the last four balls of Statham's over and 78 were needed with one last wicket to fall. But for 40 minutes Harvey and Johnston tortured all Englishmen present. In seven overs Johnston had only nine balls to face. For the rest Harvey played like a genius. He ran where there was no run and got

away with it. He hooked over Bailey's head at long leg when Bailey would have had a catch had he been where he should have been on the fence. He drove and he glanced and all the time Tyson and Statham were wearing themselves out.

Finally Bailey had to replace Statham, who had been playing an important part by bowling most gallantly into the wind for 85 minutes, and Harvey hit Bailey for two fours. Tyson, too, after 90 minutes' bowling since luncheon, was almost on his knees when at last he had Johnston before him on the first ball of an over. Johnston maddeningly hit a four one-handed to fine leg off the fourth ball but off the fifth he glanced a catch down the leg side to Evans and the umpire's finger was up.

THROUGH OTHER EYES

AUSTRALIAN PRAISE FOR ENGLAND

HIGH PRESSURE ATTACK

FROM AN AUSTRALIAN CORRESPONDENT

SYDNEY, DEC. 22

England beat Australia fairly and squarely because of Tyson's magnificent bowling, which has caused tremendous enthusiasm among all those who love skill and courage. Injured and practically carried off the field yesterday he was a matchwinner to-day; the merit of his superb bowling lies in the fact that, on a perfect pitch, he hit the stumps four times, and it has made him a hero throughout the country.

When Tyson sent back Burke and Hole in one over he set the Australians back on their heels and they never recovered. Harvey was batting so well that victory was there provided someone could stay with him, but no one could stay, simply because Tyson, splendidly supported by Statham, maintained a high-pressure attack, over after over.

Both showed how much they had learned because they attacked the off stump and kept the ball right up to the batsmen, giving them no peace, niggling at

them until finally they battered down the defences. It was superb bowling under conditions so admirably suited to batting that England can thank bowlers Tyson, Statham, and Bailey, and batsmen May and Cowdrey for victory. In saying that we must not overlook the last wicket stands in both innings, because last night Statham and Appleyard added 46 runs and the game was won by 38 runs.

Hutton deserves congratulations on the way he maintained the pressure. Once Tyson had put England on the attack, Hutton forced the issue. He used both Bailey and Appleyard for short periods, but he knew that the match winners were the two with extra speed, and wisely and convincingly he kept them on the job. It is interesting that once again the captain who sent the other side in to bat lost the match, but in this game it actually did not affect the result, for the pitch was always good and the match was won because of superiority on the field. There was no fluke about it and England's win in such a great match will do the game no end of good, besides assuring the complete success of the tour.

Australia missed Miller sadly and some changes for the third Test are inevitable, because the batting was unconvincing. For the present all Australians will give praise to England for the way they played and the way they won.

FINAL · SCORES

ENGLAND — First Innings

Hutton, c Davidson, b Johnston	30
T. E. Bailey, b Lindwall	0
P. B. H. May, c Johnston, b Archer	5
Graveney, c Favell, b Johnston	21
M. C. Cowdrey, c Langley, b Davidson	23
W. J. Edrich, c Benaud, b Archer	10
Tyson, b Lindwall	0
Evans, c Langley, b Archer	3
Wardle, c Burke, b Johnston	35
Appleyard, c Hole, b Davidson	8
Statham, not out	14
Extras (lb 5)	5
Total	**154**

Fall of wickets: 1-14, 2-19, 3-58, 4-63, 5-84, 6-85, 7-88, 8-99, 9-111, 10-154
Bowling: Lindwall 17-3-47-2, Archer 12-7-12-3, Davidson 12-3-34-2, Johnston 13.3-1-56-3

AUSTRALIA — First Innings

A. R. Morris, c Hutton, b Bailey	12
L. Favell, c Graveney, b Bailey	26
J. Burke, c Graveney, b Bailey	44
R. N. Harvey, c Cowdrey, b Tyson	12
G. B. Hole, b Tyson	12
R. Benaud, lbw, b Statham	20
R. Archer, c Hutton, b Tyson	49
A. K. Davidson, b Statham	20
R. R. Lindwall, c Evans, b Tyson	19
G. R. Langley, b Bailey	5
W. A. Johnston, not out	0
Extras (b 5, lb 2, nb 2)	9
Total	**228**

Fall of wickets: 1-18, 2-65, 3-100, 4-104, 5-122, 6-141, 7-193, 8-213, 9-224, 10-228
Bowling: Statham 18-1-83-2, Bailey 17.4-3-59-4, Tyson 13-2-45-4, Appleyard 7-1-32-0

ENGLAND — Second Innings

Hutton, c Benaud, b Johnston	28
T. E. Bailey, c Langley, b Archer	6
P. B. H. May, b Lindwall	104
Graveney, c Langley, b Johnston	0
M. C. Cowdrey, c Archer, b Benaud	54
W. J. Edrich, b Archer	29
Tyson, b Lindwall	9
Evans, c Lindwall, b Archer	4
Wardle, lbw, b Lindwall	8
Appleyard, not out	19
Statham, c Langley, b Johnston	25
Extras (lb 6, nb 4)	10
Total	**296**

Fall of wickets: 1-18, 2-55, 3-55, 4-171, 5-222, 6-232, 7-239, 8-249, 9-250, 10-296
Bowling: Lindwall 31-10-69-3, Archer 22-9-53-3, Johnston 19.3-2-70-3, Davidson 13-2-52-0, Benaud 19-3-42-1

AUSTRALIA — Second Innings

A. R. Morris, lbw, b Statham	10
L. Favell, c Edrich, b Tyson	16
J. Burke, b Tyson	14
R. N. Harvey, not out	92
G. B. Hole, b Tyson	0
R. Benaud, c Tyson, b Appleyard	12
R. Archer, b Tyson	6
A. K. Davidson, c Evans, b Statham	5
R. R. Lindwall, b Tyson	8
G. R. Langley, b Statham	0
W. A. Johnston, c Evans, b Tyson	11
Extras (lb 7, nb 3)	10
Total	**184**

Fall of wickets: 1-27, 2-34, 3-77, 4-77, 5-102, 6-122, 7-127, 8-136, 9-145, 10-184
Bowling: Statham 19-6-45-3, Tyson 18.4-1-85-6, Bailey 6-0-21-0, Appleyard 6-1-12-1, Wardle 4-2-11-0

·1956·

IT HAD BECOME CLEAR early in the summer that the Australians struggled against Jim Laker's off-spin. In their match against Surrey at the Oval, Laker, *right*, took all 10 wickets in an innings. By the time they arrived at Old Trafford for a rain-affected match they still had not learned. England began well with Peter Richardson and Rev David Sheppard scoring 104 and 113 respectively as the home side reached 459. Laker and Tony Lock removed Australian openers Colin McDonald and Jimmy Burke and then Laker took over, re-writing the record books in the

process. Laker destroyed the Australian batting from the Stretford End, taking the remaining eight wickets to finish with nine for 37. He ended the first innings with a 22-ball spell of seven for eight and the last nine batsmen managed a paltry 30 runs between them as Australia were all out for 84. In the second innings Laker went one better. He took 10 for 53 to finish with a match analysis of 19 for 90. McDonald was the only batsman to break the shackles with a defiant 89. When Laker had no. 11 Len Maddocks trapped lbw, only 33 minutes playing time remained.

Jim Laker became the toast of England when he dismissed Maddocks lbw for two, right, to take his 19th wicket in the Old Trafford Test and win the match. Controversy raged, however, over the state of the pitch.

ENGLAND'S FLYING START IN FOURTH TEST MATCH

---

307 FOR THREE ON PITCH ALREADY BEGINNING TO HELP BOWLERS

From Our Cricket Correspondent

Everything went right for England on the first day of the fourth Test match against Australia at Old Trafford, and by the end of it they had reached 307 for three wickets. That is not an unassailable position, but it is an immensely strong one, particularly as the pitch, even at this early stage, is not turning back its spin. Indeed, Laker and Lock must already feel a tingling in their fingers at the prospect of bowling on it later in the match, and England have reason to believe that their performance yesterday may be an important stride towards retaining the Ashes.

Perhaps as significant a moment as any during the day was when May, for the third time this season, won the toss. The wicket, contrary to expectations, had no semblance of life. It was, instead, a blissful place for batsmen as it was heartbreaking for bowlers, and England made the most of their good fortune by batting with unaccustomed skill and welcome success. Richardson and Cowdrey sent them away with a fine opening partnership of 174 in 190 minutes, which was the highest against Australia since Hutton and Barnett made 219 together at Nottingham in 1938. Before that only Hobbs and Rhodes, Hobbs and Sutcliffe, and Hayward and Jackson had made more for England's first wicket against Australia, so that England's pair of the present have moved into exalted company. When they were gone two more young amateurs carried on the stroke-play.

TRIBUTE JUSTIFIED

During the day there were as many as 37 4's and a 6, many of them classically executed, and it says much for Sheppard

Rev. David Sheppard, one of England's first innings centurions.

---

that his innings was as attractive as any. It was a tribute in the first place to choose him, and it is a reflection of his class that in his sixth innings of the summer he has already made 59 against Australia and is still in possession. It is not often that the opportunity comes of writing so generously of England's batting, and when

they or any other country do score 111 before luncheon and over 300 runs in a day, it calls for rejoicing.

But Australia bowled as indecisively as they can have done for a long while. They appeared downhearted that the pitch was so slow, and if, as seems likely, it crumbles within the next day or two, they will have grounds for feeling that the dice are loaded against them. Yesterday Laker and Lock would have got more from the turf than Benaud and Johnson because they have greater powers of spin. They might even have been unpleasant, but that is not really relevant. The point is, that in a Test match of five days in fine weather, the toss should not be all-important, and both sides in their first innings, at any rate, should expect to find similar conditions. Perhaps that may yet happen, but one doubts it.

WITHOUT PACE

The England selectors decided to omit Trueman. Weighing Trueman's value against Oakman's was an intricate business, but one look at the pitch seemed to justify the choice. Miller's gesture after bowling his first over certainly showed how he, for one, felt about it. It was a suggestion, if not of despair, at least of disappointment, for the pace about which there had been so much talk was nowhere to be found.

The bowlers had a job to make the ball rise much above the bails, the slips soon moved up a couple of steps, and, more important perhaps, there was dust flying away from the bowlers' marks. Much of the grass which was growing on Wednesday had been shaved away by the hand mower, and no great powers of far-sightedness were needed to recognize the possibility that the ball might be turning quite sharply by the weekend. After an hour Johnson himself made one or two deviate off the arid patches, and everyone must have realized how lucky England had been to win the toss.

Cowdrey and Richardson began at once to hit the ball with the middle of the bat, and soon the score was ticking along at a merry rate for a Test match. Miller, after a couple of rather lackadaisical overs bowled in a sweater, gave way to Archer, and

Lindwall tried in vain to entice something from the pitch. But there was not even any early moisture as encouragement or compensation, as there was at Leeds a fortnight ago. And the opening pair, when they knew that they were, as they say, in clover, quickly responded with some splendid strokes. In the first hour one remembers most of all a force for 4 off Archer which Cowdrey placed away between mid-wicket and mid-on, and a vivid cover drive by Richardson which lost none of its beauty for going straight to a fielder.

In 55 minutes 44 runs were made, and when Johnson himself and Benaud took over there was a burst of scoring. For a quarter of an hour these two simply could not find a length, and a spate of long hops and full pitches were gladly devoured by Cowdrey and Richardson. One, it is true, almost bowled Cowdrey as he hooked at it, and another went past Archer at slip, but in 17 minutes 31 were scored, and England's second 50 came in only 35 minutes.

Cowdrey went to 48 with a hook and an on-drive off successive balls from Benaud, and then, at five past one, he reached his 50 with a force to the leg boundary off Johnson. To those who have become used to prods and pushes at the start of a Test match, and even to English collapses, this was a rich and refreshing mixture, and by luncheon the total had reached 111. Richardson by then had also passed his third 50 of the series, but not before surviving what must be called a chance to the gully. He slashed at Archer, and the ball almost stuck in Benaud's right hand as he threw himself at it. Probably only someone with Benaud's remarkable reaction would have made a catch of it.

MAJESTIC CONTOURS

In the afternoon Richardson outstripped Cowdrey, who never again quite got into his stride. Now the Australians bowled better, and they set themselves to curb England's progress. During the morning Australia's cricket had been strangely dowdy, the bowling prodigal and without penetration, and England had revelled in it. Now Miller

moved round the wicket and sought to bring down Cowdrey by tempting him outside the off stump. Twice Cowdrey edged him past the gully as he drove with the face of the bat noticeably open, and once he mishooked Miller just in front of Craig, who was running in from long leg. But still Cowdrey retained his composure. There were no boastful gestures, only majestic contours and much natural elegance. The left-handed Richardson is smaller and less imposing, but he was batting extremely well, and again the two of them were missing nothing between the wickets.

Richardson swept Johnson twice for 4 in the first over after luncheon, and two drives off Lindwall and several forces off the back foot made a lovely noise as they came off his bat. He refused, too, to nibble at anything far outside his off stump, and there was no stopping him as he took the partnership past the 150 mark. The time was 160 minutes, and this although Cowdrey hereabouts was pinned on 67 for half an hour, with Johnson throwing his off breaks up wide of the wicket. Just when he was on the move again he was caught by Maddocks driving at Lindwall. Langley, incidentally, had, of all things, managed to aggravate his injured finger on Wednesday night by sleeping on it, and Maddocks had taken his place behind the stumps. Within half an hour he also had a hand in sending back Richardson.

MATURE TECHNIQUE

In the meantime Sheppard had made his appearance, and Richardson had experienced an enviable moment, the fulfilment of his first hundred against Australia. He jumped to 98 with a hook and a tickle off Benaud, but he was made to work hard for the last two which came eventually out of 191 after he had been batting for 218 minutes. When one saw him open the season with a century for Worcestershire against the Australians there were a good many rough edges, and he seemed to be dangerously fallible to the outswinger. Yesterday the maturity in technique and the confidence he has acquired since then were very marked, and

he has the application to go with them. One would say that after this innings, and certainly on easy wickets, he will make plenty of runs for England.

From England's point of view Richardson got out at an unfortunate moment, for when he edged an attempted cut the new ball was due in five runs time. Sheppard then was five and May had the rare pleasure of entering when the innings was soundly launched. Soon the new ball was safely behind him, and two hours later the two Cambridge Blues were still there. Until they had digested their tea they took things cautiously, May especially, but then they started to splay the ground with superb strokes. Sheppard, upstanding and right behind the line of the ball, banged Lindwall past Harvey at cover point, and he hooked Benaud and then stepped away and forced him mightily off the back foot.

ANGRY LEG BREAK

With an hour to go the 250 was hoisted, and Sheppard was making most of the running, but this was the signal for May to let go some wonderful drives off Archer and a number of shots off his legs which filled everyone with admiration. Sheppard, too, hooked Archer for 6 over square leg to take him to 50, and except when a leg break from Benaud spun angrily England were in complete command. It seemed that Sheppard and May would remain so until stumps were drawn, when suddenly, with 20 minutes left, May fell foul of a leg break from Benaud. It was one of those that fizzed off the pitch, May playing forward could not control it, and Archer making ground, took a high right-handed catch at slip.

It was decided now to send in Bailey, who had been sitting on the players' balcony during the morning with his pads on until the opening stand was well under way. The idea evidently was to call upon him in the event of an early wicket, but to use him now as a night watchman seemed perhaps unnecessarily cautious. Yet even he took to hitting boundaries, and doubtless he will return to-day with instructions to push things along so that England can drive home the great advantage they have won.

Day Two

The Manchester Guardian 28/7/56

AUSTRALIA HUMBLED

Laker's Great Bowling

FORECAST. — Cloudy, with chance of thundery rain or thunderstorms.

England : 459
Australia : 84 and 53 for one

By Denys Rowbotham

After tea at Old Trafford yesterday an excited crowd, again of over 30,000, witnessed one of the most remarkable collapses in the history of English and Australian Test cricket. In 35 minutes, after being 62 for two, the Australians lost their last eight wickets for 22 runs, Laker took seven of these wickets for eight runs, scarcely credible in 22 balls.

The stark result was that at 5.25 the Australians followed on 375 runs behind England's first-innings total. How incomprehensible and unexpected all this was the day's last 65 minutes showed. For though May did not call on Lock and Laker for some twenty minutes Australia had lost only one second-innings wicket, that of Harvey, at the close.

Some hint that the Australians might expect trouble was provided by Benaud and Johnson in the morning. For 45 minutes these two flighted the ball extremely well to a much more consistently accurate length than either had achieved on Thursday. Already Benaud's visible turn to the off, an occasional ball which popped or fizzed, and Johnson's ability now to turn his off-break from the Stretford end showed how quickly the wicket might be wearing.

Bailey, after first being reduced from driving to strict forward defence by Johnson's clever changes of rich flight and length, soon was out. Johnson flighted a ball beautifully to a length and Bailey, who had pushed forward, was bowled; he had played for the off-spin which did not come and so inside the ball.

SHEPPARD IN COMMAND

Hereafter, but for the same commanding batting with which Sheppard had delighted everyone on Thursday and a superb display of quick-footed, perky, but extremely judicious hitting by Evans, England might have floundered badly after her good start. For ten minutes after Bailey's dismissal Johnson, who had all but drawn Washbrook half-forward and across fatally to his first ball, now beat him comprehensively and had him leg before as he played back. This ball of full length turned sharply.

Johnson also was running an occasional ball away to the slips, much as South Africa's Tayfield did last summer, and in another fifteen minutes he trapped Oakman with this ball. Oakman twice had used his great height to drive Johnson, then pushed forward to a ball flighted just shorter which moved away from him, and was caught off the edge at slip.

So England was 339 for six and only the power of Sheppard's broad yet upright handsome off-driving, the quickness with which he jumped to drive wide of mid-on, and the violence of an occasional spacious hook had hinted of the authority which was England's on Thursday. Evans quickly changed all this. That even Sheppard more than once had been drawn forward by flighted balls which popped and turned and only just failed to find the edge of his bat hardly seemed to enter Evans's calculations. For these calculations were based on the use of feet which would move so quickly that no spin or pop, so long as judgement was accurate, would be left the time to operate.

For half an hour Evans's judgment did not err. He was beaten by the first ball Benaud bowled to him, to which perhaps absent-mindedly he pushed forward. Thereafter he did not push forward again. He turned Benaud for a single, lay back and square-cut Johnson for another, and then after Sheppard had square-cut Johnson and leaned forward and swept Benaud contumaciously, he launched his attack upon Johnson. He leaped at his and lofted him to mid-wicket. He danced forth again and clumped him straight to the sight-screen. He jumped and drove him for two further singles and then jumped and lofted Benaud straight for six. He turned a single, raced out once more to Benaud, and finding himself stranded, applied four-wheel brakes severely and skidded to a late cut for four.

Nothing, it seemed, could keep him still as he jumped and drove both bowlers, checked and turned them if he moved out too far and then cut them saucily each time they pitched short. He lofted Benaud for a second six—this time over the city end sight screen—and then cut him savagely for four the next ball. Though Johnson trapped him at last five minutes after this, he had made 47 out of 72 in half an hour.

He had also done something more. By quick footwork he had destroyed Benaud's strict control entirely and taken much of the threatening accuracy out of Johnson. So that though Laker was run out at five minutes to one the impassive Lock was able to defend with academic correctness and make more than one effective sweep and cut while Sheppard moved majestically to his century and England to a score of 449 at lunch.

AFTER THE FIREWORKS

Once Evans's fireworks were over, indeed, Sheppard settled with rare resolution to his work. Twice in succession he jumped and drove Johnson through the covers with shots of a vintage MacLaren would have recognised. Then he swept him four and drove him straight for two and reached his century with a late cut like an axe blow. Lindwall and Miller with the new ball tested somewhat his reflex actions and Archer finally bowled him after lunch when for a second time he tried to drive him. But Sheppard had done England proud and when he was out, and England's innings ended almost at once afterwards, the score of 459 looked good enough for the Ashes.

How good it was to look two and a half hours later could hardly be guessed at the time. Benaud had made a few balls lift and spin spitefully and Johnson sometimes had achieved a turn sharp of angle. But Evans had shown what quick footwork could smother and only fitfully had Sheppard's defence from a firmer back foot been really tested. Statham and Bailey, though more accurate, could win no more from the wicket than had Lindwall, and when first Laker and then Lock replaced them they did not tax Burke and McDonald more than Johnson and Benaud had taxed Sheppard and England's middle batsmen in the morning.

One thing, however, was surprising one. On this grassless wicket from which turn would come through wear on the bare reddish places May bowled Laker from Benaud's end and Lock from Johnson's end. This seemed like throwing away the good work of powdering that already had been done by bowlers of comparable spin. Certainly when May changed his bowlers round at four o'clock the whole character and temper changed with a stark suddenness scarcely credible. In Laker's second over a good length ball turned sharply and McDonald, who played forward, edged his shot and was snapped up by Lock at close fine-leg. Then in this same over Harvey played for off-spin and was bowled inside his forward shot by the ball Laker pushes through more quickly with his arm. Lock similarly was causing the ball to lift uneasily to Burke, whose forward shot now began for the first time to cock the ball forward.

Even so, Burke and Craig looked still confident, if now wary. Both were turning and driving neatly and compactly off their bodies and neither their demeanour nor the Australian score of 62 for two at tea prepared one for the avalanche that so quickly was to follow. It began indeed almost before one had swallowed one's last teacake. Lock's first ball after the interval popped like some spitting snake. Burke's half-cock shot could not avoid it and, quite helpless, he was caught at first slip. Laker's first ball beat Craig's back shot completely and he was palpably leg before wicket. Six men and Evans crouched like torturers round Mackay. Laker popped and turned again and Mackay was caught at wide second slip. Australia in two overs had become 62 for five.

TEAM PANIC

To write all down has taken longer than the happenings, and though these three wickets might have owed much to the wicket's vagaries what came next looked like the result of wholesale and perhaps unprecedented team panic. Miller lofted Lock straight away for six like a man certain his last moment was upon him; he lunged forward to Laker next over and it was. Benaud struck a huge blow at Laker and Statham judged the catch perfectly at long-on. Archer jumped to drive and Laker, who now was flighting the ball like some Machiavellian artist in temptation, had him stumped by several yards. And then, within ten minutes, Laker contrived to beat the forward shots of Maddocks and Johnson by stratagem or subtlety not discernible even to the expectant eye.

So the Australians somehow had got themselves out for 84 and lost their last eight wickets in something near record time. How unnecessary it was their last hour's resistance surely proved. For though May did not begin with Lock and Laker, both were bowling within roughly twenty minutes. Both, too, were turning the ball occasionally again with bite and lift. Yet until McDonald retired after half an hour with a knee injury suffered against Statham in the first innings neither he nor Burke had given England a chance. Organised back-footed and forward defence had stunned or smothered most balls bowled to them. With McDonald's retirement, however, a disaster did occur, for Harvey hit loosely at Laker's first full-toss and to his shame and chagrin hit straight to Cowdrey at mid-wicket. A pair of spectacles and Australia 28 for one.

But Burke now jumped and off-drove Laker royally and thereafter with Craig kept his head cool, his judgment sane, and his feet mobile enough not merely to survive until the close but to add in half an hour another 25 runs. So there should not be surrender without a struggle to-day. Even so should Burke go early Australia's middle and late batsmen will have to discover an organised technique, a capacity for swift and accurate judgment, and a coolness and phlegmatic outlook far different from that they showed yesterday if defeat is to be avoided to-day. So long as the weather holds this dry, bare wicket can become only more difficult.

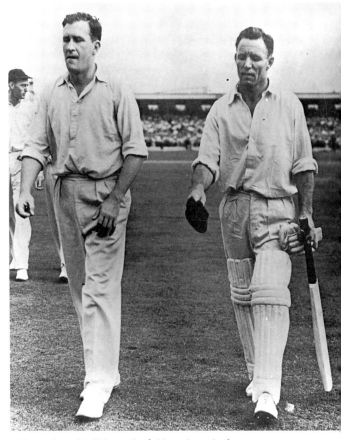

Laker and Lindwall leave the field at the end of Australia's first innings.

Test Wicket Condemned by Australian Press

Only 45 minutes' cricket was possible in the fourth Test Match at Old Trafford yesterday. In the 13 overs—10 of them maidens—bowled between ten past two and five to three, Australia scored six runs for the loss of Burke. During the lull, the state of the pitch is providing plenty of comment; many Australian papers yesterday carried protesting headlines.

ALAN ROSS says that despite the dust, "the fact remains that the present pitch has not played badly. England's score is not all that misleading.

"The fast bowlers had to be written off, but Laker has scarcely made a single ball lift, and Lock, reputedly the best bowler in the world on a powdery wicket, only very few.

"So far Lock has bowled 26 overs and taken one wicket for 50. That does not argue a graveyard."

The Australian Press takes a different view. Under the heading EXPLANATION CALLED FOR ON WICKET, Tom Goodman, writing in the influential Sydney Morning Herald, says: "There were derisive cries from pockets of Australians spread among the large crowd when groundsmen swept the pitch and dust arose in thick clouds."

He thinks Australia's team leaders would be "failing in their responsibility if they do not ask for an explanation concerning the state of this wicket."

Other Sydney headlines read:—

STIR OVER DOPED PITCH THEORY.—Sun.

PITCH TURNS TEST INTO FARCE—HONOURS TO U.K. ON FARCICAL WICKET.—Daily Mirror.

IT'S LAKER AGAIN—BATS COLLAPSE ON BAD PITCH.—Daily Telegraph.

All papers praise Laker, but most say the sudden deterioration in the pitch needs investigating. W. J. O'Reilly writes: "Let's have it straight—this pitch is a complete disgrace. What lies in store for Test cricket if the groundsmen are allowed to play the fool like this?"

The Telegraph's R. S. Whitington says: "This Old Trafford pitch is a disgrace to those who produced it or ordered it." Lindsay Hassett, the former Australian captain, says the wicket was unworthy of a county match, but adds: "Let us give England full credit for providing on a temporary wicket one of the most attractive batting exhibitions seen for many years in Test cricket."

The Real Trouble : Failure of Nerve

From ALAN ROSS

Old Trafford July 28

One has become accustomed now, at about the aperitif hour, to this ritual Saturday procession to the Test Match wickets, as if a major operation were about to take place.

The captains proceeding first as grave as surgeons; umpires like specialists in consultation behind them as though fearful of what examination might reveal; finally, the groundsman like an orderly awaiting their instructions.

Once at the pitch the prodding, undertaken with the ball of the thumb, begins. It is followed by closer visual scrutiny and depressions by the feet. If the pitch does not wince too audibly, the shaving process starts

HUSHED, RESPECTFUL

When completed, there is further laying on of hands, followed by a blanket bath, this morning's affair being particularly thorough. Next there is the formal disagreement between the captain-surgeons, further prolonged consultations between specialist-umpires, and finally, after agonising deliberations, a verdict.

The crowd, who were to-day allowed in to witness these preparatory manoeuvres, from time to time offer vocal encouragement, though generally their attitude is that of students in an operating theatre, their manner hushed and respectful.

This time the preliminary verdict, offered after an hour's contemplation at 1.30 p.m., was that a second diagnosis would be made at a quarter to two. At ten past two the operation eventually got under way.

Statham, in his opening over of the afternoon, bowled from the Stretford end under recognisable sun, hit Burke twice on the legs, the first time painfully striking the instep with a full pitch.

Lock, from the railway, began with two maidens to Craig and was then replaced by Bailey, off whom after 20 minutes Craig scored the first run. At twenty to three Laker took over from Statham, using three short legs, no slip and the rest of the field fairly deep. Burke immediately made an optimistic appeal against the light, which was rejected, and in the same over played an off-break stiffly and gently into Lock's hands at leg-slip. McDonald, continuing his overnight innings, lay back and cut Laker to the cover boundary, a stroke better than almost any played by an Australian yesterday.

Rain now came bustling up very fast out of a deluding sky, and in no time at all the water on the wicket was as clearly defined as on the Manchester Canal and about as muddy. The ground flooded, and a sizable crowd returned to Old Trafford railway station as quickly as it had hurried in after lunch.

NO HEART, NO SKILL

The match, which from the start has not been a happy one, has therefore made little progress. Since 1905, no Test between England and Australia has resulted in a win for either side at Old Trafford, and whether the present one can break that gloomy record remains to be seen. Certainly, on their showing so far, Australia do not deserve to escape: since making their disappointment at the wicket plain from the start, they have since scarcely bothered to put a face on it.

One has a right to expect from Test cricketers a certain degree of adaptability; the Australian batting during their brief innings on Friday night was bereft of all heart and skill.

The slowness of the pitch and its early dustiness were patently miscalculated: too much grass had been taken off it and it was from the beginning devoid of natural juice. The fast bowlers in turn showed it to hold nothing for them, and for Johnson, whose attack is essentially a pace one, losing the toss was a serious business.

Fortunately, cricket is not a game in which precise conditions can ever be stipulated, so that ill-balanced sides, able to perform only when weather and wicket are perfect, cannot hope to get away with it indefinitely against more versatile opponents.

TURF CONSULTANTS

Wickets on which a player like Mackay, by holding his bat straight and barely moving it, can bat for many hours, and

even score runs, make nonsense of cricket as an art form. If one is going to discount completely its more subtle skills and graces, then let wickets be specially prepared by turf consultants to a uniform specification, and transported to all Test match grounds in suitable containers.

From lunchtime on Thursday the wicket had taken a certain amount of spin. Between the innings, the dust brushed off

Laker in action.

it was like a storm in the Sahara. No one could pretend that this was ideal: but preparing wickets is not an exact science, and until it is one has to deal in approximations.

The Australians, unfortunately, set off on the wrong foot. Their bowling, that of the spinners especially, was extraordinarily untidy on Thursday, and once the runs began to come they showed a definite decline in spirit. But fielding was of a high standard, and on Friday Johnson found something like his best form.

But by then it was too late. The subsequent Australian collapse to Laker was a psychological one, a pure failure of nerve.

DESPAIRING SWINGS

Technically, the Australian batting has been extremely bad, veering between timid back play that allowed the spin its full value and despairing swings.

It is not unfair to suggest that an average English county side would have backed itself to make 250 runs in similar conditions. Burke was rarely in trouble and McDonald, until playing a careless stroke, looked full of runs. The remainder took their fate for granted.

England, of course, were particularly suited to the conditions. But, for once, we have bowlers equally capable of using any given wicket; and since the selectors have stuck to the expedient principle of picking each team for the match in question, and of pinning their faith in class batsmen, whether in full practice or not, the batting, too, has acquired a width and distinction it has not possessed since the war.

Australians were commonly supposed to be immune to the off-spinner, but obviously they are now more at the mercy of the ball that turns into them than the one that leaves them.

INADEQUATE

The truth is that since Hutton, setting complete store by Tyson and Statham in Australia, succeeded with an all-pace attack, the Australian selectors, not unnaturally banking on England being largely dependent on these two again, have laid their plans accordingly.

Conditional to this, with no spin bowler approaching the O'Reilly, Grimmett, or for that matter Laker-Lock, class, they had small choice in the matter.

However one looks at it, the defects of the wicket have been relative to the Australians' own inadequacy. On it, England made one of their largest Test scores for a long while, and, in doing so, showed how correct technique, based on forward play with the head down and the proper movement of the feet towards the pitch of the ball, can take care of most of the ball's movement, after it has pitched.

The batting of May and Sheppard was of rare quality, and that of Cowdrey and Richardson, in easier circumstances, full of fluency and character.

Evans has, literally by leaps and bounds, asserted that when there is a good score already on the board and the temperature is right, you cannot keep the cork in the bottle.

Day Four

The Times
31/7/56

OLD TRAFFORD FRUSTRATION

ONE HOUR'S PLAY IN FOURTH TEST

ENGLAND NO NEARER

FROM OUR CRICKET CORRESPONDENT

England approached no nearer to victory on the penultimate day of the fourth Test match against Australia at Old Trafford yesterday.

In wild and raving weather only an hour's play was possible, and during this time McDonald and Craig added a further 25 runs without undue difficulty. It was as though someone had arranged a game of cricket in mid-winter, with a few spectators huddled miserably in their seats and clinging frantically to their hats. Not surprisingly the play was comparably unrealistic, and England in their frustration must feel that this is a match which they are not ordained to win.

Through the weekend the thunder had roared, the rain streamed down, and yesterday morning as the wind howled round the city of Manchester there seemed little chance of any play at all. From time to time great storms kept bursting over the ground, yet amazingly enough the pitch was sufficiently dry for action to begin at a quarter to three.

All kinds of paraphernalia had been used to make this possible. The gale, too, had helped, and for England it was far better to bowl on a pudding and from loose footholds than not to bowl at all. They had everything to gain and nothing to lose, and there were those who thought the ball might turn.

SLOW TO RESPOND

But it seems that a pitch which has been dried artificially is slow to respond to spin. It was so at Trent Bridge, and again at Headingley, and yesterday Laker and Lock found that their teeth were drawn. Bailey and Statham, for their part, tried in

Old Trafford was no match for the "wild and raving weather."

vain to make the ball lift, and the result was that in the two periods of play there were only two false strokes. Both were by Craig and both off Lock, the first passing just wide of Bailey at backward short leg and the second piercing the gap between the wicketkeeper and first slip.

Perhaps if the rain had held off once the game had begun, the pitch by evening might have been lending a hand to spin. But it was too much to hope that every dark cloud would avoid the ground, and one came to stop play soon after McDonald, at 25 past three, had appealed against the general conditions, which must have been thoroughly unpleasant for batting. That was when the score was 77 for two, and by the time the players were out again, at 10 past four, tea had already been taken.

A quarter of an hour later everyone was scurrying back to the pavilion, and the specially loaded bails used to defy the wind were taken off for the last time. Craig then had batted admirably for 134 minutes, McDonald for 110, and if and when they go out this morning they will be embarking on the fourth playing day of their innings, for both took strike as long ago as Friday evening. Since then England have been able to capture only one more wicket, but they are still as well placed as they were before the last day at Headingley.

Then Australia had also lost two second innings wickets, but the weather there was less unsettled. To-day it may need only a couple of showers which are forecast to rescue Australia and drown the game once and for all.

Day Five

Daily Telegraph & Morning Post

1/8/56

Fourth Test Victory

LAKER TAKES 19 WICKETS FOR 90 RUNS

Australia Beaten by Innings and 170 : Long McDonald-Craig Stand

From E. W. SWANTON

OLD TRAFFORD, Tuesday

For many nervous hours since last Friday evening it has seemed that England would be robbed of victory in the Fourth Test match.

But Manchester expiated its sins of weather this afternoon, and it was in bright sunshine tempering the wind that the game ended in an innings win, which meant the safe-keeping of the Ashes until M.C.C. next sail in their defence two years from now.

The only proper formal announcement of the result is that J. C. Laker defeated Australia by an innings and 170 runs. Unprecedented things are always happening in cricket because it is so charmingly unpredictable a pastime. But now and then occurs something of which one feels certain there can be no repetition or bettering.

Laker followed his capture of nine first innings wickets with all 10 in the second. What is left in the vocabulary to describe and applaud such a tour de force? It is quite fabulous.

Once at Johannesburg on the mat, S. F. Barnes, still happily with us at a ripe 83, took 17 for 159. That analysis topped the list in Test matches until this evening—when Laker, wheeling relentlessly on, left the statistical gentry without another comparison to make or another record to be knocked down.

Hedley Verity took 15 for 104 after the thunderstorm at Lord's in '34. Wilfrid Rhodes, another old hero still listening to the play, even if he cannot now see it, got a like number at Melbourne half a century ago.

In the recent past, Alec Bedser got out 14 Australians for 90 at Trent Bridge on their last visit. Great figures. Great deeds.

But Laker in 51.2 overs has added a ten for 53 to his ten for 88 against this same Australian side for Surrey. And in this Test he has actually taken 19 for 90.

NON-STOP BOWLING
Always Attacking

Laker's first innings performance was phenomenal enough, but its merit was perhaps clouded by the deficiencies of the Australian batting, as also by the palaver over the condition of the wicket.

There was no room whatever for argument regarding his bowling today. He bowled 36 overs, practically non-stop except for the taking of the new ball, all the time attacking the stumps and compelling the batsman to play, never wilting or falling short in terms either of length or direction.

Nor was he mechanical. Each ball presented the batsman with a separate problem. Laker never let up and neither for an instant could his adversary.

LOCK TOILS ON

It is, of course, scarcely less remarkable that while Laker was building up new heights of fame at one end Lock was toiling just as zealously, albeit fruitlessly, at the other. On a wicket on which one famous cricketer captured 19 wickets the other, scarcely less successful and

dangerous, taking one day with another, in 69 overs had one for 106.

Of course if the gods had been kind Lock could have taken more. He was not, in cold fact, at his best, and if he is suffering the reaction now from all his hard bowling in Pakistan it is not to be wondered at.

Still the comparison between figures is in one sense unarguable evidence of Laker's great performance. If the wicket had been such a natural graveyard for batsmen it is inconceivable that Lock, even below his peak, even with the other arm tied to his side, would not have taken more than one wicket.

APPLAUD McDONALD
Kept the Balance

Applause for Laker, and applause also in a scarcely lesser strain for McDonald, who, in his long vigil, rose to the occasion for Australia and fought as hard as any man could do to win his side the respite of a draw.

So long as McDonald was in the odds were still fairly balanced. When he was beaten at last directly after tea the latter-end batsmen carried on in the same spirit, and there was a bare hour to go when Maddocks, the number eleven, played back and slightly across to Laker, fell leg-before and advanced up the wicket to shake the hero by the hand.

One of the Australian party summed up the day, as the crowd that massed round the pavilion dispersed and Laker, glass in hand, had turned from the balcony to dressing-room by saying:

"Well, it was a good scrap after all." There was relief in his voice just as there was jubilation in the surrounding English faces.

SOUND DEFENCE
McDonald and Craig

The captains having formally disagreed, there was a delay of 10 minutes before play was continued this morning. The wicket was just about as sluggish as yesterday.

The weather, however, was not so violently unpleasant, for the wind, though still quite brisk, had dropped, and the clouds were higher with even a hint or two of blue sky.

McDonald and Craig, by high-class defensive play, withstood the session of an hour and 50 minutes without many moments of difficulty. They played themselves in against Bailey and Laker, who were subsequently relieved by Lock and Oakman.

Runs being of no object, except possibly to get the two batsmen to the ends they preferred, and the ball being hard to force away, the Test became one of the batsmen's concentration and judgment as to length.

TRIAL FOR OAKMAN
No Breaking Through

In this neither was found wanting, and it cannot be said that England much looked like breaking through. May gave Oakman a try, probably because from his unusual height he might get an off-spinner to lift.

He kept the ball well up on the off-side and induced some strokes off the front foot into the covers. Oakman, however, is not a digger-in, and is a relatively better bowler on a hard wicket.

May took the new ball as soon as he could, which was at a quarter to one. Bailey brought back one or two and found Craig's inside edge, and Statham and he perhaps held out slightly more hopes than the spinners.

Just before lunch Evans and Lock, those tireless propagandists, when the latter was bowling tried their hardest by expression and gesture to suggest that the dormant pitch was stirring. But McDonald and Craig came in calm and unscathed, having, incidentally, added 28 runs.

CRAIG GOES
Start of Collapse

There were early signs after lunch that the batsmanship might be more severely tested. Craig was twice beaten by lifting balls from Lock, who naturally enough was sharing the bowling with Laker.

After a quarter of an hour Craig went back to the latter and was lbw to an off-break. Thus he retired full of honour after an innings of four hours and 20 minutes,

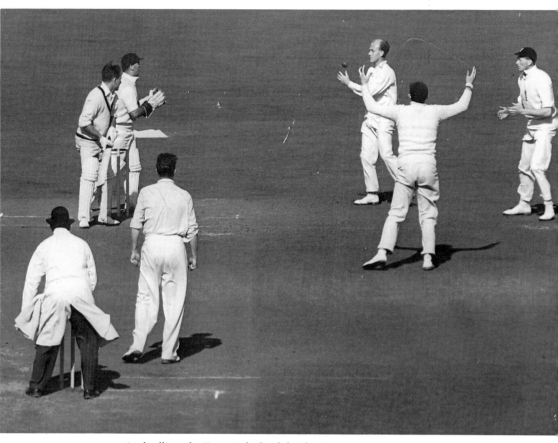

Lindwall caught Tony Lock, bowled Laker 8.

in which his stature had grown surely and steadily. The breaking of the stand was the signal for the second Australian collapse of the game. Within half an hour Mackay, Miller and Archer had all followed, all to Laker, and all for ducks.

Granted the ball was doing a little more during this phase in answer to bursts of sun, these batting failures underlined the worth and value of the third-wicket partnership. Where before the judgment of length and direction had been good enough to ensure a smooth, well-considered defensive stroke, now the new batsmen were floundering about and either using their pads or offering a last-minute jab.

SIX CLOSE FIELDERS
Mackay Encircled

Mackay was surrounded by slips, silly mid-off, and short-legs, six in all within a

five-yard radius. Once could hardly see how he could survive, for in going forward he plays so far in front of the front leg. This had been evident against the slow bowlers even while he was putting up his celebrated resistance at Lord's.

Now Mackay probed out, and edged a short sharp catch to Oakman, the middle of the slips. I have never seen a batsman whose value rose and fell so abruptly according to the state of the wicket. On a good one he wants blasting out. When the ball is doing anything it is hard to see how he can last five minutes.

As it was, Mackay to-day, like Harvey on Friday, bagged a pair.

One expected Miller to try to shift Laker's close leg fieldsmen as he had done at Leeds. Instead he seemed intent on fending away with the pads, using the bat only as a last resort. It was this manoeuvre which undid him, for he decided at the last moment he must put the bat to a yorker on the leg-stump, missed it, and was bowled.

It was an innings singularly out of character.

McDONALD LOOKS ON
From Lock's End

Laker had Archer pushing out at an off-break and steering it round the corner. McDonald, at the other end, steady and more or less serene, thus saw Australia's barometer drop from the healthy regions of 114 for two to 130 to six.

He himself, it so happened, during this phase was almost exclusively opposing Lock, who was giving him the chance to indulge his feelings every now and then with a short ball which was usually hit for runs.

Benaud now got stuck with McDonald, determination in every line, fastidious care also, for he took guard sometimes once or twice an over as though suspicious that Evans might have surreptitiously moved the position of the stumps.

Benaud also gardened assiduously, which was prudent enough, seeing that the ball was taking turf.

It earned him a little mildly derisory applause.

BOWLING SWITCHED
To No Avail

May did his best to scotch the threat of a McDonald-Benaud stand by changing round his main spinners, introducing Bailey and giving Oakman another spell which he was scarcely able to justify.

Benaud was nearly yorked by Bailey. However that was as near another wicket as anyone could come.

McDonald was seemingly impervious, immovable, and this pair came in to tea, having stayed together an hour and 20 minutes.

Australia were still breathing.

But McDonald did not take root afterwards and it was the inevitable Laker who got the most valuable wicket of all. This was a sharp off-break which for once went too quickly for McDonald, who edged it to the sure hands of Oakman in the middle position just behind square. So

ended a valiant effort lasting without a chance for more than five hours and a half.

AFTER BENAUD—
—a Swift End

Lindwall made a steady partner for Benaud and at 5 o'clock these two looked ominously settled and determined: there was still Johnson and Maddocks to come.

Laker, having taken 19 wickets in the match, leaves the field and enters history.

It was not yet "in the bag." But Benaud now went back where he might have gone forward and was bowled middle-and-off stumps or thereabouts.

Twenty minutes later Lindwall, like so many before him, fell in the leg-trap. Then, with Johnson looking on, Maddocks made his entry and speedy, gracious exit. So the game ended. The post-mortems no doubt will linger on. But whatever is added one thing cannot be gainsaid: Laker was magnificent.

FINAL · SCORES

ENGLAND — First Innings

P. E. Richardson, c Maddocks, b Benaud	104
M. C. Cowdrey, c Maddocks, b Lindwall	80
Rev. D. S. Sheppard, b Archer	113
P. B. H. May, c Archer, b Benaud	43
T. E. Bailey, b Johnson	20
C. Washbrook, lbw, b Johnson	6
A. S. M. Oakman, c Archer, b Johnson	10
T. G. Evans, st Maddocks, b Johnson	47
J. C. Laker, run out	3
G. A. R. Lock, not out	25
J. B Statham, c Maddocks, b Lindwall	0
Extras (b 2, lb 5, w 1)	8
Total	459

Fall of wickets: 1-174, 2-195, 3-288, 4-321, 5-327, 6-339, 7-401, 8-417, 9-458, 10-459
Bowling: Lindwall 21.3-6-63-2, Miller 21-6-41-0, Archer 22-6-73-1, Johnson 47-10-151-4, Benaud 47-17-123-2

AUSTRALIA — First Innings

C. C. McDonald, c Lock, b Laker	32
J. W. Burke, c Cowdrey, b Lock	22
R. N. Harvey, b Laker	0
I. D. Craig, lbw, b Laker	8
K. R. Miller, c Oakman, b Laker	6
K. Mackay, c Oakman, b Laker	0
R. G. Archer, st Evans, b Laker	6
R. Benaud, c Statham, b Laker	0
R. R. Lindwall, not out	6
I. Maddocks, b Laker	4
I. W. Johnson, b Laker	0
Total	84

Fall of wickets: 1-48, 2-48, 3-62, 4-62, 5-62, 6-73, 8-78, 9-84, 10-84
Bowling: Statham 6-3-6-0, Bailey 4-3-4-0, Laker 16.4-4-37-9, Lock 14-3-37-1

AUSTRALIA — Second Innings

C. C. McDonald, c Oakman, b Laker	89
J. W. Burke, c Lock, b Laker	33
R. N. Harvey, c Cowdrey, b Laker	0
I. D. Craig, lbw, b Laker	38
K. Mackay, c Oakman, b Laker	0
K. R. Miller, b Laker	0
R. G. Archer, c Oakman, b Laker	0
R. Benaud, b Laker	18
R. R. Lindwall, c Lock, b Laker	8
I. W. Johnson, not out	1
L. Maddocks, lbw, b Laker	2
Extras (b 12, lb 4)	16
Total	205

Fall of wickets: 1-28, 2-55, 3-114, 4-124, 5-130, 6-130, 7-181, 8-198, 9-203, 10-205
Bowling: Statham 16-9-13-0, Bailey 20-8-31-0, Laker 51.2-23-53-10, Lock 53-30-69-0, Oakman 8-3-21-0

·1960·

THE START OF A MAGNIFICENT series could not have been more exciting with the Brisbane meeting resulting in the first ever Test tie. Garfield Sobers put West Indies in a commanding position with 132 out of 453, Alan Davidson taking five wickets. Australia's reply was even more impressive, Norm O'Neill (181) and Bob Simpson (92) helping the home side reach 505. Davidson followed up his five wickets in the first innings by taking six for 87 in the second as West Indies slumped to 284. Australia needed 233 to win in 310 minutes but at 57 for five the target looked beyond

them. When captain Richie Benaud joined Davidson at the crease the instructions were to go for victory. They took the score to 226, when Davidson was run out by Joe Solomon for 80. When the last over began they needed six runs. When Benaud tried to get them in one stroke Wes Hall, *left*, took his fifth wicket. Wally Grout was run out off the fourth ball going for the winning run. Lindsay Kline arrived, nudged what looked like the all-important single but Ian Meckiff was run out by Solomon, fielding at square leg and with only one stump to aim at, to tie the match.

The moment a Test was tied. Ian Meckiff, stretching for the winning run, is beaten by
Joe Solomon's direct hit.

Day One

The Sydney
Morning
Herald

10/12/60

BRISBANE, Friday

The West Indies had one of their finest days ever in cricket when they scored 359 runs with a loss of seven wickets against Australia in the first Test at Brisbane Cricket Ground today.

This was a golden day of golden batting—a day made memorable for many lucky people by the handsome and commanding batting by young Garfield Sobers and his veteran partner, Frank Worrell.

Sobers, a 24-year-old left-hander, played one of the greatest Test innings of our time.

Australia will need a good start in the attempt to gain a substantial first-innings lead to compensate for possible last use of a pitch that is likely to take more spin as the match, scheduled for five days, advances.

Sobers scored 132 runs (21 fours) in just under three hours, having reached his first century against Australia and his tenth in Test cricket, in 125 minutes.

His 100 included 15 fours.

Sobers' batting was distinguished by brilliant stroke play and remarkable power.

Sobers and his 36-year-old captain Frank Worrell, who scored 65, shared in a near-record fourth wicket stand of 174 runs in 152 minutes after the West Indies had lost their first three wickets for 65.

Even with the early setbacks, the West Indians scored 130 runs in the two-hour session before lunch.

They followed with 142 runs in the two hours between lunch and tea.

MAJESTIC

This was really remarkable going.

Aided by a fast outfield, the West Indians hit 48 fours plus a six by young left-hander Peter Lashley—198 runs in boundary shots.

The crowd of 10,678 feasted on the great batting of Sobers and his majestic partner Worrell.

Even the perspiring Australian bowlers, and the fieldsmen with hands sore from stopping—or trying to stop—powerful strokes, voted it a "wonderful day's cricket."

SOBERS MASTERLY IN SCORING 132 DURING "GOLDEN DAY OF GOLDEN CRICKET"

From TOM GOODMAN

Frank Worrell - power and majesty.

They were unstinted in their praise of Sobers.

Worrell played a thoroughly admirable part.

TROD WICKET

He brought discipline into the batting and steadied Sobers at a crucial stage of the innings after two of his early batsmen, Conrad Hunte (24) and Rohan Kanhai (15) had been caught off rash strokes.

Sobers and Worrell had been dismissed within seven minutes of each other, soon after 3 o'clock.

Then little Joe Solomon from British Guiana, playing his first Test against Australia, batted most creditably to reach 65 and help consolidate the position.

Solomon was out, unluckily, six minutes before "stumps".

In playing a forcing shot to square leg off spinner Bobby Simpson, he trod on his wicket and dislodged a bail.

Wicketkeeper Gerry Alexander, who had shown unusual restraint for an hour and three-quarters, will resume tomorrow with Sonny Ramadhin.

Ramadhin hit Lindsay Kline's last ball of the day to the boundary.

OUTSTANDING

Heavyweight Alexander could do some damage to the Australian attack if he gets another start tomorrow.

Alan Davidson, who captured the first three wickets at a cost to him of 33 runs off six overs, finished 4/102.

He did a big share of the toil with 22 overs, and was the outstanding bowler.

But the other fast left-hander, Ian Meckiff, was most disappointing.

He failed to produce his top pace—he is just not thumping down that extra fast ball, the fairness of which some English observers used to query.

Meckiff had some ragged overs.

He was very lucky to claim the wicket of Sobers with a dreadful full toss, outside the leg stump, at a stage when skipper Richie Benaud was ready to take him off.

The ball, hit too softly, flew from the top edge of Sobers' bat and was easily caught by Kline near the square leg umpire.

Garfield Sobers scored 132 in a fourth wicket stand of 174 with his captain, Worrell.

Kline, preferred by the selectors to Johnny Martin in the final Eleven, showed fairly good control, although Sobers pelted him as well as the others.

Benaud, who found it difficult to counter Sobers, came through the ordeal of 19 overs with no sign of his recent throat infection.

The pitch, perhaps because of some lingering moisture, showed some variation in height in the early stages.

Davidson made some balls lift off a good length. But the pitch soon became easy in pace. The sun shone warmly.

THREE "W'S"

Garfield St. Auburn Sobers, from the little island of Barbados which produced the West Indies famous three "W's",

thoroughly established himself in Australian eyes with his magnificent batting which followed a recent unlucky period.

Sobers' only other score of note on this tour was 119 against Western Australia.

His previous highest score against Australia was 64 at Kingston (Jamaica) in 1955, when he was 18.

He and Clyde Walcott then had a fourth wicket partnership of 179 runs—the best for that wicket for West Indies against Australia.

Sobers and Worrell today failed by only five runs to equal that stand.

Sobers' big performance in Test cricket came with a rush after he had turned 21.

He holds the Test record with a score of 365 not out against Pakistan.

OFTEN DARING

He is now playing his 33rd Test against all countries, and with today's innings, he has aggregated 3,052 runs.

We will be seeing a lot more of this coffee-coloured young man of medium height and we will be grateful for it.

His stroke play today was often daring, often elegant: he placed the ball extremely well, and, with perfect timing, imparted great power.

He made only two dangerous false strokes—an edge off Davidson early past fourth slip, and another edge off the same bowler when 128.

One will remember forcing shots past point and some terrific straight-drives off Benaud.

Day Two

The Sydney Morning Herald

12/12/60

TEST IS OPEN

First Few Hours Will Be Crucial For Aust.

From TOM GOODMAN

BRISBANE, Sunday.—The first hour's play tomorrow will be a crucial period in the first Test, which is proving a remarkable match.

The West Indies have taken the honours of two days' play.

But their captain, Frank Worrell, says the match is "wide open."

Worrell said tonight: "We will know more about it at the close of play on Monday.

"If the Australians manage to bat all day they will have relieved their position considerably. Our job is to get them out—and we will be straining to do that tomorrow."

Three days remain for play. Australia, facing the West Indies' grand first-innings score of 453, have 196 runs up for three wickets, having lost Colin McDonald, 57, Neil Harvey, 15, and Bobby Simpson, 92.

Norman O'Neill, 28, and Les Favell, will resume their fourth-wicket partnership at 11 a.m. tomorrow. They will seek to counter the hazards of express bowler Wesley Hall with the new ball and with the help of a slight ridge at the southern end of the pitch, which yesterday helped first Australia's Alan Davidson and later Hall to "lift" the ball from a good length.

Australian batsmen have so far faced up rather grimly to their big task of overhauling the West Indies' score and obtaining a substantial lead to counter the possible disadvantage of last use of the pitch.

DRIER PITCH

But if the new ball (due when four more runs have been scored) is survived by O'Neill and Favell, these batsmen, with strong support to follow, should set about building up the score.

Worrell admits that apart from his trump card, Hall, much of the West Indies bowling yesterday was aimed at retarding scoring with, as play advanced, accompanying field placing.

The pitch has not yet offered any distinct help for spin.

But as the warm sunny weather continues the pitch will be getting drier. By tea time tomorrow the players should be able to judge whether the strip is likely to disintegrate.

Wesley Hall remains Australia's number one menace. His figures are 0-51 but with his sustained hostility he had a profound effect, physical and psychological, on our batsmen yesterday.

That slight ridge on the pitch was enough to make him dangerous; he cracked Colin McDonald in the region of the heart with two balls—one of good length, the other shortish.

Mainly through their influence, particularly their enterprising batting capped by Kanhai's double century of sustained brilliance against Victoria and the classical partnership of Sobers and Worrell in this Test, cricket in the Australian summer has turned the corner.

Their batting in this match went deeper than they expected, what with number 10 man Hall cracking up 50 runs to supplement the grand 60 by staunch wicketkeeper Gerry Alexander.

BIG ASSET

Their bowling and fielding do not match their batting. But the excellent bowling form of left-hander Sobers yesterday caused their team leaders to cast off any doubts they may have had about their deletion of the second fast bowler, Chester Watson, from this match on a pitch lacking real pace.

Australia's depth in batting—it carries a wealth of experience—could be a big asset in the ensuing hours of play, more so if

Wesley Hall scored a valuable 50 and finished the match with nine wickets.

O'Neill and Favell really get going. These two are capable of carving up an attack—but first they must get Hall out of the firing line.

Already the Australian selectors have been given some food for thought.

Primarily, there has been Ian Meckiff's lack of dash and consequent loss of confidence. He bowled badly here in the First Test against England but he was faster

Colin McDonald, hit on the chest by Hall, recovered to score 57.

then than he is now.

He is just not in form and therefore is below true Test quality. Too much concentration on purity of delivery?

The selectors will be interested in the significance of Gordon Rorke having been given by Ian Craig only six overs against Western Australia in Sydney, whereas Frank Misson had 14 overs.

Misson could be on the fringe of Test selection; certainly he must be on the list of possibles for the English tour next year.

FIRST TEST IS IN THE BALANCE

Fighting Innings by Norman O'Neill

From Percy Beames

BRISBANE, Monday

The fate of the first Test between Australia and the West Indies is delicately poised—luck could easily swing the result either way—but, at present, the most likely result is a draw.

Australia nearly gained control when Norm O'Neill turned on a fighting marathon batting performance to defy the attack for just on seven hours before he was caught for 181 runs.

The last Australian dismissed, O'Neill's fighting innings was the main factor in the side scoring 505 to gain a first-innings lead of 52 runs.

Only two balls were delivered by Alan Davidson when the West Indies began their second innings.

After the second delivery umpires upheld an appeal against the light by Conrad Hunte and play ended at 5.25 p.m.

West Indies captain Frank Worrell said the pitch was still pretty good and he thought a lot more runs would be scored.

So far, there has been no evidence of spots wearing to allow the spinners to come into their own.

In the whole day's play yesterday there were no more than half a dozen deliveries that turned to any appreciable extent, and only one of these did damage.

The unlucky batsman was Ken Mackay, when a ball from Sobers spun around his bat and he was bowled.

Technically, O'Neill's innings was anything but a great one.

It lacked aggressiveness and power, and was further blemished when luck played its part in allowing chances to slip through the fingers of fieldsmen.

O'Neill was lucky also when a ball rolled on to the leg stump without dislodging the bail and, on occasions, when he slashed at balls outside the off-stump without making contact.

However, in value, it was without doubt the most valuable he has played for Australia.

Previous to now, O'Neill has batted with the outlook of a young, enthusiastic boy, who delighted in hitting the ball to every part of the field with gay abandon and power.

Today he showed himself as a mature, remorseless gatherer of runs—a batsman who no longer gives thought to providing entertainment.

How well he succeeded was proved in that he stayed until the last man, Lindsay Kline, came in before finally sacrificing his wicket.

He was easily caught at mid-off when he swung wildly at Wesley Hall.

FIRST TEST

It was his first Test century in Australia and his fourth in Test cricket.

Last year, when he toured with Australia, O'Neill made a century against Pakistan and two against India.

He has made more than 1000 runs in Test cricket.

First lucky break O'Neill enjoyed was on 47, when he cut Worrell hard to the right hand of Gary Sobers at first slip and the catch was dropped.

Five runs later he tried to sweep Sobers to the leg fence, missed and the ball rolled from his body and lodged against the leg stump.

Another two runs later he chased a ball from Valentine outside the off stump,

West Indies 'keeper Gerry Alexander drops Norman O'Neill on 57 off Alf Valentine.

intending to crack it hard past point, but merely touched it.

Wicketkeeper Gerry Alexander juggled the catch, but to the consternation of every West Indian player, he dropped the ball.

LATE CHANGE

Possibly to offset these lucky breaks a little, the game did swing rather

dramatically in the last 36 minutes of play.

Australia, with Alan Davidson giving O'Neill grand support, had passed the West Indies' 453 total with five wickets in hand.

After the tea adjournment Frank Worrell took the new ball and gave it to Hall, who had badly disappointed earlier in the day with his new-ball bowling.

When he began the day, Hall found he could not hold the ball comfortably because of perspiration.

He lost confidence and his erratic, listless efforts in five overs cost 37 runs.

He bowled better when he began his after-tea spell, but even so did not promise much until, with the Australian score at 469 and holding promise of reaching 600, Davidson played carelessly and was caught behind.

From that point, things ran against Australia and in 36 minutes five wickets crashed for the addition of only 36 runs.

Hall's final figures were 4/140, having captured the wickets of O'Neill, Davidson, Benaud and Grout.

However despite his final spell, Hall was still far below his best and there was nothing fearsome about his speed.

STRAIGHT BALL

Benaud, who became Hall's second victim, simply missed a straight ball, and Grout walked right in front of his wicket when trying to turn a straight ball down to fine leg.

The other wicket to fall was Ian

Meckiff, who was beaten by a good throw from the field when taking a run without worrying much about the return.

The bowler who was one of the West Indies' most dangerous was Frank Worrell, who had both O'Neill and Mackay dropped.

It is not easy to induce Mackay to hang out his bat at a ball outside the off-stump when it is bowled with the intention of

The combined efforts of Alexander and Conrad Hunte are not enough to dismiss Ken Mackay.

providing a catch to the wicketkeeper or the slips, but Worrell managed to do so.

Mackay snicked the catch, but Alexander flung himself in front of Hunte, at first slip, and grassed the chance.

Fortunately, Sobers then came to the side's rescue one run later and repaired the damage.

Worrell Accurate

Worrell bowled with sustained accuracy, good direction, subtle change of pace, and every now and again managed to wring a little more spin than expected from the pitch.

His greatest problem was that, with Hall unable to work up to any aggressive mood, there was no other bowler in whom he could place much faith.

PARTNERSHIP

Valentine might have been the man had he kept the ball up to the batsman all

day and, more important still, had he bowled over and not around the wicket in concentrating on an offside field.

Australia's overnight position, 3/196, had been given a much healthier look by the time the O'Neill-Favell partnership was broken.

This happened after 84 runs had been added in 93 minutes, with Favell contributing 45.

Favell was not the confident, aggressive batsman so often seen when batting for South Australia but rather an edgy batsman seemingly worried by the fear of failure. But his worst show of nerves came later when facing Valentine after reaching 33.

Twice he went down the pitch and swung straight and hard to lift the slow bowler over the fence in successive balls.

They were fine, powerful hits, but obviously betrayed the anxiety and tension Favell had built up in himself.

Next ball he pushed Valentine towards square leg, and dashed down the pitch. O'Neill stayed his ground and sent Favell back, but it was ruled by Umpire Hoy that Favell had failed to beat Ramadhin's return.

Meanwhile O'Neill had reached his 50 in 148 minutes, with six fours. It was a slow half-century for O'Neill.

Mackay, who took over from Favell, looked a more assured player, but without once recalling the stroke player of the Queensland game, when he made 173.

By the time he left, bowled by Sobers, Australia's score had moved on to 381, with O'Neill on 127. When he did score, it was not because of any creative stroke play, but simply a straight-out case of taking toll of the poor ball.

O'Neill had been batting 235 minutes and had hit 15 fours when he reached his century. Most of his boundaries were from shots in front of or behind point, or strong pulls.

Only occasionally did he take any license with the drive—in previous years one of his chief batting strengths.

Davidson, who came in with the score at 5/489, without question overshadowed both Mackay and Favell.

Soon after he began batting he had to face Hall, but neither this nor the fact the fast bowler had the new ball, worried him.

O'Neill had passed his 150 in 326 minutes, with 20 fours, and was 169 when Davidson left. After that he got little of the strike, for wickets tumbled with unexpected suddenness. It was a pity his innings ended as it did, for he thoroughly deserved to finish unconquered.

But his willingness to throw his wicket away at the end merely emphasised what his batting had shown all day—that the interests of his side were his first consideration.

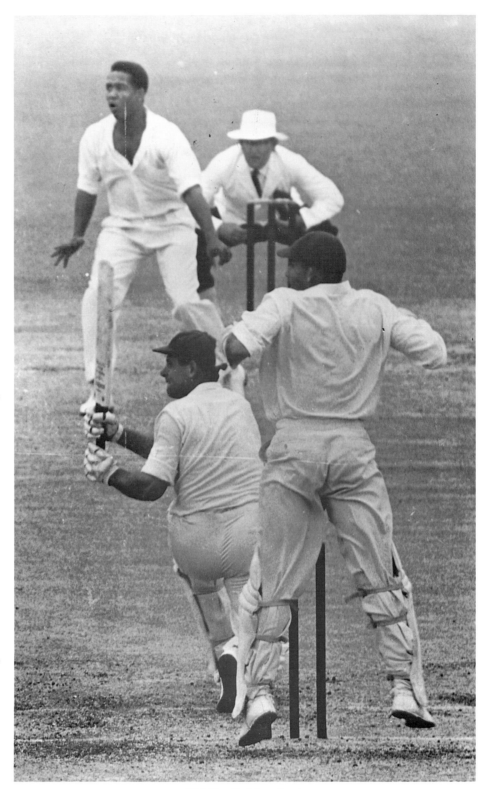

O'Neill pulls Sobers for 4.

Day Four

Barbados Advocate

14/12/60

Caribbean boys make heavy weather of Australia attack

1st test victory beckons Aussies
... But Hall capable of upsetting 'apple-cart'

BRISBANE, Tuesday.

Australia begin the last day of the first test with victory beckoning as they have only 207 to chase plus whatever the West Indies last pair can add.

Nothing in the behaviour of the wicket gives the ground for belief that West Indian spinners can get enough help to fiddle Australia out cheaply. But the possibility of a dramatic breakthrough by speedman Wesley Hall remains despite his high quota of misdirected balls in the first innings.

Hall, whom the crowd cheered in recognition of Saturday's half-century, is nought not out but bowlers will have first shot at Alf Valentine the world's most vulnerable tailender.

With two bowlers unfit (Meckiff strained ankle, Kline sore back) and injured batsman McDonald resting his bruised chest, the Australians were cracking up quicker than the pitch. I suspect Meckiff has nursed his trouble throughout the match and it has affected his bowling more than any change which English critics imagine they see in his arm action.

On shoulders designed by nature for the task, left-hand Alan Davidson carried the burden of attack so manfully through 160 balls today that five more wickets take his tally to 10 for the match.

Leg-spinner Richie Benaud, still taking tablets to clear up a throat infection, never ceases trying but had to wait until his 24th over before his quicker flipper surprised his first victim.

Davidson loosed an inswinger of unplayable lateness to fling down the pillar of West Indies innings captain Frank Worrell, whose fine 65 is his sixth consecutive half-century on Australian wickets.

I again admired the steadfastness of Joe

Sobers is yorked by Alan Davidson for 14 in West Indies' second innings.

Solomon, 47, in barring Australian progress at one end for nearly four hours.

In mid-afternoon Worrell took off his cap not to the bowler, but to brush from the pitch a loose scrap of turf from their bootscrapers. The Skipper was concerned lest scraps affect the bounce of the ball from Australian spinners.

After this impromptu housewifely act Frankie shook the dust from his burgundy cap and replaced it on a head which he kept down to the task of saving the side from slipping into a losing position. The tidier end of the pitch was more dangerous. It was there that the first six wickets fell to the seamer—five of them to Davidson.

SECOND TIME

For the second time in the match Kanhai 54 chased the left-hander's outswinger far outside the off stump and edged a catch to wicketkeeper Grout.

A yorker which got through lefthander Garry Sobers (14) knocked West Indies hopes much harder than it did the stumps. Davidson's late inswinger with the new ball at 210 seemed to find the inside edge of Worrell's bat making Grout move to his left to hold his sixth catch of the match—his fifth off Davidson.

The left-hander swung one the opposite way to bowl left-hander Peter Lashley for 0.

In many overs today West Indians had to score against tighter field placing than Benaud had used in the first innings. I thought the changes were primarily to cope with each batsman's strength and weakness in accordance with the state of the game, but they might have been tinged with sardonic reaction to West Indies tighter fields and touches of leg theory.

It was the first time since Benaud became captain that I had seen less than a full umbrella field of slips and leg slips set for both new ball bowlers.

After Conrad Hunte off-drove Davidson's eighth ball to the fence one umbrella man was moved to midoff and stayed there for Rohan Kanhai after Cammie Smith (6) was caught at cover (and sent to bed in his hotel with acute tonsillitis).

For Kanhai's favourite gully shots Davidson's slip cordon was increased to five. Some of the gaps which West Indies strokesmen enjoyed in the first innings were blocked in the soft echo of tight fields which helped cause the heckling of Australian batsmen on Saturday because they could not rival the West Indians' stream of fours.

Tighter out cricket, coupled with loss of prized wickets before West Indies gained a 100-lead caused their 200 to-day to creep up off 57 overs in four hours compared with 38 overs in less than three hours on Friday.

EARLY BLOW

Davidson struck an early blow for Australia when he had Cammie Smith caught at short extra cover in his second over today. Then Kanhai came in to join Hunte and started batting as though he had been batting for hours.

He and Hunte pushed the score along ahead of the clock and 50 was sent up in 40 minutes with Hunte 26 and Kanhai 13.

Davidson as usual was bowling to three slips and a gully with three leg slips and only two men in front of the bat.

He was moving the ball across the batsmen's body to slip and Hunte and Kanhai went after him. They sent up the 50 partnership in 28 minutes and then Benaud made his first bowling change.

He brought on himself for Meckiff and replaced Davidson with Mackay. At 28 Kanhai slashed at a Mackay outswinger but Benaud could not hold the catch. In Benaud's next over Kanhai off-drove him powerfully to the boundary; an exquisite stroke and the crowd applauded.

Hunte turned Davidson for four to midwicket but in the same over he tried to drive him square and snicked the ball to Simpson who held the catch. West Indies were two down for 88. Sobers played over gully to the boundary, but at 14 he tried to turn a yorker to leg and the ball crashed in to his stumps. Worrell dangled his bat at the first ball from Davidson and Grout leapt in front of first slip and dropped the catch. Lunch was taken with the score 119; Kanhai not out 51, Worrell not out one.

After lunch Kanhai added three runs to his score and then chased a ball from Davidson wide of the off stump and gave Grout an easy catch.

This brought Worrell and Solomon together. Mackay bowling at medium pace, keeps the ball just outside the off stump and this had the effect of slowing down the scoring rate for Solomon let most of the deliveries go through to the keeper.

DIGGING IN

This period was the slowest of West Indies batting with Worrell and Solomon digging in and refusing to take any risks.

Benaud kept ringing the changes and used seven bowlers in his attempt to break the Worrell-Solomon partnership. He brought Mackay back into the attack then switched to Davidson and Meckiff with Simpson sending down three overs but Solomon in his wisdom resorted to the patience of Job and presented a dead bat to anything on the wicket.

He was batting for 88 minutes before he square-cut Davidson for four and that was only because Favell misfielded the ball on the boundary. It was good to see the West Indians showing so much fight in trying to get themselves through the difficult stage of the match.

Worrell was the chief architect of this recovery. He played the spinners in masterly fashion, and held the middle batting together while taking advantage of the scoring opportunity.

He reached his fifty with a single to cover in 119 minutes during which he scored 7 fours. Then the 50 partnership was realised in 77 minutes. The pitch was taking spin but slowly, and some deliveries were keeping low. Worrell and Solomon were together at tea with the total 204.

After tea the new ball was taken immediately and Davidson bowled to Worrell. In Davidson's second over after tea he got Worrell's wicket with an outswinger that lifted and found the inside edge of the bat, giving Grout another catch. This wicket fell at 210.

Lashley played the third ball of that over but the fourth beat him by pace and he was clean bowled without scoring.

Australia were now well back in the game with two hours and 15 minutes of play remaining.

EFFORT NEEDED

This meant that another great effort by Alexander and Solomon was called for and the West Indian vice captain decided to get himself dug in. He scored five singles in his first hour at the wicket while Solomon smothered the leg-breakers of Benaud and the medium paced out-swingers of Mackay.

Benaud persisted with Mackay and himself while the batsmen waited for the loose ball. Then with 20 minutes of play remaining Alexander hit across a spinner from Benaud and was bowled with his score on five.

West Indies were now very much in trouble with a lead of 192 and only the tail to bat.

Ramadhin started by sweeping Simpson to the fine leg boundary and then he snicked another to long leg for two. Then another calamity befell the West Indies when Ramadhin edged a leg break from Simpson to Harvey at slip and was caught for six with the total on 250.

West Indies ended the day with a lead of 207 with one wicket remaining. Simpson trapped Solomon leg before with ten minutes of play remaining as Valentine and Hall survived the remainder of play.

Day
Five

The Sydney
Morning
Herald
15/12/60

ONLY ONE BALL TO GO

'Fabulous' End To Test; First Tie On Record

From TOM GOODMAN

BRISBANE, Wednesday

Australia and the West Indies today tied the first Test at the Brisbane Cricket Ground. It is the first tie ever in Test cricket.

In an incredible finish, Australia's last three wickets (two run-outs) fell in the last over of the day.

The last wicket fell when Ian Meckiff was run out off what normally would have been the second-last ball of the match.

It was then four minutes after 6 p.m., the normal finishing time.

West Indies fast bowler Wesley Hall had begun the last over of the day before 6 p.m. and under the laws of cricket, it had to be continued until the innings ended or he completed the over.

Only 4,100 people saw this most fabulous of all cricket finishes.

MAGNIFICENT STAND

But they made enough noise for 30,000 in the last 12 minutes of play, during which Australia lost four wickets—and that after the magnificent fighting stand by Alan Davidson and Australia's captain Richie Benaud.

The crowd rushed the ground, swarming over the pitch, now to become famous as the "Test match tie" pitch.

The crowd then gathered in front of the players' pavilion calling for the heroes.

This most dramatic and most extraordinary Test match was all the thrilling close finish Test matches rolled into one.

The "man of the match" for the West

Joe Solomon from British Guiana was the West Indies' man of the match.

Indies was that quiet little fellow with the small moustache, Joe Solomon, from British Guiana.

Solomon was already a batting hero of this Test.

He became one of cricket's immortals when he threw-out Meckiff in that final moment of crisis.

He knocked the wicket down from square-leg, side-on and 15 yards away.

He could see only the side of one stump.

What is more, he had thrown out Davidson some minutes earlier from mid-on. Dead-eye Joe.

AUSTRALIANS ON THEIR KNEES

The Australians, needing 233 runs in 310 minutes to win today, were on their knees when they had lost their first five batsmen for a paltry 57 runs.

Sonny Ramadhin ended a Davidson-Mackay stand at 3.20 p.m. by bowling Mackay.

Davidson and Benaud, in a wonderfully controlled seventh-wicket partnership, added 134 runs.

At 5.52 p.m., Davidson was thrown out by Solomon.

Australia, 7 for 226, needed seven more runs for victory with eight minutes left before the scheduled time for drawing stumps.

Garfield Sobers was the bowler sharing the new ball with Hall.

Wally Grout stole a single from Sobers' seventh delivery and Benaud took a single from the eighth to give him the strike against Hall.

So, Australia stood 7/227—six runs short of the target—when Hall, with loping strides, began the memorable last over.

The clock above the scoreboard showed 5.55 p.m.

Then these things happened:—

First ball: Grout struck on pad, and they ran, dangerously, a leg-bye.

Second ball: Benaud swung at it, but the ball flew off the shoulder of his bat and he was caught behind the wicket, 8/228 at 5.57 p.m. Five runs wanted.

Third ball: Hall charged to the bowling crease with long arms whirling: but Meckiff played the ball safely.

Fourth ball: It flew past Meckiff on the leg side and he and Grout raced for a bye. Hall gathered the ball and threw at the wicket but missed.

THIRD RUN ATTEMPT FATAL

Fifth ball: Grout skied it forward of square leg. Kanhai came running in. It was his catch, but Hall charged across the

Jubilation for West Indies as O'Neill is caught by Alexander off Hall in Australia's second innings.

turf with arms outstretched, got to the ball but dropped it. The batsmen ran a single—8/230.

Sixth ball: Meckiff swung the ball high to square leg and Hunte raced after it as it neared the boundary. The batsmen crossed twice, but as Grout tore through for a third run, Hunte's great return to the wicketkeeper beat him home, and he was run out. Meckiff scored the two completed runs. The scores were level.

Seventh ball: Kline, a sick man (he had been treated for a chill), gallantly played the ball towards square leg, and the two batsmen raced for what would have been the winning run. But little Solomon coolly threw down the wicket at the striker's end and Meckiff was run out.

As the players were leaving the field, the crowd surging around them, Benaud trotted out to greet his rival captain, Frank Worrell, and cricket writers stood in the press box.

They had never seen anything like this finish before. They knew they would never see it again.

The chairman of the Australian Board of Control, Sir Donald Bradman, who is an Australian selector, said:

"This was the greatest Test of all time. There were thrills every day. And what a finish today. You couldn't see anything better than that."

Richie Benaud said: "It was fabulous. The best game I've ever known. When we needed 40 runs in even time to win, it seemed to me that both teams had played so well, a draw would be fitting. Nobody could have dreamed of a tie."

CUTTING THINGS TOO FINE

Frank Worrell said:

"I felt that a draw would be a great result. But a tie! That was cutting things too fine.

"I hope cricket will have many more such games.

"I am very proud of my boys. Every man played his part."

Many thousands of Brisbane people saw the thrilling finish in their homes as the last two hours of play were televised.

FINAL · SCORES

WEST INDIES — First Innings

C. C. Hunte, c Benaud, b Davidson		24
C. W. Smith, c Grout, b Davidson		7
R. B. Kanhai, c Grout, b Davidson		15
G. St A. Sobers, c Kline, b Meckiff		132
F. M. M. Worrell, c Grout, b Davidson		65
J. S. Solomon, hit wkt, b Simpson		65
P. D. Lashley, c Grout, b Kline		19
F. C. M. Alexander, c Davidson, b Kline		60
S. Ramadhin, c Harvey, b Davidson		12
W. W. Hall, st Grout, b Kline		50
A. L. Valentine, not out		0
Extras (lb 3, w 1)		4
Total		453

Fall of wickets: 1-23, 2-42, 3-65, 4-239, 5-243, 6-283, 7-347, 8-366, 9-452, 10-453
Bowling: Davidson 30-2-135-5, Meckiff 18-0-129-1, Mackay 3-0-15-0, Benaud 24-3-93-0, Simpson 8-0-25-1, Kline 17.6-6-52-3

AUSTRALIA — First Innings

C. C. McDonald, c Hunte, b Sobers		57
R. B. Simpson, b Ramadhin		92
R. N. Harvey, b Valentine		15
N. C. O'Neill, c Valentine, b Hall		181
L. E. Favell, run out		45
K. D. Mackay, b Sobers		35
A. K. Davidson, c Alexander, b Hall		44
R. Benaud, lbw, b Hall		10
A. T. W. Grout, lbw, b Hall		4
I. Meckiff, run out		4
L. F. Kline, not out		3
Extras (b 2, lb 8, w 1, nb 4)		15
Total		505

Fall of wickets: 1-84, 2-138, 3-194, 4-278, 5-381, 6-469, 7-484, 8-489, 9-496, 10-505
Bowling: Hall 29.3-1-140-4, Worrell 30-0-93-0, Sobers 32-0-115-2, Valentine 24-6-82-1, Ramadhin 15-1-60-1

WEST INDIES — Second Innings

C. C. Hunte, c Simpson, b Mackay		39
C. W. Smith, c O'Neill, b Davidson		6
R. B. Kanhai, c Grout, b Davidson		54
G. St A. Sobers, b Davidson		14
F. M. M. Worrell, c Grout, b Davidson		65
J. S. Solomon, lbw, b Simpson		47
P. D. Lashley, b Davidson		0
F. C. M. Alexander, b Benaud		5
S. Ramadhin, c Harvey, b Simpson		6
W. W. Hall, b Davidson		18
A. L. Valentine, not out		7
Extras (b 14, lb 7, w 2)		23
Total		284

Fall of wickets: 1-13, 2-88, 3-114, 4-127, 5-210, 6-210, 7-241, 8-250, 9-253, 10-284
Bowling: Davidson 24.6-4-87-6, Meckiff 4-1-19-0, Mackay 21-7-52-1, Benaud 31-6-69-1, Simpson 7-2-18-2, Kline 4-0-14-0, O'Neill 1-0-2-0

AUSTRALIA — Second Innings

C. C. McDonald, b Worrell		16
R. B. Simpson, c sub, b Hall		0
R. N. Harvey, c Sobers, b Hall		5
N. C. O'Neill, c Alexander, b Hall		26
L. E. Favell, c Solomon, b Hall		7
K. D. Mackay, b Ramadhin		28
A. K. Davidson, run out		80
R. Benaud, c Alexander, b Hall		52
A. T. W. Grout, run out		2
I. Meckiff, run out		2
L. F. Kline, not out		0
Extras (b 2, lb 9, nb 3)		14
Total		232

Fall of wickets: 1-1, 2-7, 3-49, 4-49, 5-57, 6-92, 7-226, 8-228, 9-232, 10-232
Bowling: Hall 17.7-3-63-5, Worrell, 16-3-41-1, Sobers 8-0-30-0, Valentine 10-4-27-0, Ramadhin 17-3-57-1

·1971·

THE FINAL TEST at the Oval was a humiliating experience for England. Not only did defeat cost them the series, but it was the first time India had won on English soil. The home side had looked vulnerable in the first Test, narrowly escaping defeat and it was the batting that was their downfall. There was no sign of the fourth day collapse, though, when England set out on the first morning with John Jameson making 82. After his departure, Alan Knott (90) and Richard Hutton (81) took the score to 355 all out. Wicket-keeper Knott and Hutton, son of the great Sir

Leonard, had added 103 runs for the seventh wicket from only 66 balls. India moved to within 71 runs of that score thanks mainly to Farokh Engineer's battling 59. Captain Ray Illingworth demonstrated how much spin there was in the wicket by taking five for 70. Disaster struck for England in their second innings. They reached 23 without loss before falling to 101 all out, Brian Luckhurst top scoring with 33 and spinner Chandrasekhar, *left*, taking six for 38. India needed a modest 173 to win, Abid Ali cutting Luckhurst for the winning boundary.

India leave the field having bowled out England for 101 in their second innings to set up victory in the series.

Day One

The Daily Telegraph 20/8/71

KNOTT COMES TO ENGLAND'S RESCUE AGAIN WITH 90

England won the toss and made 355 all out.

By E. W. SWANTON at The Oval

John Jameson hits Bishen Bedi over the top in his first innings 82.

This was a day of no mean attraction, with the added merit that two of the three central figures were men new, or all but new, to Test cricket: John Jameson and Richard Hutton.

Both played handsome parts, while Knott, who is coming on by leaps and bounds as a batsman (a phrase that is particularly applicable to his cricket whatever he is doing), performed his customary rescue act when the England innings had sagged most of the way to ruin.

The weather was hot, and Illingworth's fifth successful call of the summer was not the least fortunate, for though the pitch was easy-paced, my feeling is that it might grip spin progressively more as the game goes on.

SAME AGAIN

The reader, casting an eye over the England score-card, can be excused for supposing he is looking at an old newspaper. The pattern of this latest first innings was very much of a kind with the previous five of the summer.

The batsmen, broadly speaking, failed, whereupon the bottom half took over: notably, of course, Knott, who yet again played with the verve and quick-witted skill that impelled one famous Test cricketer to recall Denis Compton himself.

Such was the general picture, but it takes no account of Jameson, whose 82

was the bright, redeeming thing as far as the specialists were concerned.

In many respects, Jameson's innings was a rare tonic. He lost Luckhurst in the second over, nicely caught at second slip by Gavaskar, chasing a wide half volley from Solkar, whose natural line of course, left arm over wicket, is across the batsman.

JAMESON OPENS UP

Jameson then saw Edrich looking anything but certain, especially against Solkar, but he made his own valuation of the attack, and was soon putting his bat to anything that could be safely hit. The covers seemed his favourite country, coupled with a fondness for lifting the slow bowlers straight.

Twice Bedi found himself driven on the full into the members' seats, once to the mortal peril of a lady member who most unwisely turned her head from the ball. (Yes, ladies are now admitted to the Oval pavilion—ground floor only!)

If Jameson did not punctuate these and other strokes of pedigree with occasional sweeps of horrifying ugliness—for instance to several good-length balls outside the off stump, spinning away—his innings could be given full marks without reserve.

However, handsome is as handsome does, and for the most part this was batting of orthodoxly aggressive attraction. Jameson's 50 came out of 76 in an hour and a half, and his 82 took only two and

threequarter hours, and was made out of 139.

There was one other small thing about Jameson worth recording. He could actually be observed now and then to be smiling. It was pleasant to see an England batsman apparently enjoying what he was doing, and let us hope the intolerable strain of Test cricket does not catch up with him for a bit.

But back to the disasters. England at lunch were 97 for one. When Edrich, coming forward to Bedi, was caught behind it was 111 for two. Fletcher dabbed and was caught at slip, 135 for three.

Worse, d'Oliveira, perhaps forgetting Wadekar was left-handed, called for a short run on the off-side, and Jameson, who has quite a large frame to urge into motion, was sadly and narrowly run out

A simple remedy for lost time

Day Two

The Times
21/8/71

By John Woodcock
Cricket Correspondent

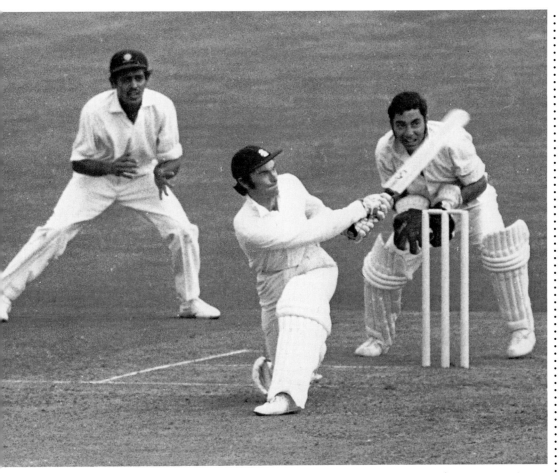

Alan Knott "played with the verve and quick-witted skill that impelled one famous Test cricketer to recall Denis Compton himself."

when his hundred seemed there for the taking.

D'Oliveira (143 for five), next was well caught by Mankad high up at mid-off driving, while Illingworth after 40 minutes of consolidation with Knott making three at the other end, hooked at a short, fast top-spinner from Chandra and was bowled (175 for six). In the same over, Chandra's wrong 'un perilously shaved Hutton's bat and leg stump; whereupon Hutton settled in and there followed the saving seventh-wicket stand.

While Hutton played straight and off-drove admirably, Knott indulged himself with all sorts of liberties. Rapidly the initiative, which had belonged so patently in mid-afternoon to India, changed hands.

These two had put on 103 in a bare

hour and a quarter before Solkar, with the new ball, caught and bowled Knott with a slower one.

Snow was soon caught behind to give Solkar his third wicket, whereupon Underwood fulfilled a valuable part, staying with Hutton while the latter went from strength to strength, ensuring England of a score that was nearer a true reflection of well-nigh perfect batting conditions.

The skill of the Indian spinners (though Solkar also bowled very well) added as usual to the pleasures of the day, and it was quite an acute off-break from Venkat that bowled Hutton and so ensured that where there might have been three English centuries in fact there were to be none.

Not a ball was bowled at the Oval yesterday in the third Test match between England and India. Steady rain, beginning in mid-morning, had shown no signs of letting up when hope was abandoned for the day soon after three o'clock.

This means that the only one of the six Test matches this summer not to have been affected by rain was that at Headingley against Pakistan. At Edgbaston, against Pakistan, and at Lord's and Old Trafford, against India, rain on the last day prevented a result; the other Test at Lord's, against Pakistan, was half washed away.

After all the expenses of their tour, Pakistan were not far from going home with only three drawn Test matches to show for it. So, now, are the Indians, though there is, of course, still plenty of time for England to win at the Oval.

If the authorities are reluctant to introduce time-limited Test matches, there is no earthly reason why a sixth day should not be set aside to be used in the event of thunder, lightning, rain, or riots.

Had this been done this season there would almost certainly have been five finishes out of five, instead of only one. There would have been less frustration and less reason for the public to feel, as many of them do, that Test matches are always drawn, anyway. By the simplest of remedies could the image be improved.

Day Three

The
Sunday
Telegraph
22/8/71

Breezy Engineer revives India

By MICHAEL MELFORD at the Oval

A lot of things seemed slightly unreal yesterday-the weather, which at times was the nearest Kennington is likely to come to a sea threat; the achievement of five and three quarter hours' play against all omens; and India's score of 234 for seven, which until the last few minutes might have been even more respectable than that.

At 21 for two, with Gavaskar gone,

But their fortunes were revived again—and this time with a good deal of panache by Engineer and Solkar.

The stand added 97 in 115 minutes before Solkar was brilliantly caught at second slip by Fletcher off d'Oliveira in the seventh over of the new ball. In the last over but one, Engineer went too, after playing the main part in halting

LATE START

If you wanted to think up a really unattractive morning for cricket the mist, persistent suspicion of drizzle and north-east wind yesterday would have made an inspired start. Yet somehow play began only 15 minutes late and the wretched Mankad and Gavaskar had to cope with Snow and Price in a gloom which made almost anyone above medium pace seem menacing.

However, the pitch was comfortable enough, and though the short ball, as usual, had Mankad especially at some disadvantage they came safely through until the 10th over when a fast, full-length ball from Price came back slightly and knocked Mankad's middle stump a long way.

In Snow's next over, Gavaskar suffered the same conclusive indignity, perhaps rather more unluckily for it was to the first ball after a long hold up caused by the peregrinations of a black dog.

No doubt one day someone will write a treatise on cricketing dogs and their influence, in which case I should like to submit the case of the Johannesburg animal who, with a thunderstorm brewing, prevented another over from being bowled before tea and probably saved Australia from defeat.

ANGULAR METHOD

Wadekar, in his angular method, at once began pushing ones and twos and occasionally treating himself to a hook. Sardesai cutting and glancing was equally unprepared to be depressed by events and without too much anxiety they dealt with d'Oliveira and Hutton and second spells by Price and Snow.

The outfield was many runs an hour slower than on Thursday but they went steadily until Illingworth and Underwood came on half an hour after lunch. Underwood at once posed a few problems and Sardesai, who spent much of his time advancing down the pitch to Illingworth, was lucky once that the ball just touched the inside edge.

When 37, he might have been caught in the gully off Underwood but what with

Mankad is bowled by John Price for 10.

India had made a start which seemed in keeping with what were to them damp and alien conditions but Wadekar and Sardesai restored order with a third-wicket stand of 93.

At 125 for five after Illingworth had removed Sardesai, Vishvanath and Wadekar in mid-afternoon without conceding a run, things looked even gloomier for them.

Illingworth, who held the Pavilion end for over two and a half hours.

The ball turned slowly but enough for an off-spinner of his ability to pose awkward problems and but for Engineer's good sense and determination not to be pinned down, the England captain's figures might deservedly have been much more memorable than three for 49.

Sardesai's driving and Wadekar's occasional pulled drive, the score advanced again at a respectable pace. Sardesai was not being dashing when Illingworth turned an off-break between his bat and pad to bowl him, but Vishwanath, in Illingworth's next over, had gone down the pitch with belligerent intent. Realising that he had made the ball into a yorker, he came down on it hurriedly, but merely squeezed it back onto the stumps.

SHORTISH BALL

At 125, Wadekar's innings of nearly three hours ended when he aimed to cut a shortish ball from Illingworth. It bounced more than most, and he was well caught off the top-edge by Hutton, moving left at slip. Thus, in 20 minutes, Illingworth had turned 114 for two into 125 for five. Engineer's breeziness at that moment when the initiative was being torn away from India, was a godsend to them.

He raced down the pitch to Illingworth and pushed him wide of mid-on. Hutton, after tea, was regularly struck in that direction. Solkar contributed some fine strokes on the on-side, and in an hour they added 60 runs.

Illingworth kept himself on for the duration of the old ball and the left-handed Solkar had some hazardous moments with the one turning away from him outside the off stump. Engineer showed a rather unsuspected restraint against the flighted ball, which usually turned a lot more and Illingworth's admirably sustained spell ended without further success.

DIM LIGHT

In spite of the dim light, Price, Snow and the new ball brought even better things from both batsmen, especially Solkar, but d'Oliveira in his first over moved the ball away from him and Fletcher dived low to his left at second slip to catch him.

Engineer remained, as busy as ever on the on-side and as ambitious as ever between the wickets. Not for him, a quiet finish with an eye on Monday morning. Instead, alas, a mishook in Snow's last over and a gentle catch to mid-on.

Play was interrupted by the appearance of "Dexter" the dog.

J. J. WARR COMMENTS . . .

Grey sky — grey cricket

The Saturday tradition of the Tests this summer continued at the Oval. It has happened that most of the dull play in the two Test series has been provided when the crowds have been at their biggest.

Allowing for the wash-out against Pakistan at Lord's, the average number of runs scored on Saturdays has been less than 200.

Circumstances and some good fast bowling by Snow and Price conspired to give India a bad start on a placid wicket. They were instantly on the defensive and the cricket became as grey as the sky.

Wadekar, with his back to the wall, responded by dispensing with his back lift against the quicker bowlers. He was at the crease two hours before he scored his first boundary.

Illingworth always squeezes the last drop of advantage from this sort of situation and until the slow bowlers appeared he made run-scoring particularly difficult.

Sardesai averages over 40 in his Test career and he gave another solid exhibition. India never really looked like following on and the £1,500 which is awarded to the winner of this match looks like staying in the bank.

Two prizes are also being awarded to the best entertainer on each side in the series. I can only hope that Saturdays don't count.

Day Four

The Guardian
24/8/71

Chandra causes downfall

India in position to beat England

By JOHN ARLOTT

The bowling of Chandrasekhar in the third Test match at The Oval yesterday put India in a position to beat England for the first time in England and take the rubber. Today, with eight wickets left they need another 97 runs to win with the whole day at their disposal.

When Chandrasekhar was a child he had poliomyelitis, which left his right arm so withered that he taught himself to pick up and throw left-handed. Yet he bowled his wrist spin at quite remarkable speed with his damaged and substantially weaker right arm.

He traffics chiefly in googlies and top spinners with an occasional leg break as a tactical threat, and a surprising faster ball. Tall, lean, and merry-faced, he has a valuably high delivery, and a whippy wrist gives him appreciable nip off the pitch. At 26 he has played in only 19 Tests and although he toured England in 1967, he was not included in the Indian party to West Indies last winter.

Yesterday his 6-38 effectively put out England for 101, considerably less than their 134 at Lord's in 1934, which was previously their lowest Test total against India. Neither Snow nor Price could find any life in the pitch; Underwood from the Vauxhall end could hardly straighten his left arm finger spin, though opposite him Illingworth derived sufficient slow turn to reinforce his flight.

The Indian spinners, brought up on shorter commons, found the conditions to

John Edrich, yorked by Chandrasekhar for 0.

their liking. Venkataraghavan from the pavilion end made his off breaks bite, but with more snap than Illingworth. Above all, Chandrasekar's fiery wrist spin extorted a degree of life, bounce and turn far beyond any other bowler in the match. It was no doubt significant that Wadekar entrusted the main operation to these two in preference to the subtler, but crucially slower, Bedi.

India had three wickets in hand when play began and Venkat and Abid Ali, developing from the cautious to the sprightly, made 45 of the 50 morning runs before Illingworth turned a ball back between Abid Ali's bat and pad: and Venkat, playing wildly across Underwood's line, was lbw. When Bedi drove a catch to deep mid-on, England led by 71 on the first innings and Illingworth had achieved his best Test bowling figures since the Leeds Test against Australia in 1968, 26 Tests ago. He earned them by control, imaginative flight and variation.

Luckhurst and Jameson made a comfortably unhurried start against the mild new ball attack of Abid Ali and Solkar and a little after one o'clock Wadekar brought on Venkat and Chandrasekhar, who destroyed the English innings. Jameson was out purely unluckily; Luckhurst drove Chandrasekhar and the bowler, putting down a hand to field, diverted it into the stumps and Jameson was run out for the third successive time in his four Test innings.

EDRICH YORKED

In the last over before lunch, Chandrasekhar yorked Edrich in the manner of Douglas Wright, a wrist spinner of similar method and pace. Fletcher pushed forward into the next ball, a googly, and Solkar from short leg threw himself forward and rolled over with the catch.

So immediately after lunch Chandrasekhar, with two balls remaining in an over, was on a hat-trick. Wadekar set six fieldsmen closely about the bat. D'Oliveira smothered the first ball and jabbed the second to slip, where Sardesai dropped the sharp chance. In Chandrasekhar's next over he was missed again when Solkar, diving, could not hold the catch at forward short leg.

Luckhurst played responsibly and coolly, reading Venkat accurately and improvising late defence against Chandrasekhar. D'Oliveira, outwardly calm and playing strokes to disperse the close field, was in truth less assured than he looked, and eventually he mis-hit Venkat high to deep mid-on. Knott, by now entitled to failure in a Test innings, was rapidly taken at short leg by the alert Solkar. Fifty-five for five was a dangerously bad start even for the current England team.

Chandrasekhar swept away all hope of a recovery with three more wickets in three overs for no runs. He caught and bowled Illingworth with his slower ball; decisively, he had the patient Luckhurst caught at slip from a cut; and took a low but easy return catch off Snow. Hutton and Underwood, careful but quick to hit the loose ball, made a brief stand. Wadekar replaced Chandrasekhar with Bedi, who at once had Underwood caught at square leg sweeping. After that over Chandrasekhar came back to have Price lbw, and the English innings was over.

At 4.15 Mankad and Gavaskar set out towards the 173 India needed to win. In Snow's second over, Gavaskar played no stroke at a ball he thought to be passing down the leg side; it proved to be a late outswinger and he was plainly and dejectedly lbw. Mankad and Wadekar saw away the fast bowlers and reached 37 in something over an hour before Mankad pushed forward to Underwood and edged a catch which Hutton, at slip, pushed up with his left hand and caught with both. Wadekar, the left-hander, began to punch his bottom hand through his stroke and, with Sardesai devoted at the other end, there were no serious alarms as they made their way to 76 off 41 overs by the close.

India's second innings breakthrough came when Jameson was run out for the second time in the match, this time when Chandra deflected Luckhurst's drive onto the stumps.

Day
Five

The Times
25/8/71

India's three exciting hours to fame

By John Woodcock
Cricket Correspondent

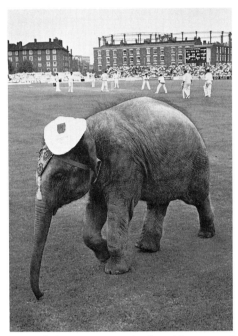

*Bella the elephant, left, lends her support during the great Hindu festival of Ganesh, the god with
an elephant's face. Wadekar, right, and Chandrasekhar acknowledge the cheers of the crowd.*

India's victory, received amid scenes of great enthusiasm, stands as one of the finest achieved by a visiting side to this country. It is something they have been striving for since they first played Test cricket 39 years ago, and it came from an apparently hopeless position.

Just think of it. They had been saved from defeat at Lord's and Old Trafford by rain, and last Friday evening no one gave them the slightest chance of winning. With a first innings total of 355 England, it seemed, were secure from defeat. With Australia, West Indies, New Zealand and Pakistan already under their belt, they were moving to another cold and calculated victory. Or so we thought. But Chandrasekhar fooled us all, and yesterday India kept their nerve where Pakistan and Australia have recently lost theirs.

England fought as they have been guaranteed to fight. Never was a match more reluctantly conceded, and this was all to England's credit. It was a desperately slow pitch; so slow that Illingworth gave

Price not a single over and Snow only six. He relied upon himself and Underwood to win the match, and for once there were too few runs to play with. Hardly a ball turned, and Snow might as well have bowled a poached egg as a bouncer.

Yet when Wadekar was run out without a run added to the overnight score of 76 for two, it looked as though England might get away with it again. D'Oliveira, from cover point, took advantage of a moment's hesitation to beat Wadekar's dash safety after Sardesai had called him for a single. For some time after that Underwood, Illingworth and D'Oliveira probed away, hopefully, thoughtfully, patiently, persistently. And with the luck they needed through the slips Viswanath and Sardesai survived.

For the most part Illingworth gave Underwood the pavilion end, from which

the ball was more likely to turn, and Underwood, for all his accuracy, lacked the flight or spin to win the day. Laker and Lock would have fancied their chances no doubt, but Locks and Lakers are few and far between. Illingworth ringed the bat, to try to delude the batsmen, and his fielders gave him all they had. But Sardesai and Viswanath, and then Engineer, were too good for them.

When Underwood got a ball to turn at Sardesai and Knott took a good catch, there was still a chance for England. So there was when Underwood stuck out his left hand to take a spectacular return catch from Solkar. That was 134 for five and, as Illingworth said later, he believed then that England could win if they made short work of Engineer, which they failed to do.

Sardesai defended stubbornly for two hours, 40 minutes, and with great skill

Viswanath kept England at bay for almost three hours. Without these two India would not have won. And without Engineer they would have won less comfortably. He came in with 39 still needed, and of these he made 28 himself.

Having got out going for the winning runs, Viswanath was not there to be garlanded as Engineer was. He was caught

They have contributed more liberally to our summer's pleasures. In Illingworth's time as captain, England have now won eight Test matches, drawn 12 and lost only one. Before that, under Cowdrey, they played seven more without defeat. But an unbeaten record has its complications. Now that England have lost they should think in terms of building a side which

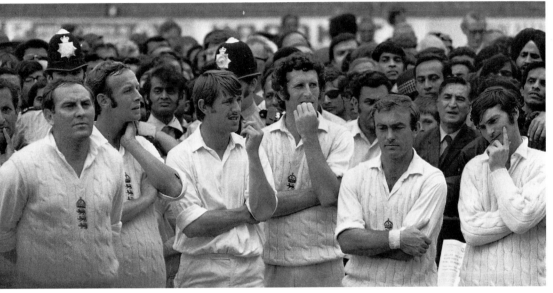

England players (left to right) d'Oliveira, Illingworth, Underwood, Luckhurst, Snow, Edrich and Knott listen to the speeches celebrating India's victory.

by Knott off Luckhurst, brought on by Illingworth as a last desperate throw. It had taken India three hours to make the 97 they needed when the day began; three tense, exciting hours which culminated with an invasion of the field by the Indians of London.

So, at last, the tightrope snapped. England have walked it several times this year. During the winter they did so at Sydney and then at Auckland.; again this summer at Edgbaston, Headingley and Lord's. They are not a good side, as England sides go, and their performances this summer have reflected, quite starkly, the hapless state of Australian cricket. But their way of playing makes them devilishly difficult to beat.

Both India and Pakistan have appeared to enjoy their cricket more than England.

plays the game with more of a smile and less of a frown.

This, of course, was a wonderful result for Indian cricket. Always they have bred fine, natural players, whose temperament has been suspect. Yesterday was their festival of Ganesh, which is one of the great Hindu festivals. Ganesh, a god with an elephant's face, comes to the succour of the distressed.

Well, it was England who were in need of his help. And if, as they should, they proclaimed their readiness to tour India this winter, they may need it again. For in a short time Ajit Wadekar has made this Indian side into a match for anyone. Within six months they have beaten West Indies and England away from home—and climbed the highest peaks in the cricketing world.

FINAL · SCORES

ENGLAND — First Innings

J. A. Jameson, run out	82
B. W. Luckhurst, c Gavaskar, b Solkar	1
J. H. Edrich, c Engineer, b Bedi	41
K. W. R. Fletcher, c Gavaskar, b Bedi	1
B. L. d'Oliveira, c Mankad, b Chandrasekhar	2
A. P. E. Knott, c & b Solkar	90
R. Illingworth, b Chandrasekhar	11
R. A. Hutton, b Venkataraghavan	81
J. A. Snow, c Engineer, b Solkar	3
D. L. Underwood, c Wadekar, b Venkataraghavan	22
J. S. E. Price, not out	1
Extras (b 4, lb 15, w 1)	20
Total	**355**

Fall of wickets: 1-5, 2-111, 3-135, 4-139, 5-143, 6-175, 7-278, 8-284, 9-352, 10-355

Bowling: Abid 12-2-47-0, Solkar 15-4-28-3, Gavaskar 1-0-1-0, Bedi 36-5-120-2, Chandrasekhar 24-6-76-2, Venkataraghavan 21.4-3-63-2

INDIA — First Innings

A. V. Mankad, b Price	10
S. Gavaskar, b Snow	6
A. L Wadekar, c Hutton, b Illingworth	48
D. N. Sardesai, b Illingworth	54
G. R. Vishvanath, b Illingworth	0
E. D. Solkar, c Fletcher, b d'Oliveira	44
F. M. Engineer, c Illingworth, b Snow	59
S. Abid Ali, b Illingworth	26
S. Venkataraghavan, lbw, b Underwood	24
B. S. Bedi, c d'Oliveira, b Illingworth	2
B. S. Chandrasekhar, not out	0
Extras (b 6, lb 4, nb 1)	11
Total	**284**

Fall of wickets: 1-17, 2-21, 3-114, 4-118, 5-125, 6-222, 7-230, 8-278, 9-284, 10-284

Bowling: Snow 24-5-68-2, Price 15-2-51-1, Hutton 12-2-30-0, d'Oliveira 7-5-5-1, Illingworth 34.3-12-70-5, Underwood 25-6-49-1

ENGLAND — Second Innings

B. W. Luckhurst, c Venkataraghavan, b Chandrasekhar	33
J. A. Jameson, run out	16
J. H. Edrich, b Chandrasekhar	0
K. W. R. Fletcher, c Solkar, b Chandrasekhar	0
B. L. d'Oliveira, c sub, b Venkataraghavan	17
A. P. E. Knott, c Solkar, b Venkataraghavan	1
R. Illingworth, c & b Chandrasekhar	4
R. A. Hutton, not out	13
J. A. Snow, c & b Chandrasekhar	0
D. L. Underwood, c Mankad, b Bedi	11
J. S. E. Price, lbw, b Chandrasekhar	3
Extras (lb 3)	3
Total	**101**

Fall of wickets: 1-23, 2-24, 3-24, 4-49, 5-54, 6-65, 7-72, 8-72, 9-96, 10-101

Bowling: Abid Ali 3-1-5-0, Solkar 3-1-10-0, Venkataraghavan 20-4-44-2, Chandrasekhar 18.1-3-38-6, Bedi 1-0-1-1

INDIA — Second Innings

A. V. Mankad, c Hutton, b Underwood	11
S. Gavaskar, lbw, b Snow	0
A. L. Wadekar, run out	45
D. N. Sardesai, c Knott, b Underwood	40
G. R. Vishvanath, c Knott, b Luckhurst	33
E. D. Solkar, c & b Underwood	1
F. M. Engineer, not out	28
S. Abid Ali, not out	4
Extras (b 6, lb 5, nb 1)	12
Total (6 wkts)	**174**

Fall of wickets: 1-2, 2-37, 3-76, 4-125, 5-134, 6-170

Bowling: Snow 11-7-14-1, Price 5-0-10-0, Underwood 38-14-72-3, Illingworth 36-15-40-0, D'Oliveira 9-3-17-0, Luckhurst 2-0-9-1

ENGLAND V AUSTRALIA
22ND - 26TH JUNE

·1972·

LORD'S
SECOND TEST

BOB MASSIE, right, who two years earlier had been playing for Kilmarnock in Scotland, and had been rejected by Northamptonshire, won this match for the Australians almost single-handedly. Massie began with a staggering eight for 84 in his first Test appearance as England struggled to reach 272, Tony Greig making 54. Australia's response hinged on the Chappell brothers Greg and captain Ian. Greg hit 131 while Ian made 56 before he became one of John Snow's five victims. The visitors had opened up a 36-run first innings lead before

Massie, the deadly debutant, did for England again. Dennis Lillee removed Geoff Boycott and Brian Luckhurst and then Massie ran through the order, surpassing his first day performance by taking eight for 53 as England were skittled out for 116. That left the Australians requiring 81 to win and they were guided home by Keith Stackpole who hit 57. Massie's performance was met with disbelief in some English quarters with accusations that the ball was out of shape and that the swing bowler had kept shine on the ball using lip salve.

Bob Massie's finest hour. He is applauded all the way to the Lord's pavilion following his destructive performance.

Day One

The Times
23/6/72

England helped out of trouble by Chappell's decision

By John Woodcock
Cricket Correspondent

England were let off the hook in the second Test match yesterday, or so it seemed, by a strange decision by Ian Chappell, the Australian captain. It happened in mid-afternoon, when England were 97 for five and in every kind of trouble.

Until then Massie and Lillee, both from the sunshine city of Perth, had threatened to bowl England out for a dangerously low score on a pitch that always had something to offer the faster bowlers. Only Smith and D'Oliveira had made any runs, and Massie had just accounted for them both. This was precisely the tonic he needed after bowling 20 overs with a break only for luncheon.

Yet Chappell chose this of all moments to take him off. With the last ball of his 20th over Massie bowled Smith. By the time he bowled again, two hours later, Greig and Knott had added 96 invaluable runs. Massie at once had Knott caught in the gully and Greig at the wicket and if by the close of play England were on their way again, Australia must still have wondered what might have been.

This could be a great Test match. Unless the weather "fines up" as the Australians say, the pitch may never be perfectly true. England should bowl well on it today, and except on paper I doubt whether Australia have much of an advantage. It could well be that in a match of moderate scoring the stand between Greig and Knott will be of much importance: Knott, whose fitness was in doubt until the last moment, and Greig, whose last seven innings against Australia,

Only Tony Greig looked comfortable against Massie's prodigious swing.

including those for the Rest of the World, have been 66, 3, 70, 22, 57, 62 and 54.

There is, of course, nothing new about England being dug out of trouble by their middle batsmen. Time and again—and against all-comers—it has happened in the last three or four years, and yesterday was a day more for bowling than batting. It was a day, too, when those who had remembered their rugs were the envy of those who had not. Considering the weather the crowd of 17,350 was not a bad one, and they saw some absorbing cricket.

Twenty-five minutes behind schedule due to rain, Illingworth won a toss which

he might just as soon have lost. Having won it he felt obliged to bat, and within an hour England were in trouble. After feeling a twinge in the nets, Arnold was omitted from the England side. By retaining Colley and leaving Inverarity out Australia strengthened their medium-paced bowling at the expense of their batting. With 50 minutes gone, and no wicket down, Australia were in danger of missing their chance. In the early overs Lillee bowled too short and Massie with little luck. But at 22 Boycott was yorked, aiming to hit Massie wide of mid-on; at 23 Luckhurst was bowled by Lillee, and at 28 Edrich was leg before to Lillee. Within 20 minutes Australia were a side revived. When Lillee pitched the ball up England still played back, and it was this that undid Luckhurst and Edrich.

By luncheon England were 54 for three. Immediately afterwards D'Oliveira hooked and cut successive balls from Lillee for four, and he was starting to make light of the difficulties of batting when he was leg before to Massie with an eye on a leg-side gap. When Smith was bowled by a full toss, hitting across it again, England were 97 for five, at which point Ian Chappell brought on his brother in place of Massie.

Against Greg Chappell Knott played himself in while Greig once again escaped capture. At tea they had added 42, mostly against the bowling of Greg Chappell and Colley, and in the second over afterwards Francis dropped Knott when he was 16, a simple chance at short midwicket off Lillee. Poor Francis. He is said never to have enjoyed fielding, and he will like it even less after this.

When, with Knott beginning to play as well as Greig, Massie returned, the two were out, and with Snow coming in with threequarters of an hour left Australia must have had high hopes of another wicket or two before the close. Instead, with some luck through the slips and much good sense, Illingworth and Snow added 49. This morning, with a new ball at their disposal, Australia will be hoping quite soon to be batting themselves, and if they bat well this, as I say, could be the very devil of a match.

Australia unable to hold advantage

By Jack Fingleton

It was tough, tight cricket with the Australians losing their early advantage when they had Boycott, Edrich, Luckhurst, Smith and D'Oliveira all out for 97. As at Manchester, the middle and early tail got the initiative back and at stumps England were in a comfortable position.

The Australians had nobody who could press home their wonderful position with five out. It should have been Gleeson, but, although this flick spinner always bowls tidily, he does not seem to get wickets and so Massie, in particular, and Lillee saw their early good work dispersed in the afternoon when Greig and Knott, Illingworth and Snow all made valuable runs.

Massie was Australia's hero. We have heard laments in many quarters that the Australians sadly missed Graham McKenzie on that helpful pitch at Old Trafford. The man they missed most, as he clearly showed yesterday, was Massie. He already has the rare distinction of getting five wickets in his first innings against England, which, I think, would approximate to a batsman making a century in his first Test. As he bowled yesterday, with good control, length and movement in the air and off the pitch, he would have been in his element at Manchester.

Ian Chappell gave Massie a huge load of work. He never shirked it. he came gliding in with a beautifully smooth action and we lost count of the times he beat the batsman completely.

There was plenty of green in the pitch at the start but it did not yield much movement. Massie can swing in any atmosphere and he cuts the ball on the best of pitches. So that there was no undue help for him in the conditions. He is just a splendid bowler. He played with Kilmarnock last summer and returned to Perth without a job. Indeed, he took the position on the Perth scoring board before getting his usual job of bank clerk.

Lillee again bowled well. His direction is improving with each game, and it was obvious that his pace was not appreciated by some of his opponents. Boycott and Edrich had a tough job against these two West Australians. Boycott and D'Oliveira were both yorked—Massie changes his pace with excellent concealment—and I thought that Boycott played an unusually casual stroke for Boycott.

Smith, who is a splendid judge of a run, and D'Oliveira staved off trouble in a valuable stand. Then Greig, who now has plenty of confidence and feels that he really belongs in the top sphere—which is always comforting for a player to know—played a splendid innings. He groped a little against Gleeson, but saw that through. He has, so far, been the series' most successful batsman.

Francis made a bad miss when he dropped Knott at 16 off Lillee. This cost Australia dear. The sun was out at this time and I wondered if the uncapped Francis was handicapped. Only Gleeson and Marsh in this side continuously wear the baggy Australian caps. The vogue of long hair has kept the cap in the dressing room because the cap will not sit on long hair.

There must have been some obscure reason why Francis put this particular one down, because it could not have been easier.

Snow and Lillee, long locks flowing in the peace of the light afternoon sun, had a tilt which puts Snow ahead on points at the day's end with another round to be decided today. Snow made some capital shots. So, too, did Illingworth, in spite of being hit a nasty blow by Lillee, who also managed to leave his imprint upon Greig.

England's score looks good to me. The pitch today will be splendid for batting, true and easy-paced. The Australians will want a quick breakthrough, but they could well lament that they fell off the bus yesterday after getting halfway with the distinction. It was not the fault of the Perth combination—Lillee and Massie.

Ian Chappell gave Massie a huge load of work. He never shirked it.

Day Two

The
Guardian
24/6/72

29,000 watch a grand recovery

Chappell wins an absorbing day

John Arlott at the second Test

A composed and faultless century by Greg Chappell led Australia clear from two set-backs to a position of strength at Lord's yesterday in the second Test. Absorbing and fluctuating cricket played before a happily appreciative crowd of 29,000 combined to lift the proceedings from the level of a game to an occasion.

In two partnerships, first with his brother and then with Edwards, the younger Chappell batted in two separate but equally convincing characters. Already, at 23, he is a mature, responsible and informed cricketer; an orthodox batsman with keen concentration.

Only Snow, at his most aggressive and, late in the day, the finger-spinners, Gifford and Illingworth, threatened to make any penetration. Australia will bat again this morning, only 72 behind England with Chappell still in possession and five wickets in hand.

The pitch was again friendly in pace, its bounce even and undisturbing and, though it allowed some slight seam movement it was soon obvious that no English bowler could employ the atmospheric conditions to swing the ball as Massie had done, or as Arnold—also essentially a swing bowler—would have expected to do.

Finishing off the English innings was something more than a formality. Massie, bowling with good control, and tactically astute variation, took outstanding wickets for a final analysis of eight for 84: a rare performance for a man playing his first Test. Tall and strongly-built, Massie has a relaxed, rhythmic run-up, a high right-arm delivery and he makes the ball swing

sharply and late. He might well have been a killer at Old Trafford. Now he had Illingworth lbw with an inswinger; hit Snow's off stump with one which began on middle and leg and then went the other way; and moved one away from Gifford's forcing stroke for a catch to the wicketkeeper. The last five English wickets had changed the shape of the game by putting on 175 runs.

In the first over of the Australian innings Francis mis-read both the length and line of an extremely fast near-half volley from Snow, played back instead of forward and was bowled. In the same over Stackpole's hasty snick dropped only a little short of the slip field. In Price's first over Stackpole aimed his instinctive hook at a short ball, mishit and gave Gifford a simple catch at square leg.

From that crisis point—seven for two—the Chappell brothers steadied the innings by cool determination and thought. Greg, the younger, addressed himself to keeping an end secure, as his correct style, watchful concentration and understanding of English conditions qualify him to do. Meanwhile, Ian, his captain, played strokes, which is his nature and his best policy.

Before he left Australia he declared he had had "a gutful of bouncers" and that in future he proposed to hook them. Now, when Price and Snow bowled short to him he hooked them boldly and capably. Five fours and a stirring six—into the Mound stand off Snow—came from that stroke; and when the ball was up to him he drove it firmly.

For more than two hours the English

bowling looked no more than a containing operation. At one period Greg Chappell's score stayed at 14 for almost an hour. On the other hand the bowlers had no encouragement and, for the first time in the match, a pair of batsmen appeared to be in secure control.

Illingworth maintained the pressure of pace as far into the afternoon as he could, alternating Snow and Price at the pavilion end and in the sixth over of a sustained and searching spell Snow broke the partnership. His bouncer was genuinely fast and shrewdly directed, Ian Chappell was fractionally late with his hook and skied it to long-leg where it was dropping short of Smith who threw himself forward and rolled over holding the catch. Walters shaped tentatively at Snow and in his next over, predictably, he edged him cross-batted and Illingworth, the finer of the two gulleys posted for the purpose, took the sharp low catch.

Once again the innings was rebuilt. From the outset of his first Test innings, Edwards showed that he is not disturbed by pace. He moved into position to play Snow without hurry and now he took over the duties of anchorman. Meanwhile Greg Chappell succeeded his brother as stroke-maker. Although he once glanced Snow with delicate precision, most of his runs came from drives played with a full flow of a straight bat round the arc from mid-wicket to cover. A four through extra cover off Price was a front foot stroke of graceful command and instinctive timing.

England's seam bowling soon ceased even to contain the batting and their first spinner—Gifford—came on to bowl the 67th over; half an hour later Illingworth himself took the other end. For the first time Chappell showed signs of unease; a sweep which did not connect and a belated cut were his first errors.

The slow bowlers gradually took a hold on the game; trying to lure Edwards into a reckless stroke, harrying Chappell. They tied up the game for three maiden overs and, almost immediately, when the fifth wicket stand had made 106, Edwards took the bait, swinging Illingworth high to mid-wicket where Smith took a well-

*Greg Chappell receives
the applause of the
M.C.C. members
following his
marvellous century.*

judged catch. In poor light, Gleeson was sent in to see the day away, and in an atmosphere of noisy tension he scampered the five runs that took Chappell to his century with no more than a couple of minutes left for play. It had been splendidly earned: and it rounded off a day happily, if surprisingly, visited by the sun.

Scoreboard

ENGLAND—First Innings
Overnight : 249-7.

R. Illingworth lbw b Massie ...	30
J. A. Snow b Massie	37
N. Gifford c Marsh b Massie	3
J. S. E. Price not out	4
Extras (lb 6, w 1, nb 6) ...	13

Total 272

Fall of wickets : 260, 265.

Bowling : Lillee 28-3-90-2; Massie 32.5-7-84-8; Colley 16-2-42-0; Chappell (G. S.) 6-1-18-0; Gleeson 9-1-25-0.

Today : 11.30-6.30

AUSTRALIA—First Innings

K. R. Stackpole c Gifford b Price	5
B. C. Francis b Snow	0
I. M. Chappell c Smith b Snow	56
G. S. Chappell not out	105
K. D. Walters c Illingworth b Snow	1
R. Edwards c Smith b Illingworth	28
J. W. Gleeson not out	0
Extras (b 5, nb 1)	6

Total (for 5) 201

Fall of wickets : 1, 7, 82, 84, 190.

Bowling to date : Snow 21-8-37-3; Price 16-3-49-1; Greig 20-4-46-0; D'Oliveira 13-3-30-0; Gifford 11-4-20-0; Illingworth 7-2-13-1.

Day
Three

The
Sunday
Times

25/6/72

Australia's Test jamboree

Two men poles apart when it comes to reporting an England-Australia Test match are Jack Fingleton, representing the Australian point of view, and our cricket correspondent Robin Marlar. So we asked them to report the struggle at Lord's together. It turned out to be a remarkable day.

ROBIN MARLAR: This is going to be known as Massie's match, Jack. Your faith in him has been absolutely justified.

JACK FINGLETON: His success has been really remarkable. They put the lights on all night in Perth once when the American astronauts wanted to take their bearings. They could well leave them on for a week after this. One must not, however, forget the magnificent innings of Greg Chappell, Ian Chappell, Marsh and Edwards. Would you agree with me that Lillee's pace has upset your countrymen, or some of them?

RM: Lillee made the breach. He was perhaps lucky to get Boycott. The ball rolled down off Boycott's body on to the wicket, and the off bail just fell. It was a terrible moment for England. Lillee deserved this success. If anything, he bowled faster here than at Manchester, and certainly straighter.

The groundsman, Jim Fairbrother, gets credit, too. Ridge there may be still, but this wicket has pace, and I feel the strokes we have seen have owed much to the conditions and been the principal cause of the crowd's immense and obvious satisfaction with the match.

JF: I too would like to say what a beautiful cricket pitch this is. It gives everybody a chance—bowlers can hope, and batsmen can play their strokes, as you say. One thing that struck me about this crowd. I have never at any match heard such warm-hearted applause from the various sections of the crowd as Massie, Lillee and Snow returned to their fielding positions. Cricket will never die while we see places like this.

RM: True, and this has been a Saturday sell-out. The gates were shut before the start, and thousands of people were unable to get in. Receipts are a world record at £81,000. A pity the match will not be sustained at this level for five days. But you can't have everything.

JF: You mention immediately the financial side of it. This figures so largely in English cricket these days. I don't complain—it takes money to run a big game. But more important to me is that Test cricket has come into its own again.

RM: Has this particular game grabbed you more than any Test in the last series in Australia?

JF: I have never been more absorbed in a Test. I didn't think much of our last series. Too many squabbles about umpiring, too many no balls, no lbws. I didn't think the players enjoyed it much either.

RM: One thing about Lord's is that the players love the place. Not surprising when you get the entire ground standing to applaud Greg Chappell all the way back to the pavilion after his innings, not only the highest so far but also an outstanding knock for temperament and skill. How straight he played! And what a reception!

Little things count. Even when leaving the ball alone, Greg Chappell looked the part, watchful and decisive as the ball went through. Against the medium-pacers he was always playing the length ball back down the pitch, his bat vertical in contrast to some of the Englishmen, who tend to push to the legside.

JF: I have long thought him our best technical batsman. This innings was a replica of the century he got in his first Test innings against England in Perth. The shutters up for a long time, then as the game changed, the switch to most glorious strokeplay. After Australia were two down for seven, the Chappells played in the highest traditions of Australian batsmanship. It was fighting stuff of the highest calibre. How their grandad, Vic Richardson, would have loved it.

RM: Back to Massie. A few short steps, 11 running strides, kept bringing him up from the Nursery end with a load of problems. He bowled a full length. All his second-innings victims fell while he was bowling around the wicket. This seems to be Australia's secret weapon. Benaud turned the match by going round at Old Trafford in 1961. Neil Hawke tried it too, but never like this.

JF: It's Massie's late swing and control that cause so much worry. But what about the slip fielding? It has been truly magnificent by both sides here, so different from Old Trafford. It must have been the background there.

RM: To Massie and Colley, the three Australian slips were not standing in the usual arc: they were stepped, second more than two yards in front of first, third a yard ahead of second. It certainly worked.

JF: The English fielding and throwing have improved out of sight since the last tour. Mike Smith's wonderful catches! And one noticeable thing—how splendidly all the bowlers have fielded straight drives.

The three most attractive Australian innings in the series so far have been this one by Greg Chappell, and two by Marsh.

RM: On the English side, Tony Greig's strokeplay is a match for anyone at the moment. After three successive fifties, he was due for a failure like Stackpole. Marsh is certainly fun—not a good player to English eyes outside the offstump, but he's a powerful fellow and what strokes! He twice took 10 in an over here, hooking d'Oliveira for four and then driving him into the Warner Stand for six. Then, when Price bowled from the Nursery End—a rarity for him—Marsh hooked him astonishingly over mid-on, and then put the next ball among the boozers in the Tavern. They loved it.

JF: I disagree with you about Marsh. I think his technique is very sound. He is not what anybody would call a slogger, although he's hit six sixes in three innings. I would call him a scientific hard hitter. Some of his drives brought back memories of Frank Woolley.

RM: Frank was here on Friday, still guardsman straight at 85. Would you have handled England in the field in that first Saturday session as Illingworth did?

JF: I perceive that you don't agree with his tactics? In what way? (Interruption: Boycott is out.

RM: Hell, that puts a different complexion on it.

A rare wicket for Dennis Lillee; Boycott bowled for 6.

JF: No, that is good for us. This will finish a wonderful Test.)

RM: I thought he might have let Marsh and Colley have more of Snow early on. D'Oliveira is a wonderful change bowler. Greg Chappell, perhaps, relaxed his concentration against a gentler pace and dragged the ball on to his wicket. I think I would then have said: 'Thank you and sweater.' Australia took 18 off Dolly's four overs, and put on 40 before Snow came back. Mind you, it is easy from the Press-box.

JF: Marsh swashbuckled every English bowler at Manchester. Snow has no fears for him. A skipper has a tough job. Most thought our Chappell took Massie off too early in the first innings, the very over

after he had got a wicket. One thing I will say—I think Illy places a field as well as anybody I've seen. He studies each batsman. Runs are never easy with him.

RM: I agree. He put himself in the gully on Friday to catch Walters, and it worked. Do you think England bowled as well with the second new ball as they did with the first?

JF: Gleeson would say even better. He played and missed a dozen times. Yes, your chaps did spray it, but don't forget that Greg started the day with 105. This means he started with a big whack of confidence. This has been a deplorable game for openers. As a bowler, will you analyse?

RM: The bowlers have to have some gravy some time. Massie bowled the same full length in the second innings as he did in the first, and he succeeded even though the wicket was not so helpful on the third day. Lillee bowled very fast.

I'm not sure whether England have the order right. Edrich told me earlier in the season that he is prepared to go down to No. 3. After four failures, I'm sure Luckhurst wishes he had from the start.

Luckhurst is one of the top three here, and his failures have hurt England. Perhaps Lillee feels he has him taped now.

JF: What we have to recognise is that in Arnold, Snow, Lillee and Massie we have four magnificent opening bowlers. They don't give the batsmen any peace. Opening against them is a tough job. Yes, Boycott was unlucky. I don't think he likes that man being placed almost in his hip pocket. Greg Chappell might have been unfortunate in also playing on, although then the ball hit his bat.

Match in a nutshell

Barring catastrophe, Australia will level the series on the fourth day tomorrow by beating England in the second Test at Lord's. England are just 50 ahead with their last pair together.

Massie, in his first Test, has taken more wickets in a Test than any Australian—15 for 122 and seven for 38 yesterday. Only Smith, who stayed from 18 to 81, could long survive the attack of Lillee, Massie and Colley in England's second innings.

Lillee took the first two wickets, and in the 95 minutes to tea England lost four wickets for 25. The match was then as good as lost.

None of the English batsmen was out to an irresponsible stroke. With the exception of Boycott, all were drawn on to the front foot and beaten by pace, movement, angle or a combination of all three.

In the morning session Australia went from 201 for five to 298 for nine, and England took 20 minutes after lunch to get the last wicket. Australia led by 36.

Greg Chappell hit 14 fours in his 131. Marsh hit two sixes and six fours in his sparkling 50. Snow took two wickets in three balls, and finished as England's most successful bowler with five for 57.

If England had lost the toss... If England had mopped up quickly yesterday morning... If Boycott had not failed... England expected to win this one. The day's events left Alec Bedser, chairman of selectors, cheerful but suffering slightly from shock.

Day
Four

The Daily
Telegraph
27/6/72

MASSIE'S MATCH SQUARES THE SERIES FOR AUSTRALIA

Australia beat England by eight wickets with more than a day and a half to spare, thus squaring the series 1-1.

By E. W. SWANTON at Lord's

No Monday miracle here! A greater contrast with the sweat and strain of Saturday could indeed scarcely be imagined as the England last-wicket pair on a balmy summer morning demonstrated that runs were easily come by on this excellent pitch and Australia then coasted to their inevitable victory.

There it is, then. The series is squared. Australia have won convincingly at Lord's, and nothing is surer than a rare fight lies ahead at Trent Bridge, at Headingley, and finally at the Oval.

This is obviously very much to the good, as also it is that for Australia a reproach has been removed. Eleven Tests against England had passed without a victory, their longest sequence in history.

The barren spell is behind them and it scarcely needs saying that Ian Chappell's side will now be twice as hard to beat.

When after Gifford and Price had added 30 runs in half an hour (a substantial proportion of them off the middle of the bat) Massie brought things to a close—by aid of the eighth catch of the innings either in the slips or by the wicketkeeper—he made his match analysis 16 for 137. This second test will be forever remembered for these figures if for nothing else.

BIGGEST TAKINGS

It will be noted in the record books, too, as producing the largest sum ever taken at a cricket match, around £83,000.

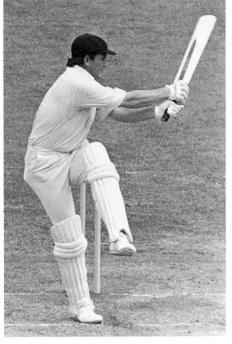

Keith Stackpole makes the winning hit.

What is at least equally important is that the crowds have had good value for money.

Limited-over cricket is excellent as far as it goes but it is a version that must always be subservient to the real thing, and the highest expression of the real thing is Tests between the major cricket countries led by England and Australia.

Granted the essential of a good wicket,

it should be possible to leave the rest safely to the players. We must hope, by the way, that the other three groundsmen do as good a job as the first two.

There is a fortnight and more before Trent Bridge and the England selectors will be glad of the chance to observe current form in the hope of improving their side.

There can be no wholesale swapping but, in at least two or three places, the opportunity exists if a few sturdy cricketers—young, please, for preference—can seize the moment.

ON-SIDE NUDGERS

In particular, the selectors will want to note the performances of batsmen those counties possessing genuine fast bowlers. One can think of several on-side nudgers with respectable averages to whom one would give scant chance against this Australian attack.

There were around 7,000 to see the two and a half hours' cricket of the fourth day, bringing the attendance, including members, somewhere just above 100,000 and the last-wicket stand—England's highest of the innings—stretched the play long enough to make their journeys better worth while.

When Australia went in soon after 12 o'clock, Stackpole, though Snow induced a missed connection or two and Price at 20 had Francis out square-cutting, soon seemed to have the situation comfortably under control.

Stackpole took three off-side fours off successive balls from the wayward Greig and hit Price for a fourth, while Ian Chappell batted with unusual restraint at the other end.

CAUGHT WITH APLOMB

At 51 d'Oliveira, as he so often does, induced a chance to slip off his outswinger and Luckhurst took it with much aplomb to dispose of Chappell.

Illingworth missed Stackpole at third slip off Snow when he had made 35 and after lunch, when only a handful were needed, Stackpole slashed Price through the covers with a stroke that Boycott might have made an effort to catch if the game had been at stake.

FINAL · SCORES

ENGLAND — First Innings

G. Boycott, b Massie		11
J. H. Edrich, lbw, b Lillee		10
B. W. Luckhurst, b Lillee		1
M. J. K. Smith, b Massie		34
B. L. d'Oliveira, lbw, b Massie		32
A. W. Greig, c Marsh, b Massie		54
A. P. E. Knott, c Colley, b Massie		43
R. Illingworth, lbw, b Massie		30
J. A. Snow, b Massie		37
N. Gifford, c Marsh, b Massie		3
J. S. E. Price, not out		4
Extras (lb 6, w 1, nb 6)		13
Total		272

Fall of wickets: 1-22, 2-23, 3-28, 4-84, 5-97, 6-193, 7-200, 8-260, 9-265, 10-272

Bowling: Lillee 28-3-90-2, Massie 32.5-7-84-8, Colley 16-2-42-0, G. S. Chappell 6-1-18-0, Gleeson 9-1-25-0

AUSTRALIA — First Innings

K. R. Stackpole, c Gifford, b Price		5
B. C. Francis, b Snow		0
I. M. Chappell, c Smith, b Snow		56
G. S. Chappell, b d'Oliveira		131
K. D. Walters, c Illingworth, b Snow		1
R. Edwards, c Smith, b Illingworth		28
J. W. Gleeson, c Knott, b Greig		1
R. W. Marsh, c Greig, b Snow		50
D. J. Colley, c Greig, b Price		25
R. A. L. Massie, c Knott, b Snow		0
D. K. Lillee, not out		2
Extras (lb 7, nb 2)		9
Total		308

Fall of wickets: 1-1, 2-7, 3-82, 4-84, 5-190, 6-212, 7-250, 8-290, 9-290, 10-308

Bowling: Snow 32-13-57-5, Price 26.1-5-87-2, Greig 29-6-74-1, d'Oliveira 17-5-48-1, Gifford 11-4-20-0, Illingworth 7-2-13-1

ENGLAND — Second Innings

G. Boycott, b Lillee		6
J. H. Edrich, c Marsh, b Massie		6
B. W. Luckhurst, c Marsh, b Lillee		4
M. J. K. Smith, c Edwards, b Massie		30
B. L. d'Oliveira, c G. S. Chappell, b Massie		3
A. W. Greig, c I. M. Chappell, b Massie		3
A. P. E. Knott, c G. S. Chappell, b Massie		12
R. Illingworth, c Stackpole, b Massie		12
J. A. Snow, c Marsh, b Massie		0
N. Gifford, not out		16
J. S. E. Price, c G. S. Chappell, b Massie		19
Extras (w 1, nb 4)		5
Total		116

Fall of wickets: 1-12, 2-16, 3-18, 4-25, 5-31, 6-52, 7-74, 8-74, 9-81, 10-116

Bowling: Lillee 21-6-50-2, Massie 27.2-9-53-8, Colley 7-1-8-0

AUSTRALIA — Second Innings

K. R. Stackpole, not out		57
B. C. Francis, c Knott, b Price		9
I. M. Chappell, c Luckhurst, b d'Oliveira		6
G. S. Chappell, not out		7
Extras (lb 2)		2
Total (2 wkts)		81

Fall of wickets: 1-20, 2-51

Bowling: Snow 8-2-15-0, Price 7-0-28-1, Greig 3-0-17-0, d'Oliveira 8-3-14-1, Luckhurst 0.5-0-5-0

Bob Massie took sixteen wickets in his Test debut. It was the high point of his short career.

·1977·

AUSTRALIA WON THE centenary Test by 45 runs, the same margin by which they had won the first encounter on the same ground 100 years earlier. They batted first and were quickly in trouble at 51 for five before Greg Chappell hit a defiant 40. When he was out to Derek Underwood, he became the Kent spinner's 250th Test victim. Australia's modest first innings score of 138 started to look more imposing as Dennis Lillee and Max Walker set about their work, Lillee finishing with six for 26 and Walker four for 54 as England slumped to 95 all out. The

second innings performances were considerably more impressive. Australia reached 419, with Rod Marsh (110 not out) becoming the first Australian wicket-keeper to score a hundred in Tests between the countries, and declared with nine wickets down leaving England needing 463 to win. That score did not look out of the question as Derek Randall, left, and Dennis Amiss added 166 for the third wicket before Amiss fell for 64. Randall, the fidgeting firecracker from Nottinghamshire, went on to score 174 off 353 balls, the first and best of his seven Test hundreds.

Dennis Lillee,
a fearsome sight
for international
batsmen for over
a decade.

Day One
The Observer 13/3/77

England's day of glory

from PETER DEELEY in Melbourne

The 61,000 fans who came here hoping for English blood in this centenary Test went away almost silent and demoralised at the end of the first day after seeing their batting heroes destroyed — all out for 138. And when, late in the day, it was England's turn to bat Dennis Lillee failed to live up to the hysteria the crowd turned on for him, though he did have opener Bob Woolmer caught when the tourists were just 29.

Pre-match pageantry had hardly prepared a huge crowd for the drama that was quickly to follow. before the game there was both nostalgia and sentiment as 20 present and sentiment as 20 present and former Test captains came on the field with massed bands for a ceremonial line-up. Then Greig won the toss with a specially minted coin, and his gamble to put Australia into bat may rank as the bravest he has ever made.

That he was right, and that the pitch had some early spite in it, was proved in spectacular fashion in the pre-lunch session. Lever, bowling from the pavilion end, was unable to extract as much lift as Willis. But in Lever's third over, Davis played inside the line of a ball on the leg stump and the umpire was emphatic in his decision. The whole England side rushed over to swamp Lever with congratulations.

Lever's first ball to Cosier, the next man in, got up and hit him on the arm. And Willis followed suit in the next over with a ball which had the crowd baying for his blood. It reared up only fractionally short of full length and McCosker stood there trying to play it down defensively. Instead the ball flew through, caught him on the bottom of the jaw and then fell onto the wicket. McCosker was helped off holding a sponge to his bloody jaw and lower lips. And

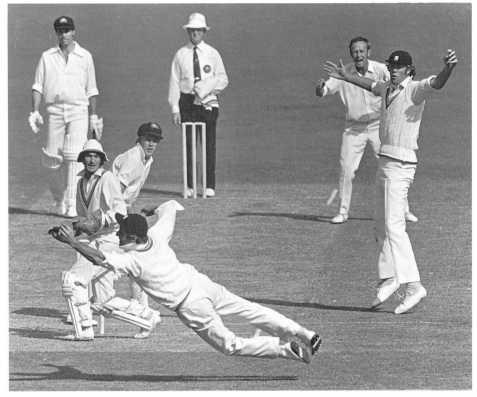

Mike Brearley dives full length to hold on to an edge from Kerry O'Keeffe off the bowling of Derek Underwood.

although the ball was no bumper, when McCosker was later taken to hospital an X-ray disclosed that his jaw had been fractured.

Chappell arrived with the scoreboard reading 12 for two Willis's first ball fizzed over his head and the Australian captain, leading his country for the first time against England, looked distinctly unamused.

Lever had Cosier groping with one delivery which only just missed the top edge of the bat. Then off the last ball of the same over Cosier tried to hook Lever, but only spooned the ball high up towards the vacant leg-slip position. Fletcher dashed across from the slips to get under the ball, and Australia were now 23 for three and only seven overs gone.

The new batsman, David Hookes, a 25-year-old teacher, could scarcely have imagined a more frightening situation in his worst nightmare. But Hookes has been breaking batting records all summer here and he showed undoubted class early on by taking 10 runs off one Lever over, including two inspiring cover drives for four.

Old replaced Willis at the end of the first hour. In Old's second over Hookes played hesitantly at a ball leaving him and gently clipped a catch into Greig's hands at slip. Forty-eight for four — and even worse was to come. Doug Walters, too, was in no mood to be tied down — and it proved his undoing. He tried to cut Willis, who had been brought back, got a thick edge and the ball shot high into the air behind the slips. Greig had plenty of time to run back and take the catch.

So ended a disastrous first session for Australia. Five of their main batsmen had gone and their run total — 57 — was the lowest in a two-hour first-day opening session that even the collective memory of the greats on this ground could recall.

The first semblance of a misfield came when England had been out there for three hours. Knott letting a low shooting ball from Willis by for four byes.

While Chappell had been tied down for three hours for his 27 runs — in the process getting the boos and jeers the crowd had been saving up for the tourists — Marsh was still inclined to lunge and sweep. It brought about his dismissal when he slashed a ball from Old on his off stump and pulled it round his ears down the leg side. Knott brought off one of his spectacular dives and held the chance with scarcely room to squeeze his gloves between ball and turf.

Gilmour went very quickly to Greig's third catch, getting a thick edge to one from Old, and O'Keeffe faced only three balls before he groped forward to Underwood, and Brearley took the best catch of the innings launching into full flight at slip.

There was little resistance from Australian tail, Chappell, who had been caution personified, suddenly lifted his head on a straight ball from Underwood and was comprehensively bowled. It must have been one of the most restrained innings of his life: 237 minutes for 40 — and not a single four.

Remembering Willis's treatment of McCosker, the whole ground was a blaze of noise as Lillee ran in to open the Australian attack to Woolmer.

Woolmer and Brearley dealt competently rather than confidently with several bouncers. Then Lillee put down two to Woolmer in one over and had him caught with the next ball at slip, the batsman's feet well away from the pitch of the ball. Derek Underwood survived both speed and deep evening shadows and England went off only 109 runs behind with nine wickets in hand in this first round.

A devil of a game

Sir Leonard Hutton comments

This was, without doubt, the greatest cricket scene I have ever seen. A huge crowd on a perfect Melbourne sunny day turned out to see the game of the century. I, along with other former England captains and also Australians, stood with the two teams before the start of play what was to me a rather moving occasion. I stood between Cope and Fletcher on this magnificent turf while the national anthem was played. I could feel the nervousness of the England players. It was rather like Wembley Stadium before the Cup Final.

Greig made a great start for England when he won the toss and showed his aggressive spirit by asking Australia to take strike, giving his own pace bowlers the chance to bowl on a first day, pre-lunch Melbourne wicket with its reputation of being full of the devil.

After the first three or four overs I felt uneasy about Greig's decision. Willis had problems with his direction, but Lever had a nice lively pace. I thought for a moment this was not the Melbourne wicket of old. Had a mistake been made? Should we have faced the Australian demon bowler Lillee from the very outset?

Then, to my surprise, Davis managed to miss what I thought a pretty straight delivery from Lever, Davis might have played slightly across this ball, which was a little above medium pace. But this was the wicket England needed, for it put new life and hope into the opening attack. A number of friendly bouncers had been bowled by Willis without giving the batsmen any problems at all when, out of the blue, Willis made a short-pitched delivery hurry through and lift to McCosker, who tried his pull shot only to deflect the ball via his face on to the stumps. Not a good stroke from an experienced batsman at that state of the game.

Australian batsmen are very fond of the pull stroke. As they are compulsive gamblers so there are compulsive hookers and pullers — and Australia seems to have their fair share at the moment. Cosier and Walters gave their wickets away with this stroke, one of the hardest to play, before

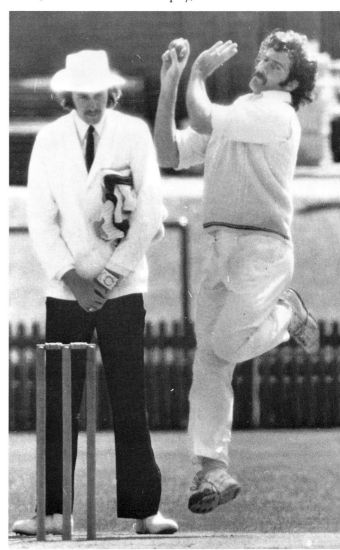

Lillee gets sideways-on to unleash another fearsome delivery.

Glasses poised to toast a batsman

From Colin Cowdrey

MELBOURNE, March 13

getting the pace of the wicket. They chanced their arm and payed the penalty.

Chappell's innings was full of sound common sense in the difficult circumstances. It is to be hoped that his colleagues take note in the second innings and inwardly digest the example shown by their captain. This Melbourne wicket was without doubt a good wicket by any standards. England bowled well, giving very little away. The field placing was good and fielding was outstanding in all departments. Greig's catching of Gilmour, Knott's of Marsh and Brearley's catch at slip left-handed to dismiss O'Keeffe were all masterpieces.

Many old players — and many of this large crowd — were interested to see Hooke's first appearance in a Test match. He got a really fine reception when he made his way to the wicket. This young man could well give England a lot of trouble in the years ahead. He plays very straight and showed in this short stay that he has true class.

To bowl out Australia on this wicket was a fine performance. Old and Underwood were both outstanding and gave very little away. England's fielding was of the highest class; no chances were missed and Knott enhanced his already remarkable reputation.

England's opening batsmen faced a very aggressive opening attack in the final difficult hour. But Australia undoubtedly missed Thomson. Batting against Walker was almost a respite after facing Lillee. If Walker hit you it would hurt: but if Lillee hit you the memory and the pain lingered on.

Lillee bowled a couple of nasty bouncers to Woolmer who was looking for a third when he failed to get across to a good length ball pitched fifteen to eighteen inches outside the off-stump. This wicket for Lillee clearly ilustrated the value of the bouncer.

I came here expecting that Australia would win — though not easily — principally because of Lillee and Chappell. But this wicket is going to get better and better and I think the advantage is in England's favour — particularly as McCosker is injured.

Off the field the celebrations do not look like abating. Glasses clink and memories flood back as old friends pause to chin-wag in a relaxed, leisurely way. On the field the two teams are at each other's throats, locked in a desperate struggle for runs.

This is as hard a Test match as one could imagine. From the ring it is something of a puzzle why the ball should be so much master of the bat. In India Willis, Lever and Old spearheaded our triumph and here they were revelling in conditions to suit them. A mat of grass holding the moisture and an unexpected variation of bounce made for tentative batting. The fielding was superb on both sides and so far there has been only one chance to slip away, with Knott, Marsh, Brearley, Greig and Chappell outstanding in picking up outstanding catches.

At the end of the first day 54 overs had been bowled, Australia dismissed and England off to a sound start. Today, under a cloudless sky, Australians feared the worst. Hobbs and Sutcliffe might have batted for ever in the conditions. I was sitting with Ponsford and Hutton, with Boycott in the next row. I had a feeling that each one of them might have broken some bowlers' hearts today. But it was not to be.

Long before lunch the Australian crowd were in full voice chanting Lillee and Walker as they ran in to bowl. This is a war of nerves for batsmen, the new and unattractive aspect of the art of

Packed stands at the MCG made this, in Sir Len Hutton's opinion: "the greatest cricket scene."

Randall doffed
his cap as a Lillee
bouncer whistled
past his ear.
Next ball he was
out for 4 — round
one to Lillee.

batsmanship. Walker was in his element, swinging the ball about and varying his pace. But every eye was on Lillee, the Australian virtuoso and athlete supreme. He posed every sort of problem and his figures did not really flatter him. England can only be thankful to have been spared Thomson's blast from the other end, as could well happen again in England next summer.

It was fitting and appreciated by the large crowd that Bob Parish, chairman of the Australian Cricket Board, escorted Harold Larwood and Bill Voce on to the middle at the interval. They were given a wonderful ovation. Voce took his jacket off and marked out his run much to the amusement of the crowd. I could not help noticing that he had elected to bowl into the breeze, taking up where he had left off 45 years ago. I longed to turn the clock back and see them bowl an over each, but

The Don might not have shared my sentiment.

The crowd have been aching for an exhibition of class batsmanship from someone. Sadly, Amiss and Fletcher were out before they were in. Walters showed us some glimpses of his best in the second innings, but Chappell has looked rather at odds with himself. Davis played well under the pressure of playing for his place to England. It was the young Hookes, in his first Test match, who has showed us some of the best strokes so far.

I was glad to see that Randall had plenty of time against the fast bowlers. Unwisely, he doffed his cap as a bouncer from Lillee whistled by. The gallery enjoyed it, but they liked it even more when he was out next ball. Greig walked in to a noisy reception, part cheering and the rest not so polite. He induces this sort of love-hate relationship and thrives on it.

Lillee took an age setting and resetting the field for his first ball to Greig, placing a fielder just behind the square-leg umpire as a decoy. Then came the fastest ball of the day, well pitched up at the off stump.

Greig's response was to attack. He threw himself at it like Arnold Palmer laying into a one-iron into the wind at Birkdale, both legs off the ground. Happily, he was late with the shot and the ball just sidled by the off-stump. It was a staggering stroke for the England captain to be contemplating at this juncture. It would have pleased Frank Woolley, no doubt, and Charlie Barnett. They believed in taking the bowling by the scruff of the neck. There was no chance of this happening today. Yesterday the England flag proudly, almost in disbelief. But now the game is back with Australia. Dare we hope for another dramatic change-round tomorrow?

Australia 430 ahead after Marsh, Hookes end bowlers' reign

'Lefties' set up win

By PETER McFARLINE, our
Chief Cricket Writer

Bold left-handed batsmen Rod Marsh and David Hookes broke the bowlers' domination of the Centenary Test yesterday and set Australia up for victory.

At stumps last night, Australia was 8/387 in its second innings, giving it an overall lead of 430 with tomorrow and Thursday to play. Today is the rest day.

Marsh was 95 not out, needing only five runs to become the first Australian wicket-keeper to score a century in Anglo-Australian Test matches.

The gallant Rick McCosker was his partner on 17 not out.

The Australians added 263 runs for the loss of five wickets in the six hours play.

If that seems slow, it must be remembered that the England bowlers managed to limit themselves to only 57 overs for the day — an appallingly slow rate.

Australia's early batsmen, Ian Davis and Doug Walters, consolidated the team's position with watchful defence in yesterday's first session.

The game was still fairly well poised at lunch-time, with the score 4/166. Walters then was on 66 and Hooke 26.

Walters was out four minutes after play resumed, giving Hookes the chance to take hold of the steady England attack and pummel it unmercifully.

The 21-year-old Adelaide physical education student, playing in his first Test did exactly that.

The needling given to him by captain Tony Greig throughout his innings provided the catalyst.

Hookes played defensively at the first two balls of Greig's sixth over. The next five all finished on the MCG pickets as his score rocketted from 26 to 56.

The third ball went straight over the

David Hookes, playing in his first Test, made 56 in 59 deliveries.

bowler's head for 4. The fourth, a shortish delivery, was swept finely for number two.

Cover fieldsman Derek Randall had barely moved when the fifth delivery was past him.

Hookes reached his 50 with an on drive thought the vacant mid-wicket area off the sixth and the covers were again violated on the seventh.

The last ball was played to cover point and Greig grabbed his cap and sweater from umpire Max O'Connell, grateful to vacate the bowling crease.

It is hard to imagine any batsman making such an impact on a match in his debut.

Comparisons are hard to find but it is believed the last time five consecutive fours were hit in a Test match was in 1921 at the MCG when Victor Richardson performed the feat against England captain J. W. H. T. Douglas.

OUT NEXT OVER

Hookes was out in the next over caught bat and pad by a tumbling Keith Fletcher at short leg off Derek Underwood.

His 56 had come off only 59 deliveries with nine 4s in 125 minutes.

His start had been faltering, especially against the short-pitched ball on or about off-stump, but his final impact was staggering.

The sight of Hookes left an interesting imprint on the England bowlers, who gradually lost their line, and to the fieldsmen, who made several errors towards the end of the day.

And it gave Marsh the incentive to find the batting form that has all but deserted him at Test level in recent times. He hit the ball cleanly during his 225 minute stay at the crease, and his 95 has come from only 144 deliveries with nine 4s.

The stocky wicketkeeper set an Australian record on Sunday, and could well make this his most memorable match with just five more runs tomorrow.

He reached his 56 in only 77 deliveries with a classic straight hit to the boundary off Chris Old, and shared in three good partnerships.The first was 37 and 42 minutes for the sixth wicket with the dashing Hookes.

Then came 23 for the seventh wicket with Gary Gilmour, who made 19 before aiming a wild swipe at Lever — only to hear the death rattle of his stumps.

Then marsh and Lillee added 36 in 87 minutes for the eighth.

The pair had no trouble weathering the second no ball which was taken by Old at 6/244, although Lillee at 16 was dropped by Old in the gully by Willis — a chance that would have been held on Saturday or Sunday.

When Lillee departed for 26, well caught by Amiss in the covers off Old, McCosker held on courageously.

CROWD RESTLESS

Although the crowd was restless to see Marsh reach his century before stumps, there was really no hurry. He took 38 minutes over his last 14 runs.

Australia has much to thank patient opener Ian Davis, 64 in 239 minutes, and Waites, 66 in 217 minutes for their good second innings recovery.

Both showed early yesterday that the wicket held little to fear and their concentration rarely lapsed.

Both showed responsibility to the cause, although Walters was dropped at 16 and 60.

Nevertheless, they showed that the Centenary Test was not past —? bowlers.

England now has a formidable to save, let alone win, this match.

Only one side, the 1914 Australians, has managed to make more than this in the fourth innings to win an England Australia Test.

I don't fancy England's chances of re-writing the history books.

Hookes by any other name...

By
JACK FINGLETON

David Hookes is not a second Bradman nor a second Harvey nor a second Frank Woolley.

To me he is David Hookes of Adelaide, worthy of his name standing on its own merits after his electric batting at the MCG yesterday and I do hope people do not burden him with the handicap of being known as a second somebody or other.

I am pleased I wrote yesterday that Hookes showed he was a Test batsman as soon as he came to the middle on Saturday.

One with a blind cricket eye could see that. He got out when Old came up with a short, rising ball to which an experienced batsman would have dropped his wrists.

Bless me if yesterday after Ian Davis had played a most commendable innings, Greig didn't blatantly bowl immediately for Hookes to commit a similar indiscretion.

Greig had a cordon of four slips and he bowled for the lad to snick.

I don't know what ailed Doug Walters at that moment.

He should immediately have walked down the pitch to quieten Hookes and said; "David, they are going for you in the slips again. Let them go. "

Walters didn't do what an old hand should have done to a newcomer.

Hookes batted his way out of that but the moment of truth came when Greig suddenly decided in his 13th over to bowl off-breaks around the stumps.

Like the old soldier he is, Greig took infinite time and care to adjust his fields, a man a few yards here and a few yards there, all intended obviously to put more pressure on Hookes.

The lad's answer was to hit the best shot of the game to that stage by lofting Greig high over mid-off, an imperious shot.

Next he swung him fine for another four. But better was to come.

The next was a glittering cover drive, then a beautiful stroke on the on-side to bring up his 50, then another crashing four through the covers again and the crowd understandably went wild.

Five fours in five balls and then the next and last ball of the over could have been another boundary only Amiss

Rod Marsh unleashed some fearsome strokes in his unbeaten 110.

roundly hooted, was in the way.

Greig took his sweater, hid his face in it and pretended to cringe away. Hookes was out the next ball he was splendidly caught by Fletcher at short leg of Underwood.

Like playing at the rising ball, he will learn to play a dead-bat to such a ball. He

is only 21, and what confidence this success will give him in the highest sphere has yet to be seen.

He is a bright intelligent lad who missed much cricket last summer when he went back to school to matriculate for the teacher's college.

This really, was the first time this historic match came alight from a batting view-point.

I happened across a recent Test batsman of ours who told me that the pitch was allowing movement; and the ball wouldn't come on to the bat, a common saying in cricket to day.

It not only came on to Hookes' old bat, well bound, but it left it with incredible speed. He is a sheer delight and will

always be learning. His name is resounding around the cricket world today and he is the best thing to happen to this match.

Apart from Dennis, of course, he brought life to it.

Dennis shares with me the belief that he is a mighty good batsman as he showed yesterday.

It was splendid to see Marsh succeed and he also proved that the ball will come up to the bat if the batsman moves to it.

Walters, Davis, Marsh, who might have got a Test century here a few years ago had not the closure been made when he was in the nineties, all played delightful innings.

But the hero of the match was Hookes whose name suggests one of the best shots of the game if played sensibly.

Cheeky Randall canes
Lillee and shows up
Aussie weakness

Day Four

The Daily Mail 17/3/77

From ALEX BANNISTER in Melbourne

The gloom which enveloped the English camp after the recurring catastrophes in the Centenary Melbourne Test was suddenly lifted yesterday by the exciting impertinence and skill of Derek Randall.

Apart from his own brilliant 87 not out, the 27-year-old Nottinghamshire batsman laid bare the Australian secret that they are virtually a two-man bowling side.

On the eve of the selection of the party to defend the Ashes in England next season, it was made clear on a pitch becoming progressively slower that after Dennis Lillee and Max Walker their attacking resources are limited.

Randall's second achievement was to restore the pride and fighting spirit of a side physically on its last weary legs and mentally jaded.

The winning target of 463 in ten hours 50 minutes, including those last 15 eight-ball overs, might as well have been 1,000 at the time, but by the close it was down to 272 with Randall still there after the best 222 minutes of his career and nine thumping crowd-silencing boundaries.

CRUCIAL

'I have never seen Derek bat better,' said skipper Tony Greig. 'I told him not to get out at 40 or 60 as he often does, and to keep going. His batting was tremendously exciting for us because we

*Round two to
Randall...
The Nottinghamshire
batsman hooks Lillee
for four during his
magnificent innings
of 174.*

are desperately short of batsmen of true class. We will now fight to the death.'

Randall's first assault was on Walker, and the crucial stage came in Lillee's fourth spell. An over produced no fewer than six short-pitchers — and 12 runs. Substitute Ray Bright might have caught him at gully if his arms were twice their length but Randall hooked and drove as if he had never heard of Lillee.

Lillee gave Randall 'the stare,' which is supposed to turn the batsman to jelly, and Randall gave the stare back with an impish grin on his face. Randall was never intimidated, never cowed, and never restricted in his stroke play and praise be, here was an English batsman vigorously putting bat to ball.

The second wicket stand between Mike Brearley, who played his resolute part to perfection, and Randall produced 85 in 123 minutes. Randall faced 88 deliveries for his first 50 in his fifth Test and walked off at the close with his bat on his shoulder as if he had been enjoying an afternoon spree at Trent Bridge.

Dennis Amiss had a traumatic beginning, pushing his first ball from Walker uppishly by short square leg, and against Lillee hopped around as if in pain — possibly mental anguish. But Amiss is a born fighter. No top-class batsman has been in as many peaks and troughs, and he has never lacked fierce but quiet determination.

Lillee can be relied on to make a supreme effort for a breakthrough, but if England can hang on in the crucial morning session, the Queen's visit will coincide with a dramatic struggle.

Day Five

The Times
18/3/77

A dish to set before the Queen

From Colin Cowdrey

Melbourne, March 17

As the light began to fade after five gloriously sunny days of enthralling cricket, Knott was dismissed by Lillee, his fifth wicket and eleventh in the match, and Australia had won the centenary Test match by 45 runs.

By some coincidence, on March 17, 1877, a hundred years ago to the day, England were set a target of 154 and also lost by 45 runs. Today it was a stiffer task. In scoring 417, England achieved the highest total in the fourth innings of an Anglo-Australian Test match and in doing so have won all hearts.

The first hour was fascinating, for Chappell had a problem. With Gilmour injured, Lillee was the trump card. He had to be thrown in to the fray to make the early break, if possible, but the new ball was available in 12 overs. O'Keeffe was bowled tidily and took two vital wickets later on. Walker, faced with the prospect of some marathon spells later in the day, was discarded temporarily.

Needing just 13 for his first Test hundred, Randall was confronted with a burst from Lillee. If he was nervous he showed no trace of it. Brearley had provided the helpful word early in his innings and now he was fortunate to have the steadying influence of Amiss at the other end. In the event he played quite superbly, a deft sweep, a glorious late cut and he was soon on 99, facing Lillee. Next ball he tucked him away to fine leg for his first Test hundred and became the fourteenth batsman to score a hundred in his first Test match against Australia. The Yorkshireman, Willie Watson, was the last to do so in 1953.

I was delighted for him after his rigours in India where his previous best in a Test match had been 37, but he had made a huge contribution to the team's success by his enthusiasm.

It would have been understandable if he had shown the odd lapse of concentration in the excitement of his achievement but he just played better and better as he went along. He is something of an irrepressible Jack-in-the-box both in batting and fielding but today he assumed a responsibility to fit the occasion. His timing never left him; only fatigue slowed him down and, in part, contributed to his downfall.

All the while Amiss looked a class player with plenty of time. He seems to have the broadest bat in English cricket today and Lillee did not unruffle him as much as I expected. His sudden dismissal by a ball that kept rather low was the turning point of the day. True, that while Greig and Randall were together we could still have won but somehow I had the feeling that we were beginning to live too dangerously.

When Randall made 161 he edged Greig Chappell low and wide where Marsh appeared to have scooped his glove under the catch. As he rolled over and over the umpire upheld the appeal and Randall departed a disconsolate figure. Without delay Marsh leapt to his feet and rushed down the wicket to tell his captain that the ball had bounced. The umpires conferred and Randall was recalled. It was indeed a chivalrous gesture at such a critical moment of the match.

O'Keeffe traps John Lever.

Just before tea England were slowed down by some good bowling from Chappell himself and he elected to gamble with O'Keeffe. In his first over, Cosier dived full length to take a magnificent catch off bat and pad and Randall's historic innings had closed on 174. The whole ground rose to him.

Through tears of joy he went out through the wrong gate, finding himself at

contempt. He is a genius of improvisation.

But the day finished with Lillee summoning up energy and fire from I don not know where. He was bowling faster at the end than he was at the beginning and deservedly he was carried aloft, first by players and then by some of his ecstatic countrymen, while a dozen or more policemen surrounded him to keep him intact.

F I N A L · S C O R E S

AUSTRALIA — First Innings

I. C. Davis, lbw, b Lever		5
R. B. McCosker, b Willis		4
G. J. Cosier, c Fletcher, b Lever		10
G. S. Chappell, b Underwood		40
D. Hookes, c Greig, b Old		17
K. D. Walters, c Greig, b Willis		4
R. W. Marsh, c Knott, b Old		28
G. J. Gilmour, c Greig, b Old		4
K. J. O'Keeffe, c Brearley, b Underwood		0
D. K. Lillee, not out		10
M. H. N. Walker, b Underwood		2
Extras (b 4, lb 2, nb 8)		14
Total		**138**

Fall of wickets: 1-11, 2-13, 3-23, 4-45, 5-51, 6-102, 7-114, 8-117, 9-136, 10-138
Bowling: Lever 12-1-36-2, Willis 8-0-33-2, Old 12-4-39-3, Underwood 11.6-2-16-3

ENGLAND — First Innings

R. A. Woolmer, c Chappell, b Lillee		9
J. M. Brearley, c Hookes, b Lillee		12
D. L. Underwood, c Chappell, b Walker		7
D. W. Randall, c Marsh, b Lillee		4
D. L. Amiss, c O'Keeffe, b Walker		4
K. W. R. Fletcher, c Marsh, b Walker		4
A. W. Greig, b Walker		18
A. P. E. Knott, lbw, b Lillee		15
C. M. Old, c Marsh, b Lillee		3
J. K. Lever, c Marsh, b Lillee		11
R. G. D. Willis, not out		1
Extras (b 2, lb 2, nb 2, w 1)		7
Total		**95**

Fall of wickets: 1-19, 2-30, 3-34, 4-40, 5-40, 6-61, 7-65, 8-78, 9-86, 10-95
Bowling: Lillee 13.3-2-26-6, Walker 15-5-54-4, O'Keeffe 1-0-4-0, Gilmour 5-3-4-0

AUSTRALIA — Second Innings

I. C. Davis, c Knott, b Greig		68
K. J. O'Keeffe, c Willis, b Old		14
G. S. Chappell, b Old		2
C. J. Cosier, c Knott, b Lever		4
K. D. Walters, c Knott, b Greig		66
D. Hookes, c Fletcher, b Underwood		56
R. W. Marsh, not out		110
G. J. Gilmour, b Lever		16
D. Lillee, c Amiss, b Old		29
R. McCosker, c Greig, b Old		25
M. H. N. Walker, not out		8
Extras (lb 10, nb 15)		25
Total (9 wkts dec.)		**419**

Fall of wickets: 1-33, 2-40, 3-53, 4-132, 5-187, 6-244, 7-277, 8-353, 9-407
Bowling: Lever 21-1-95-2, Willis 22-0-91-0, Old 27.6-2-104-4, Underwood 12-2-38-1, Greig 14-3-66-2

ENGLAND — Second Innings

R. A. Woolmer, lbw, b Walker		12
J. M. Brearley, lbw, b Lillee		43
D. W. Randall, c Cosier, b O'Keeffe		174
D. L. Amiss, b Chappell		64
K. W. R. Fletcher, c Marsh, b Lillee		1
A. W. Greig, c Cosier, b O'Keeffe		41
A. P. E. Knott, lbw, b Lillee		42
C. M. Old, c Chappell, b Lillee		2
J. K. Lever, lbw, b O'Keeffe		4
D. L. Underwood, b Lillee		7
R. G. D. Willis, not out		5
Extras (b 8, lb 4, w 3, nb 7)		22
Total		**417**

Fall of wickets: 1-28, 2-113, 3-279, 4-290, 5-346, 6-369, 7-380, 8-385, 9-410, 10-417
Bowling: Lillee 34.4-7-139-5, Walker 22-4-83-1, Gilmour 4-0-29-0, Chappell 16-7-29-1, O'Keeffe 33-6-108-3, Walters 3-2-7-0

Spectators carry Lillee aloft at the end of his 11 wicket performance.

the end of the path leading to the special box where the Queen and the Duke of Edinburgh were sitting. Within a few yards of them he discovered his mistake and stopped in his tracks and, much to the amusement of all, bowed before beating a hasty retreat across the public seats. It was a happy touch for the day belonged to him.

It might be arguable that Lillee's great bowling could have earned him the prize of Man of the Match, but without doubt Randall was the man who had made the match complete.

There were not four gladder hearts in Melbourne today than Larwood, Voce, Hardstaff and Simpson, giant names from Trent Bridge.

If the game tilted fairly sharply towards Australia after tea Knott made it clear that they were not going to have it all their own way. He played a series of astonishing shots, treating Lillee with utter

But alas, his medical advisers have determined that he is not quite intact although you could never have guessed it today. Sadly for the English public but to the relief of the English batsmen, he has withdrawn from the forthcoming tour of England.

We have had a remarkable week and life will be rather flat until we have had time to absorb it all. I do not know when I have enjoyed the last day of a Test match more than this one. It had everything, both captains playing their part in the challenge, both wicketkeepers making their mark, some wonderful fast bowling, good sustained spells of leg spin bowling, some fine fielding, a generous gesture and a large crowd.

The result was open until near the end. When Randall and Greig were raking the embers just before tea there was still the prospect of an English victory. What a dish to set before the Queen.

ENGLAND V AUSTRALIA
16TH - 21ST JULY

·1981·

HEADINGLEY
THIRD TEST

TRAILING 1-0 IN THE series, England arrived in Leeds for the third Test with Ian Botham, *right*, deposed as captain after making a pair at Lord's. Mike Brearley was back in charge but England suffered another dismal start as Australia piled up 401 for nine declared, John Dyson scoring 102 and captain Kim Hughes making 89. Botham, without the pressures of captaincy, took six for 95 and then scored 50 in England's reply but it all looked in vain as they were forced to follow on needing 228 to make Australia bat again. When they collapsed to 135 for seven, England appeared doomed and bookmakers were offering a staggering 500-1 against an England victory. Then Botham masterminded one of the great fightbacks in Test history. He cracked 100 off 87 balls and went on to score 149 not out and, with the help of 'rabbits' Graham Dilley (56) and Chris Old (29), left Australia needing 130 to win on the final day — surely a simple target, but more than England could have been hoping for. At 56 for one they were cruising, until an inspired Bob Willis, having changed ends, took eight for 49 to secure an amazing 18-run victory.

Ian Botham ducking under a beamer from Geoff Lawson as his ultimately heroic innings starts to become more than an irritation to Australia.

Day One

The Daily Telegraph

17/7/81

DYSON CELEBRATES AFTER ENGLAND LET CHANCE SLIP

By MICHAEL MELFORD at Headingley

England dropped their catches at Headingley yesterday, as they did at Trent Bridge, so Australia could work their way into a strong position on the first day of the Third Cornhill Test. John Dyson's previous highest score in 11 Test matches was 53, but, accumulating largely off the back foot, he batted doggedly for all but the last quarter hour of the five hours 10 minutes' play.

His 102 steered Australia to a score of 203 for three, which in the prevailing conditions was good going. Dyson was dropped at 57 and Chappell, his partner in a second-wicket stand of 94, was missed twice in the early stages of their two hours 40 minutes together.

England's bowlers were tidier than on many occasions recently and they were out of luck, but the bounce varied enough and the ball moved enough to suggest that this might be a pitch on which the Australian bowlers, with their extra pace, will prove a handful. Nearly two hours of play was lost in the first part of the day, but the extra hour was played on an evening of brilliant sunshine.

LACK OF VARIETY

It was a fair guess that a three-week drought would end on the morning of a Test match, but one over was fitted in after a punctual start before the light faded for the first time. The players were soon back, but when it faded again, followed by heavy showers, the hold-up lasted for 35 minutes before lunch and 70 minutes afterwards. Hughes had taken the unusual step of having another look at the pitch after winning the toss, accompanied by Marsh, before he decided to bat.

Various factors probably created doubt, including the over-cast weather in which the England bowlers were likely to be kept fresh by stoppages for bad light or rain.

England had somewhat surprisingly left out Emburey on a dry looking pitch with cracks in it. Such disappointment, which the lack of variety caused, was slightly relieved when the faster bowlers—Old, especially—kept the ball well up and generally made the batsmen work hard.

Just before rain ended the 65 minutes play in the morning Botham bowled one over and brought his third ball back to have the left-handed Wood lbw.

In the afternoon Botham and Old bowled very well for an hour, moving the ball about and creating a new uncertainty. Only 11 runs were scored in the first half hour and Chappell, when three, survived a difficult chance off Botham to Gower diving left at third slip.

CHAPPELL DROPPED

Before tea Willey, who had a finger injury at Lord's and did not bowl there, had three overs but it was Willis off whom Chappell had his next escape, dropped by Botham. It would be unrealistic to expect Botham to be instantly transformed into the fairy prince for whom all goes well.

He had certainly been running up more smoothly than for much of the last year, but when the first catch came his way at second slip, it hit him on the chest and bounced away. Chappell was then seven and the score 90.

With what seemed a reasonable piece of thinking, Brearley moved Gatting, who has been catching everything, to second slip and switched Botham to the gully. As if inspired by some impish fate, Dyson cut Dilley into the gully and Botham missed the catch two-handed to his left.

Occasionally Willey pitched short and was hit cleanly off the back foot, but batting became no easier as the unevenness of the bounce became more marked. Old, as the most accurate, caused the most uncertainty.

Eventually Chappell tried to force a ball from Willey off the back foot. It was probably not quite short enough for the purpose and he was caught at the wicket.

Hughes came in with 75 minutes left and was on hand to congratulate Dyson as he reached his priceless 100. Dilley came on for a new spell and his first ball was of a good, full length. Dyson, driving over and across it, was bowled.

John Dyson hits out during his innings of 102.

Botham keeps England hopes alive

Day
Two

The Times
18/7/81

By John Woodcock
Cricket Correspondent

The second day of the Third Test match, sponsored by Cornhill, like the second Test at Lord's and also the first day of this one, contained little of the quality or the cut-and-thrust to be expected when England meet Australia—at any rate Botham, happily, took five wickets after tea. Until they declared at 401 for nine, with 20 minutes left, Australia just plodded along, against much ordinary bowling, helped by a further blackening of England's catching record.

Though nothing like as bad as the one at Trent Bridge, this is not the best pitches. Australia's batsmen were rapped on the thighs often enough for England's to be sure not to mislay their thigh pads this morning. Besides this, the occasional ball kept low. With their one-match lead in the series Australia were content to take no risks. They batted as though sure enough that a total of around 400 would be an insurance against defeat, as no doubt it will be.

The days are gone when they are immediately vulnerable if the ball is moving about. Hughes batted very solidly for his 89, Yallop with much tenacity for his 58. By running between overs England just about managed 15 overs to the hour. Of the overs they bowled in their five hours in the field, Willey was allowed one. I sensed that, until Botham got among the wickets, even the English players thought fairly little of it all.

No-one will be more disturbed by the standard of England's fielding, especially their catching, than Brearley. In his first two years as captain England scaled the heights, missing little that came their way at slip and saving countless runs on the ground.

It is all very different now. At various times in the present series Hendrick, Gooch, Woolmer, Gatting, Willey, Botham, Dilley, Brearley, Emburey, Old and Boycott have been at slip. Yesterday it was Gooch who nodded there: Hughes, when he was

Botham: "was running in quite as in his palmy days."

66, put down off an easy one. The best slip catcher in England is probably Tavare, a fact that the England selectors will have to start, very soon, to bear in mind.

The local view was that a Bradford league side would have bowled better than England did yesterday morning. Their line was dreadful. Although it was Dilley who took the only wicket to fall, when he

removed Bright, the nightwatchman, no-one was less straight, all day, than he.

Most counties, with the help of their overseas players, would have bowled better than this. I imagine even that an attack of Hendrick, Jackman, Selvey and Allott, or of Arnold, Lever, Jarvis and Jesty would have been disappointed to let Australia declare. Of one thing you may be fairly sure—Australia will bowl more accurately than England did.

As on the first day enough time was lost early on for play to continue until seven o'clock. This time the morning stoppage lasted for 35 minutes, that in the afternoon for 70 minutes. There was less sun now than on Thursday, which made the day only more cheerless. In the third over of the morning, before the first of the rain, England took a new ball, Old sharing it with Dilley rather than with Willis as he had on Thursday. By lunch, when there had been 85 minutes play, Australia were 250 for four, having started at 203 for three.

The afternoon, consisting of 20 overs, produced 59 runs. Once in a while Hughes uncorked a fizzing stroke through the covers but, these apart, there was precious little to remember. England bowled better than in the morning but without success. It was nearly five o'clock by the time they took their second wicket of the day. Having batted for four and a half hours Hughes, aiming to leg, spooned up a return catch to Botham.

That was at 332. At 354 Border was leg before to Botham, on the front foot, and three runs later Yallop, wafting at Botham, was caught by Taylor off the under edge. After Marsh and Lawson had added 39 Botham had Lawson caught at the wicket off a lifter and when, as the long day drew towards its close, Botham bowled Marsh, Hughes declared.

By then Botham was running in quite as in his palmy days. It was good to see—an encouragement to him and to Brearley, and to England when they needed one.

Day Three

The Sunday Telegraph

19/7/81

The Lion gets tail in a twist

TONY LEWIS reports from Headingley

Australia should rest comfortably on their day off knowing that they have shaken the lion by the tail and rendered him almost toothless and in his own den too. Following Australia's declaration of 401 for nine, they bowled out England without straining too hard for 174, taking a first innings lead of 227 and enforcing the follow-on. Bad light stopped play twice, at nought for one and finally at six for one.

Their advantage has come mainly from the accuracy of their bowlers. England's seam bowling had been inaccurate, but the Australians, Lillee, Alderman and Lawson settled into a steady line and length which had the English batsmen having to play at the ball most of the time. With the luxury of 400 runs behind him, Hughes could keep his close fielders lined up from first slip to square gully.

Maybe England ran out of luck too. Graham Gooch certainly did. He faced four balls yesterday, and was out to two of them. When England followed on 227 runs behind Gooch was brilliantly caught by Alderman, diving from third slip across in front of second.

Immediately Gooch was out and up the pavilion steps, the umpires found the light unsuitable for batting. Off they came. It is the sort of decision which tempts the most genial professional, as Graham Gooch is, to shoot himself in the showers... or maybe shoot the umpires.

Play was stopped by bad light at 5.20 and the players did not reappear before the scheduled finish at six o'clock. The large crowd were hoping that the umpire's inspection, just before six, would find the conditions suitable for the extra hour to be taken. It was not to be so.

However, shortly before six o'clock the sun re-emerged and a few minutes after the hour, was blazing down on Headingley. It was a perfect evening for cricket. The playing rule says that the teams have to be on the field, if the extra time is to be made available.

The crowd was furious. Cricket was about to self-destruct again. Many who

Mike Gatting is lbw to Lillee for 15.

had travelled far and paid good money were left complaining that the players should be available throughout the extra hour in case the weather improved, as it had here. Cushions were thrown and, once again, cricket's administrators were cursed. When will the game realise that it is offering professional entertainment! — not simply a workaday routine for the performer only.

The Test began with two days of mystery. The Australians found most of the answers; England groped as if they were trying to find a way out of a maze and, in the end, had to be helped out by Kim Hughes's declaration; the spectators knew all the questions but none of the answers.

Why had England left out Emburey? If it was to be a match won by the seamers then three would surely be enough. Another doubt was whether they had the right seamers there anyway. The accuracy of Old, Hendrick or Jackman and the swing of Botham should have been enough to see any side out for 200. Dilley and Willis fired gentle cannon, mainly in the wrong direction.

More questions. Why was Willey brought into the attack to bowl 13 overs, taking one wicket for 31 runs on a pitch which was not supposed to be assisting spin?

The one understandable aspect of the game was Australia's determined batting. Dyson's century made up for his past failures. He was watchful and made the most of the luxury of being able to monitor most of the balls as they passed wide of the wicket. His partnership with Hughes could be the most significant effort of the whole series.

They were the players who took their sides's total to fantasy proportions in "English" conditions. Yes, the most repeated question on the ground was "how on earth can you get 400 at Headingley when the ball is moving about?"

When England's turn came to bat, the problems of staying at the crease were obvious. Gooch went early, Boycott and Brearly batted with huge concentration, but not quite enough luck. Boycott, in fact, got so far behind a ball from Lawson that he left his leg stump unprotected.

A bouncer from Terry Alderman forces Boycott to take evasive action.

The ball cut back sharply from the off and knocked over the slender target. I cannot imagine that Boycott is bowled behind his legs more than once a decade. So, with three wickets down for 42 a normality settled over the play. The three-pronged Australian seam attack kept the ball up to the bat, the slips lined up for the edges, but whenever decent attacking strokes were possible, Gower and Gatting leading the way, the ball flew over the hard ground for valuable runs.

Lillee who had opened the attack from the Kirkstall Lane end followed Alderman from the main stand end. He immediately gave Gatting some trouble. Wood dropped a straightforward catch at first slip.

Thereafter the day belonged to Australia, barring a few flourishes from Gower and Botham. Botham played and missed like everyone else, but he also strung together some of the most belligerent strokes.

He had rightly worked out the high odds against occupying the crease for a long time by defensive methods and all Headingley wished him the good fortune to get away with his counter attack. His end had to come with a snick, which it did off Lillee's bowling. He left the arena with firm stride knowing that he was the old Botham, contributing massively to England's effort.

However, the Australians were not to be denied their victims. Rod Marsh too, entered the record book. In 71 Tests he has beaten Alan Knott's record of 263 victims behind the stumps which was set in Knott's 93 Tests. Yesterday Marsh took the ball, which tended to go through at varying heights, with his usual agility. He could thank his bowlers, too.

Alderman has an easy run up and a whippy wrist action. He kept a full length and generally, ran the ball away from the right-handers. Lillee tended to bowl a little on the short side at first, but then, at his hasty medium pace, he attached himself to the most telling line, on or just outside the off stump.

Gower, Taylor and Botham edged balls to Marsh, Willey played over a yorker which shot on to his stumps off his foot. Old went to a second slip catch and Dilley departed to a stroke of his own invention which lobbed a catch back to Lillee the bowler.

Day
Four

Daily
Express
21/7/81

Botham's a miracle!

PAT GIBSON reports

The amazing Ian Botham had the mourners dancing in the aisles at Headingley last night with the greatest comeback since Lazarus.

Botham took up his bat and walked in with England slipping towards defeat in the third Cornhill Test and the Ashes as good as lost.

Three and a half hours later he had transformed a wake into a carnival with an almost miraculous 145 not out—the highest score of even his remarkable Test career.

The chances are that, with England still only 124 ahead with one wicket left, Australia will win today and take a 2-0 lead in the series.

Yet for the moment Botham has made it a time for English rejoicing by throwing off the chains of captaincy and becoming what he was before—a colossal cricketer to whom nothing seems impossible.

In his first match since losing the job he had already taken six for 95 and scored 50, but those efforts paled beside this incredible performance.

England, needing 227 to avoid a humiliating innings defeat, had slumped to 105 for five when he marched boldly in to join Geoff Boycott.

STRUGGLE

When Boycott's characteristic struggle to save England off his own bat ended after three hours 35 minutes with the deficit still 94, it looked as though the match would be lost by tea.

But Botham, relishing the challenge far more than he could possibly have done if he'd been captain, not only launched into a counter attack but drew a gallant response from Graham Dilley.

Between them, Botham, standing up and driving anything overpitched or pulling anything short, and Dilley, revealing an almost classical square drive, put on 117 in only 80 minutes.

It was only seven runs short of England's record for the eighth wicket against Australia set by Patsy Hendren and Harold Larwood at Brisbane in 1928.

Chris Old joined Botham in a ninth-wicket partnership of 67 in 53 minutes and finally Bob Willis contributed a single to an unbroken last wicket stand of 32 to increase the Australian frustration.

Dilley, with nine fours in his highest Test score of 56, and Old supported him admirably, but England owed everything to Botham and his remarkable reincarnation.

The statistics alone tell the story of his astonishing century that came off only 86 balls in 158 minutes.

His first 50 took him 112 minutes but he went from 39 to 103 in only 17 strokes—a six, 14 fours and two singles.

The entire England team came out on to the balcony to applaud as he raised both arms in triumph before the proceeded to drive, pull, steer and slog another half dozen boundaries.

Many consider that Botham's incredible fight back was inspired by the carefree hitting of his first partner Graham Dilley.

No matter how they came, Botham's runs turned the match on its head.

At the end when he had been batting 210 minutes and struck one six and 25 fours, the crowd massed in front of the pavilion, singing "For he's a jolly good fellow" and waving Union Jacks.

CAPABLE

The scene could not have made a greater contrast to what had gone before when only Boycott seemed capable of saving England. He quickly lost Mike Brearley, David Gower and Mike Gatting as the Australian bowlers again threatened to make short work of the English batting.

Peter Willey stayed 75 minutes in a fifth wicket stand of 64 but when he was caught at backward point and a surprised Boycott was judged lbw to become the fourth of the persevering Terry Alderman's five victims we thought it was all over.

Then came Botham...

'NOW LET'S GET ANOTHER 50 OR 60 RUNS'

Kathryn Botham, who always felt the failure more keenly than her husband, Ian, last night revelled in his glory.

The pretty brunette was at Headingley along with most of the Botham family.

And as hundreds of fans gathered in front of the pavilion, to cheer the maker of an astonishing century, she said:—

"It's like a fairy tale.

"I'm so pleased for him, because we have all gone through a lot recently."

While his three-year-old son, Liam, used one of Dad's bats in a post-match practice on the outfield, Botham himself was reluctant to discuss the innings.

Clearly touchy about what he calls his Catch 22 situation—if he admits that he only plays well when not captain, he will never regain the job—he would only say: "It was one of my most satisfying innings.

"When Graham Dilley and I came together, we just decided to have a go and took it from there. But it might be interesting if we can get another 50 or 60 tomorrow."

Botham finished his innings with a split bat and Australian manager Fred Bennett added wryly: "We would have been in trouble if he'd had a complete bat."

Day Five

The
Guardian
22/7/81

Paul Fitzpatrick on a famous victory in the third Test at Headingley

England evoke a golden age

Not since the golden age of cricket have England won a Test to compare with the one they won by 18 runs against Australia at Headingley yesterday.

Not since A. E. Stoddard led his side to victory by 10 runs in Sydney in 1894, the only previous instance of a Test side following on and winning the game, has an English cricket public been given quite such cause for celebration.

This third Cornhill Test will be remembered for many things—chiefly for the soaring performances of Ian Botham, and the marvellous bowling yesterday of Bob Willis—but perhaps the thing that will give it an imperishable place in cricket history alongside the tied Test of Brisbane 1960 was the utter improbability of the victory.

England, it will be remembered, scored 174 to Australia's first innings 401 for nine declared; and at one stage on Monday they were still 92 runs short of making Australia bat again with only three second-innings wickets standing.

To be at Headingley yesterday was to be part of a drama as gripping as anything the fertile mind of Wilkie Collins could have dreamed of. It was impossible to take the eye away from a single delivery; every run that edged Australia towards their target of 130 heightened the anxiety of an absorbed crowd; every wicket England captured added another heartbeat of tension until by the time that Willis uprooted Bright's middle stump to end the game most nerves could have stood no more.

Only Test cricket could have produced such a fascinating plot as this; no other game could have allowed such an unlikely and outrageous swing of fortune as England experienced. Only a drama that is allowed to unfold over five days could permit such a twist in the plot so wild as to be almost unthinkable.

After three and a half days of largely dull preamble, England were finished,

ready, it seemed, to subside to an innings defeat; ready, humiliatingly, to go 2-0 down in a series only three matches old. Kim Hughes already had visions of himself as the latest proud owner of The Ashes. With three matches still to go his dream is now a long way from realisation.

The man who did most to fling logic the full length of the Kirkstall Lane was Ian Botham, with an innings that was the

of an unforgettable innings of 149, but Willis was not able to keep him company for much longer yesterday. A push forward at Alderman, an outside edge, a catch to second slip and Willis's resistance had ended, leaving Australia to score a modest 130 runs to win... a target to be treated with respect but not one surely to perturb unduly pragmatic Australians.

The Headingley crowd had seen the

Rod Marsh waits in vain for Botham to falter.

modern embodiment of Jessop. That blistering, sustained attack on the Australian bowling turned the game upside down on Monday afternoon, but in spite of its magnificence it seemed at best a heroic gesture. If England were to have the slightest hope of winning another 50 or 60 runs would be needed yesterday and with only Willis left to support Botham that seemed unlikely.

Botham struck another four, his 27th

rebirth of Botham. They now saw Bob Willis peel away the years and give a display of pace bowling culled from his youth, before the days of suspect, creaking knees. No one has tried harder for his country over the years.

His performance surpassed anything that he has produced in Test cricket previously. Throughout his spell he found movement, bounce, life, and pace; too much pace for eight Australians. No

Englishman has ever returned a more impressive set of figures at Headingley—eight for 43, an analysis to give Willis a glow of pride when he is "old and grey and nodding by the fire."

Willis is a laconic chap, except, it seems, when he is asked on the television to give his views on the English press. He weighs questions carefully, delays the answer until you think he is not going to answer at all, and then usually produces some telling or humorous comment.

Did he think he would ever play Test cricket again when he left the West Indies in February for repair to a troublesome knee? "I never thought I'd play cricket again, let alone Test cricket," he replied. What motivates him? "I want to keep playing for England. That sounds phoney, I know, but it's the truth." Who could doubt that yesterday?

The Warwickshire captain is used to reading his obituary notice in the columns of national newspapers. If England had lost this game he might have expected to see it there again. But his desire to keep playing for England will now be fulfilled for a few more Tests yet.

Young pace bowlers with aspiration to an England place—the Allotts, Hughses and Newmans—will have to look elsewhere for a possible opening. This vacancy is definitely filled. As Brearley said: "I didn't think Willis could still bowl like that. He surpassed himself."

Ron Allsop tried and failed to produce a wicket at Trent Bridge that was fair to both batsmen and bowlers but would produce exciting cricket; Keith Boyce adopted a similar policy at Headingley and he too failed.

Everyone was agreed, Willis even, that the wicket was loaded in favour of the bowlers. "If you hit the cracks," Willis said, "the ball either squatted or went vertical." But although here was a track that no batsman could trust there were surely, as Dyson, Hughes, and Yallop, Botham and Dilley had proved, surely 130 runs in it.

There was really no one else to whom Brearley could have given the new ball. It had to be Botham. His rich vein had to be tapped as long as possible and sure enough

Botham raised English spirits by having Wood, who struck the first two balls from the Somerset all-rounder for four, caught at the wicket in the third over.

There followed a similar phase of cricket to the Australian first innings when Dyson, again looking technically sound and temperamentally assured, and Chappell, carefully, stoically gave the innings its spine.

Bob Willis gives Trevor Chappell the glare of intent.

But no sooner had a back bone been established than it was snapped by a furious spell of bowling that brought Willis three wickets in 11 balls without a run scored off him.

England for the first time could entertain the audacious thought of a win while Australia must have suffered their first serious misgivings.

An awkward, lifting delivery to the outside edge of Chappell's bat gave Taylor the second of the four catches which brought him the world record number of dismissals. Hughes, never comfortable,

could not keep down a rising delivery that caught the throat of his bat and brought Botham to a fine, tumbling catch at third slip.

Yallop, also unable to angle his bat enough over another ball of chest height, was caught alertly by Gatting at short leg. At 58 for four, Australia must have felt for the first time like unwilling victims in a plot they had no power to resist.

Border, getting an inside edge to a delivery from Old that uprooted his leg stump, became the third Australian batsman successively to collect a duck and when the obdurate Dyson, after two hours' solid resistance, fell trying to hook Willis, Australia were 68 for six and sliding fast. With Willis pounding in from the Kirkstall Lane end, a bounce in his step and bent on destruction, there was no respite either.

Marsh might so easily have done for Australia what Botham on a much grander scale had achieved for England. He is a batsman who could have put the game back into Australian hands with a few powerful swings of his woodcutter's arms.

Swing he did but only high down to fine leg, where Dilley, glancing down swiftly to make sure his feet were firmly inside the boundary line, judged a difficult catch to perfection.

Lawson, a promising batsman but still young, had neither the nerve nor the experience for the occasion and plodded fatally at Willis. Only two wickets remained and now 55 runs were needed and England, it seemed, astonishingly, would win with something to spare.

The margin in the end, however, was a mere 18 runs, and English followers could have stood nothing closer. Bright is a sound bat, Lillee is experienced, and between them—Lillee by unorthodox but perfectly justifiable methods, Bright by more legitimate means—whittled away the deficit until Lillee tried to hook Willis to the midwicket area but succeeded only in looping the ball up to mid-on, where Gatting took his second outstanding catch of the innings.

Botham was brought back and watched Old drop Alderman twice in an over before Willis, fittingly Willis, ripped out Bright's middle stump.

The Headingley
crowd saw Bob
Willis peel away the
years to help win the
unwinnable Test.

Willis the indestructible is the saviour of the summer

Frank Keating

Things like this are always better when you know they could not have happened to a nicer chap. Simply, Bob Willis, winter's has-been, has resurrected the whole summer, saved a whole series. With a little help from his friend, Ian, mind you.

Bright-eyed and bushy-haired, long-legged and wonky-kneed; we have never once seen him charge in off his mark have we, without those high-stepping knees working up the head of steam as stampingly methodical and relentless as those prancing iron bars attached to the flywheel of that first puffing Rocket that was flogged from Stockton to Darlington.

The Willis family hail from up that way. He was born in Sunderland but his journalist father ended up in Surrey. Bob was brought up in Cobham, stockbroker, mock Tudor, mock-life belt.

I had occasion to spend a couple of Christmases in Cobham a few years ago. One festive afternoon we went for a walk across the old Recreation ground in downtown Stoke d'Abernon. That very afternoon I was aware that under some blazing tropical sun Bob's two great Cornish-pasty boots were slapping themselves down on some foreign field for England. Talk about heart and sole.

We digested our mincepies and dug our new-gloved hands deeper onto overcoat pockets as frost rolled in and I fancied I heard those two great feet clattering in over the frost-hard turf of England, grunting and gritting as well...

The Rec was where Willis learnt his cricket after his day at grammar school.

And then he gangled home to play his whining Bob Dylan records and moonily dream of things like eight for 43 for England that was to come 60 Test matches later.

Early in February, we lined up to say goodbye for Bob before breakfast in the Trinidad Hilton Hotel. The legs had given up again and everyone knew that this was the very end. Kaputt. Finis. Good luck, mate. Don't stick around the county slog too long.

Yesterday I was minding my own business watching a pleasant enough county game in the West, up in the bar above the pavilion and behind the plate-glass window. Small match in Bristol, not many there. Suddenly—honest—tennis balls, satchels, luncheon bags, bags, and school caps went in to the air from the tiny knot of schoolboys huddled down at third man. England had done it! No, said someone in the bar, Willis had done it.

The extra hour on a day affected by the weather in a Test, will, in future, become part of the normal playing time. This move follows the decision by the Headingley umpires to abandon play for the day just before 6.0 p.m. on Saturday.

Under current regulations, conditions must be fit for play at the scheduled time of close for the extra hour to come into effect. On Saturday, the umpires and the law-makers were unfortunate that the sun broke through soon after 6.0 pm and that play would have been possible throughout the next hour. Now, if more than an hour is lost during the day, 60 minutes will be added on with no conditions.

FINAL · SCORES

AUSTRALIA — First Innings

J. Dyson, b Dilley	102
G. M. Wood, lbw, b Botham	34
T. M. Chappell, c Taylor, b Willey	27
K. J. Hughes, c & b Botham	89
R. J. Bright, b Dilley	7
G. N. Yallop, c Taylor, b Botham	58
A. R. Border, lbw, b Botham	8
R. W. Marsh, b Botham	28
G. F. Lawson, c Taylor, b Botham	13
D. K. Lillee, not out	3
Extras (b 4, lb 13, w 3, nb 12)	32
Total (for 9 dec.)	401

Fall of wickets: 1-55, 2-149, 3-196, 4-220, 5-332, 6-354, 7-357, 8-396, 9-401

Bowling: Willis 30-1-72-0, Old 43-14-91-0, Dilley 27-4-73-2, Botham 33.2-11-95-6, Willey 13-2-31-1, Boycott 3-2-2-0

ENGLAND — First Innings

G. A. Gooch, lbw, b Alderman	2
G. Boycott, b Lawson	12
J. M. Brearley, c Marsh, b Alderman	10
D. I. Gower, c Marsh, b Lawson	24
M. W. Gatting, lbw, b Lillee	15
P. Willey, b Lawson	8
I. T. Botham, c Marsh, b Lillee	50
R. W. Taylor, c Marsh, b Lillee	5
G. R. Dilley, c & b Lillee	13
C. M. Old, c Border, b Alderman	0
R. G. D. Willis, not out	1
Extras (b 6, lb 11, w 6, nb 11)	34
Total	174

Fall of wickets: 1-12, 2-40, 3-42, 4-84, 5-87, 6-112, 7-148, 8-166, 9-167, 10-174

Bowling: Lillee 18.5-7-49-4, Alderman 19-4-59-3, Lawson 13-3-32-3

ENGLAND — Second Innings

G. A. Gooch, c Alderman, b Lillee	0
G. Boycott, lbw, b Alderman	46
J. M. Brearley, c Alderman, b Lillee	14
D. I. Gower, c Border, b Alderman	9
M. W. Gatting, lbw, b Alderman	1
P. Willey, c Dyson, b Lillee	33
I. T. Botham, not out	149
R.W. Taylor, c Bright, b Alderman	1
G. R. Dilley, b Alderman	56
C. M. Old, b Lawson	29
R. G. D. Willis, c Border, b Alderman	2
Extras (b 5, lb 3, w 3, nb 5)	16
Total	356

Fall of wickets: 1-0, 2-18, 3-37, 4-41, 5-105, 6-133, 7-135, 8-252, 9-319, 10-356

Bowling: Lillee 25-6-94-3, Alderman 35.3-6-135-6, Lawson 23-4-96-1, Bright 4-0-15-0

AUSTRALIA — Second Innings

J. Dyson, c Taylor, b Willis	34
G. M. Wood, c Taylor, b Botham	10
T. M. Chappell, c Taylor, b Willis	8
K. J. Hughes, c Botham, b Willis	0
G. N. Yallop, c Gatting, b Willis	0
A. R. Border, b Old	0
R. W. Marsh, c Dilley, b Willis	4
R. J. Bright, b Willis	19
G. F. Lawson, c Taylor, b Willis	1
D. K. Lillee, c Gatting, b Willis	17
T. M. Alderman, not out	0
Extras (lb 3, w 1, nb 14)	18
Total	111

Fall of wickets: 1-13, 2-56, 3-58, 4-58, 5-65, 6-68, 7-74, 8-75, 9-110, 10-111

Bowling: Botham 7-3-14-1, Dilley 2-0-11-0, Willis 15.1-3-43-8, Old 9-1-21-1, Willey 3-1-4-0

·1985·

ENGLAND'S NINE-WICKET victory in the fourth Test meant that they were the first side to come from one down to win a series in India. David Gower lost the toss but England were in a commanding position within an hour of the start when Neil Foster and Norman Cowans reduced India to 45 for three and they were all out for 227 in a little over five hours. Foster finished with six for 104 in his first Test of the tour. England then established a huge lead of 380 when Gower declared at 652 for seven, their highest score against India. Graeme Fowler survived two dropped catches to make 201 and his partnerships with Tim Robinson (178) and Mike Gatting (241) were both record stands for England against India. Gatting's 207 meant that he and Fowler were the first Englishmen to score double centuries in the same innings. When India resumed, Foster took the wickets of Sunil Gavaskar, Dilip Vengsarkar and Kris Srikkanth in his first four overs, but a century by Mohammed Azharuddin, his second in two Tests, pushed the total to 412, Foster finishing with match figures of 11 for 163. It took England only eight overs to score the 35 runs required.

Graeme Fowler and Mike Gatting during their magnificent partnership.

Day
One

The Times
14/1/85

Foster shines on a day which has everything

From John Woodcock
Cricket Correspondent
Madras

It is not often that one can say at the end of the opening day of a Test match anywhere, let alone in India, that there was never a dull moment, but it was so here yesterday. India were bowled out in the first innings of the fourth Test for 272 and when the sun went down England, in reply were 32 for no wicket.

The pitch was the key to it, no less than the approach of the two sides. It has pace and occasional bounce, just enough of both to encourage bowlers and batsmen alike. The ball also swung quite a lot. There was one exceptional innings — from Amarnath — as well as some marvellous English fielding; and there were six wickets for the indomitable Foster making his first appearance of the series. Cowdrey too, justified his inclusion by the contribution he made as a third seam bowler. His first 14 overs bowled off the reel, were prodigious in their endeavour.

India batted for much of the time as though no one had told them that this was not a one-day international. At lunch they were 102 for three, having been 45 for three after 12 overs. There were those who said it was not vintage Test cricket; that in the conditions Hadlee would have done this or Marshall that. But England bowled with a fine spirit and India batted as the mood took them. When Fowler and Robinson went out to face 10 awkward overs before the close they saw them through with resolution, the only scares coming with the last two balls when Siva twice beat Fowler. It should be a fine match now, yet when England lost the toss, with the pitch looking full of runs I had feared the worst.

Both sides roared straight into action, Gavaskar forced the second ball through

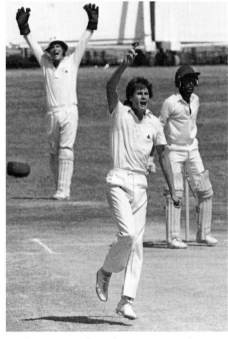

Neil Foster appeals without success at the start of his finest bowling performance for England.

the covers off the back foot and Fowler, sprinting after it, turned four into three with an astonishing save. That set the tone of the day. In the second over, bowled by Foster, Gavaskar scored two boundaries, one a magical stroke off his legs besides surviving an appeal for a catch at the wicket. It was not an entirely confident appeal. In Foster's next over he was hooked vividly for four by Gavaskar, who then, having survived another close call, this time for leg-before, had his stumps shattered. Gavaskar was across the line of a good length ball. It was Foster's 13th Test wicket, but the first to be bowled.

Off the first ball of the next over Srikkanth, driving at an out-swinging half volley from Cowans, was given out, caught at the wicket. The decision which was a

long time coming, surprised the batsman. Vengsarkar was off the mark with a square slash for four off Foster, Amarnath, with a sparkling hook for four off Cowans. It was heady stuff, enjoyed by a good crowd in holiday mood. It is a superb modern ground now, circular in shape, spacious and colourful, and yesterday there was a breeze blowing through it.

By the time Vengsarkar was third out, just before morning drinks, he had edged Foster between second and third slip at catching height and played one stroke of such magnificence that the great Hammond would have been proud of it. But from time to time the ball had been hitting the splice of Vengsarkar's bat, when he was playing back, and Foster now got one to bounce a shade more steeply. It took Vengsarkar by surprise and the catch went straight but quite sharply to Lamb at second slip.

Though still full of incident, the second hour came as a disappointment to England after the rewards of the first. Not for the life of me could I see the sense of giving Edmonds and Pocock seven overs before lunch, especially with the ball not turning. The first morning of a Test match in Madras is when every self-respecting fast bowler is wanting to get his hands on the ball. Pocock's three overs cost 23 runs. The batsmen were glad of them though it was against Cowans that Amarnath made his most dashing strokes, both hooks, one of them high into the cavernous stands. In this second hour Cowdrey came as near as anyone to taking the next wicket, first with an amazing piece of fielding then by bowling the virtually unplayable ball to Azharuddin, pitching on the leg stump and flying high over the off.

Amarnath was so sure that his firm on side push would pass well wide of Cowdrey at short square leg that he set off, all unconcerned, on a run. Within a trice Cowdrey, with a diving save and reverse flick, had missed the batsman's wicket by a hairsbreadth, with Amarnath far from home. Bowling at a brisk medium pace Cowdrey beat the bat as much as anyone. What his bowling lacks is discipline, not punch. His length and line may not have been quite tight enough to make the very most of the moment, but my goodness how he tried. His grandfather played at Chepauk, but never his father. They would have found a lot to be pleased with in Christopher's wholehearted effort yesterday.

Azharuddin and Amarnath set off after lunch just as they had ended the morning, looking for every chance of runs. Azharuddin improves with every innings he plays and Amarnath was in cracking form. When, in the sixth over of the afternoon, Amarnath hit four successive balls from Edmonds for four, England had to hang on. Gower brought back Foster, who despite taking two of the wickets to have fallen, had bowled only seven overs. Almost at once he had Amarnath caught at the wicket, chasing something way outside off stump. Amarnath and Azharuddin had added 110 for the fourth wicket.

Three overs later Cowdrey removed Azharuddin's leg and middle stumps and in the over after that Shastri went much as Amarnath had. By walking, these two made the umpires job easy. There followed the second sizeable partnership of India's innings, one of 74 in even time between Kapil Dev and Kirmani. Happily for India, and the game in general, Kapil is the same joyous and uninhibited batsman he was when last he played for India. They can drop him from the side but they will not subdue him. He is always giving the bowler a chance and the spectator a thrill.

Like Amarnath, he was playing with dangerous confidence when he drove Cowdrey to long off, for Cowans, running to his left in the shadow of the stands, to hold an excellent catch. Amarnath hit 14 fours and a six in his 78, Kapil eight fours in his 53.

The last three Indian wickets came in 10 overs, two of them to Foster and one to Cowans. Cowdrey, at square leg, caught a hard hook from Siva, knocking the ball up at the first attempt and finding it again just in time. Finally Chetan Sharma, not to be left out of the strokemaking, skied an attempted hook to second slip. Kirmani had played faultlessly for two hours and India's runs had come at four an over, in all directions and with every kind of shot.

FOWLER MAKES INDIA PAY FOR THEIR LAPSES

Day Two

The Daily Telegraph 15/1/85

By. MICHAEL CAREY in Madras

England dominated yesterday's events in the fourth Test at Madras with a growing certainty and ruthlessness they have rarely shown in an overseas contest in recent years, and ended the second day with a lead of 21 and nine wickets in hand.

Graeme Fowler's unbeaten 149 was the focal point of a display which built effectively on the work of the bowlers, and after a record opening partnership of 178 with Tim Robinson, he and Mike Gatting saw a memorable day out with an unbeaten 115 which left England at 293 for one, made from 90 overs.

Assuming England continue to make batting the applied science it was yesterday, India can think only in terms of saving the game. If England can occupy the crease beyond tomorrow's rest day, they will be able to apply enormous pressure, even on a pitch that may remain good.

Whatever happens next in a totally absorbing contest — not least when viewed through English eyes — Fowler's innings can already be classed alongside the one Robinson played in Delhi as superhuman effort in terms of stamina and concentration, particularly in the more demanding heat and humidity here.

PERSPIRATION PROBLEM

By the end, he had been there for some six and half hours, facing 290 balls and hitting 18 fours and required several changes of apparel, plus the insertion of drops in his eyes at every break to assuage the problems of perspiration streaming into them and making them sore.

Unprescribed but no less valuable were the other drops donated by India which allowed Fowler to escape when 10 in only the second over of the day, then again at 36 and 75.

Yet as ever, Fowler never became nonplussed by these episodes and, if a comparison with a Yorkshireman may be forgiven over the Pennines this morning, that is one attribute he shares with Herbert Sutcliffe.

Kirmani, who missed him at the start, also allowed Robinson to escape when 44 and by the time their partnership was broken it had not only beaten the 159 of Geoff Pullar and Peter Richardson — the previous highest for the first wicket against India — but threatened to avenge the infamous day here three years ago when England toiled without taking a wicket.

As it was, Fowler's highest Test innings made him only the third Englishman to score a century in Madras — after Cyril Walters and Graham Gooch.

And as Gatting helped him through the final stages of his great day he was, perhaps influenced by weariness, playing even straighter and showing fine judgment outside his off stump.

His first escape, fumbled off the outside edge by Kirmani, came at a time when it was not quite clear why Shastri had started the day by sharing the attack, rather than Sivaramakrishnan who had posed one or two problems the previous evening.

When Siva did appear, he was not permitted to settle by either Fowler or Robinson, though he later exploited the rough outside the left-hander's off stump.

The appearance of Chetan Sharma, looking very plain, reinforced the belief that England had done well the previous day to dismiss India for less than 300 and the openers found they could cruise along at more than three an over, simply by lying in wait for the loose delivery.

The only problem might have been over-ambition in the face of much mediocrity and after Fowler had steered a short ball from Chetan Sharma through Vengsarkar's hands at gully, Robinson went after a very wide one, got a touch and saw Kirmani fail to hold the chance as he dived a long way in front of slip.

Otherwise all was serene as the pair completed England's first three-figure opening of the series in 29 overs. When Yadav appeared, somewhat belatedly it seemed, Fowler stepped out and drove him sweetly for a straight six which damaged an English photographer's camera on the front row of the Press box.

FOUR OVERTHROWS

Inevitably, things quietened down later, and in the third hour England made only 39 runs from 16 overs, during which Fowler, slashing hard at Shastri, saw Kapil fail to hold a sharp slip chance, while as he entered the 90s he also seemed to have problems with timing.

Robinson, apart from a willingness to hook more than usual, had gone on solidly, but immediately after a drinks interval, pushed forward to a flighted leg-break from Siva and this time Kirmani held the catch, almost four hours after the innings had started.

Fowler then went to his hundred by courtesy of four overthrows from Siva, wiped his brow, took a fresh guard (mentally if not physically) and once Gatting had overcome a tendency to early excesses — which included an attempt to cut Siva's googly — the pair settled down

Fowler's 201 was an England record in a Test against India — until Mike Gatting reached 207.

to make sure the position was not squandered.

Another slight alarm came when Gatting, offering no stroke to Kapil at three, saw the ball come back some distance over the top of the stumps. But the day's second three figure partnership came in 29 overs with little other hope being offered to the bowlers.

Gatting, putting the half volley away in uncomplicated fashion and also finding plenty of bowling that could be swept or forced off the back foot, reached his half century from 92 deliveries with a staidness that was highly acceptable as the close neared, while the new ball, taken at 258, posed more problems for India than it did for England.

Day
Three

The
Guardian
16/1/85

Matthew Engel reports from Madras on the fourth Test

Gatting and Fowler double up Indians

The England innings at Madras yesterday assumed Himalayan proportions, comparable with the greatest performances in the history of English batsmanship. England and India go into the rest day of the fourth Test amid the debris of English broken records and Indian broken hearts.

Above it all stand Mike Gatting and Graeme Fowler, both of whom began this series with their quality as Test players in doubt and who have now become the first England batsmen in 108 years and 610 matches to score double centuries in the same Test innings.

With two days of the Test remaining England are, astonishingly, 611 for five, 339 ahead of India. The only worries one has are whether any of this will prevent this game being any less drawn than that in Calcutta and whether one might not wake up with a screaming hangover and find that we are really back in Christchurch.

The bare figures are suffocating. Fowler scored 201, which was a record for any Englishman in a Test in India and stood for around three hours until Gatting passed him on the way to 207. The total was not only England's highest in India but their highest in any overseas Test since the Second World War and the timeless Test at Durban in 1938-39, which went on almost as long.

The interim scores will be statistical benchmarks for years to come. England were 563 for two before Lamb was out. Even in Hutton's Test at The Oval in 1938, the third wicket fell at 546. The highest score at which England have ever lost their second wicket was 425 at Melbourne in 1911-12. Fowler was second out just six runs short of that.

For two days, everything has gone right for English cricket. But will it mean

anything come Friday night? The wicket is now playing extremely easily, except for the first faint traces of bowlers' rough. The local theory is that the heavy rain which fell on Madras last week will bind the wicket a good deal better than the usual salty water poured on when the pitch is being prepared.

Batting may be just as straightforward 48 hours hence as Fowler and Gatting have made it look.

Much is bound to depend on the Indian's state of mind, after they have had the rest day to recover. Ideally, England ought to have whizzed the Indians in for a few overs from a fresh Cowans and Foster last night when their demoralisation was still fresh.

Now England may well bat on briefly tomorrow morning after getting the heavy roller on to try and hasten the ravages of time.

The 654 of Durban may yet be surpassed.

Had India gone in again, Gavaskar would have been able to bat. He was off the field from lunchtime onwards, after an allergy made his hands swell and go green. Most fielding captains are allergic to 611 for five.

The first three partnerships of the England innings were worth 178 (Fowler and Robinson on Monday), 241 (Fowler and Gatting) and 144 (Gatting and Lamb). After that Edmonds and Foster were sent in to slog. Only once before have the first two England wickets put on 150 each — against India at Edgbaston in 1974. This match was particularly relevant: David Lloyd, Fowler's fellow-Accringtonian, scored 214 not out, and the one figure Fowler really wanted to beat, for purposes of light-hearted banter until old age, was that one.

He has nothing else to feel sorry about. Oh, he still played and missed outside off stump on rare occasions, but the strength of his run-getting was on the off-side between square and extra cover. He resisted his habit of lofting the off spinner over mid-on until he was past 180 when he smashed two sixes off Yadav in the same over, removing him from the attack and conceivably from the Indian team.

He did not give another chance, there was nothing clear-cut all day until Foster was put down at long-on and, apparently, gave one less than one had thought on Monday.

Fowler says he did not nick the ball early on when Kirmani dived and missed,

Gatting demonstrates his power on the way to his total of 207.

Fantastic Foster

England hero here to stay

From PETER SMITH in Madras

and was undoubtedly telling the truth. He has never been afraid to admit his failings. Other people have often been afraid to give him full credit for his skill and character.

Whether or not the return of Gooch and the rest knocks him out of the Test team, he will be a force in English cricket for years to come.

But in the end, he was overshadowed. Gavaskar described Gatting's innings as magnificent, and there is no point looking for another word.

In the morning, when the Indians bowled more tightly than at any stage of the match, he was content to wait. Only 75 runs came in the session, the quietest period of an unquiet match.

With Gatting, though, you know that if the ball is there to be hit, he will hit it. He built his innings with the utmost care, reached his century in five hours — and it was after tea that he set out to do what he can do as effectively as any other contemporary English batsmen, Gooch included, which is trample on an already broken attack.

Having waited 31 Tests for his first 100, the 200 target three Tests later never bothered him — twice in the 190s he reverse swept Shastri and when he reached 200 the spectators applauded him as generously as they would have done the local boy Srikkanth.

The crowd indeed was most appreciative throughout — they warmly applauded Lamb when he reached 50 and they also enjoyed the Sunday stuff at the end when England concentrated on quick runs.

Gatting holed out at long-on. Gower, who was originally padded up to go in No. 3, held back to let Edmonds and Foster go in and slog. Lamb and Foster got out swiping the inswingers of Amarnath, the acting captain who brought himself on after 145 overs when all the other options had failed.

Gower eventually arrived at No. 7. It would have been nice had he joined in more, but he is presiding over the resurrection of English cricket's self respect, and that is something of which we can all be proud.

Foster showed: "sheer guts, courage and determination."

Whatever happens today, this fourth Test thriller will be inscribed forever on the big heart of Neil Foster.

The chance of victory Foster set up so magnificently with his pace bowling on the first day looked even more real thanks to his sheer guts, courage and determination on the fourth.

The 22-year-old Essex six-footer yesterday added four wickets to his six to give him 10 wickets in a first-class match for the first time — and he seems certain to play a huge part in England's fortunes during the next decade.

RECORD TOTAL

Foster's four were the only wickets England collected after asking India to score 380 runs to avoid an innings defeat and fall 2-1 behind in the series with just one match to play. By the close, they were still 134 runs adrift.

But what a marvellous four wickets they were! Three of them fell in the space of 18 deliveries after England had batted on for another 41 runs before declaring on 652 for seven. It was their highest-ever total against India, and the fifth highest in Test history. Within 12 deliveries of India setting off along their escape route, Foster's lean, hard frame was lost beneath the delighted figures of his colleagues as Sunil Gavaskar, India's captain, was caught by Mike Gatting at first slip.

It was a start beyond England's wildest hopes. But even better was to come with the first ball of Foster's third over. Dilip Vengsarkar played a genuine leg glance only to see Paul Downton dive full length to his left and clutch the ball out of the air.

RESTLESS

India's 19 for two became 22 for three 10 deliveries later when the restless Krishna Shrikkanth — who had already hooked a wayward Norman Cowans for six — attempted a repeat. This time the ball gloved him, looped in the air and Chris Cowdrey ran in gratefully from backward square leg to take the catch for which he had been positioned.

Foster might even have held another soon after. This time as a catcher, leaping like a salmon on the long leg boundary to take a Mohinder Amarnath hook against Cowans only to stumble over the boundary line.

That was a blow, because Amarnath then played with an assurance matched by the 21-year-old Mohammed Azharuddin who deserves to be bracketed with Foster as a hero on another day of sparkling cricket.

So savagely did they fight back in the 210 minutes they shared together that England manager Tony Brown was forced to leave the ground as their partnership approached 200!

Brown said: "I had not seen any of the wickets fall in the morning because I was away on business. When the stand started to look a little frightening, I decided to see if my absence might do the trick again. I'm glad it did."

Amarnath was just five runs from only his second Test century in India when he hooked again at Foster and was caught.

THAT'S MY BOY SAYS NO. 1 FAN

Neil Foster's mother Jean will be up at 5.30 this morning to listen to the BBC's ball-by-ball commentary from Madras.

'I'd like to see Neil take some more wickets but the main thing is that we win,' she said. 'If we can do that, I won't mind if he doesn't take another, though naturally we're thrilled he's got ten so far.

'Neil started playing right from the time he could walk,' she said. 'My husband used to take him along to matches he was playing in and he grew up in the game.

'He's good at most games. He could have been a professional footballer with Ipswich but he preferred cricket.'

Spinners in crucial breakthrough against India

ENGLAND GO 2-1 UP IN SERIES & SET RECORD

By MICHAEL CAREY in Madras

England obtained the memorable and historic victory their all-round supremacy had earned them in the fourth Test in Madras yesterday, defeating India by nine wickets to take a 2-1 lead in the series with one Test remaining—in Kanpur, starting on Jan. 31.

The measure of England's success is that no visiting team had ever previously come from behind to take a lead in a series in India, let alone one whose early days here were plagued with all kinds of doubts and uncertainties and off-the-field distractions.

If England can produce another well-rounded team effort, punctuated with the superb individual contribution they enjoyed here, in the final contest, David Gower may become only the third England captain, after Douglas Jardine and Tony Greig, to win a series on the sub-continent.

That, however, may depend on the type of pitch produced. Normally Kanpur has the blandest batting surface and England have not been involved in an outright result there since they won 30 years ago.

Nor have they ever lost there, but it was no surprise to hear India's captain, Sunhil Gavaskar, saying last night that he hoped for conditions which would give his side a chance of saving the series.

FEWER OBSTACLES

England, however, hold a considerable psychological advantage which will not have been weakened by their performance in Madras.

Victory was always more than a possibility once they had dismissed India in only 68 overs on the first day and their progress yesterday encountered fewer obstacles than anyone dared hope, considering the quality of the pitch and the fast-scoring conditions.

The removal of the overnight pair, Shastri and Azharuddin, by the spinners inside 10 overs was a huge bonus. Later Kapil Dev threatened the delicate time and runs equation of the day before falling to Cowans but India were still 19 behind with their last pair Kirmani and Sharma together.

They ensured England would have to bat again by adding 51, equalling India's record in these series, but England required only 33 to win and these were made comfortably off eight overs by Robinson and Gatting after Fowler had been caught behind.

Curiously enough, a carefully considered decision not to take the new ball immediately also played a crucial part in England's success, much as it had in their victory in the second Test in Delhi.

It was due after two overs and both Azharuddin and Shastri, wearing their helmets, clearly expected it. But Gower perhaps sensing that both would have been happier with it coming quickly on the bat, stayed his hand and his spinners did him proud.

Pocock had regained all his old sleight of hand and accuracy after his problems of

Phil Edmonds leads a concerted but unsuccessful appeal against India's Mohammed Azharuddin,
who went on to score 105.

Thursday and perhaps because both he and Edmonds were more relaxed—and refreshed—they gave the ball more air and perhaps extracted more from the pitch than hitherto.

At any rate, both did enough to induce catches off bat and pad and with the departure of Shastri, with his ability to lie doggo for lengthy periods, England not only had two ends to attack but must have felt for the first time that the door was open.

POWERFUL STROKES

Kapil Dev, however, batted thoroughly well. The pressure on him, after the events of recent weeks, must have been enormous but he defended correctly and every now and then attacked the spinners with strokes that were crisply and powerfully struck.

With Kirmani's busy support, he saw 82 added for the seventh wicket in 18 overs. If there had been much more of this

India would have been in the clear by lunchtime and, influenced by Kapil, capable of taking the game right away from England.

But after 24 overs of spin, Foster and Cowans returned to the fray when India were still 53 behind, though there was no immediate bonus, Kirmani continuing to nudge and cut and Kapil once launching into a tremendous drive over cover off Cowans.

In the next over, though, Cowans, running in more convincingly than at any time in the match, got everything right at last with one superb delivery which, pitching around off stump, bounced and left Kapil who was beautifully caught at first slip by Gatting.

Foster, who finished with match figures of 11-163, followed this one over later by having Sivarma palpably lbw as he shuffled across to a ball which did not bounce much and held its line. So when Yadav,

suffering from arthritis in the neck, was caught behind off Cowans India were 361 for nine.

Kirmani remained splendidly defiant, missing little that could be hit hard off the back foot, while Chetan, perhaps because of earlier dismissals, began to attract rather more than his fair share of short-pitched bowling, especially from Cowans.

After what England went through last summer, it might seem churlish to labour the point, but with Foster also lapsing into shortness this was not the most intelligent or glorious period of England's day, though there was no doubting the extent of Sharma's courage.

With both batsmen cheerfully casting aside thoughts of Kirmani dominating the strike, the bowling was flogged around for a while, with Fowler in the covers making a valiant attempt to reach a difficult chance offered by Kirmani when he played another flailing drive at Cowans.

EDMONDS FINISHES IT

Inevitably the spinners returned and after the pair had equalled the 10th wicket record for India established by Nadkarni and Chandrasekhar in Calcutta, 1963-64, Edmonds, maintaining a full length despite everything, had Kirmani caught by Lamb at backward point. England now turn their attention to trying to win the one-day series, in which they lead 2-0. The next match is in Bangalore tomorrow, with the side unlikely to be named until the morning of the match.

England will not need reminding that, their abundant spirit apart, there is no connection with what they have just achieved and what will be required tomorrow. But they succeeded in the first two matches despite frailties in several departments and a tightening up all round would give them the efficiency to add this series to the immense satisfaction of their deeds in Madras.

FINAL · SCORES

INDIA — First Innings

S. M. Gavaskar, b Foster	17
K. Srikkanth, c Downton, b Cowans	0
D. B. Vengsarkar, c Lamb, b Foster	17
M. Amarnath, c Downton, b Foster	78
M. Azharuddin, b Cowdrey	48
R. J. Shastri, c Downton, b Foster	2
Kapil Dev, c Cowans, b Cowdrey	53
S. M. H. Kirmani, not out	30
N. S. Yadav, b Foster	2
L. Sivaramakrishnan, c Cowdrey, b Foster	13
Chetan Sharma, c Lamb, b Cowans	5
Extras (lb 3, nb 4)	7
Total	**272**

Fall of wickets: 1-17, 2-17, 3-45, 4-155, 5-167, 6-167, 7-241, 8-243, 9-263, 10-272

Bowling: Cowans 12.5-3-39-2, Foster 23-2-104-6, Edmonds 6-1-33-0, Cowdrey 19-1-65-2, Pocock 7-1-28-0

ENGLAND — First Innings

G. Fowler, c Kirmani, b Kapil Dev	201
R. T. Robinson, c Kirmani, b Sivaramakrishnan	74
M. W. Gatting, c sub, b Shastri	207
A. J. Lamb, b Amarnath	62
N. A. Foster, b Amarnath	5
P. H. Edmomds, lbw b Shastri	36
D. I. Gower, b Kapil Dev	18
P. R. Downton, not out	3
C. S. C. Cowdrey, not out	3
Extras (b 7, lb 19, nb 17)	43
Total (7 wkts dec.)	**652**

Fall of wickets: 1-178, 2-419, 3-563, 4-599, 5-604, 6-640, 7-646

Bowling: Kapil Dev 36-5-131-2, Sharma 18-0-95-0, Yadav 23-4-76-0, Sivaramakrishnan 44-6-145-1, Amarnath 12-1-36-2

INDIA — Second Innings

S. M. Gavaskar, c Gatting, b Foster	3
K. Srikkanth, c Cowdrey, b Foster	16
D. B. Vengsarkar, c Downton, b Foster	2
M. Amarnath, c Cowans, b Foster	95
M. Azharuddin, c Gower, b Pocock	105
R. J. Shastri, c Cowdrey, b Edmonds	33
Kapil Dev, c Gatting, b Cowans	49
S. M. H. Kirmani, c Lamb, b Edmonds	75
L. Sivaramakrishnan, lbw, b Foster	5
N. S. Yadav, c Downton, b Cowans	5
Chetan Sharma, not out	17
Extras (b 1, lb 4, nb 2)	7
Total	**412**

Fall of wickets: 1-11, 2-19, 3-22, 4-212, 5-259, 6-259, 7-341, 8-350, 9-361, 10-412

Bowling: Cowans 15-1-73-2, Foster 28-3-59-5, Cowdrey 5-0-26-0, Edmonds 41.4-13-119-2, Pocock 33-8-130-1

ENGLAND — Second innings

G. Fowler, c Kirmani, b Sivaramakrishnan	2
R. T. Robinson, not out	21
M. W. Gatting, not out	10
Extras (lb 1, w 1)	2
Total (1 wkt)	**35**

Fall of wickets: 1-7

Bowling: Kapil Dev 3-0-20-0, Sivaramakrishnan 4-0-12-1, Shastri 1-0-2-0

Pat Pocock strikes to end Azharuddin's stubborn resistance.

ENGLAND HAD PLAYED 29 Tests against the West Indies since 1974 without a win. The West Indies had not lost any match at Sabina Park, Kingston in 34 years. Graham Gooch's team changed all that. They began the first day of the first Test in sensational fashion, destroying West Indies' feared batting, Angus Fraser in particular bowling admirably for his best international return of five for 28. The home side, out for 164, were made to suffer further by Allan Lamb, *right*. The England vice-captain made 132 and with Robin Smith (57) helped England reach 364, a lead of 200. For once, England's batsmen did not fear the home side's hostile battery of fast bowlers, although Courtney Walsh took five for 68 and bowled excellently. West Indies made a better fist of things in their second innings, reaching 222 for five, with Carlisle Best making 64 before becoming one of Gladstone Small's four victims. Then they collapsed at the end of the third day before rain, frustratingly for England, washed out the fourth day's play. On the fifth day, England wrapped up the tail (the last five wickets for just 18 runs) and Wayne Larkins hit the winning single to ensure victory by nine wickets.

Allan Lamb celebrates his century at Sabina Park, for the second time.

Day
One

The
Sunday
Telegraph
25/2/90

Five-wicket Fraser breathes fire into England no-hopers

Tony Lewis in Jamaica

Reporting good news for England in a Test match played against West Indies is a strange and confused feeling. The facts are plain: West Indies all out for 164 and England 80 for two at the close, which came six overs early because of bad light.

Less clear is how euphoric to be. Has it all been a ghastly joke. Will the big fast bowlers grind England down as ever? There were signs by the end that the Caribbean machine was beginning to tick over smoothly again. Gooch was brilliantly caught down the leg side by Dujon and Stewart parried a short ball from Bishop to second slip.

The bounce of the ball was sometimes low and, as always happens, the faster bowlers produce the more lethal shooters. Spin is not a factor in this Test. There may be an over or two from Richards before the end but the seamers are going to be hammering the ball down for hour after hour, day after day.

England's heroic effort began in unlikely circumstances because Greenidge and Haynes had put on 62 for the first wicket. Thereafter England's professional approach paid off, bowling just outside off stump and letting the West Indians take the chance of playing their shots to a crowded off-side field.

Capel got a little swing, Fraser plugged away and ended up with five wickets for 28. Small, too, was excellent and controlled. The odd burst of speed came from Malcolm, who was erratic, but collected the big prize of trapping Viv Richards leg before.

Removing a West Indian side for 164 was beyond England's wildest hopes. Their reply was determined and, thanks to the fast outfield, dotted with boundaries. England probably did well enough with the bat to give confidence to the remainder of the order in the dressing room.

Gooch played perfectly, turning the balls sweetly off his hip for boundaries but was out in that most unlucky way, caught down the leg-side from a flick of a deflection. Dujon's diving catch was a classic of gymnastics.

Stewart's first Test began well enough but he was caught in two minds when Bishop dug in a ball and had him fencing it out to Best at second slip. Larkins and Lamb took the score to 80 as the sun retreated, and play was called off as batting became a risky business.

The session between lunch and tea was enthralling: 72 runs were scored while four wickets fell. The session after tea was nothing short of sensational. When last did England have West Indians scampering to put on their pads in the dressing room? Who would have predicted that young men like Angus Fraser and David Capel would have been a destructive factor?

The first afternoon casualty was Richie Richardson. Capel had got his away-swingers to go a little and had Richardson playing and missing. Next ball, a short one hammered in and, rising, hit Richardson on the gloves as he tried a scooping sort of hook. Small took the catch which lobbed to backward square leg.

Carlisle Best went next prodding at a ball which ran away from him outside off-stump and getting an edge to Russell: 92

for three. A second wicket fell on the same score when Haynes tried to relieve his frustration by driving at Small. He did not get to the pitch of the ball and gave the bowler a return catch.

England danced as the West Indians panicked. Vivian Richards strolled out to bat with the air of a king inspecting his troops in disarray and regally he set about restoring their poise and purpose with a stream of five fours.

Caribbean nerves were hardly eased, though when Richards survived two vehement appeals: one for leg before off Small and a "catch" behind off Fraser. England were not amused in the least.

But he fell on his own sword. Devon Malcolm tempted him to the hook shot by dropping a ball short and setting two fielders back on the deep backward square leg boundary. A normal batsman would have acknowledged caution: not Richards, he hooked at an imaginary ball because the real one did not bounce as high as he expected and he was out leg before.

Then Angus Fraser produced a miracle all of his own. He removed Hooper and Marshall with the first and sixth balls of his first over after tea; and, next over, he had Bishop caught at slip.

Hooper self-destructed, mis-pulling the diligent Fraser to Capel who took a comfortable catch at wide mid-on. Then Marshall was bowled and the large crowd fell silent. Dujon stroked a few runs before Bishop edged his first ball to Larkins at first slip. Suddenly it was 150-8, and when the score reached 164, Fraser mopped up Walsh and Patterson to finish with 5-28.

By including the extra batsman, rather than a spin bowler, England's approach was defensive but this was sensible. A draw would be a most satisfying conclusion here in Jamaica because few of the England party are at the top of their form. Even if they were they would have to play, as Gooch put it, "out of their skins."

If England are to win the series it is likely to be by the odd Test and that would surely be the third one on the Port of Spain pitch in Trinidad which is slower and helps spin.

Remember how a spinner of Border's ordinary talents bowled the West Indies to defeat? Gooch will need Medlycott, his left-arm spinner, confident and in form by that time, if there is to be any hope of emulating the Australians.

Gooch could be well satisfied with the bowling performance of Small. He kept a line strictly on or outside off-stump and, on one occasion, surprised Greenidge with a bouncer which struck the batsman's left shoulder and passed the outside edge of his bat. He was tidy and gave Gooch control in a first spell of 7-2-25-0.

At the other end Malcolm who had been billed as England's attempt to meet fire with fire, was hostile, gave both batsmen uncomfortable moments but also sent down some half-volleys and some short balls which fed Greenidge's endless appetite for the square cut.

Greenidge played some memorable strokes, all the more worthy because the first hour of a Test innings is so loaded with the fear of failure. He flipped a high square cut square — one bounce to the boundary — and driving Small, again for one bounce, for four through mid-on. England needed early wickets but they were not coming.

No opening partnership has performed as long as Greenidge and Haynes. They came together in 1978 and have opened for the West Indies in almost every match since. Greenidge is among the finest openers of all time, positive and often savage in his stroke-play, while Haynes is a tremendous hooker of the ball and has improved his all round game.

The outfield was fast. During the off-season youth soccer is played at Sabina Park and the cricketers have complained about a rough fielding surface. So an extra heavy roller has been used. Sometimes the batsmen only coaxed the ball but it still raced for four.

Despite their almost telepathic understanding, however, Fraser still managed to keep a good line and length, but Malcolm, despite his bursts of genuine speed in front of his home-town crowd was erratic. It must be said, however, that he would have been helped by an earlier placing of a mid-off.

Malcolm almost trapped Haynes with the old one-two: a bouncer which caused

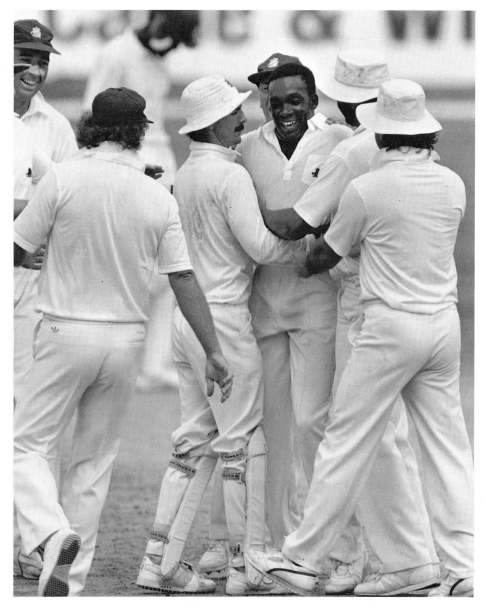

Gladstone Small is mobbed by team-mates after catching Des Haynes off his own bowling.

a painful blow to the elbow followed by a quick ball which had Haynes slashing outside off stump. A catch flashed just out of Stewart's reach in the gully.

As it was Fraser, who did a superb job, was bowling when the first wicket fell in astonishing fashion. Greenidge turned the ball to fine leg. Malcolm, having moved awkwardly to it, fumbled. Off went Greenidge for the second run but Malcolm, now recovered, sent in a low, flat throw of

breathtaking speed and accuracy and Greenidge was left stranded.

Richardson was looking to paddle a short ball to leg when he was caught off his glove and Haynes, seeing a rare ball straight on the stumps, launched into a fatal drive to give a caught and bowled.

It was hard to believe one's eyes: West Indians fidgetting nervously, fencing at shadows, surviving throaty shouts for leg before. Was it really happening?

Day
Two

The Daily
Mail
26/2/90

Lion-tamer Lamb

**From PETER JOHNSON
in Jamaica**

England's hero masters those feared pacemen

Allan Lamb's eight-year search for his first Test century on foreign soil ended yesterday with England in an unaccustomed seat of power.

By the time their eldest adopted son had fulfilled the most elusive ambition of his career in his 46th overseas innings, England had backed the West Indies into so tight a corner that the threat of a blackwash — the tourists' ultimate dread — had faded from even the most timid mind.

Twenty years as kings of the cricketing jungle have made the West Indies a dangerous beast when wounded. Yet the 172-run partnership shared by 36-year-old Lamb and his younger South African compatriot, Robin Smith, has left them with little choice but to fight for survival.

When the sun went down on a stunned Sabina Park, England led by 178 runs and every batsman had obeyed the stirring new edict that they must defend their stumps first, their bones second.

Lamb set the example with a 132 as unflinching and full of truculence as any of his previous Test hundreds. This was unique in two respects. First, because he had never before made a Test century outside England, and, secondly, because a scoreboard miscalculation twice left him perched on 99. A man of nervous disposition might have wilted after realising that he had gone through his celebration for nothing. Lamb merely hooked fast bowler Ian Bishop for four and repeated it, grinning.

In all he hit sixteen boundaries and eventually went — caught at slip off Courtney Walsh — a very tired, contented man. For more than six hours he had underlined the point made by England's bowlers the previous day — that beneath the superman image of this West Indies side are some vulnerable mortals.

Lamb thrived on that fallibility. He was only 30 when he edged Bishop at eminently catchable height. It was heading comfortably for first slip Carl Hooper when wicketkeeper Jeff Dujon half-heartedly stuck out a hand and turned a chance into a calamity.

Skipper Viv Richards, sensing that, glared at the shame-faced Dujon and thumped his fists against his sides.

His frustration had been simmering from the moment England set out in pursuit of the West Indies inadequate 164. When you have looked down on the likes of England for so long it hurts to find yourself under their heel. It becomes doubly hard to bear when the main power is being wielded by two South Africans who, in Richards's view, have entered Test cricket by the back door.

There came a time, before Smith's 57 was cut short by a slip catch off Bishop, when the West Indies attack came as close as it ever has to being innocuous.

The formidable pace battery had been tried in every conceivable permutation and managed only the solitary wicket of Larkins — and many thought him unlucky to be adjudged leg-before.

By then Lamb was deeply entrenched on a wicket we are told will become more hostile as the match progresses. It showed signs of it late yesterday as Nasser Hussain, fencing at a lifting ball from Bishop, paid the price of his inexperience.

But not even the loss of five late wickets could spoil England's joy as they finished on 342 for eight — their highest score in the Caribbean for sixteen years.

Allan Lamb cuts to the boundary during his match-winning innings of 132.

England's dream comes closer

Day Three

The Times
27/2/90

From Alan Lee
Cricket Correspondent
Kingston

Playing like men in a dream from which they fear to wake, England yesterday reached out for fantasy and found that it was real. Their first victory over the West Indies in 16 long and painful years is now much more than fanciful possibility. It will almost certainly happen sometime tomorrow, though how long it will need for the result to be believed and absorbed is another matter.

Applying themselves with a commitment which they had needed much earlier, West Indies yesterday fought grimly for survival but, despite Carlisle Best's first Test fifty, the first-innings deficit of 200 was too awesome a handicap to carry on an increasingly untrustworthy pitch. When the third day ended they were only 29 runs ahead with eight wickets down and nowhere to go. Best and Viv Richards, standing stony-faced against unaccustomed odds, gave England cause for concern with a fifth-wicket stand of 80 after tea. But, with his side still eight runs short of avoiding an innings defeat, Richards drove over a full-length ball from Malcolm and was bowled.

This critical moment, joyously acclaimed by England players now obliged to believe in themselves, added romance to a story already laden with scarcely credible drama. Malcolm, a gambler's pick for the tour and a contentious inclusion here on his native island, had dismissed the great Richards twice in the match and now, with four second-innings wickets, he is close to winning it. The heckling he received from sections of the crowd suggests some Jamaicans, at least, will find it hard to forgive him.

Malcolm, whose line has been better than anyone could have expected, had earlier removed both West Indian openers as they set out on the improbable mission of batting for two days to save the game or, arguably, a day and a half to put England under pressure. Neither objective had looked likely once West Indies had lost four prime wickets for 112 to an England attack laudably maintaining the essential disciplines in the 92°F heat. If Best and Richards caused a ripple of self-

51 balls and scored 14 runs when Walsh tempted him with a short one. Trying to fetch it through the vacant mid-wicket area, he mis-timed the shot and Patterson, at mid-on, took a simple catch. Out third ball against Jamaica a week ago, Malcolm

The critical moment. Viv Richards is bowled by Devon Malcolm to leave West Indies at 192 for five and staring at defeat.

doubt, this was swiftly banished as the remaining recognized batsmen were removed in the overtime period demanded, for the third successive day, by a slow over-rate.

It had taken West Indies 50 minutes to claim the two remaining England wickets at the start of play. In the process they conceded precisely the 22 runs England needed to score a further psychological point. A deficit of 200 somehow intimidates so much more than 199.

Russell had faced 39 of the morning's

failed even to survive one yesterday, Walsh defeating his crab-like defence. One of Gooch's innovations is the team huddle. Whenever they take the field his players gather round the captain for the sort of pep-talk one would not, until recently, have associated with the lugubrious Gooch. Yesterday's huddle must have contained a special message, for this was a God-given opportunity which England did not dare waste.

They needed a wicket before lunch and they got it. Haynes, having just clipped

Angus Fraser registers his delight at winning an lbw decision against Richie Richardson. The Middlesex paceman finished with match figures of 6 for 59.

Malcolm fluently through mid-wicket for four, chose to repeat the shot against an in-swinging yorker which hit the base of his leg stump.

An over later, Small's probing line so nearly gained reward, Richardson edging between wicketkeeper and first slip. Russell should have taken responsibility but made no move; Larkin's reaction was too late.

It could have been an expensive miss but the admirable Fraser ensured it was not. It was he, after lunch, who began to consistently hit the length from which the bounce could not be predicted. Two successive balls from him scuttled through at ankle height before Richardson, seeing one dropped marginally short, went for the pull and was leg before.

Greenidge, almost two and a half hours into an innings of severe self-denial, saw Malcolm pitch one up on off stump and could no longer resist the bait. Launching into his cover drive, he drilled the ball straight to Hussain, who gratefully clutched it to his chest.

When Carl Hooper was caught at first slip, via a fumble at second, in the last over before tea, Richards faced one of the rare crises of his captaincy tenure: the West Indies are well used to finishing Tests inside three days but not, customarily, on the losing side. He marched in, missing the crowd's usual gladiatorial welcome, and set about the century the situation demanded.

For 111 minutes it looked ominously possible. Richards only once allowed himself to plant that front foot outside off stump and whip the ball through mid-on in that inimitable way by which he signals his superiority. The rest was strict, disciplined batting; little Best a willing ally despite the knee injury with which he had collapsed in mid-run before tea.

The end of Richards was effectively the end of the West Indies. Soon, Best was drawn forward by Small, rousing himself for a final assault from the Pavilion end, and Gooch, at second slip, hurled the catch skywards. Then Dujon, who had looked more confident than anyone, was simply beaten for pace by the inspired Malcolm.

Another slip catch, this time by Larkins off Small, dispatched Bishop before, in bright sunlight but with shadows creeping across the pitch, the umpires decreed that 45 minutes of extra play was quite enough. England were not concerned. With two days left, they have the luxury of time on their side.

Day
Four

The Daily
Telegraph
1/3/90

Champagne and England victory are kept on ice

By Peter Deeley in Kingston

The Bollinger Special Cuvee remained on ice at England's team headquarters here yesterday. Jamaica's wettest February in recent times ended with a splash washing out the fourth day of the First Test leaving England still waiting to complete a memorable victory.

The best vintage available in the Caribbean had been summoned up by David Gower, the former England captain — here as a columnist — as a tribute to the efforts of his successor Graham Gooch.

But despite the work of the ground staff, there were still puddles in the outfield late into the afternoon, and the bowler's run up at one end was still slippery.

On their fourth inspection the umpires finally called off play shortly after 4 pm local time. Prospects for today — the final day — are better but not brilliant, with the chance of scattered showers.

So England can only hope that the gates — and the champagne — are opened to them this time. West Indies, with two wickets left, are only 29 runs on.

The tourists took their frustrations in good heart, though impatience with events showed out in the middle at one stage when Gooch sat on the roller and Allan Lamb, his vice captain, perched on a spade as if in protest.

Viv Richards, wearing a Free Now T-shirt depicting Nelson Mandela, indicated his feelings about play when he made heavy weather of walking on to the outfield in open-toed sandals. It was particularly galling to see brilliant sunshine for most of the day a few miles away glinting on the water.

When some of the England party arrived in the morning they had found that water had seeped under the covers and on to the bowler's run up at the northern end of the Sabina Park ground. Although the rain had stopped at 7.30 am, the downpour had gone on through the night.

Once it had cleared, a ground staff of 25 were out in force. But such weather is infrequent in Jamaica and there is no mechanical apparatus, like our "whale", with which to mop up. The system here is rather more rustic. Recently mown grass was raked into a series of giant anthills and painstakingly scraped up into wheelbarrows.

To some it might seem the staff were dragging their heels since this was the only way West Indies could avert defeat. There were five pools of water in various parts of the outfield to which no drying work was being done.

But Mr Stewart was satisfied that everything possible was being done "within the limits of local conditions, although I do not think the covers were up to the job.

"The ground would be a hive of activity if we were at home but one has to respect local knowledge. They like to see the water soaking away by its own efforts before they start sweeping," Mr Stewart said.

Allan Lamb, left, and Graham Gooch wait for the pitch to dry to allow them to get on with winning the match.

Day Five

The
Independent
2/3/90

England halt the one-horse race

Martin Johnson reports
from Kingston, Jamaica

The sun mercifully shone, and it was all over before what turned out to be an entirely liquid lunch. Against the fiercest bowling side in the world it was never less than heavy odds-on that England's cricketers would all be nursing headaches during this tour, but not from celebration hangovers.

England did not just scrape past the winning post in the first Test here, they cruised past it with what, in racing parlance, would be termed a double handful. If there has ever been a more remarkable result in the history of Test cricket, it is hard to call it to mind.

The nine-wicket win was a triumph for old-fashioned English cricketing virtues — a lot of sweat and a lot of discipline. There remains no doubt that the opposition have more talent, and they will not take kindly to having their tail so emphatically tweaked. However, if England continue to play as well as they have done here, it will be a fascinating series — and whatever happens now, all 16 of them will never enjoy a fonder memory.

This was a far bigger shock, to everyone perhaps but the players themselves, than England's victory in the opening Test in Brisbane on Mike Gatting's tour to Australia, and far more special than retaining the Ashes in Melbourne three years and two months ago — which was the last occasion they won a Test match of any real significance.

It hardly mattered yesterday that the members of the "I Was There" club can hold all their annual meetings in a telephone kiosk, and of the few hundred

Wayne Larkins steered England home to victory.

who witnessed it there were almost as many who live closer to Kingston upon Thames than Kingston, Jamaica. No one buys tickets for the fifth day of Test matches in this part of the world — leastways not until now.

Having cleared the weather hurdle, and Graham Gooch must have spent most of the previous night peering anxiously out of his bedroom window, England vaulted the next one by clearing up the final two West Indian wickets in only 18 minutes and 20 deliveries.

It was always a comfort to know that Malcolm Marshall had only a couple of batting duffers for company, and when Courtney Walsh attempted something indescribably agricultural against the 14th ball of the day from Gladstone Small, he looked round to find his off stump several yards away.

If this, given Small's superb bowling here, was highly appropriate, so too, given the West Indies' often shoddy cricket, was the loss of their last wicket in the match in identical fashion to the first, a run-out. Patrick Patterson pushed Devon Malcolm quietly away on the on side, and his posthumous response to Marshall's invitation for a single left him around 16 yards short when David Capel's lob arrived back at the bowler's stumps.

England were thereby left with 41 to win, and may not have needed reminding that when New Zealand required only 33 against the West Indies two years ago, Tony Gray and Courtney Walsh reduced them to 20 odd for five before they eventually scrambled home. Viv Richards predictably let loose his two quickest bowlers in Patterson and Ian Bishop, but England have had too many complete hidings from the West Indies not to complete this one in style.

They almost made it by 10 wickets, and it was disappointing when, with just half a dozen more needed, Gooch recorded his eighth consecutive Test score of under 20 by mis-timing a catch to square leg. Gooch has captained England in only three Test matches, but the way he has marshalled his forces this time after managing to complete the 1986 tour without a single recorded smile has been

impressive, and it would have been nice had he been there to make the winning hit.

That privilege ultimately fell to Wayne Larkins, who clearly regarded 41 to win as licence to take on the short stuff with a series of blows intended to knock out Sky's satellite dish. He was almost decapitated by one from Walsh — almost losing his wicket as well when the helmet that flew off jerking his head back bounced just wide of leg stump — but five of England's six boundaries came from his dashing blade before something more sedate produced the winning single.

The ensuing scenes in the visiting dressing-room have not exactly represented the everyday story of England Test folk in recent years, and even Alec Bedser, who can normally be relied on to come up with something like, "We'd have beaten this lot by an innings", was pumping hands with delight.

Gooch, never one to get carried away, was a mixture of elation and realism afterwards. "We played well, and they didn't play quite so well," he said, "but it is obviously a special feeling to beat the West Indies after all this time. We had no special formula, but just concentrated on what we can do well. I learned under Keith Fletcher at Essex that if you ever take the field believing you'll be beaten, you will be, and while there may be some low points to come, we'll never give up, that's for sure."

His opposite number said that he always believed England were a better side than they were given credit for (Richards conveniently forgetting he described the selectors as potty when Gower and Botham were left out) and that his own team "needed a kick up the arse".

Richards, in a thinly veiled reference to complaints about the West Indies' bowling tactics over the past 15 years, added: "I didn't hear a lot about bouncers and over-rates. We take our hidings well." Richards does not, though, expect to take too many more. "We will," he said, "win this series. You can bet on that." Most of us have, actually, but all of a sudden — wondrous to relate — it is no longer a one-horse race.

F I N A L · S C O R E S

WEST INDIES — First Innings

C. G. Greenidge, run out	32
D. L. Haynes, c & b Small	36
R. B. Richardson, c Small, b Capel	10
C. A. Best, c Russell, b Capel	4
C. L. Hooper, c Capel, b Fraser	20
I. V. A. Richards, lbw, b Malcolm	21
P. J. L. Dujon, not out	19
M. D. Marshall, b Fraser	0
I. R. Bishop, c Larkins, b Fraser	0
C. A. Walsh, b Fraser	6
B. P. Patterson, b Fraser	0
Extras (b 9, lb 3, nb 4)	16
Total	164

Fall of wickets: 1-62, 2-81, 3-92, 4-92, 5-124, 6-144, 7-144, 8-150, 9-164, 10-164
Bowling: Small 15-6-44-1, Malcolm 16-4-49-1, Fraser 20-8-28-5, Capel 13-4-31-2

ENGLAND — First Innings

G. A. Gooch, c Dujon, b Patterson	18
W Larkins, lbw, b Bishop	46
A. J. Stewart, c Best, b Bishop	13
A. J. Lamb, c Hooper, b Walsh	132
R. A. Smith, c Best, b Bishop	57
N. Hussain, c Dujon, b Bishop	13
D. J. Capel, c Richardson, b Walsh	5
R. C. Russell, c Patterson, b Walsh	26
G. C. Small, lbw, b Marshall	4
A. R. C. Fraser, not out	2
D. E. Malcolm, lbw, b Walsh	0
Extras (b 23, lb 12, w 1, nb 12)	48
Total	364

Fall of wickets: 1-40, 2-60, 3-116, 4-288, 5-315, 6-315, 7-325, 8-339, 9-364
Bowling: Patterson 18-2-74-1, Bishop 27-5-72-3, Marshall 18-3-46-1, Walsh 27.2-4-68-5, Hooper 6-0-28-0, Richards 9-1-22-0, Best 4-0-19-0

WEST INDIES — Second Innings

C. G. Greenidge, c Hussain, b Malcolm	36
D. L. Haynes, b Malcolm	14
R. B. Richardson, lbw, b Fraser	25
C. A. Best, c Gooch, b Small	64
C. L. Hooper, c Larkins, b Small	8
I. V. A. Richards, b Malcolm	37
P. J. L. Dujon, b Malcolm	15
M. D. Marshall, not out	8
I. R. Bishop, c Larkins, b Small	3
C. A. Walsh, b Small	2
B. P. Patterson, run out	2
Extras (b 14, lb 10, w 1, nb 1)	26
Total	240

Fall of wickets: 1-26, 2-69, 3-87, 4-112, 5-192, 6-222, 7-222, 8-227, 9-237, 10-240
Bowling: Small 22-6-58-4, Malcolm 21.3-2-77-4, Capel 15-1-50-0, Fraser 14-4-31-1

ENGLAND — Second Innings

G. A. Gooch, c Greenidge, b Bishop	8
W. Larkins, not out	29
A. J. Stewart, not out	0
Extras (lb 1, nb 3)	4
Total (for 1)	41

Fall of wickets: 1-35
Bowling: Patterson 3-0-11-0, Bishop 7.3-2-17-1, Walsh 6-0-12-0

· I N D E X ·

·INDEX·

· I N D E X ·

·INDEX·

ACKNOWLEDGEMENTS

Thanks to everyone who supplied the photographs and illustrations noted below; and in particular Ken Kelly, Roger Mann, David Frith, Peter Perchard and Abigail Sims for their invaluable help. Special thanks are due to Eve Horan at Hulton-Deutsch who time and time again came up with "just one more photo..."

The Aldus Archive: 87
Allsport: 10, 34, 86, 144
The Cricketer International Magazine: 119, 141
Patrick Eagar: 165, 166, 167, 169, 172, 173, 175, 176, 178, 179, 180, 183, 184, 185
David Frith: 14, 16, 48, 84, 120
Hulton-Deutsch: 8, 12, 13, 15, 17, 18, 20, 23, 25, 27, 30, 33, 44, 45, 46, 47, 51, 52, 53, 55, 56, 59, 67, 70, 76, 78, 80, 81, 82, 83, 88, 90, 91, 92, 93, 95, 97, 98, 99, 101, 102 (both), 103, 104 (both), 105, 113, 118, 124, 125, 126, 127, 128, 137, 138, 142, 143, 145, 146, 147, 148 (both), 149, 150, 152, 153, 154, 155, 156, 157, 158, 159, 160, 161, 162 (both), 163, 177, 182
The Illustrated London News: 9
Ken Kelly: 77, 85, 122
Roger Mann: 57, 58, 60, 61 (both), 62, 65, 66, 72, 73, 75, 108, 109, 110, 112, 114, 116
Bob Martin 208, 211
Adrian Murrell 174, 186, 187, 188, 189, 190, 191, 192, 193, 194, 195, 196, 198, 199, 200, 202, 203, 204, 206, 207, 209, 212, 213, 214, 215, 216
Press Association: 164
Sport and General: 74, 106, 123, 131, 135, 140, 141, 171
Surrey County Cricket Club: 94, 130
Topham: 107, 115, 117, 132